Remembering a Massacre in El Salvador

 **Other titles on Latin America available from the University of New Mexico Press:**

Independence in Spanish America: Civil Wars, Revolutions, and Underdevelopment (revised edition)—
Jay Kinsbruner

Heroes on Horseback: A Life and Times of the Last Gaucho Caudillos—
John Charles Chasteen

The Life and Death of Carolina Maria de Jesus—
Robert M. Levine and José Carlos Sebe Bom Meihy

¡Que vivan los tamales! Food and the Making of Mexican Identity—
Jeffrey M. Pilcher

The Faces of Honor: Sex, Shame, and Violence in Colonial Latin America—
Edited by Lyman L. Johnson and Sonya Lipsett-Rivera

The Century of U.S. Capitalism in Latin America—
Thomas F. O'Brien

Tangled Destinies: Latin America and the United States—
Don Coerver and Linda Hall

Everyday Life and Politics in Nineteenth Century Mexico: Men, Women, and War—
Mark Wasserman

Lives of the Bigamists: Marriage, Family, and Community in Colonial Mexico—
Richard Boyer

Andean Worlds: Indigenous History, Culture, and Consciousness Under Spanish Rule, 1532–1825—
Kenneth J. Andrien

The Mexican Revolution, 1910–1940—
Michael J. Gonzales

Quito 1599: City and Colony in Transition—
Kris Lane

Argentina on the Couch: Psychiatry, State, and Society, 1880 to the Present—
Edited by Mariano Plotkin

A Pest in the Land: New World Epidemics in a Global Perspective—
Suzanne Austin Alchon

The Silver King: The Remarkable Life of the Count of Regla in Colonial Mexico—
Edith Boorstein Couturier

National Rhythms, African Roots: The Deep History of Latin American Popular Dance—
John Charles Chasteen

The Great Festivals of Colonial Mexico City: Performing Power and Identity—
Linda A. Curcio-Nagy

The Souls of Purgatory: The Spiritual Diary of a Seventeenth-Century Afro-Peruvian Mystic, Ursula de Jesús—
Nancy E. van Deusen

Dutra's World: Wealth and Family in Nineteenth-Century Rio de Janeiro—
Zephyr L. Frank

Death, Dismemberment, and Memory: Body Politics in Latin America—
Edited by Lyman L. Johnson

Plaza of Sacrifices: Gender, Power, and Terror in 1968 Mexico—
Elaine Carey

Women in the Crucible of Conquest: The Gendered Genesis of Spanish American Society, 1500–1600—
Karen Vieira Powers

Beyond Black and Red: African-Native Relations in Colonial Latin America—
Edited by Matthew Restall

Mexico OtherWise: Modern Mexico in the Eyes of Foreign Observers—
Edited and translated by Jürgen Buchenau

Local Religion in Colonial Mexico—
Edited by Martin Austin Nesvig

Malintzin's Choices: An Indian Woman in the Conquest of Mexico—
Camilla Townsend

From Slavery to Freedom in Brazil: Bahia, 1835–1900—
Dale Torston Graden

Slaves, Subjects, and Subversives: Blacks in Colonial Latin America—
Edited by Jane G. Landers and Barry M. Robinson

Private Passions and Public Sins: Men and Women in Seventeenth-Century Lima—
Maria Emma Mannarelli

Making the Americas: The United States and Latin America from the Age of Revolutions to the Era of Globalization—
Thomas F. O'Brien

Raising an Empire: Children in Early Modern Iberia and Colonial Latin America—
Ondina E. González and Bianca Premo

Christians, Blasphemers, and Witches: Afro-Mexican Rituals in the Seventeenth Century—
Joan Cameron Bristol

Series advisory editor:
LYMAN L. JOHNSON,
University of North Carolina at Charlotte

Remembering a Massacre in El Salvador

The Insurrection of 1932,
Roque Dalton, and the
Politics of Historical Memory

Héctor Lindo-Fuentes,
Erik Ching,
and
Rafael A. Lara-Martínez

University of New Mexico Press
Albuquerque

© 2007 by the University of New Mexico Press
All rights reserved. Published 2007

12 11 10 09 08 07   1 2 3 4 5 6

Library of Congress Cataloging-in-Publication Data

Lindo-Fuentes, Héctor, 1952–
Remembering a massacre in El Salvador : the Insurrection of 1932,
Roque Dalton, and the politics of historical memory /
Héctor Lindo-Fuentes, Erik Ching, and Rafael Lara-Martínez.
    p. cm. — (Diálogos)
Includes bibliographical references and index.
ISBN 978-0-8263-3604-0 (pbk. : alk. paper)
1. El Salvador—History—Revolution, 1932. 2. El Salvador—History—
Revolution, 1932—Historiography. 3. Collective memory—El Salvador—
History—20th century. 4. Dalton, Roque, 1935–1975 5. Mármol, Miguel.
Miguel Mármol. I. Ching, Erik Kristofer. II. Lara Martínez, Rafael. III. Title.
F1487.5.L56 2007
972.8405'2—dc22
                                        2007012888

Book design and composition by Damien Shay
Body type is Minion 11/14
Display type is Brioso Pro and Type Embellishments

CONTENTS

LIST OF ILLUSTRATIONS	xi
ACKNOWLEDGMENTS	xiii
ACRONYMS AND ABBREVIATIONS	xvii
INTRODUCTION	1
CHAPTER ONE The Uprising and the Matanza of 1932	23
CHAPTER TWO The Historical Background	69
CHAPTER THREE The Life and Writings of Roque Dalton Prior to Miguel Mármol	97
CHAPTER FOUR Dalton, Mármol, and the Notebooks	137
CHAPTER FIVE Left-Wing Politics and Memories of 1932	183
CHAPTER SIX Right-Wing Politics and Memories of 1932	217
CONCLUSION	251
APPENDIX:	
Document 3–1 Roque Dalton, excerpt from "Testimony of the Committed Generation," *La Prensa Gráfica*, 1957	263
Document 3–2 Roque Dalton, excerpt from *El intelectual y la sociedad*, 1969	265
Document 3–3 Roque Dalton, excerpt from *El Salvador*, 1963	266

Document 3–4   269
Roque Dalton, excerpt from the introduction to *El Salvador: Monografía*, 1965

Document 3–5   271
Roque Dalton, excerpt on the issue of Anastasio Aquino, *El Salvador: Monografía*, 1965

Document 3–6   273
Roque Dalton, excerpts from "People, Places, and Events of 1932," *Historias prohibidas del Pulgarcito*, 1974

Document 4–1   284
Roque Dalton/Miguel Mármol, excerpts from *Miguel Mármol*, 1972

Document 4–2   291
Roque Dalton/Miguel Mármol, selection from Dalton's handwritten notes on the 1932 uprising

Document 5–1   295
Jorge Fernández Anaya's report on El Salvador, September 1930

Document 5–2   302
Report by Comrade H before Caribbean Bureau of Investigation, late 1932

Document 5–3   308
Reply by Comrade R to Comrade H, Caribbean Bureau of Investigation, late 1932

Document 5–4   311
Response by Comrade H, Caribbean Bureau of Investigation, late 1932

Document 5–5   314
Report on El Salvador from Santa Ana Comrades, 1936

Document 5–6   320
Miguel Mármol's brief historical notes on the labor movement in El Salvador, 1948

Document 5–7 325
David Luna, excerpt from 1963 *Tribuna Libre*,
"The Uprising of 1932"

Document 5–8 328
Roque Dalton, excerpt from unpublished 1972 manuscript
on the history of the Communist Party of El Salvador

Document 6–1 333
"A Landowner's Account," 1932

Document 6–2 337
Message of President Hernández Martínez before
the National Assembly, February 1932

Document 6–3 340
Excerpts from Joaquín Méndez,
Los sucesos comunistas, 1932

Document 6–4 344
Excerpts from Jorge Schlesinger's
Revolución comunista, 1946

Document 6–5 350
"How Is a Dictatorship Born?" editorial from
La Tribuna, 1952

Document 6–6 353
Excerpt from Enrique Córdova's Memoir,
"General Maximiliano Hernández Martínez,"
written in 1960s

Document 6–7 356
"Is Confrontation Inevitable?" editorial by
Sidney Mazzini in *Diario de Hoy*, 1977

NOTES 359

WORKS CITED 381

INDEX 399

LIST OF ILLUSTRATIONS

Intro-1	Roque Dalton in Prague ca. 1966–1967	3
1–1	Victims of the Matanza, from *Revolución comunista*	39
1–2	Cover of *Revolución comunista*	46
1–3	Lynching of Ama in *Revolución comunista*	59
2–1	Map of El Salvador indicating the main sites of the 1932 uprising	70
3–1	Roque Dalton on his high school diploma, 1952	99
3–2	Roque Dalton being released from prison, early 1960s	104
3–3	Headline *Diario de Hoy*, October 30, 1964	105
4–1	A page of Dalton's original notebook	144
4–2	A page of Dalton's original notebook	147
4–3	A page of Dalton's original notebook	148
4–4a	A page of Dalton's original notebook	154
4–4b	A page of Dalton's original notebook	155
4–5a	A page of Dalton's original notebook	158
4–5b	A page of Dalton's original notebook	159
4–6	A page of Dalton's original notebook	161
4–7	A page of Dalton's original notebook	165

4–8	A page of Dalton's original notebook	166
4–9	A page of Dalton's original notebook	168
4–10	A page of Dalton's original notebook	170
4–11	A page of Dalton's original notebook	172
4–12	A page of Dalton's original notebook	175
4–13	A page of Dalton's original notebook	178
4–14	A page of Dalton's original notebook	180
5–1	Miguel Mármol, ca. 1960s or 1970s	196
5–2	Dalton with Roberto Retamar in Cuba, ca. early 1960s	211
6–1	Headline of *El Día*, January 21, 1932	220
6–2	Page from *Diario de Hoy*, January 16, 1967	236

ACKNOWLEDGMENTS

This project is a group effort that has grown out of many years of professional work by three scholars who came together because of a shared commitment to the subject matter. It would be impossible to recognize the tremendous number of people and institutions that have helped each of us carry out our research over the years. So, at the risk of failing to acknowledge the many intellectual, personal, and financial debts we have accrued, we will limit ourselves to the people and institutions that have been most immediately involved in the completion of this specific book.

First, we owe a great debt to the family of Roque Dalton for allowing us access to Dalton's personal archive. We were the first scholars to see the archive, and we acknowledge the unprecedented opportunity that we have had in doing so. We have done our best to provide an honest and open interpretation of what we found. Throughout this process, our appreciation for the quantity and quality of Dalton's work has only grown. He was a remarkable author and a political activist who paid the ultimate price for his commitment to make El Salvador a better country.

Susan Greenblat-Campos translated most of the annex materials that were originally in Spanish. She demonstrated an unflinching attention to detail and insisted on getting it "just right," despite our repeated assurances that what she had done was enough.

Carlos Gregorio López-Bernal, the former director of the history program at the University of El Salvador (UES), has been a long-standing colleague in the study of Salvadoran history. In addition to facilitating Ching's Fulbright at the UES in the spring of 2005, he also organized a public lecture at the university that allowed us an opportunity to present our initial findings to a university audience. Carlos Gregorio and the rest of the staff in the history program at the UES have worked diligently to keep the study of history alive in postwar El Salvador.

Knut Walter, a long-standing colleague and friend in El Salvador, has aided in our research and subsequently in this book in ways too innumerable to recount.

Héctor Pérez Brignoli provided us with three valuable primary documents from his personal collection. They have made the book much stronger, and we gratefully acknowledge his generosity.

Alfredo Ramírez served as a research assistant in El Salvador and proved to be an ever-competent, reliable self-starter who made many valuable contributions to this book. Jaime Barba helped to organize an open forum on Roque Dalton at the UES that provided us with another opportunity to share our work. He also provided a commentary on leftist politics in 1970s El Salvador that resulted in some changes to one chapter. Geovani Galeas interviewed us on his program on public television in El Salvador, which gave us both an opportunity to share our findings and also to meet interesting people who contacted us after the shows. Mario Vásquez offered many valuable insights on the project during personal conversations.

We would like to thank Curbstone Press for allowing us to reprint a portion of the English translation of *Miguel Mármol*, and also Carlos Henríquez Consalvi and the Museum of Word and Image (MUPI) in San Salvador for allowing us to use some images from their collection. We received patient and excellent help from staff members at various libraries and archives, including but not limited to the National Archive (Archivo General de la Nación) in San Salvador, the National Library (Biblioteca Nacional) in San Salvador, the library of the David J. Guzmán National Museum in San Salvador, the Walsh Library at Fordham University, the James Buchanan Duke Library at Furman University, and the Russian State Archive of Social and Political History, Moscow, Russia (RGASPI). Svetlana Rosenthal of RGASPI was especially helpful.

As for reviewing and editing this book, our first and foremost acknowledgment goes to Lyman Johnson, editor of the Diálogos series of the University of New Mexico Press. His comments were incisive and invariably helpful. He dedicated a great amount of time to editing various versions of this book, especially the initial draft. The final result is by far and away a much stronger and better product as a result of his efforts. Professor Judy Bainbridge, a senior member of the English faculty at Furman University, read the entire manuscript to provide an "outsider's" perspective. Her insights and comments were most helpful. We would like to thank the two anonymous reviewers through the University of New Mexico Press who provided worthwhile comments that led to improvements. Our thanks to Alex Giardino for an excellent copyedit.

Some of the funding that made this project possible was provided by Council on International Education Exchange's (CIEE) Fulbright Program that allowed Ching to spend an academic term in El Salvador in spring of 2005. Furman University's Research and Professional Growth Program and its Creative Advance Planning grant program also funded research for Ching and provided him leave time to write. Fordham University and New Mexico Tech have also provided financial and professional aid to Lindo-Fuentes and Lara-Martínez in various ways for the duration of this project.

ACRONYMS AND ABBREVIATIONS

ARENA	Alianza Republicana Nationalista (Nationalist Republican Alliance)
CC	Comité Central (Central Committee)
CCE	Comité Central Ejecutivo (Central Executive Committee)
CE	Comité Ejecutivo (Executive Committee)
CI	Communist International, or Comintern
CN	National Council
CTG	Confederación de Trabajadores de Guatemala (Confederation of Guatemalan Workers)
ERP	Ejército Revolucionario del Pueblo (People's Revolutionary Army)
FMLN	Frente Farabundo Martí para Liberación Nacional (Farabundo Martí National Liberation Front)
FPL	Fuerzas Populares de Liberación Farabundo Martí (Farabundo Martí Popular Liberation Forces)
FRTS	Federación Regional de Trabajadores Salvadoreños (Regional Federation of Salvadoran Workers)
ORDEN	Organización Democrática Nacionalista (Nationalist Democratic Organization)
PCS	Partido Comunista Salvadoreño (Salvadoran Communist Party)
PRTC	Partido Revolucionario de Trabajadores Centroamericanos (Revolutionary Party of Central American Workers)

RN	Resistencia Nacional (National Resistance)
SRI	Socorro Rojo Internacional (International Red Aid)
UES	Universídad de El Salvador (University of El Salvador)

Bibliographic and Endnote Abbreviations

AGN	Archivo General de la Nación, San Salvador, El Salvador
CN	Colección de Nulos
FO	Foreign Office
GDC	Guatemala Documents Collection
LC	United States Library of Congress
MG	Ministerio de Gobernación, El Salvador
PRO	Public Record Office, London, England
RG	Records Group
RGASPI	Russian State Archive of Social and Political History, Moscow, Russia
SI	Sección Indiferente
SNIE	Special National Intelligence Estimate
SS	Sección Sonsonate
USNA	United States National Archive, Washington, DC
WNRC	Washington National Records Center, Suitland, Maryland

INTRODUCTION

> History turns into myth as soon as it is remembered, narrated, and used, that is, woven into the fabric of the present.
> —Jan Assmann, *Moses the Egyptian*

In late January 1932, thousands of poor peasants in western El Salvador rose up in rebellion. Armed mostly with machetes and a few guns, they attacked roughly one dozen municipalities, including direct assaults on army garrisons in the provincial capitals of Sonsonate and Ahuachapán. The rebels failed to seize the two cities, but they did gain control of more than half a dozen smaller, but still populous townships. They directed their attacks on sites of local power, such as municipal offices and homes of the elite. The rebellion lasted about three days before the military collected itself and regained control of the occupied towns. During the army's counterattacks, the rebels retreated quickly before the soldiers' superior weaponry. By the time the rebellion was suppressed, the rebels had killed between fifty and one hundred people.

The reoccupation of rebel-held towns marked only the beginning of the state's devastating response to the uprising. During the next two weeks, the army and local paramilitary bands embarked on a massive killing spree. They massacred peasants indiscriminately throughout the entire western region. In towns that had witnessed heavy rebel activity, the army gathered peasants into municipal plazas under the pretext of granting them safe passage and machine-gunned them en masse. Lynch mobs comprised of local citizens and military reservists chased down individuals and shot or hung them. By the time it was all over, the number of dead may have been ten to thirty thousand. The wide discrepancy in estimated figures is the result of no one having bothered or dared to count the bodies strewn throughout the countryside, lying exposed along roadsides, or buried in mass graves. Having since been dubbed the the "Matanza," or the massacre, this episode of mass killing has the dubious distinction of being acknowledged as one of the most extreme cases of state-sponsored repression in modern Latin American history.

Among other things, the Matanza helped consolidate the military's hold on power in El Salvador, which it had seized in a coup just two months earlier. The military went on to retain control over the government for fifty years, constituting the longest period of uninterrupted military rule (1931–79) in modern Latin American history. Even after the military left power in 1979, it retained tremendous political influence until the end of a devastating twelve-year civil war, from 1980 to 1992. As these events suggest, twentieth-century El Salvador has been a land of extremes, and 1932 stands out as a sad exemplar of this reality.

One of the people who survived the massacre of 1932 was Miguel Mármol. He was a young man from a poor family that lived in a fishing hamlet not far from the capital city of San Salvador. A shoemaker by trade, he became a labor activist in the 1920s and eventually helped found El Salvador's Communist Party in March 1930. The police arrested Mármol shortly after the uprising broke out because they suspected him and all other communists of having organized the insurrection. Soldiers took Mármol and eighteen other prisoners to a ditch outside San Salvador to execute them by firing squad. Mármol was shot four times, but he survived, largely because so much blood had been spilled on him that as a police officer was preparing to deliver the coup de grâce a superior told him not to waste the bullet. Mármol went on to serve as a ranking member of the Communist Party until his death by natural causes in 1993.

In 1966, Mármol attended a meeting in Russia and spent two weeks in Prague on his return trip. There, he unexpectedly met another Salvadoran communist, the young journalist and poet Roque Dalton. The two men had not met previously, although Dalton had

INTRO-1
Roque Dalton during his exile in Prague, 1966–67.

heard stories about this legendary survivor of 1932. They struck up a fast friendship. Eventually, during a series of interviews Mármol told Dalton his life story. From the notes of these meetings, Dalton wrote a roughly five-hundred-page text that was first published in Costa Rica in 1972 under the title *Miguel Mármol: Los sucesos de 1932 en El Salvador* (Miguel Mármol: The events of 1932 in El Salvador).[1]

Fascinating, politically charged, and written in the first person, *Miguel Mármol* was one of the earliest examples of testimonial literature, a genre of international proportions that emerged primarily out of Latin America during the civil conflicts of the 1970s and 1980s. Testimonial literature was typified by a disenfranchised person telling his or her life story to a literate outsider who had the training and contacts to compile and publish the story. Testimonials are inherently political because they express the voice of someone normally excluded from public discourse. In particular, testimonials tend to stress the brutal reality of living in severely hierarchical societies ruled by military regimes. Miguel Mármol's narrative never achieved the international recognition of its successors, especially *I, Rigoberta Menchú,* the story of a Guatemalan Indian woman first published in 1983 that contributed to her receiving the Nobel Peace Prize in 1992. But Mármol had little conceptualization of these broader literary issues, and although Dalton did, testimonial literature was still in its infancy in the mid-1960s. The two of them had stumbled upon one another accidentally in Eastern Europe in the midst of the cold war and were navigating uncharted waters. They were simply trying to tell a story that they believed to be politically relevant back home.

Indeed, *Miguel Mármol* had tremendous political implications for El Salvador, even though it was not published there in its entirety until after the civil war. *Miguel Mármol* challenged one of the great ironies of 1932—the eerie silence in the decades after the Matanza. The events were rarely discussed publicly, yet most everyone in the country knew about them because stories had been passed down in personal conversation and oral tradition. The versions of events contained in these traditions varied significantly with each person and group, but most every Salvadoran at least knew that something tremendous and horrifying had happened back in the early 1930s. In this way, 1932 represented an element of shared national identity, in which knowing something about the events helped to define what it meant to be Salvadoran.

Miguel Mármol quickly emerged as the master narrative of 1932. Accounts had been published before, and others would be published afterward, but none of them achieved the influence or recognition of Mármol's. Although conservative anticommunists hated Mármol's politics, they agreed with his basic story line, that the Salvadoran Communist Party and the ideology of communism were pivotal to the uprising. The right reinterpreted 1932 as a victory over communist subversion, whereas Mármol and the left defined it as an act of heroism by the Communist Party and the brutal preservation of elite privilege. In this regard, *Miguel Mármol* at once reflected and promoted the political polarization that defined El Salvador in the 1960s and 1970s and that sent the country hurtling down the path to civil war in the 1980s. That the memory of 1932 played a decisive role in defining later battle lines is evidenced by the nomenclature of the opposing sides in the civil war. The rebel guerrilla force named itself after Farabundo Martí, a leftist activist in the early 1930s who was executed by the military during the Matanza. One of the most brutal death squads in the 1970s and 1980s named itself the General Maximiliano Hernández Martínez Brigade, after the president in 1932 who oversaw both Martí's execution and the Matanza.

Interpreting 1932 and the Making of Communist Causality

It is difficult to overstate the scale of 1932 and its importance to Salvadoran history. Rebels killed or wounded dozens of people, attacked military garrisons, occupied towns, and looted or destroyed businesses, government buildings, and private homes. In response, the army killed thousands of people in a few days, preserving oligarchic rule and establishing military authoritarianism as the governing norm. Some people viewed these events with gratification, even if they found the violent process unfortunate. Others considered the events horrendous and lived in constant fear that the state would unleash mass terror once again. Regardless of who looked at them, the events of 1932 left an indelible impression on generations of Salvadorans.

Since 1932, Salvadorans and internationals alike have been trying to make sense of what happened, but meaning has proven elusive. Candid public discussion of the events was suppressed, archives were off-limits, documents were destroyed, lost, or stolen, and many people who witnessed the events were exiled or killed or remained silent. However, some evidence survived. Journalists wrote reports, eyewitnesses shared their accounts, the U.S. and British legations filed official briefings, and various authors and artists made 1932 a subject of inquiry. Still, until the early 1990s, the public record on 1932 was small, which made the few published accounts, like *Miguel Mármol*, all the more important because they represented the precious arena where the memory of 1932 existed in public. In the early 1990s, with the end of the cold war and El Salvador's civil war, new evidence surfaced, including government records from archives in El Salvador and the papers of the Salvadoran Communist Party from the Comintern archive in Moscow, Russia. Most recently, a team of international scholars gathered dozens of oral testimonies from elderly eyewitnesses and some descendents of survivors who have preserved their family memories as oral traditions. It would be an overstatement to say that the evidence now available on 1932 is comprehensive or that published accounts are completely convincing. Unaware readers who venture into the record of 1932 will find a dizzying array of argumentative twists and turns. But over the years, two issues have dominated interpretive debates: communism and ethnicity.

Many factors explain why communism would assume a central role in interpretations of 1932. Geopolitical conditions in the 1920s and early 1930s encouraged onlookers to view rebellions like that of 1932 in El Salvador as communist. Never mind that El Salvador hardly resembled the industrialized capitalist society that Marx envisioned as ripe for revolution or that the nation had a tiny and disorganized communist party. Just a few years earlier the 1917 Revolution had brought Russia, then one of the largest and potentially wealthiest countries in the world, under communist rule. The new Russian leaders vowed to promote global revolution. To this end, they established the Comintern, or Third Communist International, an organizational committee based in Moscow and comprised of communists from across the globe. They worked diligently to coordinate local party activities throughout the world.

Advocates of communism in Latin America looked upon the Russian Revolution and the formation of the Third International with great expectation. They saw Russia as a beacon of hope and approached their local plans with renewed enthusiasm. Opponents of communism in Latin America viewed the Bolshevik victory in Russia with trepidation. Already opposed to Marxism in principle, they became rabid anticommunists, convinced that the Soviet Union was behind a global conspiracy, sending money and advisors into the world to incite class conflict and foment global revolution. These anticommunists feared that their societies would be caught up in an international firestorm and that long-standing local issues would now assume global dynamics. Much like today's war against terror, the surge in anticommunist hysteria in the 1920s, known as the first Red Scare, mobilized citizens to defend their societies against a supposed onslaught.

When rebellions like that of 1932 in El Salvador occurred in the midst of this first Red Scare, many onlookers were inclined to interpret these events in the context of the global clash between communism and capitalism and to assume that communists, either national or international, were responsible for causing them. Indeed, many superficial aspects of the 1932 uprising followed the script of social revolution; thousands of poor people violently attacked centers of local power, and most of the roughly fifty to one hundred people killed were representatives of El Salvador's power structures—the army, the government, and the rich. Some of the earliest reports of the uprising described the rebels as communists who shouted slogans and carried placards in favor of communism. One of the first newspaper headlines in El Salvador that focused on the uprising read, "Communist Hordes Burn and Loot Various Locations," and the front page of the *New York Times* reported, "Red Revolt Sweeps Cities in Salvador."[2]

In later decades, international conditions further encouraged analysts to look back upon the 1932 rebellion and portray it as communist-inspired. The first Red Scare abated in the 1930s with the emergence of fascism in Europe and the eventual alliance between the United States and the Soviet Union against Hitler and Mussolini in WWII. But after the conclusion of the war, and with the onset of the cold war in the late 1940s, a second, more virulent Red Scare materialized. The success of the Cuban Revolution in 1959 and the rise of left-wing militancy across Central America in the 1960s and 1970s brought the new Red Scare home to El Salvador in full force. Anticommunists marked these developments with renewed trepidation, whereas adherents of communism became all the more convinced that social revolution was inevitable. Both sides hunkered down for a long and increasingly violent battle. To many Salvadorans, it seemed that a pattern was emerging, in which communism played a key role in the nation's history, dating back to 1932.

Political conditions inside El Salvador encouraged later interpreters to look back upon the rebellion of 1932 as being led by communists. Ironically both communists and their enemies came to agree that the uprising of 1932 was caused by communism. This belief, which we call the argument of "communist causality," became an ideological focal point for both the right and left in El Salvador, especially in the years leading up to the civil war of the 1980s. The right accepted communist causality because it portrayed their forefathers as the historic defenders of the nation, who fought back the barbaric threat of communism and preserved El Salvador as a Catholic nation respectful of *propiedad privada* (private property) and ruled according to the values of the leaders of the *empresa privada* (business community). Furthermore, the right used this argument to justify its hard-line stance against mass mobilization in the 1960s and 1970s, including the use of death squads to eliminate supposed "communist" insurgents. The left accepted communist causality because it depicted communists as the historic leaders of the masses, the protectors of the downtrodden, and the vanguard in the fight against capitalism. The left also used this argument to promote itself as the leader of the surge in mass militancy after 1960. In other words, both the left and the right in El Salvador considered 1932 to be the precedent for their contemporary battle lines. Perhaps more than any other reason, this convergence of opinion between ideological enemies explains why communist causality came to dominate interpretations of 1932.

Nevertheless, there are reasons why communist causality was challenged by other arguments, mainly that of ethnicity. One reason is that by 1932 the history of labor unionism and communist activism in El Salvador had been short. The first nationwide labor union did not form until 1924, and the Communist Party was not founded until March 1930, less than two years before the insurrection occurred. As an agricultural country with a nominal industrial base and a small urban work force, El Salvador did not fit the traditional Marxist notion of a country poised for social revolution. In fact, various Salvadoran and international communists argued that El Salvador had to go first through a bourgeois, capitalist revolution and sweep away the vestiges of feudalism before a true socialist revolution could occur.

Regardless of communism's short history in El Salvador, anticommunism was alive and well in the 1920s and 1930s. The government used it to justify crackdowns on dissident workers, and El Salvador's conservative intellectuals discussed the threat that the Russian Revolution represented to their society. But before 1932 El Salvador did not experience the same degree of anticommunist hysteria as its more industrialized counterparts in North America and Europe, where economic downturns after WWI and during the Great Depression caused widespread misery and boosted membership in leftist political parties. To many onlookers in the 1920s and early 1930s, it seemed that Marx had been all too prescient more than a half century earlier when he said that the growing misery of the industrial proletariat in Europe would be the engine of social revolution.

El Salvador too suffered during those tumultuous years of the 1920s and early 1930s, but many Salvadorans considered communism to be only one of many factors shaping their society. In addition to communism, they were concerned about ethnic conflict over land, regional patronage networks struggling for autonomy against a centralizing state, and nation-building programs that suppressed ethnic diversity in the name of national unity. Arguably, the issue of ethnicity and the possibility of Indian rebellions were of greater concern to elite Salvadorans in the late 1920s and early 1930s than were communism and the possibility of socialist revolution. Some Salvadorans considered the Mexican Revolution, with its focus on landownership and ethnic mobilization, to be more relevant than the distant Russian Revolution. Indeed, conditions in western El Salvador resembled those in Mexico; the region had a history of ethnic conflict in which Ladinos (members of the dominant culture regardless of race) defined Indians as threats to progress, and Indians, in turn, identified Ladinos as repressive, elitist racists who were determined to eradicate Indians from society. The ideology of communism did not necessarily fit into that long history of ethnic conflict.

On the whole, Salvadorans have preferred to downplay the issue of ethnicity in their history. By the early 1900s, the increasingly popular idea that most Salvadorans were of mixed ancestry (*mestizos*) provided one reason to ignore ethnic differences. By the mid-twentieth century, the climate of the cold war after WWII further encouraged Salvadorans to put aside ethnic explanations of the past and focus on the clash between capitalism and communism. However, imagine if later interpreters of 1932 had not had the cold war environment to shape their vision. Imagine if after WWII Stalin had been marginalized in Russia, Central Europe had been torn asunder by ethnic conflict, and countries in Latin America, such as Bolivia and Peru, had followed a similar pattern of ethnic unraveling. If these events had transpired, ethnicity might have replaced communism as the primary explanation in global politics. Under such conditions, interpreters might have looked back upon 1932 as just another historic example of ethnic conflict rather the first in a series of communist conspiracies, and we would now be discussing "ethno-causality" rather than "communist causality" as the dominant explanatory framework.

Of course, global events did not transpire that way. The cold war happened and the clash between capitalism and communism pushed aside ethnicity as the preferred explanatory variable. But the point of presenting this counterfactual is to illustrate our main argument in this book, that present exigencies affect historical interpretation. A clear example of the relationship between political conditions and scholarship can be seen in U.S. historiography after 1945. In the 1940s and 1950s, the United States emerged as a global superpower, once and for all surpassing its European cousins. Because the ascendancy of the United States coincided with the cold war, the United States linked its superpower status to the defense of capitalism and democracy as well as to the suppression of socialism and the containment of the Russian Revolution. Historical scholarship reflected these developments with what has come to be known as "consensus history," or "American exceptionalism." Historians adhering to these perspectives described U.S. history as rooted in liberal ideals such as freedom, democracy, and economic growth through the marketplace. They called this history "exceptional" in order to set the United States apart from Old World Europe, which supposedly suffered from the lingering effects of feudalism and conflicts from the early modern era. As part of the New World, the founders of the United States supposedly escaped these legacies and invented a new progressive nation destined to become a global leader.[3]

Consensus history and American exceptionalism came under attack in the 1960s and 1970s from so-called new historicism, which emphasized social history over political history and which stressed the importance of people previously left out of past analyses, such as working people, women, and African Americans and other minorities. Adherents of new historicism looked at the darker side of U.S history, its hierarchies and repressive traits, and offered an alternative to consensus history. Not coincidentally, the emergence of new historicism coincided with the conflicts of the civil rights movement and protests against the Vietnam War. As these movements brought new actors onto the political stage, demands for a more complete history, one that avoided the sanitized and celebratory "consensus" of the 1940s and 1950s, increased. Ellen Fitzpatrick, a scholar of these trends in scholarship, concludes that there is a direct link between political conditions and historical writing: "Political currents, social trends, cultural conflicts and intellectual upheaval—the very history of the United Stats in the twentieth century—have been profound determinants of historical tradition and memory. Historians are no more immune to these forces than any other group of Americans."4 One element of Fitzpatrick's argument that holds great salience to our study of El Salvador is that the school of consensus history in the United States was not necessarily developed consciously or with the coordinated intention of its advocates. In other words, they didn't revise U.S. history simply for the sake of contemporary political objectives and without regard for the pursuit of historical "truth." Rather, consensus history emerged because the historians who conducted the studies believed that they were uncovering a reality of the U.S. past that had been ignored by prior scholars. A similar commitment guided the adherents of new historicism.

The way communist causality came to dominate interpretations of 1932 offers another example of a relationship between political exigencies and historical interpretation. Before the onset of the cold war, communism and ethnicity received roughly equal attention as an explanation for the events of 1932. However, once the cold war settled in, and especially after the Cuban Revolution in 1959, communist causality pushed ethnicity aside and began to dominate analyses. But today, after the cold war and the civil war in El Salvador have ended, communism no longer seems as relevant and scholars of 1932 are reconsidering ethnicity as a causal variable. Not so coincidentally, Indian communities in El Salvador are pushing for greater political recognition, and part of their efforts includes redefining 1932 as a decisive moment in their history of struggle. In short, political conditions and trends in scholarship often affect one another.

During its heyday, communist causality so dominated explanations of 1932 that it can be called a "metanarrative," an argument so widely accepted and consistently repeated that it suppressed all other interpretations. In social science theory, a metanarrative is an argument that defines debate rather than being defined by it, that shapes investigation rather than being subjected to it.5 In the case of 1932 in

El Salvador, the metanarrative of communist causality led investigators to study the communist origins of the uprising, rather than asking if the uprising had been communist in the first place.

But even in the midst of a metanarrative, dissenting arguments do not disappear entirely. They survive as "counternarratives," or what historian Jan Assmann would call a countermemory, "a memory that puts elements to the fore that are, or tend to be, forgotten in the official memory."[6] In regard to 1932, counternarrative arguments downplayed communism and looked to other explanations for the cause of the uprising, such as regional identity, religion, class, gender, and especially ethnicity, all of which had little or nothing to do with Russia, Marxism-Leninism, or the Communist Party of El Salvador. The counternarratives of 1932 can be difficult to locate in the sources, and sometimes they require a close reading to be discovered. In fact, sometimes they exist in the same sources that advanced communist causality, such as the book *Revolución comunista* (Communist Revolution) by the anticommunist Guatemalan journalist Jorge Schlesinger. Published in Guatemala in 1946, the book's main argument is that the 1932 uprising was communist. But a careful reading reveals repeated references to ethnicity and descriptions of the rebels as Indians. In other words, the counternarrative of ethnic conflict survived amidst Schlesinger's overarching promotion of communist causality. Anyone who read his work would have come away, either consciously or unconsciously, with an appreciation for the importance of ethnicity to the events. Only with the advantage of hindsight can one discern these trends and see how individual arguments accumulate into collective patterns, often without the conscious intent of the authors who wrote them. Our argument is that the rise of communist causality to metanarrative status has less to do with the historic evidence and more to do with political conditions in El Salvador that made it an acceptable argument to most people.

Historical Memory

The main goal of the present book is to answer two deceptively simple questions: How have the events of 1932 in El Salvador been remembered, and what factors determined those memories? We contend that ideological and political conflicts in El Salvador in the decades after 1932 allowed communist causality to become the dominant memory of 1932, even though close analysis of the evidence provides ample reason to question communism's role. We also argue that alternative memories, such as ethnicity, survived and created a fluid interpretive environment in which communist causality was at least occasionally challenged in the marketplace of ideas. To prove these points, we examine an array of sources covering the events of 1932, including but not limited to books, oral interviews, and newspapers. We pay special attention to the *Miguel Mármol* testimonial, in part because of its importance in the rendering of 1932, but also because we have a new source of special richness. Thanks to the generosity of the Dalton family, we have been granted first-ever access to Roque Dalton's personal archive, which includes the handwritten notes that he took during his interviews with Mármol in Prague in 1966. By comparing the notes to the final published version of *Miguel Mármol*, we are able to demonstrate that the story of 1932 contained in the final publication changed from that recorded in the original interview. Mármol's seemingly singular narrative voice in the book actually reflects the contribution of multiple voices, most notably Dalton's. We expand our examination outward from *Miguel Mármol* to include an array of other sources, which allows us to argue that the complexity of *Miguel Mármol* encapsulates the various elements that contributed to diverse narrative organizations of the memories of 1932 in twentieth-century El Salvador.[7]

At this point, an astute reader might want to ask us the following question: Instead of studying the memory of 1932, why don't you study the events of 1932 in order to discover the truth and set the record straight? In the present book, we take an approach that Jan Assmann calls "mnemohistory," that is, it "is concerned not with the past as such, but only with the past as it is remembered."[8] When some sections of the book provide more traditional historical accounts, they do so to show why the memory of 1932 was rendered important and shaped by a present context. We also show that the memories of 1932 influenced the direction of Salvadoran history.

The idea that memory is a social product that shapes personal identity but is also shaped by political and social contexts has a long and venerable past. Since the late nineteenth and early twentieth centuries, when historian Ernest Renan (1823–92) underscored the importance of forgetting for the creation of a sense of national identity, and sociologist Maurice Halbwachs (1877–1945) argued that memory is always a social product, thinkers in different disciplines have appreciated the acts of remembering and forgetting as complex, highly social experiences.[9] The memory of an event and the so-called facts of an event are intimately intertwined and mutually dependent. Paul Ricoeur (1913–2005) recognized the difficulty of differentiating between actual events and memories when he wrote, "We have nothing better than memory to signify that something has taken place, has occurred, has happened before we declare we remember it."[10] For Ricoeur our knowledge of the past exists in the form of memories. Rather than the past consisting of objective facts and memories being either accurate or inaccurate reflections of them, Ricoeur argues that "facts" come into existence when we turn them into a memory. Memory mediates consciousness. So, regardless of whether we participated in an event, witnessed it, or study it years later, our knowledge of the event exists as a memory in our minds. When memory mediates the processing and storing of the past, it does so by utilizing words and frameworks provided by the social context. Therefore, studying the "facts" cannot be divorced from the process by which we create and store memories, as shown by the earlier example of the rise and fall of "consensus" history in the United States.

The following assertion by one of El Salvador's deputies to the National Assembly in March 2004 illustrates our point. A group of university students from the United States traveled to El Salvador on a study-abroad program and met with the deputy (the equivalent of a congressman in the United States) as part of their trip. The deputy was a high-ranking member of the Nationalist Republican Alliance (ARENA), a conservative political party founded in 1981 that has won each of the four presidential elections since 1989. The deputy discussed with the students the history of ARENA and its current platform and made repeated references to the 1932 uprising. When a student asked him how many people the rebels killed in 1932, the deputy responded, "twenty thousand." Thinking that the deputy had misheard the question, the student clarified that he was asking how many people the rebels killed, not how many the army killed during the Matanza. The deputy responded that he indeed understood the question, saying,

"The rebels had killed 20,000 during the uprising and the army responded with a comparable number during the massacre."[11]

We can assume that the deputy was not lying or trying to deceive his audience, but instead he was expressing a version of the past that seemed appropriate to him. He can be accused of ignorance, of not having consulted readily available books with accurate information that would have shown him that the rebels had killed fewer than one hundred people rather than twenty thousand. But that explanation is insufficient. The deputy probably felt himself quite informed on the subject, based on what he had heard when he was growing up and what he had occasionally read in newspapers. He may have heard competing descriptions of the events, but somehow what registered in his mind as accurate was the particular account that he shared with the students. The question then becomes, what led him to reject certain versions of 1932 as false and accept others as true? As a young man who had not lived through the events of 1932, his understanding was based on the historical memory of the various social groups to which he belonged, each with a vested interest in remembering 1932 in a particular way. Although it is difficult to know which of these social groups were most influential in shaping his historical memory, it is likely that his political affiliation (ARENA), his ethnicity (non-Indian), and his class (wealthy) were influential. The relevant issue in this example is not so much the extent to which the deputy's knowledge was right or wrong, but rather the process by which his memory of 1932 came into existence. The challenge is to determine which groups or sociopolitical variables were speaking through him when he answered, "twenty thousand."

The ARENA deputy's response is more comprehensible when we consider memory as a social commodity. As much as we like to think of our memories as belonging to us as individuals, in fact they belong to all the different groups with which we affiliate, however distant that affiliation might be. Whether the group is our family, circle of friends, community, region, nation, political party, employment group, worship group, literary group, generation, race, class, or gender, it affects our personal identity and thus how we recall the past. Groups have an investment in how its individual members remember things, and subsequently, they promote conformity to a collective ideal. This pressure to conform can be the result of a coordinated effort, perhaps by leaders of the group. More often the pressures are uncoordinated, haphazard, and decentralized, but they are no less influential in shaping our sense of self and our manner of recollecting the past. In short, memory is at once personal and collective.

Another example from El Salvador shows how the memory of a group can shift in accordance with social and political conditions unbeknownst to individual members. The province of Morazán in eastern El Salvador witnessed some of the most intense fighting during the civil war of the 1980s and its population endured numerous army atrocities. The best documented of such atrocities was the massacre at El Mozote in December 1981, when an infamous army battalion, the Atlacatl, murdered hundreds of unarmed peasant villagers. While conducting fieldwork in the region years later, the anthropologist Leigh Binford discovered that his informants attributed other massacres to the Atlacatl as well. But Binford realized that the events they were describing happened before the Atlacatl had been created, and thus this unit could not have been culpable. The peasants were not lying to Binford, but rather were telling the story of the civil war as they remembered it. Their memories had shifted without their awareness according to their political and social conditions.[12]

But just as memories can surrender to pressures for change, so too can they resist them. Memories function similar to narratives in that they order past events and relate them to audiences. In a way, a memory is a story put into linguistic form. Recent theories of narrative and language suggest that memories, like language, are neither fully open nor closed systems.[13] Rather they reside at a halfway point between peoples' intentional desires to change the story and previous versions of the story that act as bulwarks against alteration.

If the linguistic theories of Ferdinand de Saussure (1857–1913) and the literary theories of Mikhail Bakhtin (1895–1975) are applied to the study of memory, what emerges is a concept of memory as being simultaneously individual and collective, and malleable and inflexible.[14] According to Saussure, we belong to linguistic communities, and through constant interaction with the members of those communities, we collectively agree upon the meanings of the words we use. Bakhtin made a similar argument about interpretive communities and used the term "dialogic" to refer to the constant give-and-take relationship between the members of group as they arrive at mutually agreed upon meanings. By extension we can see ourselves as belonging to many different "memory communities" that have vested interests in how their individual members recall the past. Therefore, we are involved in a dialogic relationship with the members of our memory group(s) over what form our memories will take when we turn them into narrative expression. If, for example, the ARENA deputy had said that the rebels in 1932 killed only fifty people and caused minimal damage, but the army slaughtered thousands of innocent people during the Matanza, he would have betrayed the established norms of the ARENA memory community, which depends on steadfast anticommunism and a belief that while communism destroys society, the army defends it. In other words, the deputy thought about 1932 within parameters established by his context, which limited his range of interpretive options.

Our memories might surrender to pressures for change, or they might resist those pressures, but in either case, memories are the negotiated terrain between what actually happened and how we express what happened in a social context. To return to what Paul Ricoeur said, our memories are all that we have of an event, so the objective and foundational "truth" of an event rapidly dissipates, leaving us with only our memories in the form of linguistic and narrative expression. Often, then, debates over what happened in the past turn out to be linguistic and narrative contests, taking place where memories are articulated and shared with other people.

One has to ask hard questions when it comes to the issues of how memory works and how it is affected over time and by social contexts. In addition to the linguistic, literary, and social theories mentioned above, recent work by experimental psychologists and brain researchers question how people recall events. They utilize the experimental method, statistical analysis, and brain scans, or in other words, what is typically called "hard science," yet their work reinforces and complements many of the insights of Renan, Halbwachs, Saussure, Bakhtin, and Ricoeur.

Daniel Schacter, the chair of Harvard's Department of Psychology, has surveyed hundreds of articles containing the most relevant scientific literature on memory and reported his results in *The Seven Sins of Memory: How the Mind Forgets and Remembers*.[15] One of the "sins" identified by Schacter is labeled "bias." As the author explains, psychological research shows that "people whose views on political issues have changed over time often recall incorrectly past attitudes as highly similar to present ones. In fact, memories of past political views are sometimes more closely related to present views than to what people actually believed in the past."[16] Another memory problem identified by Schacter is also particularly relevant for our subject matter. It is the problem of suggestibility. One of the instances when this problem occurs is when information is elicited by a second person, such as in interviews, police interrogations, and survey questions. Individuals have a tendency to incorporate in their memories information that comes from other sources, be it suggested overtly (as happens sometimes in police interrogations), or indirectly (other versions of the same event, or politically inspired speculations put forth by interested parties). Leading questions and certain phrasing can suggest answers because most people avoid dissonance and prefer to be in agreement with their interlocutors. Information and photographs in newspapers and images on television can also affect people's recall of an event. This is particularly problematic when the events in question have been amply discussed or reported. Such is the case with the impact and persistence of 1932 in public and private discussion.

Analyzing memory is no simple task, even when it comes in the form of a firsthand recollection, like a memoir or a personal conversation. In fact, any expressive form, including architecture, statues, paintings, music, drama, oral testimonies, and film, among many others, can serve as a site of contested memory. The general public may think of academic scholars as operating outside this debate, as trained professionals who are immune from social pressures, demonstrating the accuracies or inaccuracies of any given historical memory. But academics are not so privileged; they too belong to memory groups. Their interpretive process is subject to the same social pressures as anyone else, be it a professional historian or an average "person on the street" who has not devoted much thought to how historical memory comes into being.

Historical memory assumes political importance because it can be used to legitimize policies and actions. Every group has certain memories that serve as a touchstone for its identity. For Salvadorans on both the left and the right, that memory is 1932. For the French it might be the Revolution of 1789; for people in the United States, the American Revolution, the civil rights movement, or September 11; for Russians, the Gulag; for South Africans, Apartheid; for Jews, the Holocaust. Memories of the same event need not be unitary; in fact, they seldom are. When key memories are invoked in the public arena, they may define battle lines. Groups may defend their memories, or their particular interpretations of the past in order to preserve their sense of collective identity. Sometimes they fight their battles in oral testimonies, written words, public monuments, or images, such as photographs and motion pictures. Other times, sadly, they fight with guns or other weapons, as people kill their adversaries, or sacrifice themselves to defend the collective memory of their group. People do not readily sacrifice themselves for memories that they see as political fabrications, but rather for ideas they believe to be truthful. Most people do not want to fight and die for lies. They want to defend and they actively seek out the truth. But, once again, the question is what leads them to accept a particular version as true?

The link between political action and historical memory is apparent in the most diverse contexts. The wars in Yugoslavia during the 1990s provide an excellent example of the mobilization of memory for political confrontation.[17] Historians refer to Slobodan Miloscvic's infamous 1987 speech to commemorate a victory of the Ottomans over the Serbs in the battle of Kosovo in 1389 as a turning point in the dissolution of Yugoslavia. The Yugoslav leader used the memory of an event five hundred years earlier to inflame Serb nationalist feelings, and thus he ultimately put his country on the road to self-destruction. In the end Yugoslavia was fragmented by enraged groups fueled by memories. As Ilana R. Bet-El puts it:

> These were memories of aggressive acts committed by the others: Croats upon Serbs and Muslims; Muslims upon Croats and Serbs; Serbs upon Croats and Muslims and Albanian Kosovars; Albanian Kosovars upon Serbs. Sin

upon sin, national memories conjured up as if they were real, personal memories, locking each ethnicity into itself, making all the others abhorrent, unjust and fearful. Words of the past became weapons of war.[18]

The fact that "words of the past," alternative narratives of distant events, can become "weapons of war" is the reason why the exploration of historical memory is as important as the exploration of "what actually happened."

Organization of the Book

We have divided the book into six chapters. The first chapter is dedicated to an extended narrative of the 1932 uprising and the Matanza based on the incomplete sources available. Within that description, we offer a discussion of the rationale behind the unprecedented massacre. In Chapter 2 we provide a historical background to put in context both the events of 1932 and the different "presents" that defined how they were remembered over time. Chapter 3 focuses on the life and work of Roque Dalton. We provide biographical information on Dalton and look at the corpus of his written work, especially his early writings on Salvadoran history that most directly affected his interpretation of 1932. In Chapter 4 we plunge into a comparison of Dalton's handwritten notes with the final published version of *Miguel Mármol*. Dalton recorded his interviews with Mármol in roughly seventy pages of handwritten field notes in a notebook, and then over the next six years he turned them into a cohesive five-hundred-page narrative. The comparison between the notes and the manuscript reveals Dalton's editing choices, allowing us to investigate the political and ideological rationales behind them. We focus on how a first-person testimony, loaded with distinct cultural elements of oral tradition, was turned into a seamless, linear chronology.

Chapters 5 and 6 examine the internal interpretive histories of the political right and left in El Salvador in regard to 1932. Chapter 5 is dedicated to the left and looks at an array of Communist Party and other left-wing documentation to show the existence of contentious internal debates over how the uprising of 1932 should be conceptualized. It reveals that intraleft factionalism over issues relating to the ideology of insurrection played a decisive role in shaping how individual left-wing interpreters, including Roque Dalton, conceived of the uprising. In addition to documents from the Communist Party in the early 1930s, the chapter introduces a previously unknown document written by Miguel Mármol in 1948 in which he connects internal party differences to the existence of rivaling approaches to 1932. Chapter 6 looks at the political right and shows that right-wing spokespersons conflated fears of ethnic and sexual violence with the specter of communism to delegitimize the rebels in 1932 and to undermine later support for left-wing insurgency. This had the unintended effect of retaining the issue of ethnicity as an explanatory variable for 1932, even as the right itself was rallying around anticommunism. The final chapter highlights our main arguments about identity, memory, and politics with brief references to preceding chapters. It also provides examples from contemporary El Salvador to show that memories of 1932 remain politically relevant today.

The Appendix is a document section consisting mostly of primary documents that either have never been published or have never been made available in English translation. The documents, ably translated by Susan Greenblat-Campos, were selected to illustrate our arguments and should be considered an integral part of the book. Hopefully, they will also assist imaginative college professors in developing material for rich classroom discussions.

CHAPTER ONE

The Uprising and the Matanza of 1932

> The past is not simply "received" by the present. The present
> is "haunted" by the past and the past is modeled, invented,
> reinvented, and reconstructed by the present.
> —Jan Assmann, *Moses the Egyptian*

In late January and early February 1932, El Salvador passed through a period of violence and terror that left an indelible imprint on its history and its inhabitants' psyches. Thousands of poor Indian and Ladino peasants across the western highlands attacked more than one dozen towns, destroying property and killing dozens of people in the process. In response the Salvadoran Army went on a murderous rampage across the western countryside, leaving thousands and perhaps tens of thousands of people dead in its wake. The goal of the present chapter is to describe the events of 1932 and examine debates over two pressing issues: the identity of the rebels and the reasons for the massacre. We rely on previously unavailable evidence, including the records of El Salvador's Communist Party stored in a formerly closed archive in Moscow, Russia, to illustrate that interpretations of the events have always been diverse and complex. In particular, the new evidence shows that many contemporary participants did not consider communism to be the most important explanatory variable. The fact that communist causality emerged as a metanarrative in later decades illustrates the importance of unraveling the process by which collective historical memories of 1932 came into existence.

The Setting

The 1932 uprising was centered in El Salvador's western countryside (see map, p. 70), a distinct region, but also one that shared similarities with the rest of the country. El Salvador was a predominantly agricultural nation with an overwhelmingly rural, poor population, and so, regardless of where people lived throughout the country, they tended to reside in rural districts on the outskirts of small regional towns. Western El Salvador was no exception to this rule. In 1932, El Salvador had 285 towns, almost all of which were small, isolated places that functioned as administrative and commercial centers for sprawling peasant populations. Wealthier residents of a region tended to live in town, in nice homes situated on or near the central plaza. Poorer peasant residents lived in simple, but functional one-room homes built of wooden poles and packed earth with straw or thatch roofs located on homesteads either on the immediate outskirts of town or on scattered properties throughout the surrounding countryside.[1]

In 1932 the majority of El Salvador's towns lacked paved streets and running water, and electricity was limited, although most towns were connected by telegraph lines to regional capitals. The rural areas had limited infrastructural development, and typically the only way to get goods into or out of them was on the backs of people or animals. Some of the larger plantations, and especially those where the owners were resident, had large homes, groomed lawns, and higher-quality access roads.

All rural areas were divided into administrative districts called *cantones*, which fell under the jurisdiction of a nearby town. Typically, each town had between ten and twenty cantones, but a canton was simply a geographical division for administrative purposes. Cantones had no centers or official buildings, nor did they offer services or government; in short, they were simply countryside. Even though the peasants who lived there were counted officially as residents of the nearby towns, most of them identified their canton as their place of residence, reflecting the fact that the majority of their daily existence revolved around the demands of rural labor. The peasant residents of cantones traveled to town occasionally to buy and sell goods, worship, and conduct official business, such as voting or registering a birth or death in the family. But they spent most of their lives in the countryside cultivating land. They either worked as laborers on nearby plantations or eked out a precarious existence on their personal farm plots known as *milpas*. A British adventurer who rode through El Salvador on horseback in 1933 during a continental trek to Chile, described the appearance of a typical Salvadoran peasant:

> The native men are dressed in loosely fitting white trousers and a shirt or blouse of the same color; as a rule these clothes are hanging in rags and are very dirty. They wear wide-brimmed straw hats with high crowns and rarely go out without a machete in their hands or hanging from their waists, like swords, in leather sheaths.[2]

El Salvador's peasants often lived near or with extended family members, and much of their life revolved around an immediate community of friends and family who functioned as a safety net, a necessary survival strategy in a country lacking basic public services.

El Salvador was notorious for having one of the highest population densities in the Western Hemisphere, which meant that even its rural areas were heavily impacted by people. In 1932, the country had approximately 1.5 million people living on slightly more than eight thousand square miles of land, giving it a population density of nearly 200 people per square mile, or twice that of the United States today. El Salvador's high population density is partly explained by the fact that the country had long been a main agricultural producer in Central America. People had been cultivating its soils for centuries, and they did so with special intensity in the late nineteenth and early twentieth centuries as the market for coffee soared. By 1932 few places in El Salvador remained remote from human contact, and the countryside consisted of a complex mishmash of plantations, cultivated plots, walking trails, irrigation ditches, and homesteads. Another North American who traveled through El Salvador in the early 1930s, this time by car, joked that "if one lights a cigarette in one village, he will be in the next before it is finished."[3]

Notwithstanding its similarities to the rest of the country, western El Salvador in 1932 was distinguished by two characteristics, Indians and coffee. As late as 1800, Indians accounted for as much as 50 percent of El Salvador's total population, but by the early twentieth century their numbers had dwindled to 20 percent or less. The reduction of Indian identity was a long, complex process that we will not examine in detail here; suffice it to say that pressures on indigenous culture were a common problem throughout the Western Hemisphere in the nineteenth and twentieth centuries. Young generations of indigenous people abandoned the cultural traits of their forefathers and become more "mestizo," or in the parlance of Central Americans, "Ladino." As the percentage of people who considered themselves indigenous in El Salvador diminished, the geographical areas where Indians predominated became more concentrated and distinct. Western El Salvador, and especially its central highlands, was one of those places. Most of the regions that rose up in rebellion in 1932 had a majority Indian population, and some of them, such as the town of Nahuizalco, were more than 90 percent Indian.

Most of El Salvador's Indians were poor, working peasants, and they were not particularly distinguishable from their Ladino counterparts. Regardless of their ethnicity, all peasants faced the challenges of poverty, illiteracy, and lack of access to resources, especially land. To the untrained eye, an Indian peasant community looked the same as a Ladino peasant community. The Indians may not have spoken Spanish as their first language, and some of them, women mainly, may have dressed in brightly colored clothing that was often a marker of Indian identity.

Indians in early twentieth-century El Salvador had a shared sense of identity with other Indians in a community setting and an uneasy relationship with Ladino society. Most Indian communities were run by long-standing religious and governing organizations known as *cofradías* that played important roles in their members' lives by binding them together in a sense of common purpose and togetherness.

Some of the largest and most influential Indian communities in El Salvador were located in the western highlands, around towns like Nahuizalco and Izalco. Historically, an Indian community and its cofradía were held together by their stewardship over a large track of communal land that members cultivated for survival to support collective objectives like support of religious and political obligations. But by 1932, communal lands in the country had been converted into private properties as a result of new laws passed in the early 1880s, which diminished Indian cohesiveness. Nevertheless, by 1932, Indian communities and their corresponding cofradías remained a vibrant part of the sociopolitical fabric of western El Salvador.

In addition to being home to large numbers of Indians, the highlands of western El Salvador were distinguished as a major center of coffee cultivation. The western highlands stretched roughly twenty-five miles wide and thirty miles long and began at the Guatemalan border in the west and ran east to the Santa Ana volcano, just behind the town of Izalco. The region included many volcanic mountains and hillsides, and even though the tallest peak did not surpass eight thousand feet in elevation, the many slopes between three and six thousand feet offered some of the richest coffee-growing soils in the world. In the latter half of the nineteenth century, the market for coffee rose rapidly in response to population growth and the Industrial Revolution in Europe and North America. Entrepreneurs and landowners in El Salvador responded by planting any and all suitable lands in coffee.

Prior to the late nineteenth century, the western highlands did not produce an export crop, so the pressures of producing for the global marketplace had not arrived there. El Salvador's main cash crop, indigo, was grown on flat lowland farms in the center and east of the country. Nevertheless, the west was still an important region in El Salvador. It served as the transit point to Guatemala, had been the site of many military campaigns throughout the first half of the nineteenth century, and its sizeable population was a valuable source of votes and soldiers. Subsequently, the western peasantry, and the Indian communities in particular, had a long and vibrant history of involvement in regional and national politics. But, the surge in coffee prices in the latter half of the nineteenth century turned western El Salvador into the country's primary revenue producer and brought a whole new series of transformative pressures. Many communal Indian lands had ended up in the hands of private Ladino coffee growers, and Indian and Ladino peasants were confronted by increasingly disparate distributions of resources and power. On the eve of the 1932 insurrection, coffee accounted for as much as 90 percent of all El Salvador's export revenues, and the series of changes that had occurred in the western countryside during the preceding five decades were staggering.

The 1932 rebellion was caused by the pressures that commercial coffee production imposed on the western highlands and its peasant residents. Issues of land, labor, local political control, market fluctuations, racism, and militarism converged into a highly volatile situation that eventually exploded in open revolt. The rebels were poor peasants, Indians for the most part, and they targeted symbols of local power, such as government buildings, businesses, homes, military garrisons, and local Ladino elites. The rebellion was organized in the rural cantones of approximately one dozen municipalities throughout the western highlands. The targets of attack were town centers where local elites and politicians lived and conducted their business. The main areas of rebel activity can be divided into six geographical zones running from west to east: Tacuba, Ahuachapán, Juayúa/Salcoatitán/Nahuizalco, Sonsonate/Sonzacate, Izalco, and Colón (see map, p. 70). Each of these areas had a distinct rebel force, so we can say with confidence that there were at least six, and perhaps more, centers of insurgent mobilization. The extent to which the distinct rebel groups coordinated their activities or responded to a central command structure remains a subject of intense debate. But one indication that at least some coordination existed is that the different rebel groups launched their attacks simultaneously.

The Events

The rebellion began in the late night and early morning of January 22 and 23. The typical pattern of attack consisted of many dozens and perhaps hundreds of rebels armed mostly with machetes and sticks, but also with a few poor-quality firearms, converging on a town's central plaza. They usually targeted the telegraph office first, hoping to cut communication with the heavily fortified military garrisons in the departmental capitals of Sonsonate, Ahuachapán, and Santa Ana. The common method of attacking telegraph offices consisted of hacking down the locked doors with machetes and trying to gain entry before the telegraph operators could send warning. Also attacked in the initial onslaught were military and police posts and municipal halls. With the exception of Sonsonate and Ahuachapán, the number of soldiers stationed in each of the targeted towns did not exceed one dozen. Even though the rebels were poorly armed, they had a numerical advantage and the element of surprise. This allowed them to successfully occupy more than a half dozen towns, including Tacuba, Salcoatitán, Juayúa, Nahuizalco, Sonzacate, Izalco, and Colón. With the exception of Salcoatitán, which had fewer than two thousand inhabitants, the towns occupied by the rebels were populous, important regional centers. Izalco's population of twenty thousand was only slightly less than that of the departmental capital, Sonsonate. Nahuizalco had fifteen thousand residents, Juayúa eight thousand, Tacuba seventy-five hundred, and Colón fifty-five hundred. Ahuachapán, with slightly fewer than thirty thousand residents, was the largest city attacked. By comparison, the capital city of San Salvador had one hundred thousand inhabitants.

Once in control of a town, the rebels turned on private homes and businesses. They burned some structures, but mostly they resorted to breaking into buildings and looting their contents. Rebels targeted certain individuals who symbolized the abuses of local power, including Miguel Call, the *alcalde* (mayor) of Izalco, Emilio Redaelli, the coffee merchant in Juayúa, and General Rafael Rivas, the military commander of Tacuba. But for the most part, the rebels did not indiscriminately assault civilians. During the entire uprising, the rebels killed fewer than one hundred people, including soldiers during military engagements. The rebels did, however, force some of the wives and daughters of local elites to grind corn and prepare tortillas for them, a normally demeaning job reserved for servants. Various rumors claimed that the rebels planned to gang rape elite women in various municipalities, but that accusation seems more a product of elite hysteria than rebel intention. As one scholar has noted, it seems too convenient that all the supposed rapes were scheduled to occur on the same day that the military arrived.[4]

The first towns to be attacked were Izalco, Juayúa, and Salcoatitán in the early morning hours of January 23, around 12:30 a.m. The number of rebels involved in each assault is difficult to determine owing to wild discrepancies in reports, but it is likely that they numbered in the hundreds at the beginning, and maybe even thousands at the height of the uprising. Supposedly, the rebels in these locales were led by two of the more renowned leaders, Chico Sánchez in Juayúa and Feliciano Ama in Izalco. Ama was an Indian, and he was commonly identified as a *cacique* (leader) of an Indian community in Izalco. Sánchez was also commonly identified as an Indian leader, or at least a person with strong ties to the Indian population around Juayúa. Another supposed leader in Izalco was Eusebio Chávez, a Ladino carpenter and evangelical Christian. Another leader in Juayúa was Rosalío (Felipe) Nerio, also sometimes identified as an Indian cacique from the surrounding area.

Eyewitness reports of the uprising are rare, but one of the few to have survived came out of Juayúa. It was provided by a Baptist missionary from the United States named Roy McNaught, who wrote a brief description of his experience for a U.S. magazine that was published less than two months after the events. McNaught reported that he was awoken shortly after midnight on January 23 by loud banging. He looked out his window and saw approximately eighty men attacking the telegraph office. He said rebels then attacked the police station and killed one officer and wounded another. The rebels' next target was Emilio Redaelli, who McNaught called "the richest man in town." He says the rebels burned Redaelli's house and one of his two stores, shot him, and wounded his wife and son. McNaught wrote that as the flames of the house rose, "the cries of the poor woman came to us as we listened in our patio, making us realize the horror of the scene that was being enacted only a few blocks away." He says that Redaelli's home was the only one burned, but many other homes and stores were broken into and looted throughout the night.[5]

Another rich account of the experience in Juayúa came from the Salvadoran journalist, Joaquín Méndez, who toured the entire western region less than one month after the rebellion and wrote a book-length report of his findings. His tour was approved by the government, so his account favors his sponsors; nonetheless, his descriptions are worthwhile. He offered transcripts of many interviews with local residents. His description of the initial assault on Juayúa follows closely that of McNaught. He also provided a list of the damages to businesses and homes caused by the rebels. According to the list, the Redaelli family suffered the heaviest losses at 85,000 colones (the exchange rate was 2.5 colones to 1 U.S. dollar). Other significant losses included the Mercedes Cáceres family home at 40,000 colones and the home of Lorenzo Ríos and Julia Salaverría at 50,000 colones. In total, Méndez listed thirty properties and a total financial loss of more than 300,000 colones.[6]

The nearby town of Salcoatitán was attacked at roughly the same time as Juayúa. Given that Salcoatitán and Juayúa are only three kilometers apart and were attacked simultaneously, it is likely that the area had one rebel group that divided itself into two fronts. The nature of the attack on Salcoatitán resembled closely that of Juayúa. A description of the attack and damages was provided by the local military commander in a written report a few weeks after the uprising; it is one of the few such reports to have survived into the historical record. The commander wrote:

> After invading the town, they [the rebels] set fire to the municipal building, destroying it completely, and then proceeded to break down the doors of the homes of Señor Antonio Salaverría, Dr. Tiburcio Morán, Señorita Rosenda Rodríguez, don Benjamín Inocente Orantes, don Moisés Canales, don Francisco Pérez Alvarado, and the local bar. In the home of José Dolores Salaverría they broke the windows above a balcony. In all of the aforementioned houses, in addition to inflicting serious structural damage, the rebels destroyed all sorts of furniture and objects of value.[7]

The pattern of attack on Izalco followed that of Juayúa and Salcoatitán. The available reports are secondhand, but they claim that the rebels attacked the town from the west. Izalco was divided into two neighborhoods, one Indian (Dolores), the other Ladino (Asunción); both had their own central plaza and church. The main road into Izalco came from the south and first passed through

Dolores before arriving to Asunción, six blocks further to the north. Beyond Asunción were coffee plantations and the lower slopes of the Izalco volcano. Like most municipalities throughout the region, Izalco's town proper was not large, roughly ten square city blocks. If available reports are accurate, the rebels approached from the west side of Asunción, and one of their first victims was the new alcalde, Miguel Call. Apparently he and a friend, Rafael Castro Cármaco, a local politician from the nearby town of Chalchuapa, were standing in the street about three blocks west of Asunción's central plaza. The rebels must have gathered in the rural cantones on the western outskirts of Asunción. Upon finding Call and Castro in the street, they attacked them with machetes, immediately killing Call and badly wounding Castro. Castro later died in a Sonsonate hospital. A local resident who was interviewed by Joaquín Méndez one month after the rebellion estimated the number of rebels at two thousand.[8] After killing Call, the rebels attacked the telegraph office, the police station, and the municipal hall. Once in control of the town, they broke into a number of homes and businesses and looted them. When Méndez arrived to Izalco in late February, the damage was still evident, and he photographed doors that had been hacked open and various belongings that had been scattered about and destroyed.

Whereas Juayúa and Salcoatitán were unable to send a telegraph warning to Sonsonate, the telegraph officer in Izalco managed to send notice before the rebels destroyed his office. In response, the military commander of the Sonsonate garrison, Colonel Ernesto Bará, organized an expeditionary force to go to Izalco's aid. He placed Major Mariano Molina in charge. Shortly before sunrise on January 23, Molina assembled his troops in the plaza in front of the garrison after sending scouts into town to requisition vehicles. One of the scout groups headed north toward the nearby municipality of Sonzacate, where they encountered a large contingent of rebels. The rebels had just attacked Sonzacate and were now heading south toward Sonsonate and the garrison. The rebels overtook the car, causing the soldiers to retreat on foot. They and the rebels arrived to the garrison almost simultaneously and caught Major Molina and his soldiers off guard in the plaza with the garrison's main gate wide open. Fierce hand-to-hand fighting ensued as the soldiers retreated to the interior of the barracks. Apparently, some rebels managed to enter, but soldiers repulsed them and closed the gate. Safely behind the barrack's walls, the soldiers suppressed the attackers with machine-gun fire. Unable to match the firepower of the machine guns, the rebels broke off their assault and retreated to Sonzacate, but not before attacking a nearby police station and looting various properties in the vicinity. The number of casualties during the attack has been estimated at between fifty and seventy rebels killed, five soldiers killed, and roughly half a dozen soldiers wounded.

At about the same time that rebels attacked Sonsonate, another rebel force attacked the military barracks in the departmental capital of Ahuachapán. A similar scenario played out there; well-armed soldiers safely behind the walls of their grim, medieval-looking garrison repulsed the rebels, who nevertheless launched three determined attacks throughout the night. Even though the assaults on Sonsonate and Ahuachapán failed, they were tactical victories, and they explain why the rebellion lasted as long as it did. Military commanders in the garrisons hesitated to leave until they were sure that an attack was no longer imminent. This delay eliminated the military's advantages of speed and firepower, giving rebel groups in outlying towns more time. For example, the rebels who had attacked Juayúa and Salcoatitán on the morning of January 23 occupied the town of Nahuizalco the following afternoon because no military force forestalled their advance. Similarly, the rebels in Tacuba held the town for almost three full days before troops from Ahuachapán left the barracks and trekked to the department's remote outskirts.

The two other towns attacked in the early morning of January 23 were Tacuba and Colón, representing the western and eastern edges of rebellion. In fact, Colón was not even located in the western highlands. It was situated approximately twenty miles to the east, on the back side of the San Salvador volcano, on the side of the transnational highway, which at that time was little more than a dirt trail, leading to El Salvador's two main cities, Santa Tecla and the capital San Salvador. Colón's experience in the rebellion diverged slightly from the other towns in that the rebels did not remain in the town after gaining control. However, the initial occupation of the town followed the pattern established elsewhere. The rebels overwhelmed the local forces in short order. Two survivors who provided testimony to journalists and the military were the telegraph operator, Félix Rivas, and the wife of the local military commander, Colonel Domingo Campos. Rivas says he was awakened by the sound of his door being broken down by clubs and machetes. Both he and his wife were badly wounded, including having his hands cut off and one of his eyes put out. Colonel Campos's wife claimed that she recognized the people who attacked her husband as a group of men who had been meeting at the house of a local campesino in the canton of Las Moras. She called them the leaders of the insurrection.

But instead of staying in Colón, the rebels left approximately two hours after the attack began. A local citizen described the scene that he found after arriving to the town from a nearby plantation at 3:00 a.m., including smoldering and damaged buildings and wounded and dead people, but no rebels. Instead, the attackers had marched up the road toward Santa Tecla, the capital of La Libertad Department, presumably to attack the city. But before they arrived, a military patrol coming down the hill from Santa Tecla confronted them. A brief firefight ensued, and the rebels were forced to retreat to Colón. By the time they arrived at the town at roughly 8:00 a.m., local citizens had regrouped and repulsed the returning rebels, who then apparently dispersed into the surrounding countryside.

The experience of Tacuba followed the typical pattern of attack in Izalco, Juayúa, and Salcoatitán. The rebels took local authorities by surprise and gained control over the town in short order and then stayed there until the military arrived to dislodge them. According to reports, the local guard post in Tacuba had nine National Guardsmen under the command of Major Carlos Juárez present at the time of the attack. Apparently, six guardsmen deserted upon hearing of the impending assault. The other three defended the post until they ran out of ammunition. Reportedly, rebels threw rocks onto the tile roof of the guard post from a high vantage point, causing it to collapse on Juárez and the two guardsmen. After storming the post, the rebels killed all three occupants and beheaded Major Juárez. Another primary target was the home of General Rafael Rivas, the local military commander, who was described by one source as "a crusty old soldier who had retired to Tacuba." After the rebels broke down his door, he defended himself with a pistol and killed four attackers. But the rebels captured him, took him outside, beheaded him, then placed his head on a pike and paraded it around town.[9]

The last major site of rebel attack was the municipality of Nahuizalco in Sonsonate Department. According to one account, at 9:00 in the morning on January 23 a car drove into the town filled with rebel leaders from Juayúa and Salcoatitán, including Felipe Nerio, who announced that the town had until 10:00 p.m. to join forces with the rebels or suffer the consequences. But the rebels returned at 3:00 in the afternoon, and failing to find the town sufficiently supportive, they burned down the municipal hall and some businesses and attacked a handful of citizens, killing two and wounding at least two others. A local landowner reported to the newspaper *La Prensa* that he ran into a large mob of rebels in the surrounding countryside who were making their way toward town. He said that among the group were a number of men and boys who worked on his plantations. He said the rebels let him go but threatened that he would be one of the first to die in the attack on the city. The landowner was incredulous of the rebels, claiming that that he had paid them well and regularly, but they still rose up in rebellion.[10] One of the rebels' main targets in Nahuizalco was the Brito clan, a family of Ladinos that had moved into the region in the late nineteenth century and had become wealthy and politically powerful. They were leaders of the small, but wealthy Ladino population in Nahuizalco and had been locked in an ongoing conflict with the local Indian community over control of municipal government for many years.[11] Francisco Brito was the town's alcalde at the time of the uprising, and in a telegram to Sonsonate on January 29, he summarized the situation facing local government in the aftermath of the rebellion.

> The Alcaldía [municipal hall] and Police Station of this city were totally burned down on the 23rd by the communists; absolutely nothing remains of them; the municipal seals and whatever money was being stored in the municipal office were either burned or stolen. Today we are holding our meeting in the home of the Deputy Alcalde.[12]

The insurrection was crushed in the span of about twenty-four hours between the afternoons of January 24 and 25. The national government in San Salvador sent a massive reinforcement column by train after drawing troops from the eastern portion of the country. But the bulk of the force did not arrive to Sonsonate until January 25, and by that time the military garrisons in Sonsonate and Ahuachapán had suppressed the rebellion. Soldiers from Sonsonate engaged the rebels first. Certain that he was no longer facing imminent attack, the commander of the Sonsonate garrison sent a patrol under the command of Colonel Tito Calvo toward Izalco on the morning of January 24. The patrol encountered a large group of rebels camped in Sonzacate, and a fierce battle ensued that resulted in losses on both sides, including Lieutenant Francisco Platero, head of the machine-gun unit. Outnumbered, the patrol retreated to the barracks, and the commander prepared a larger and more coordinated response. The second expeditionary force left that afternoon under the command of Colonel Marcelino Galdámez. This time Sonzacate was vacant. Various fires were still burning throughout the town, but the rebels had apparently dispersed into the rural environs.

Galdámez's force continued north to Izalco. Reports on what transpired there are conflicting. One report indicates that the troops from Sonsonate were joined by an advance force from San Salvador or Santa Tecla. Another report indicates that rather than entering Izalco, the soldiers set up a defensive position at the bottom of the southern slope that led into town and waited for the rebels to attack them. The rebels then supposedly rushed down from the Dolores neighborhood directly into the army's fire and suffered tremendous casualties from machine-gun fire. Regardless of whether the rebels launched that attack, the fact remains that the soldiers from Sonsonate quickly defeated Izalco's rebels and regained control of the town. One of the more renowned figures captured during the counterassault was Feliciano Ama. Great debate surrounds Ama and whether he was a rebel leader, and if so, why. Nevertheless, shortly after he was captured, soldiers looked the other way as a local lynch mob took him out of his jail cell and hung him from an olive tree in Asunción's central plaza.

The troops who gained control of Izalco left the village late in the afternoon of January 24 and headed toward Nahuizalco, located approximately seven miles uphill to the west. At the turnoff to the town, they encountered a rebel force and routed it in a roughly thirty-minute battle. Again, reports conflict as to what the soldiers did next. One report claims they advanced on Nahuizalco and regained control of the town that evening around 8:30. Other reports claim that by the time the battle was over darkness had fallen, so the troops decided to make camp on the roadside and wait until morning. Either way, by the morning of the twenty-fifth, Nahuizalco was back in government hands. The troops then proceeded to Salcoatitán and Juayúa that afternoon, arriving around 3:00. Rebels tried fruitlessly to prevent their entrance into Juayúa by laying trees across the road and digging trenches, but the soldiers were undeterred. By the end of the day they had regained control of both towns after a brief battle with the rebels. That same morning (the twenty-fifth) an expeditionary force left the barracks in Ahuachapán and headed to Tacuba, which also was returned to government control.

By the end of the day on January 25, the rebellion had been put down and the rebel-controlled towns were back in government hands. The speed with which the rebellion was suppressed proves that the rebels never had the military capacity to challenge the Salvadoran Army in open combat. The only setback that the army suffered was in Sonzacate when the first advance patrol under Tito Calvo was caught off guard by a large number of rebels. But beyond that instance, the rebels never stopped the army's advance. The rebels' only advantages were numbers and surprise. Whenever the army had time to prepare, its speed and overwhelming firepower resulted in victory.

Those same advantages put the entire peasant population of the western countryside at the army's mercy during the next two weeks. The initial defeat of the insurrection was mere prelude to the series of horrifying events that followed, which have become known in local vernacular as simply "el 32." The main government reinforcements under the direction of General José Tomás Calderón arrived to Sonsonate on January 25. Thereafter, the military subjected the western countryside to a brutal reprisal. Swift-moving and heavily armed military units swept through the densely populated countryside, killing peasants indiscriminately. One of the army's more renowned tactics to streamline the killing was to order all the male inhabitants of a town's surrounding cantones to report to the main plaza in order to receive safe-conduct passes; soldiers then lined them up and machine-gunned them en masse.

In the next ten days to two weeks, soldiers and paramilitary units murdered thousands of people throughout western El Salvador in retribution for the insurrection. The archival record in El Salvador is sadly silent on these events (probably because the military destroyed or hid incriminating documents), but one of the few surviving documents that contains an explicit reference to the killing came from the local military commander in Salcoatitán. He reported, "Those who were deserving were executed on orders from higher authorities." That admission by the commander is one of the only known statements to link the mass murder directly to superior orders. He also said that the pursuit of suspected rebels was still proceeding, nearly six weeks after the uprising. "It is lamentable," he wrote, "that many of the fugitives have still not been located despite the best efforts of our teams in various places throughout the region."[13]

An elderly resident of Salcoatitán, Salvador Pérez (born in 1914), granted us an interview in the year 2000 in which he claimed to have witnessed a mass killing in the town's central plaza. He claimed that he and his family lived in a home near one of the corners of the plaza and that they had fled into the surrounding coffee plantations during the rebel attack. They returned to their home after the military regained control of the town. He said that one day shortly after their return, he and his family watched out a window of their home as soldiers gathered a large number of peasants into the central plaza. He said, "The soldiers lined the men up against the wall of the church and shot them." He watched until the shooting began, at which point his family closed the shutters. But he heard the shots and then looked out to see dead men in the plaza and some men still alive, moaning and writhing.[14]

As the example of mass killing in Salcoatitán was repeated in one town after another throughout the western region, bodies of dead people began to pile up along roadsides and in scattered heaps. Whenever possible, soldiers or local citizens buried them in mass

1–1   Photograph depicting victims of the Matanza of 1932 from Jorge Schlesinger's book *Revolución comunista*. The photo was provided to him by the Salvadoran government.

graves, but the number of dead overwhelmed local capacity, and many corpses remained exposed for days. So many corpses remained unburied by the end of the first week of February that the minister of health sent instructions to local authorities, ordering them to bury cadavers and giving them specific dimensions of the holes they should dig.

> In regard to the necessary sanitary measures to be followed relating to the new internments to be conducted…part burials were done in trenches of variable dimensions, up to thirty meters long, one to two meters wide, and one and a half to two meters deep. This office thinks it is necessary to make the dimensions uniform for reasons of health. The accumulation of no more than fifty corpses in a single grave allows for better decomposition and less absorption into the soil. Even better would be isolated graves, two cubic meters in size, in which no more than eight to ten corpses would be placed. This information is particularly important for the municipalities of Juayúa, Nahuizalco, and Izalco.[15]

Ultimately, no one kept track of the numbers killed, or at least if the military maintained a record, the documents have not been released to the public. It is for this reason that estimates of the number killed range so widely between ten thousand and thirty thousand. Certainly a portion of the people killed had participated in the rebellion, but the vast majority of victims were innocent civilians with no involvement in the events. Roy McNaught provided insight into the vague criteria used by the military to determine if a person deserved to die. He said that across the street from his home lived a poor family of eight people in a tiny shack. He said that the family did not participate in the rebellion, but on the second day of rebel occupation they joined in the thieving and stored some ill-gotten goods in their shack. When the soldiers arrived, they searched the shack, found the goods, and took the father outside and shot him. McNaught wrote, "The same thing happened to many others."[16]

A Canadian naval officer provided similar insights. He had landed at the port of Acajutla in Sonsonate Department on January 23 as part of the British government's attempt to guarantee its citizens safety during the revolt. The commander traveled by train from Sonsonate to San Salvador on the twenty-fourth and reported, "Many dead bodies of Indians were observed along the railway lines, especially around Sonsonate." He also said that residents tried to prove loyalty to the government with white flags: "Nearly everyone walking about carried a small white flag which they waved continuously to show they were not red [a rebel], many residences also had large white flags displayed in a conspicuous place." The commander doubted the effectiveness of the strategy because "one body was observed lying dead with the white flag still in his hat."[17]

Mass executions lasted approximately two weeks, and then, just as quickly as they began, they ended. The military decided that the region was sufficiently pacified, or that whatever message it was trying to deliver had had been sent. So the army's central command returned the reinforcements to the central and eastern regions of the country and left the same number of troops throughout the western region as before the uprising. However, the military supplemented its defenses by creating a civilian defense force called the Guardia Cívica (Civic Guard) to guard against further rebel activity. Civic Guard units were required to guard their town day and night and report any suspect activity. Every able-bodied male in a town was expected to serve, and the costs of feeding and clothing the guards was to be incurred by the municipality through donations from town residents. Guard units remained active throughout the entire western region during the remainder of 1932 and throughout much of 1933 in some localities. Various guard units sent out alarms about a supposed resurgence of rebel activity, but in fact no further acts of rebellion occurred. The insurgents had been hunted down, and the remainder of the population had been beaten into submission.

Rather than resurgent rebels, the main problem facing the national government in the weeks following the uprising was angry local Ladinos seeking retribution on peasants, and especially Indians. Civic Guard units were often implicated in the abuses. The uprising had been a highly personal affair, and the response took on a similarly personal tone. The municipalities attacked by the rebels may have had sizeable populations relative to other areas of the country, but they were still small, intimate communities. The elites and peasants who lived there resided in close proximity, and they often knew one another through labor or commercial relations. A common trope of elite renditions of the uprising was that the rebels were local workers who had been treated fairly but still responded in the ungrateful manner of taking up arms. One example of this trope came from the landowner in Nahuizalco (mentioned earlier) who claimed that some of the rebels who threatened him were his laborers. A similar story came out of Ahuachapán, where a local landowner by the name of Juan Germán was killed in front of his family by Juan Ramos, "a servant and retainer of the family who had been Don Juan's companion from his youth and had even accompanied him to Guatemala when he went there to study."[18] Even if these specific stories were exceptional, the elites throughout the west responded as if they were the norm. They believed that by challenging their authority the rebels had rejected society's moral and governing norms. Armed with a vision of retributive justice and taking advantage of the chaos of the Matanza, elites struck back. They joined paramilitary units and oppressed local peasant residents. For example, Ladino authorities in Izalco tried to crack down on indigenous religious practices barely one week after the uprising by proposing that all indigenous religious relics throughout the village be confiscated and locked away in the local parish. They said that the celebrations associated with the relics incite actions "contrary to our laws... [and] prejudicial to the honorable inhabitants of the city."[19] Other reports arriving from Izalco claimed that Ladino elites were beating and jailing indigenous people indiscriminately and charging them exorbitant fees to be freed. Members of Izalco's Civic Guard units were accused of participating in these events.[20] Later reports stated that Izalco's Ladinos were monopolizing the region's water supplies and refusing to allow Indians access to irrigation water for their crops.[21]

Another example of retributive actions by local elites came from Nahuizalco. Two weeks after the uprising, reports began arriving to San Salvador of myriad abuses being perpetrated by local Ladino officials against the region's poor populace, Indian and Ladino alike. The government sent an agent to the town to investigate, worried that if the accusations were true the authorities in Nahuizalco were exacerbating hostilities in the region. The agent, Lieutenant Enrique Uribe, presented himself to Nahuizalco's authorities as the new *subcomandante*, but he withheld the fact that his real mission was a secret investigation into their activities. Uribe discovered that the stories about the abuses were true. In his report to San Salvador, he said that the Ladino officials were terrorizing the peasant population with "arbitrary and violent actions." Following the military's withdrawal from the region after the Matanza, local paramilitary bands formed and roamed the countryside in search of so-called communists. Members of the Civic Guard comprised the greater whole of these bands, but they were joined by other local Ladinos and soldiers. They described their activities to Uribe as "patriotic service." But Uribe saw it otherwise:

> The authorities prior to my arrival...applied justice in a manner so poorly interpreted that the medicine became worse than the sickness afflicting the patients.... No one has escaped their criteria; far from establishing harmony and tranquility in the region, they have sowed the seeds of terror and dread, not only among the Indians but among some

Ladinos as well. In regards to their treatment of the Indians, these local officials have discredited the name of the Supreme Government as well as the honorable citizens of this community.[22]

Of course it is highly ironic that a member of Salvadoran Army, which had just perpetrated one of the most extreme examples of mass terror in modern Latin American history, would accuse paramilitary bands in Nahuizalco of undermining civic order by acting violently and arbitrarily against the region's peasants. But such were the complexities of El Salvador in 1932. The national government had decided that the mass killing should end, and it did not want local authorities disobeying and taking matters into their own hands.

Who Were the Rebels?

One of the most consistent arguments during the past seventy years about the 1932 uprising is that the rebels were organized and led by communists. We said that one of the main reasons this argument of "communist causality" became so persistent is that both the left and the right in El Salvador agreed on it. Of course, the definition of communist meant different things to different people. For example, some interpreters, mostly extreme conservatives, defined communist causality as foreigners backed by the Bolsheviks in Russia who targeted El Salvador as a site for revolution. The communist foreigners supposedly snuck into the country, proselytized to the masses, and incited them to rise up in rebellion, even though the masses probably understood little or nothing about Marxism. Other proponents of communist causality, leftists and rightists alike, de-emphasized the role of foreigners and focused instead on domestic organizations, the Communist Party (Partido Comunista de El Salvador, PCS), its sister organization the Socorro Rojo Internacional (International Red Aid, SRI), and the country's main labor union, the Federación Regional de Trabajadores Salvadoreños (Regional Federation of Salvadoran Workers, FRTS).[23] According to their interpretations, members of the FRTS, PCS, or SRI went to the western countryside, organized the masses, and led them in insurrection. Variations on this argument revolve around which organization or groups of people within each organization led the charge. Regardless of the differing versions of communist causality, everyone who believed it accepted the central tenet that communism was key to the events.

The great challenge before anyone trying to determine the accuracy of communist causality is the lack of historic evidence from rebels. Some survivors of 1932 have shared their experiences throughout the years, but none of them have claimed to be rebels, and no known accounts from rebels exist. Most of the rebels were illiterate, so they did not leave a written record. Also, most of them were probably killed in the Matanza, so they did not survive to tell their own story or pass it down to friends or family members as oral traditions. The consolidation of authoritarian military rule after 1932 also suppressed rebel testimony by creating a culture of fear that would have inhibited any surviving rebels from acknowledging their participation.

The absence of accounts from rebels is a great loss to El Salvador and a challenge for researchers, but fortunately valuable evidence is not lacking entirely. Newly available documents include materials from archives in El Salvador and records from El Salvador in the Comintern archive in Moscow, Russia. All local Communist Party affiliates of the Comintern were required to correspond with Moscow or one of its regional offices, such as the Caribbean Bureau in New York City. The records in Moscow from El Salvador include roughly 350 pages of letters and reports, which contain materials from both the SRI and the PCS.

Admittedly, there are compelling reasons to accept the validity of communist causality. Even a cursory reading of Salvadoran newspapers and government documents from 1932 reveals ubiquitous references to the rebels as communists. A couple of examples are found above, and a few more will suffice to illustrate the broader pattern. For example, the local military commander in Salcoatitán called the rebels "communists" in his report from March 1932 and said that during their attack on the town they "shouted cheers in favor of communism and the Socorro Rojo [International Red Aid]."[24] The alcalde of Armenia, another town in Sonsonate Department, began his report on the aftermath of the uprising with, "in light of the recent communist events that wounded tragically the national soul."[25] Similarly, the daily newspapers in El Salvador referred consistently to the rebels as "communists" and "reds" in their accounts of the events. Joaquín Méndez, the journalist who toured the western region and wrote a book-length narrative of the uprising in March 1932, provided transcripts of his interviews with a wide array of individuals who identified repeatedly the rebels as "communists." Roy McNaught, the Baptist missionary from Juayúa, also called the rebels "communists" and "reds." In short, contemporary sources refer unfailingly to the rebels as communists.

Another good reason to accept communist causality as valid is that after its formation in March 1930, the Communist Party of El Salvador declared its primary organizational target to be the coffee workers of the western countryside. The question for the party became whether it was able to translate its expressed goals into organizational reality and become the vanguard of the western masses. Another problem was that the party's leadership remained skeptical of the viability of armed revolt in El Salvador in 1932. But many of its members, and other leftists in the country, especially in the SRI, believed that an immediate insurrection would be successful. So, even if some leaders of the PCS opposed armed revolt, perhaps other party members and the SRI organized the western countryside and led the call to arms.

A variety of documents taken from killed or captured rebels suggest a communist presence in the uprising. The Salvadoran government gave many of these documents to journalists and other pro government spokespersons to be published as part of a campaign to discredit the rebels. One of the most well-known sources to reproduce such documents was Jorge Schlesinger's *Revolución comunista* (Communist Revolution) published in Guatemala in 1946.

Schlesinger reprinted dozens of documents given to him by the Hernández Martínez government.[26] The documents included organizational plans for the insurrection and instructional manifestos that were to have been distributed to rebels throughout the western countryside. One manifesto was entitled "Urgent General Instructions," and among its listed mandates was a call to begin the rebellion at midnight on January 22, the time the uprising actually started: "On the 22nd of January at midnight sharp all of our contingents of revolutionary organizations must be mobilized and ready to

1–2
The cover of Jorge Schlesinger's book *Revolución comunista*.

assault the barracks of the departmental capitals taking immediate action for the seizing control of said barracks and police and National Guard posts."[27]

Notwithstanding the evidence that suggests communism was central to the uprising, much evidence exists to challenge communist causality. For example, the ubiquitous use of the term "communist" to refer to the rebels by local and national authorities after the uprising can be contextualized. Almost no one who used the term had a well-developed understanding of communism, nor did they provide a definition of what they thought it meant to be a communist in rural western El Salvador in 1932. Instead, they used the word "communist" according to the parlance of the day, when the word meant someone who was violent, immoral, against the law, contrary to the nation-state, or lacking in Christianity. The international discourse of the first Red Scare in the 1920s allowed local people in El Salvador to employ the term "communist" as part of a mutually recognizable dialogue about politics and insurrections, but their use of the term cannot be taken as evidence that communists were involved in the uprising or that the local peasants who rebelled had embraced Marxism-Leninism. In particular, the local elites in western El Salvador had been confronting class and ethnic hostilities for generations before discussions of communism became commonplace after the Russian Revolution in 1917. They had a well-developed sense of their social surroundings and a wide array of concepts at their disposal to describe the potentially rebellious insurrectionary working people around them. By the late 1920s and early 1930s, they freely interchanged the word "communist" with older terms like "*Indio*" (Indian), "*campesino*" (peasant), and "*gente pobre*" (poor people, or lower class).

Another reason to question the validity of communist causality is that the leadership of El Salvador's Communist Party did not believe that El Salvador was ready for revolution; therefore, it had not been preparing for an armed insurgency. The Comintern and its office in New York City agreed and had instructed communists in El Salvador to focus on mass organizing instead of armed insurrection. Party documents from the Comintern archive reveal that throughout the first eighteen months of its existence, the party neither discussed nor prepared for insurrection. Instead, it focused on internal affairs, especially recruiting members and providing them with ideological training. The Comintern archive also contains records from the SRI, and although they indicate that SRI leaders considered their counterparts in the Communist Party to be autocratic and ineffective mass organizers, they were not planning an armed insurrection either.

However, much to their surprise, the leaders of the PCS and SRI discovered in late 1931 that an insurrection of potentially massive proportions was forming in the western countryside. They sent a series of letters to their superiors in New York, requesting advice, weapons, international advisors, and money. The tone of their letters reveals desperation. "The situation is pressing," wrote the PCS in October 1931, "these comrades are under the illusion that with their machetes they are sufficiently prepared to sustain a movement of this class." The same letter revealed the party's resignation to its failure to prevent an insurrection from coalescing. "We concurred in advance with the desire of combating with our revolutionary class theories all the left tendencies which were beginning to develop at the beginning of our movement, but now we have come to the epoch in which we can not deter the revolutionary wave which is arising everywhere, determined to obtain power, dead or alive."[28] The SRI echoed the PCS's urgency. "The situation is grave," wrote the secretary general of the SRI in a letter to New York dated November 29, 1931. "Especially in Sonsonate," he continued, "the comrades only speak of insurrection; we do not want to lose the opportunity presented by this sustained force, hoping to align ourselves with it."[29]

No money or aid arrived, which is not surprising given that New York and Moscow had provided only nominal support for Central America up to that point, and Comintern officials must have been shocked to learn that a revolt was pending. Even the PCS's and SRI's requests for aid indicate a lack of control over the situation. One of the letters from the secretary general of the SRI in San Salvador confessed an inability to provide more information on the situation in the west because of "the complete divorce between country and city."[30] He informed his superiors that he had sent a delegate to the west to gather information, but this person had not yet returned or sent back any information. The PCS's leadership demonstrated a similar disconnectedness with events in the west in testimony by a ranking party leader before an investigation committee of the Caribbean Bureau in late 1932.

Looking back over the six months prior to the PCS's and SRI's request for aid in late 1931, it is not surprising that the two organizations had little control over the pending insurrection in the west. Neither organization had established deep or broad organizational ties in the western countryside. A report from the SRI leadership in April 1931 admitted that neither it nor the PCS had organized peasant leagues or rural unions.[31] A later report by a ranking member of the PCS said that as of May 1931, "The lack of a clear form of organization was responsible for the lack of militants, or revolutionary spirit in the provinces."[32] The lack of an organizational foundation in April 1931 had been preceded by a nadir of activity by both organizations. Between December 1930 and March 1931 both the PCS and the SRI went into a period of retrogression. Subjected to intensified police repression and bogged down by internal ideological disputes, they withdrew into themselves.33

However, in roughly April and May 1931 both organizations refocused their organizational objectives. Various reports reveal that a crucial meeting took place on May 15, 1931, attended by representatives of the SRI, PCS, and FRTS. The meeting resulted in "intense activity to correct the errors... of the past year. At the same time we began to work to improve organization."34 Both organizations experienced impressive growth throughout the remainder of 1931. The membership of the PCS rose to about five hundred, and one document provides a regional breakdown of party membership just prior to 1932: two hundred eighty members and seven nuclei in San Salvador; fifty-three members and four nuclei in Santa Ana; eighteen members in Sonsonate; seventy in Ahuachapán, and thirty in Santa Tecla. Notably, the party was still heavily urban, and San Salvador remained the center of party membership. The source noted the party's urban orientation by stating that party cells outside San Salvador existed only "in the capitals of the states [departments], not in the interior."35

Notwithstanding its impressive accomplishments and its declared commitment to organizing the western coffee workers, it remains likely that the party failed to establish a strong organizational foothold in the western countryside. Various reasons would account for this failure, and one of the most important is ethnicity. In light of western El Salvador's highly racialized society, the need to take ethnicity into account for organizational purposes might seem obvious, but the PCS failed to do so. It strictly interpreted society from a class perspective, which can be explained partly by the fact that as Marxists, the members of the Communist Party considered material conditions determinant and ideological variables (like ethnicity or race) secondary. Most communists believed that a focus on ethnic issues diverted attention away from the more fundamental issues of class. In one of the more revealing statements in this regard, a report from the PCS to the Caribbean Bureau stated, "Here in El Salvador there are no Indians or Blacks."36 Another factor that hindered the party's ability to recognize the importance of ethnicity and to adopt an ethnic approach to organizing was its urban and Ladino makeup. Not only was the party based in urban areas, with nearly 75 percent of all party members being from San Salvador, but also almost every party member was Ladino.[37] Practically speaking, the party lacked familial and personal ties to the western countryside, and especially to its Indian communities.

In addition to ethnicity, another limiting factor before the party was the complex land-tenure situation in the western countryside and the way it clashed with the party's ideological approach to property. The western countryside contained many large plantations owned by a small number of elites who grew coffee and employed large numbers of poorly paid workers. The existence of these plantations fit the party's idealized vision of an exploitative landowning class lording itself over a mass of underpaid, suffering workers—a sort of early twentieth-century tropical version of nineteenth-century industrial England. But El Salvador's western countryside exhibited a complex array of land and labor conditions that failed to correspond to the party's idealized framework. Thousands of small, privately owned plots ranging in size from less than one acre to as many ten acres were scattered across the western landscape. Their owners were part of the *campesinado*, or rural poor, who had acquired ownership of their small plots either by purchase or inheritance. Many of those small plots had their origins in the privatization of Indian communal lands in the last two decades of the nineteenth century.

In addition to these private smallholders, *colonos*, or sharecroppers, constituted another complexity of the western countryside. Colonos did not own their land like a smallholder, but rather they entered into a contract with a plantation owner. In exchange for a percentage of their proceeds or a certain number of labor days, colonos received rights to farm a plot on the plantation. Thus, colonos were neither proletarian laborers nor landowners, but rather a middle group.

To its credit, the PCS understood clearly this complex situation. Such knowledge could have been a major benefit to devising effective organizational strategies. After all, poverty was widespread throughout the western countryside, regardless of whether a person was a smallholder, a colono, or a proletarian laborer. The party hoped to turn this admixture of rural poor people into a revolutionary wave, but its own ideological approach hindered its ability. The party identified private landowners, no matter how large or small, as the class enemy. One of its early statements on land identified smallholders as a "small bourgeoisie; an enemy of the class-based organization of workers; we cannot take them into our confidence."[38] Believing that proletarian laborers were insufficiently numerous to secure revolutionary victory, the party occasionally focused on colonos as an organizational target. But, here again, the complex outlook of colonos clashed with the party's approach. Although some colonos identified themselves as laborers, others simply wanted to save enough money to buy their own plot of land. Ultimately, the party found itself in a bind. It considered the west to be the revolutionary epicenter, yet it characterized many of the poor people living there as class antagonists.

Finally, factionalism within the party hindered its organizational goals in the western countryside. El Salvador's Communist Party came into existence just as the Comintern's so-called Third Period, or "class-against-class" phase (1928–34), was maturing. Driven by a strict notion of ideological purity, probably inspired by Stalin's consolidation of power in Russia, the Comintern adopted a strategic approach that mandated the elimination of relations with reformists, or nonradicals. This meant that all unions and communist parties affiliated with the Comintern had to abandon contact with any nonradical organization and also insure the ideological purity of their own members. Conditions in El Salvador never reached the stage they did in Russia, with its purges, show trials, life imprisonments, and death sentences. Nonetheless, the PCS turned in on itself in a search for ideological impurities, dedicating much of its time and energies to establishing an ideological standard and then measuring party members against it. For an organization like the PCS, whose members had originated almost entirely from the once-reformist FRTS, this had debilitating potential. A "Commission of Honor and Justice" was created within the FRTS to serve as a watchdog against reformist tendencies.[39] Within the PCS, most weekly meetings were dedicated to ideological questions, investigating suspect members, or debating decisions to expel those who were considered too reformist. Both leaders and rank-and-file members came under suspicion.

Among those expelled from the cell in San Salvador was Luis Díaz, the party's first secretary general in El Salvador. It was not until roughly April 1931 that the party determined its ideological purity to be secure. Given what we now know—that nine months later the western countryside would rise up in insurrection—the party had precious little time to achieve its objective of becoming the revolutionary vanguard of the masses.

Myriad challenges before the party's desire to organize in the west beg some important questions: Did the growth of the party in late 1931 result in substantive organizational ties to western rural areas, particularly to those communities at the center of the January 1932 uprising? Had the PCS and/or the SRI bridged the divide between country and city, Ladinos and Indians, and proletarians and smallholders? Were they able to achieve this in the span of eight months, after May 1931? Much of the new evidence suggests that the answers to these questions are "no." In fact, some of the new evidence indicates that communist leaders at the time believed that the answers to these questions were "no." The new evidence includes a particularly rich source, the testimony of a ranking PCS member before an investigative tribunal in New York City in the latter half of 1932.

Anxious to determine what had transpired during the January uprising, the Comintern ordered a surviving member of the PCS's Central Committee to travel to both to New York and Moscow to testify before investigative tribunals. No records from the Moscow investigation survived, and we do not know if it even occurred, but fortunately the records of the New York investigation have survived. The party member from El Salvador is identified as "Comrade H." He first had to submit a long written report in advance of his arrival, and then once in New York, he had to sit before the tribunal and answer questions.

The transcripts of the tribunal reveal that the PCS and the SRI were aware of a flurry of organizational activity in western El Salvador in the latter half of 1931. The Great Depression was beginning to impact El Salvador by the middle of the year. Coffee prices were dropping, and coffee growers were trying to compensate by boosting production without increasing labor costs. Workers on the plantations responded to these demands with organization and eventually with work stoppages. In Comrade H's words, "The misery of the masses in this period increased daily because of the crisis and in those countries where agriculture is dominating economy [sic], we feel the crisis in one single stroke and then it is logical that the masses demand to solve their situation through means they consider most correct."[40]

Comrade H commented on the presence of organizations among coffee workers throughout the latter half of 1931. However, he was unable to provide details of the nature or makeup of these unions. He repeatedly referred to them as "local agricultural workers trade unions," and he suggested that party cadres were involved in them, but again he was unable to offer specifics. He did, however, comment in some detail on a half dozen strikes that had occurred on some of the larger coffee plantations between November and December 1931, including plantations owned by the Sol, Duke, Regalado, and Dueñas families, which were central figures in El Salvador's so-called fourteen families, the small clique of powerful families that controlled most of the wealth in El Salvador. H was not able to demonstrate substantive party involvement in any of these strikes.

H indicated that both the PCS and the SRI wanted to play an active role in this organizational ground swell. He said that the two organizations recognized the depressed economic conditions of the latter half of 1931 as being "very favorable for the broadening of our revolutionary organizations."[41] Indeed the party had some noteworthy organizational successes, largely in and around San Salvador, and in part due to the fact that the party controlled the leadership of the FRTS. These activities included strikes, such as a shoeworkers' strike, and political protests, such as the march against the government's plan to secure a loan from U.S. banks in June 1931. Throughout the latter half of 1931, the ranks of the clandestine organizations grew accordingly.

It is in regard to the critical issue of the rural unions and the degree of radical presence within them that H received the most pressing questions from his Caribbean Bureau interrogators. Not surprisingly, his responses exposed his limited knowledge of the situation, and by extension, the party's lack of involvement in the rural unions. After his early admission that the party's cells were limited to the departmental capitals, H was asked if "the party had any members in the haciendas [and] plantations?" To this he responded, "Not certain as to number but Party did have nuclei in plantations." When pressed on the issue, H said:

> On the one hand we had the masses very anxious to liberate themselves and on the other hand a Communist Party, weak, but which had influence among the masses, a Communist Party carried away by the impulse of the masses and contaminated by them instead of training them and without the Party itself being trained in the constant struggle for immediate demands, and as the last resort, having the determination to put itself at the head of them in the struggle which ended with the results which we all know.[42]

Responses like these led the investigative tribunal to conclude that the party was not responsible for and did not have control over the insurrectionary wave in western El Salvador. Thus, the tribunal concluded that in deciding to join the rebellion, the party had committed a strategic error. "Comrade R," or "Ricardo," delivered the tribunal's summary analysis. He focused on the party's inability to close the gap between its urban base and the rural western masses. However, not even Ricardo mentioned the issue of ethnicity. Not once in the entire investigation was the issue of Indians brought up.

If the new evidence suggests that the PCS was not the primary organizational impetus for the 1932 uprising, this does not mean that the party was entirely divorced from the events. There are suggestions that the PCS had some degree of organizational presence in the communities at the center of the rebellion. The evidence is cursory, but suggestive. In his testimony, H revealed that in the early days of January, when party leaders in San Salvador decided to join the uprising, they relied upon so-called Red Commanders to gather intelligence and deliver the Central Committee's directives to the rebels. None of these exchanges occurred rapidly. At best Red Commanders and their message carriers were able to travel by train, which still required many hours to arrive to the western region. But when trains were unavailable or police surveillance was high (as it was in January

1932), messages had to be carried on foot. The identities of the Red Commanders were never revealed, but it can be assumed that they were either PCS members with contacts in the rural localities, or they were local people sympathetic to the party. The party used these channels to try to coordinate the various regional pockets of insurrection. One directive that the party sent through these channels was the mandate that rebels proclaim Soviets rather than municipalities upon successfully occupying a town. The party also used these channels during its desperate attempt to postpone the rebellion after Farabundo Martí's arrest on January 18. But this attempt failed, and the uprising went ahead as planned on January 22.[43]

When pressed to provide evidence of the party's leadership in the rebellion, H could offer nothing more than the Red Commanders. Not surprisingly, the tribunal's investigators delivered a harsh critique, encapsulated by Comrade R:

> Did the CC, after it had definitely decided to organized [sic] armed struggle...issue slogans for open organs of struggles to the lead, peasant committees? No. What did they rely upon? They relied upon secret channels, so called Red Commanders, thinking this is the means for organizing, mobilizing masses for struggle for power. Well, it wasn't the means.[44]

While Comrade R's critique might be confined by his strict adherence to a Leninist concept of organizing, it nonetheless suggests the PCS's limitations in the west. The party seems to have played some sort of coordinating role by relying on its shallow, but nonetheless existing contacts to unify disparate local movements. But beyond that, much evidence indicates that the causal impetus for the uprising originated within the western communities themselves and was based on the residents' independent and local interpretations of social conditions. We also have to assume that a substantial portion of the planning followed local affiliations and channels of communication.

Further evidence on the party's limited involvement in the uprising can be found in its activities in the critical two weeks leading up to the beginning of revolt. In the first week of January party leaders concluded that rebellion was imminent and thus they had to decide whether to join. The simple fact that the party did not make a decision on the uprising until as late as January 1932 provides strong evidence that it was not the forefront of the insurrectionary drive. The decision was not an easy one. To refuse to rebel was to stand by and watch the masses wage class war alone. To join was to plunge headlong into a seemingly futile exercise. Even if they had no way to predict the brutality of the army's counterattack, party leaders knew that many lives and the immediate future of the party hung in the balance. Not surprisingly, party leaders held varying opinions and debated their decision intensely. Those in favor of rebelling finally won the day, and the party voted on January 10 to join the rebellion. In his testimony before the tribunal, H did not reveal how he voted, but looking back at that moment, he expressed sorrow for the party's unenviable position, saying that even then he knew the party's decision didn't matter because the rebellion was going to happen with or without it. "The impulse of the masses was for struggle," he testified, "and this [was the case] from the very beginning, such that...this could only end as it did."45

Once party leaders made the decision to join the uprising, they committed whatever resources, contacts, and capabilities they had at their disposal. They placed Farabundo Martí in charge of military operations and chose January 20 as the starting date. It is not clear if the CC chose this date independently or simply acceded to a preexisting decision by rebel leaders in the west. In either case, the party activated its network of Red Commanders, hoping to centralize planning and communication. We have no evidence as to which rebellious communities followed the Red Commanders' mandates. Some party members were given the task of making bombs and gathering weapons; others wrote directives on what the rebels should do once they occupied a town, like the "Urgent General Instructions" manifesto mentioned earlier. The existence of these documents does not prove a communist leadership in the insurrection, as was argued by the Salvadoran government and the various journalists who published them. Instead, they reveal a Communist Party desperately trying to insert itself as the leader of the insurrection after being compelled to join it at the last minute.

One of the party's known contributions was a pair of conspiracies in military barracks in San Salvador on or about January 17 and 18. In both cases, it planned for soldiers loyal to the party to turn their guns on their officers and give the party control over the barracks. This plan was based on the party's recent success, albeit limited, in gaining the support of a few soldiers, mostly young conscripts from the countryside. The actions in San Salvador were dismal failures. The party could not maintain consistent communication with its supporters inside the barracks, and thus, when it gave the designated signal the only response was machine-gun blasts from the barracks still safely under government control.

In the midst of carrying out these various activities, the party suffered a devastating blow when on January 18 Martí was arrested with a pair of fellow activists. Along with them the police found a number of homemade bombs and the party's insurrectionary plans. Comrade H told the Caribbean Bureau's tribunal that the CC had ordered Martí to leave the house in which he was hiding because it had been revealed to authorities. But Martí refused this order and was subsequently captured in a sweep involving as many as seventy-five officers. Once the CC learned of Martí's arrest, it desperately tried to postpone the uprising. But it was too late to get word out to the rebel groups in the west, even if those groups would have accepted the party's decision. And so, starting in the late hours of January 22 and continuing over the next three days, armed rebels attacked roughly one dozen municipalities throughout the west.

As to the number of party members that participated in the attacks, no substantive information exists. Only two of the municipalities that were attacked by the rebels, Ahuachapán and Sonsonate, had PCS cells. But whether these members participated in the attacks on those two towns is unknown. The remote municipality of Tacuba did not have a formal party cell, but of all the places with significant rebel activity, it appears to have had the most overt radical presence, probably because the Cuenca family was from Tacuba and had members enlisted in the party. Apparently two or more Cuencas were present in Tacuba at the time of the revolt, which might explain why Tacuba was the only occupied town to supposedly declare a Soviet before the military recaptured it. But in the other main centers of rebel involvement, there was no communist cell and no known communist presence. Although it is possible that party members gathered in those regions in lieu of the pending revolt.

Even if new evidence suggests that the PCS was a tangential player in the uprising, what about the SRI? Did it fill in for the absent PCS by raising the consciousness of the western masses, organizing them into an insurrectionary wave and then leading them in rebellion? There is no evidence to suggest that the SRI or Martí embarked on an organizational campaign in the western countryside distinct from that of the PCS. The SRI and PCS were not differentiated organizations; rather, they coordinated and remained closely aware of one another's activities. In his testimony before the Caribbean Bureau, Comrade H testified on the activities of both the PCS and the SRI. He described Martí as a close associate of the party, despite Martí's long-standing disagreement with party leaders about the need to delay insurrection for years. In the critical final moments leading up to the rebellion, Martí was working directly with the PCS. By all available accounts, he did not contribute anything fundamentally different than that of other leaders, such as direct access to the rebels or greater control over affairs in the countryside.

Instead of looking to communism as the causal variable in the 1932 insurrection, much of the newly available evidence suggests it worthwhile to consider autonomous organizing by the western masses, and in particular by the Indian communities for the insurrection's conceptualization and organization. Peasant communities throughout western El Salvador, Indian and Ladino alike, had a long history of political involvement. They frequently formed alliances with political organizations at the regional and national levels in hopes of promoting their local causes. One interesting example of this as late as 1931 can be seen in the case of Feliciano Ama, the Indian "cacique" from Izalco who was supposedly a rebel leader and who was lynched after capture during the Matanza.

During the campaign for the presidential election in January 1931, Ama decided to ally with the candidate Alberto Gómez Zárate. Ironically, Gómez Zárate was considered the most conservative candidate and the one most closely allied to the elites. But following a long-standing tradition of building patronage networks, Ama promised

1–3
The lynching of
Feliciano Ama in Izlaco
in 1932, as it appeared in
Jorge Schlesinger's
Revolución comunista.

to deliver Izalco's votes to Gómez Zárate in exchange for government support for local indigenous issues. Unfortunately for Ama, Gómez Zárate lost, despite Izalco's high levels of support. This vote is all the more surprising given that the victorious candidate, Arturo Araujo was a pro-labor populist from Armenia, just a few miles down the road from Izalco. Supposedly in the aftermath of Gómez Zárate's defeat, Ama began looking to form an alliance with another national-level political organization, the Communist Party. If that alliance indeed occurred, it would have highlighted the lack of importance local communities like Ama's placed on the ideology of prospective allies. Instead they sought out whichever candidate or organization seemed to offer hope of aiding them in their local struggles.

Research from the municipality of Nahuizalco shows that conflicts between Indians and Ladinos over control of municipal government had become especially intense on the eve of the 1932 insurrection.[46]

Ladinos, led primarily by the Brito family, had been engaged in long-standing electoral conflicts with the local Indian population. The conflicts seem to have begun in earnest in the mid-1880s, just as coffee started to become a viable commodity and the number of wealthy Ladino families in the region increased. By 1932, the Ladino and Indian populations in Nahuizalco had been locked in political conflict for almost fifty years. At no time was the tension higher than in late 1931 and early 1932, just prior to the outbreak of insurrection. After a municipal election in early January 1932, the Indian community insisted to the national government that the Ladinos had stolen the election. Indian spokespersons sent repeated requests to Sonsonate and San Salvador, asking the government to intervene on their behalf, but they received no satisfying response. Finally, in a telegram to the governor of Sonsonate on January 21, the indigenous spokespersons said that failure to act immediately would carry grave consequences: "Certainly it was not your intention to forget our petition, nor is it normally obligatory to respond in such short time, but failure to transmit even a verbal acknowledgement of our petition is now a threat to the social order."[47] No response came, and at midnight the next day, Nahuizalco was overrun by armed rebels. Of course, we do not know if the people involved in the political conflict were the same people who picked up arms and attacked the city. Nevertheless, the evidence is strongly suggestive that long-standing local conflicts of politics and ethnicity intensified just prior to the insurrection. A nugget of evidence from Izalco indicates that a similar scenario had been playing out there in the preceding years. In December 1929, Feliciano Ama requested that the national government nullify a local election because the victorious Ladino candidates had engaged in improprieties. The government rejected Ama's request.[48]

Evidence like this from Nahuizalco and Izalco suggests the need to consider the uprising as based in local community organizations, whether Indian or Ladino. These organizations may or may not have allied themselves with the Communist Party in San Salvador in the months or weeks leading up to the outbreak of revolt. It seems increasingly likely that the rebellion was a local affair in which the PCS and SRI tried to gain a leadership role.

Recent scholarship of a pair of North American historians, Jeff Gould and Aldo Lauria, illustrate the evolution in arguments based on new sources.⁴⁹ Relying heavily on interviews with elderly residents of the west conducted in the late 1990s and early 2000s, they credit the SRI rather than the PCS with a central role in the uprising, but their argument takes a different approach to communist causality. While they are still in the process of completing their final study, their preliminary publications suggest that local SRI chapters were malleable entities whose identities may not have been dictated by Marxist-oriented leaders in San Salvador, such as Farabundo Martí. Instead, they portray the SRI as something that local people throughout rural western El Salvador could adapt according to their own needs and interests. In other words, Gould's and Lauria's argument has the potential to explain how the SRI and PCS had an apparent presence in the west without exercising the directing role that traditional communist-causality arguments advance. Such an argument could explain why some eyewitnesses have claimed that rebels shouted slogans in favor of communism and the SRI during the insurrection.⁵⁰ The argument could also explain why new documents from the Comintern archive make mention of SRI chapters in Nahuizalco, Izalco, and Juayúa.⁵¹

Why Did the Military Perpetrate the Matanza?

Recent research shows that peasant uprisings were recurrent features in El Salvador throughout the nineteenth and early twentieth centuries.⁵² Peasants had a long history of resorting to violence when they believed all other avenues to achieving their goals had been closed to them. As a result, authorities had a long history of suppressing insurrections and dealing with their aftermaths. Typically, ruling elites responded to rebellions with decisive but constrained violence. They captured the main leaders and executed or jailed them in order to set an example. But never before, even in El Salvador's violent and heavily militarized history, had retribution occurred on the scale of 1932. The Matanza stands out as the single worst episode of state-sponsored repression in modern Latin American history, to say nothing of El Salvador's history, and it has been a festering wound on the country's psyche ever since. Roque Dalton captured the lingering effects of 1932 when he wrote famously that all Salvadorans were, "born half dead in 1932."[53] Why did the Salvadoran government respond so severely to the 1932 uprising?

Not surprisingly, finding an answer to this question has been inhibited by a lack of evidence, mainly internal military documents. But based on available materials, scholars have developed various responses. One argument is that the Matanza was an attempt at ethnocide, the elimination of an entire group (the Indians) from the population.[54] Scholars who have advanced this argument point to the rapid decline of Indian culture in twentieth-century El Salvador and contend that the Matanza was the decisive moment in the process. They argue that the Salvadoran Army used ethnic markers, such as dress and language, to target people for repression during and after the Matanza, causing indigenous people to hide their ethnic identities and adopt the cultural patterns of Ladinos, such as speaking Spanish.

Other scholars question the accuracy of the ethnocide argument. Given that Indians probably made up a sizeable portion of the rebel groups, it is highly likely that marauding military troops targeted Indians for reprisal during the Matanza. However, some scholars argue it is less likely that this was part of a broader attempt at ethnocide, either during or after the Matanza. Their research shows that once the government put a halt to the mass killings in early February, it no longer perpetrated nor tolerated overt repression of El Salvador's indigenous population. The government, in fact, reprimanded abusive Ladino elites throughout the west for exacting revenge on Indian communities and allowed those communities to petition the government for recognition and aid as they had done for decades previously.

If the military defended Indians, it did not do so out of an inherent regard for ethnic diversity or sympathy for indigenous culture—even though the president, General Hernández Martínez,[55] was considered indigenous. Rather the government defended Indians for the same reason that it defended all peasants and working people after 1932, as part of a fascist-style populism that defined working people as an inferior but organic part of the nation. As part of its fascistic populism, the Martínez regime launched a social-reform campaign called Mejoramiento Social (Social Betterment) that was designed to alleviate the suffering of working people. Regardless of the fact the Mejoramiento Social was a modest, ineffectual effort, the fact still remains that ethnocide would have contradicted fundamentally the government's attempt to portray itself as an ally of working people, indigenous and Ladino alike, after 1932.

Other arguments have attributed the Matanza to sheer sadism on the part of military commanders, to their fervent anticommunism, or to General Martínez's distinctive religious practices. Among his many esoteric beliefs, Martínez supposedly believed in a version of reincarnation in which humans would return to earth. This belief supposedly caused him to take human death lightly because once an animal had been killed it was gone forever but a human had recurring life. Because of these types of beliefs, critics saddled the president with the moniker "*el brujo*" (the witch, or the sorcerer). Certainly many reasons exist to believe that sadism, overzealous anticommunism, and any other variety of deeply twisted psychological traits facilitated mass murder in 1932. But many scholars argue that such explanations are insufficient by themselves. Instead, they believe that the scale of the Matanza was caused by a series of distinctly intense pressures bearing down on both the national government and local elites in the west in late 1931 and early 1932. They argue that none of the rebels could have predicted that the government would respond as it did, but had they wanted to avoid such a massive repression by the government, they would have had to rebel at a different moment in El Salvador's history.

According to these scholars, the final months of 1931 and the early weeks of January 1932 were especially difficult times for El Salvador. Coffee prices were plummeting, the economy was in shambles, and predictions for respite in the future seemed bleak. Banks were foreclosing on rural properties, and many landowners feared for their futures. The government had no recourse to increase its revenues, partly because the majority of customs duties was going toward making interest payments on a 1922 loan with a U.S. bank. Political conditions in the country were similarly tenuous. The government of Martínez had come to power in early December 1931 in a coup d'état that overthrew El Salvador's first-ever democratically elected president. People who had struggled for many years to reform El Salvador's traditionally hierarchical political system held Martínez in contempt for destroying their progress. In addition, Martínez was faced with the ire of the United States, which invoked the Washington treaties of 1923 that stipulated that any government in Central America coming to power in a nondemocratic matter would be denied diplomatic recognition. The position of the United States was not driven by an inherent regard for democracy in the region, but rather by an overarching desire for order and stability. The United States believed that coups threatened its economic and strategic interests, especially as they related to the Panama Canal. To pressure Martínez to resign, it sent a special representative, Jefferson Caffrey, to El Salvador in December 1931. At roughly the same time, the country was experiencing a rapid increase in workers' mobilization, particularly in the western countryside. The corresponding clashes between organized workers and military units had become increasingly violent and deadly.

During the 1932 uprising, the Martínez government was faced with an unexpected threat beyond that of the rebel masses, the arrival of foreign military personnel and the unspoken possibility of a U.S. military invasion. When the uprising broke out, U.S. and British diplomatic officials in San Salvador sent pleas to their governments saying that the situation was out of control and the Salvadoran military was compromised by communist infiltration.[56] In response, five warships, two Canadian/British and three American, arrived to El Salvador's Pacific coast. The two Canadian ships arrived on January 23, and the first two American ships on January 25, followed by a third ship a few days later. Both the British and U.S. governments, either through their diplomatic representatives in San Salvador, or through their arriving naval officers, offered to support El Salvador's government by landing troops. One of the Canadian officers went to San Salvador on January 24 to confer directly with Martínez. While en route he had a phone conversation with the British Consul in San Salvador who described the fears of the British population and said that the Salvadoran government was losing control. The consul requested that troops be landed, and in response the commander ordered a platoon of marines to disembark at the port of Acajutla.

But the troops had to return to their ship immediately because the Salvadoran government issued an order that "on no account was a foreign armed party to be allowed to land."[57] In his meeting with the commander late in the afternoon on the twenty-fourth, President Martínez rejected the aid offers in strong terms, as he would continue to do so in the coming days. He insisted that the Salvadoran military had the situation under control, and over the next few days the government went out of its way to prove the accuracy of the president's claim, dispatching large contingents of troops to protect foreign businesses and properties. A few days later, the commanding officers from the two Canadian ships were invited to lunch with Salvadoran officers in Sonsonate at the behest of the president. The Salvadorans showed their Canadian counterparts some prisoners and invited them to watch their executions.[58] The Canadians declined, but they recognized the gesture as part of the government's ongoing campaign to prove that the uprising was under control.

By the time the Americans landed on January 25, the rebellion was mostly contained, but based on initial reports coming from U.S. and British sources in the country, the U.S. military laid plans for a large military operation in El Salvador. On January 23, the navy's High Command had ordered its forces in the region to "be prepared any time after daylight tomorrow Sunday to send maximum available force of aircraft to Salvador on same mission carrying such infantry as practicable."[59] Upon his arrival to El Salvador, the commanding officer of one of the U.S. ships reported, "There is conclusive evidence that the revolt was backed by Moscow."[60]

We now know in hindsight that the United States did not want to become militarily involved in El Salvador in 1932. It was already suffering international criticism for its ongoing occupation of Nicaragua, and much of its diplomatic correspondence during the uprising demonstrates a strong concern over how governments throughout Latin America were perceiving the arrival of warships to El Salvador. But Salvadoran officials did not know the United States's reluctance to engage in military action. All they had as a basis to make decisions were the many recent examples of U.S. military incursions in the region, most notably the occupation of Nicaragua and the guerrilla war there with Sandino. Such incursions provided them sufficient evidence that the United States had demonstrated a historic willingness to use military force in the region to protect its perceived interests. The fears of the Salvadoran officials were heightened by the fact that the United States had already refused to grant diplomatic recognition to the Martínez regime. From the perspective of Martínez and other governing officials, a U.S. military occupation of El Salvador would have been devastating. They would have lost their positions, and the country's sovereignty would have been compromised seriously. Their responses to foreign diplomats and officers indicate that they were trying to avoid the uprising from providing a pretext for foreign military incursions by either Great Britain or the United States.

Scholars who have noted these myriad pressures bearing down on the Salvadoran government argue that the Matanza was so extreme because the people who perpetrated it—the Salvadoran government and local elites throughout the western region—feared for their political and financial security, to say nothing of their lives. El Salvador in late 1931 and early 1932 was an unstable place, and the people in power believed that a feeble response to the uprising could cost them a great deal. Whatever motives may have driven the mass killings, such as race/ethnicity, pure sadism, or a fear of imperialism, the national government was in a weak position when the uprising broke out, and it responded to the threat like a wounded animal.

Regardless of why the government perpetrated the Matanza, the fact remains that its overwhelming show of force helped consolidate Martínez's hold on power. His domestic opponents preferred his authoritarian rule to a peasant insurrection, and his foreign adversaries at least had confidence that he would do whatever it took to maintain order. Even the U.S. secretary of state lamented in his diary at the height of the uprising that the United States was unable to recognize Martínez: "The man who is president and who is the only pillar against the success of what seems to be a nasty proletarian revolution ... we are unable to recognize under the 1923 rule."[61]

Conclusion

The motives behind the rebellion and Matanza of 1932 remain highly complex and heavily debated. Scholars have provided varied responses as to why the uprising occurred and why the government responded with such tremendous violence. In recent years, the debates have only intensified with the appearance of caches of newly available evidence. The existence of these debates, and especially the fact that they are growing stronger, illustrates what many interpreters have long argued: the year 1932 was a turning point in El Salvador's history. In the decades after the events, Salvadorans and internationals alike struggled mightily to make sense of what happened.

CHAPTER TWO

The Historical Background

The past is never dead; it isn't even past.
—William Faulkner, *Requiem for a Nun*

The deep resonance of 1932 with contemporary Salvadoran identity can be explained not only by the enormity of the events, but also by the fact that they encapsulate the main elements of Salvadoran history in the past five centuries. Any comprehensive understanding of the uprising and Matanza in 1932 has to take into account that El Salvador has had a conflictive history marked by social disequilibrium and a perpetually complex relationship with the global economy. Some of the primary elements of that history include the violent transformation of Indian life during the Conquest, the institutionalization of a racialized hierarchy during the colonial era, the breakdown in central authority after independence in the early nineteenth century, the turmoil created by the privatization of communal lands in the 1880s, and the economic fluctuations brought on by El Salvador's incorporation into the global economy as a producer of agricultural commodities. At various times during the

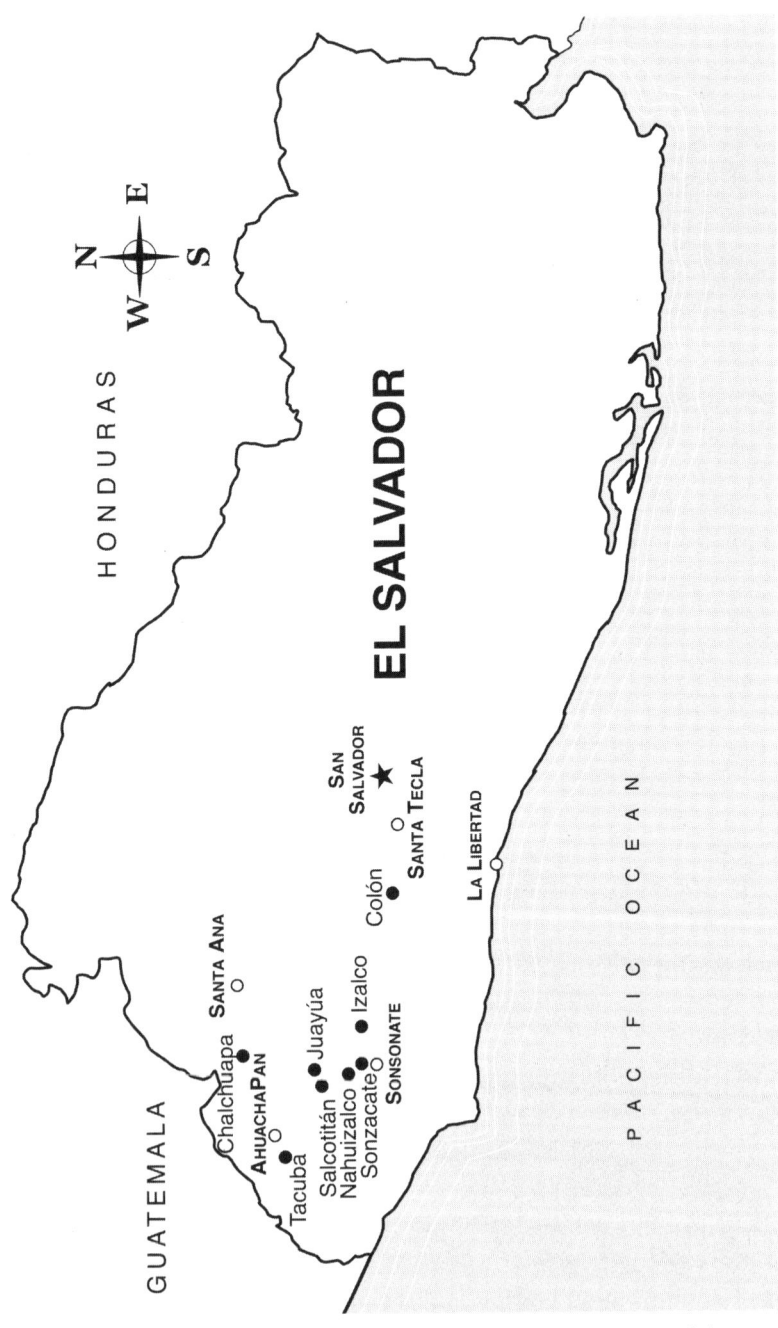

2-1   Map of El Salvador showing the locations of the main events of the 1932 uprising.

seven decades after 1932, El Salvador seemed to have chances to find an alternative to economic underdevelopment and political authoritarianism. Sadly those opportunities were lost and social crises multiplied as the country sank into a prolonged civil war in the 1980s. If the sixteenth through the nineteenth centuries laid the foundation for the events of 1932, then the tragic uprising and Matanza of that year served as prologue to the failures that followed.

Before 1932

One of the central elements to the story of 1932 is the role of Indians in the uprising. To appreciate the conditions they were facing in the early 1930s, it is necessary to look at their history dating back to Spanish colonization of the northern region of Central America. The Conquest began in 1523 with the arrival of Pedro de Alvarado, a lieutenant of Hernán Cortés, the conqueror of Mexico. Alvarado's crossing of the Paz River on the border of modern-day Guatemala and El Salvador marked the beginning of the coexistence of Spaniards and Indians on lands that would eventually become El Salvador. It also began the troubled and sometimes violently conflictive relationship between Indians and non-Indians. The Spanish consolidated power over the northern part of the Central American isthmus fairly rapidly and merged the lands that would become modern-day Central America into a single administrative unit that stretched from Guatemala to Costa Rica under the control of Spanish authorities in the capital in Guatemala. With the Conquest, the Spanish subjugated the indigenous populations of El Salvador, mainly Pipiles, relatives of the Aztecs of Mexico, and Lencas, a group with South American origins. The initial stages of colonial rule were brutal. Since the region was rich in people but poor in gold or silver, masses of Indians were rounded up, branded with hot irons, and sold as slaves to Caribbean and South American landlords. Those who were left behind were Christianized and forced to provide labor to landowners and taxes to colonial authorities. The arrival of the Spanish also brought new diseases for which the Indians had no natural defenses. Population decline was enormous. In some areas 80 to 90 percent of the indigenous population died due to disease and brutal labor requirements.[1]

The Spanish conquistadors had left Spain to find fame and fortune, but Central America challenged them. Declining indigenous populations and the absence of precious metals made organizing a lucrative economy in the region difficult. To fulfill their ambitions, the Spaniards initiated what can be called the first "globalization" of El Salvador by linking its economy to overseas markets, beginning a long process of opening El Salvador to outside forces and their inevitable fluctuations. In the sixteenth century the Spanish colonizers experimented with the export of balsam, a tree resin valued for its curative powers, and with cacao, the raw material used to make chocolate. As often happens with globalization, the opportunities presented by global markets produced challenges, such as economic instability and the troublesome fact that market changes in far corners of the globe can deeply impact the lives of everyone back home. The market for cacao, for example, declined in the seventeenth century due to competition from Venezuela and Ecuador. Landowners in what would become modern-day El Salvador had to find another product to sell. They turned to indigo, which provided the main link to the world economy until the late nineteenth century. Indigo was a blue dye made from the leaves of a plant that Mayan people had used to paint their faces in religious ceremonies and also to dye clothing. European textile manufacturers used it similarly as a dye in fabric production.[2]

Making the dye was unhealthy because its extraction required the fermentation of indigo leaves, which produced noxious fumes and attracted thick clouds of flies. In its role as protector of the Indians, the Spanish crown prohibited their employment in this unhealthy activity. Indigo producers routinely ignored the edict, and Indians continued to be forced to collect and process indigo leaves. Nonetheless, the crown's prohibition encouraged the importation of African slaves, contributing to the ethnic diversity of El Salvador's population in the late colonial period.

Throughout the colonial era, ethnicity defined a person's position in the economy and society. People were designated by ethnicity at birth, and their lives were largely determined by their ethnic labels. They paid taxes according to ethnicity, and everything from public service, to military duties, to labor organization and marriage was defined by ethnicity. By and large (and there were notable exceptions), being Spanish, either born in Europe or in El Salvador, positioned a person in the highest economic and social levels. Having mixed blood granted a person lower status than that of the Spaniards but higher than that of Africans and Indians. Whereas pre-Hispanic Indian society was hierarchical and typified by complex social inequalities, the colonial period intensified exploitative norms by institutionalizing racial difference. Spanish authorities developed a rigid and detailed racial ideology and made it central to colonial power structures, although as in any society there were exceptions to the rules, such as local Indian leaders who served as liaisons between colonial administrators or religious authorities.[3]

Religion was an instrument of power under colonialism. One of the ways Spaniards legitimized the Conquest was to save the souls of those they had conquered by converting them to Christianity. Without denying the good intentions of many priests and public officials who sought to protect Indians, it is clear that the Catholic Church was a key ally in colonial domination. Indians were made to abandon their old gods and replace them with an allegiance to Christianity. However, conversions were neither instantaneous nor thorough, which was typical of many aspects of colonial acculturation. Indigenous cultures and forms of social organization remained vibrant and alive. Indians borrowed, resisted, adapted, and often rebelled against the culture brought by the Spanish. One of the institutions that emerged during this process was the cofradía, a sodality or religious organization dedicated to worshiping a specific saint. Cofradías often functioned with minimal church supervision, allowing them to emerge as centers of Indian community identity. Cofradía leaders were community leaders, imbued with religious, social, political, and economic responsibilities. As in all aspects of colonial life, ethnicity defined the cofradías. They were not exclusively Indian, they could also be Spanish or mestizo, but rarely were they mixed.[4]

Land tenure followed the hierarchical norms and ethnic patterns of colonial society. Spanish landlords had large private properties (haciendas) devoted to both export production and subsistence agriculture. Alongside these large properties existed Indian towns, also with large tracts of land. But Indians did not own their land privately. Instead, the land belonged to the community at large and was managed collectively through the community's political institutions, usually the cofradía. The existence of communal properties was a curious by-product of Spanish colonialism that reflected a merging of cultural traditions. In part, it preserved pre-Conquest Indian practices, but it also followed the customs of Moors (Muslims), who occupied Spain between the 700s and the late 1400s. Spaniards had developed the belief that all peoples in their realm should possess sufficient resources to provide for their own sustenance. Spaniards believed this rule should apply to themselves as well as the people they conquered. Morality and ideology might have motivated this seemingly beneficent practice, but it also had practical and economic benefits because dead subjects do not make good workers or taxpayers. As a result, every township, be it Indian, mestizo, or Spanish, had the right to a tract of communal land from the Spanish crown. Indian lands were known as *comunidades,* or communities, whereas the common lands of Spanish or mestizo towns were known as *ejidos.* These communal lands could be farmed by members of the community or municipality, or they could be rented out to earn income, but they could not be sold or mortgaged. For many townships, especially Indian, communal land became a precious commodity, both a symbol of group identity and a practical source of material survival. It is a curious paradox of Spanish colonialism that it gave resources to the people it was seeking to control something they could use to resist foreign impositions. But, that was the complex reality of Spain's American empire. In addition to the communal lands and privately held estates, the third type of land tenure during the colonial era was crown-owned land, known as *tierras realengas* (the king's lands), which were sometimes left fallow and other times utilized.[5]

Administrative decentralization was another feature of colonial life that granted some empowerment to Indians and local communities. In theory, the Spanish Empire was a highly centralized structure in which all power and privilege flowed downward from the monarchy. But in reality, power was much more dispersed, and central authority had severe limits. For example, peripheral areas of Spain's American empire remained effectively isolated and beyond the bounds of the monarchy's administrators. Even those areas at the core of the empire demonstrated substantial local autonomy, where central authorities either couldn't or didn't care to exercise control. By the time independence arrived, many areas of the Spanish Empire, including El Salvador, had developed notions of distinct regional identity and power.[6]

Variations in economic production also fomented regional distinctiveness. Precious metals were the commodities most sought by Spain in its American empire. But many other products of high monetary value were also produced. One of them was indigo, and El Salvador was a major producer. The indigo market had its ups and downs, but by the late eighteenth century the European textile industry was flourishing and Spanish policies had encouraged exports. Rich landlords and merchants in Central America increased their wealth by marketing indigo, but prosperity brought tensions. People of Spanish descent born in the colonies (so-called creoles) came to resent the bureaucrats and merchants born in Spain (so-called *peninsulares*) who controlled trade and the bureaucracy. Such tensions over hierarchy were typical of most colonial societies in the late eighteenth and early nineteenth centuries. But economic decline and shocks to the Spanish political system exacerbated resentments and fueled a budding nationalism. The Napoleonic wars in Europe disrupted trade for years, and to make matters worse, in 1807 Bonaparte invaded Spain, deposed the Spanish royal family, and gave the throne to his brother Joseph. An entire system of political legitimacy that had been in place for centuries was overturned in a few months. Independence movements sprang up all over Latin America, with varying degrees of success. Central America, like Mexico, tended to be more conservative and stayed loyal to the idea of Spanish colonialism, despite numerous conspiracies by proindependence liberals. Napoleon was eventually defeated in 1815 and the Spanish king returned to the throne, but the system had already been disrupted beyond repair. In 1820 the Spanish crown received another blow when a military revolt forced King Ferdinand VII to accept a liberal constitution and to become a constitutional monarch who had to abide by laws created by an elected legislature. The Spanish monarchy was no longer the rock of stability it had been.[7]

Salvadorans played a disproportionate role in the proindependence movements in Central America. They saw themselves as the main agricultural producers in the region being unjustly controlled by parasitical colonial authorities in Guatemala. But these movements were repeatedly frustrated by conservatives who had too much to lose by breaking away from Spain and the long-established system of trade and privilege. The events of 1820 proved too much even for the Guatemalan merchants and their counterparts in Mexico. Driven by a desire to preserve their status and privilege, the elites of Mexico broke from Spain in 1821, followed shortly thereafter by the Central Americans. Although Central America proclaimed independence as a unit, the five internal subdivisions that had been created by Spanish authorities for administrative purposes perceived themselves as distinct from one another. They first experimented with a federation, but the rupture from Spain had been preceded by a long period of political instability that had weakened most institutions. With independence the system of central government fell apart and local jurisdictions began to compete for authority. Constant regional bickering interrupted by periods of civil war marked the abbreviated life of the federation. In 1839 it collapsed, and El Salvador emerged as one of five independent countries in Central America.[8]

El Salvador inherited the inequalities of the past, the ethnic distinctions, and the complex system of land tenure with Indian communities owning substantial amounts of communal land. That inheritance, together with the weakening of governing institutions, produced an atomized political system. Central authorities in San Salvador were few in number and unable to collect taxes or impose policies on assertive local powers entrenched in municipalities. Instability was rampant; between 1841 and 1861 the presidency changed hands forty-two times. The decentralized nature of power meant that local struggles were all important, whether over land, water, roads, or municipal government. Given the ethnic divisions inherited from the colonial period, in certain areas, particularly in the western region, the struggles ran along ethnic lines: Ladinos versus Indians, who accounted for perhaps as much as 50 percent of the population at independence. Ironically, given the weakness of central authority, Indian communities found greater room to maneuver and more opportunities to assert their rights during the decades after independence than at any other time in El Salvador's history. But this autonomy did not last long. As non-Indian elites began to assert or reassert their power, many of the foundations for the uprising and massacre of 1932 were established.

Changes occurring outside El Salvador in the late nineteenth century provided the central state with the resources to enhance its power. Export possibilities improved dramatically after midcentury with the incorporation of California to the United States and the emerging industrial economy in Europe. The powerful North American nation now extended from the Atlantic to the Pacific, and it needed to move products and people from coast to coast. European and North American manufacturers needed raw materials to fuel their enterprises, and the corresponding population boom that accompanied economic growth meant that millions of people were ready to consume products that could only be produced in Latin America. Maritime routes around or through Latin America became an increasingly important component of this economic surge. Ships carried goods around the Straits of Magellan or they delivered them to Panama to be carried overland by mule, or after 1855 by railroad to waiting boats on the other side. Visionaries dreamed of a shipping canal through Panama or Nicaragua, which they eventually got after the turn of the century. The end result was that the Pacific coast of the American continent, dormant for centuries, came alive with hundreds and later thousands of vessels and steam ships moving back and forth. This transformation was enormously important for El Salvador whose only ports are on the Pacific.

Regular shipping services and lower costs encouraged the export of existing commodities from El Salvador and also made it possible to add a new product to its list of exports: coffee. As coffee and indigo exports increased, the collection of import-export taxes, controlled by the central government, provided the resources to organize a bureaucracy, strengthen the army, and enforce government policies. Thus, the expansion of exports and the consolidation of the central state went hand in hand. The state had a clearly defined mission, strengthening the export economy by building roads to ports, organizing banks to finance coffee planters, and passing laws to strengthen rights to private property. Anything obstructing the cultivation of export crops was deemed regressive and targeted for change. Since coffee was grown on small trees that required many years to produce saleable beans, secure rules relating to private property were considered essential to economic growth. Indian communities, having experienced a degree of autonomy during the era of weak central governments, were now seen as an obstacle. Their communal landholdings, particularly in areas suitable to coffee cultivation, such as those in western El Salvador, became a source of ongoing conflict. Many governing elites regarded communal lands as an impediment to national development. They passed legislation in 1881 and 1882 declaring communal property illegal, forcing all municipalities and Indian communities to divide up their communal landholdings and distribute them in the form of smaller private plots.[9]

The land-privatization laws demonstrated that power was being realigned in favor of the central state and the big landowners over local authorities and small farmers. The realignment did not take place overnight. Land privatization was a cumbersome, slow process, open to corruption, and fraught with conflict. Land had always been something worth fighting for, but now that it was being distributed into private hands, the potential for disagreement increased. Divisions emerged between and within Indian communities, and between Indians and Ladinos. Nevertheless, the process proceeded over the years without debilitating unrest. The privatization legislation stipulated that the people currently utilizing common land would be given first access to it as private plots. Most of those people who had been farming communal land secured title to their former farms as privately held plots. So long as the privatization decrees did not deprive the many thousands of small farmers across the country of access to land, the privatization process was able to occur without massive civil unrest. In fact, many of the small properties that dotted the countryside in the early to mid-twentieth century originated in the late nineteenth century. Admittedly, the new private plots were not large, seldom more the ten acres necessary for a family to subsist, but the peasantry received land, giving birth to a large sector of smallholding farmers that can still be seen in parts of El Salvador today.

Because privatization meant that land became a commodity that could be bought and sold in the market place, plots of land often changed hands many times. As the initial plots proved too small to sustain peasant families over the generations, poorer families typically ended up selling their land. The result was land concentrating in the hands of an agrarian elite and the growth of a rural proletariat. Not surprisingly, this class differentiation took on ethnic characteristics, with Indians tending to make up a disproportionate percentage of the landless poor and Ladinos making up the landed elite.[10]

Different factions of big landowners alternated in control of the state until the Great Depression. One family, the "Meléndez-Quiñónez dynasty," held the presidency from 1914 to 1927 and presided over the economic turmoil associated with World War I and the coffee boom that followed. The disruption of trade with Europe during the war impacted the Salvadoran economy because the country's main trading partners were across the Atlantic. The end of the war led to an economic resurgence as coffee prices soared and the value of coffee exports more than doubled by 1922; coffee planters were richer than ever. This period also witnessed the United States replacing Europe as El Salvador's main trading partner. The trend toward land concentration that began with privatization accelerated substantially due to the "dance of the millions" as this period of export-driven prosperity was called. Another significant development during this period was the growth of cities, partly as a result of the growing need for a bureaucracy to oversee the national state and the expanding economy. Artisans, workers, and employees in the cities, particularly in the increasingly important capital, displayed a great interest in organizing and participating in politics through unions, cooperatives, and mutual societies.

The Meléndez-Quiñónez family remained in power by manipulating elections and using local patronage networks to consolidate support across the countryside, but they were careful to respect the letter of the law. When they ran out of candidates in their own family circle, and in order to abide by the constitutional prohibition against reelection, they selected a trusted collaborator to succeed them, Pío Romero Bosque (1927–31). They had no idea that he had genuinely democratic tendencies, but strangely enough he did. During midterm elections he allowed open political competition, which invigorated popular interest in politics. When his presidential term was up in 1931, he had the novel idea of not backing any candidate. The timing was such that the main issue confronting the country was the impact of the Great Depression. Once again events occurring far away had impacted El Salvador, which had become more dependent than ever on exports. The world crisis that followed the stock market crash of 1929 brought down the price of coffee, which by then represented more than 90 percent of the country's total exports. Prices were so low that some planters would have lost money had they harvested their beans, so they let them rot on the trees and sent their workers away. Planters who eked out a profit did so by either slashing wages or demanding that their workers produce more for the same old wage. Either way, heavy burdens fell on the work force. But workers who had jobs were lucky because rural unemployment was rampant. Planters who had borrowed from banks to expand their plantations during the boom period couldn't pay their mortgages, and banks running out of reserves squeezed debtors. Foreclosures and bankruptcies defined the business climate, and urban unemployment followed. The government's main source of revenue, customs duties, collapsed; as a result there was little money to pay public employees, who either went unpaid or lost their jobs.[11]

The resulting social unrest, hunger, desperation, strikes, communist propaganda, threats to property, and the apparent collapse of law and order framed the 1931 election. Not surprisingly, the winner in the election was the person who promised to take dramatic steps to alleviate the situation, particularly in the countryside. His name was Arturo Araujo. He was a landowner who had been influenced by the Labor Party when he was a student in England. During the election it was rumored that he or his campaign workers pledged to distribute land to the landless to gain support in rural areas. But once in power he lost mass support when he proved unable to fulfill his promises. His administration was disorganized, but regardless of his managerial failures, the limited government revenues made social reform impossible. Even soldiers were owed back pay. Araujo lost the backing of the army and whatever support he had from the business class when he forced banks to provide loans to the government. By

December his defenders had dwindled, and as seemed inevitable, an army coup toppled him. Araujo's vice president, General Maximiliano Hernández Martínez, took over in early December 1931. In addition to the budget crisis and the unstable political situation, the new president faced two immediate challenges: the refusal of the United States to recognize the legality of his regime, and the peasant uprising in late January 1932.

The uprising of 1932 was the culmination of a rapid increase in social and political discord throughout western El Salvador in late 1931 and early 1932. As the full impact of the Great Depression took hold, workers mobilized in response to landowners' attempts to cut costs by lowering wages, eliminating jobs, or asking remaining workers to produce more. Many of the largest plantations experienced some form of labor conflict, often in the form of strikes involving dozens, if not hundreds of workers. Some disputes were resolved peacefully, usually as a result of concessions from landowners, but many ended in bloodshed, as police and National Guardsmen cracked down on striking workers.

The insurrection was also preceded by hotly contested local elections. Normally, municipal elections occurred in December, but because of the coup, many elections across the country, and in particular in the western region, were postponed until early January. The military regime allowed the elections to follow the democratic norms instituted by President Pío Romero Bosque, allowing for broad-based political mobilization. In fact, the Communist Party backed candidates in a number of municipalities, including Ahuachapán and San Salvador. The party's candidates ran under third parties because the Communist Party was still clandestine, but they received significant popular support, partly because party leaders insisted that they avoid ideological discussions and instead focus on the population's immediate suffering. The party's candidate in San Salvador came in third, only a few percentage points behind the winner. Notwithstanding the presence of new candidates sympathetic to the Communist Party, most of the elections occurring in early January 1932 revolved around long-standing local issues. The election in Nahuizalco, for example, pitted Indians against Ladinos and resulted in the Indians demanding the government investigate supposed improprieties. When the government responded with silence, armed rebels overran the town.[12]

After 1932

The Martínez regime responded to the uprising with unprecedented brutality and widespread murder. In response to the issue of U.S. recognition, Martínez simply waited. Eventually, the United States decided that the stability of his regime outweighed the fact that it had breeched the Washington Treaties of 1923 by coming to power in a coup, so the United States granted recognition in 1934. The general survived the tremendous challenges before his regime in its early months and remained in office until 1944. During his tenure, the army began to exhibit the early signs of institutionalized authoritarianism, as the national government imposed central authority over local interests and the army began to believe that only it was qualified to govern. Military leaders knew that the challenges before the nation were great, and they believed that only the military had the strength to defend the state and the "honor" to avoid the senseless politicking associated with democracy. Big landowners and their business associates accepted the trade off, ceding direct control of the government to the army in exchange for protection. The army would stay in power in El Salvador until 1979.[13]

The combined toll of the Great Depression and the uprising had been enormous. Neither politics nor the economy functioned the same thereafter. Whatever progress had been made toward democracy under Pío Romero Bosque rapidly dissipated. The insecurity and social turmoil weakened support for ideas of political equality and civil liberty. From an economic perspective, liberal ideologies that accompanied the export boom in the late nineteenth century lost support in the face of the Great Depression and the rise of fascism in Europe. Martínez took advantage of this situation to establish a harsh dictatorship, marked by two extended "states of siege" (a suspension of constitutional guarantees), which allowed him to suppress dissent and restrict political participation. A strengthened army and newly created paramilitary groups allowed the military to play an unprecedented political role. It is estimated that one out of every five able-bodied men in the countryside was a member of army-controlled rural patrols. An efficient network of spies oversaw urban areas. Press censorship was thorough and implacable. The only political party allowed to operate was Martínez's Partido Pro Patria (Party of the

Fatherland). At the height of his power he even oversaw minor appointments at the municipal level.[14]

The government also began to intervene in the economy as never before. Driven by its fascistic undertone, the government presented itself as a populist defender of working people, embodied by its social-reform program Mejoramiento Social. Official interventionism included the defense of large landowners and the export sector. The government halted foreclosures of agricultural properties to alleviate the problems of coffee growers; it established new partnerships between the state and private business, and it created the Central Bank to take the issuing of paper currency away from private banks. The Compañía Salvadoreña del Café (Salvadoran Coffee Company) introduced state intervention in the marketing of coffee, and the national mortgage bank competed with private banks for financing properties. Both in politics and in economic management the model to be imitated ceased to be the United States and became more Mussolini's Italy and Hitler's Germany. German officers were hired to run the Salvadoran officers' school, and efforts were made to strengthen economic ties with Germany.[15]

By the outbreak of World War II, the international context had changed radically. The Great Depression was over, and the United States wanted support from all the Latin American republics. The U.S. State Department pressured Latin America's leaders to break ties with Axis countries and support the Allies. Even Martínez was not willing to oppose the United States at such a high-stakes moment, and El Salvador joined the Allied cause. The Germans in the officers' school were replaced with personnel from the United States, and German-owned properties throughout the country were expropriated. With El Salvador now firmly in the U.S. camp, the words of Franklin Delano Roosevelt acquired greater resonance. The problem for El Salvador's military rulers was that he talked about democracy and the Four Freedoms. The obvious contradiction between his rhetoric and the realities of authoritarian military rule proved too much for the Martínez regime. Moreover, the general's eccentricities, conveniently ignored in the crisis of the 1930s, became troublesome, especially when they impacted public policy. For example, during an epidemic, the general refused to take standard sanitary measures and instead ordered public lights to be covered with blue cellophane, believing that blue light provided adequate prevention. Roque Dalton provided another example of the general's oddness, when he related that his father, Winnal Dalton, offered to buy shoes for school children on the behalf of the U.S. expatriate community. The general refused the offer, arguing that children benefited from the earth's vibrations being absorbed through their naked feet.[16]

To prolong his term in office Martínez used every trick in the book. First he managed to get the National Assembly to let him finish Araujo's term. By the time he ran for office on his own in 1935 he had established complete control over the electoral system. At the end of his "first" term in office in 1939 he and his supporters changed the constitution to allow for his reelection and created a mechanism by which the legislature (as opposed to the popular vote) could choose new presidents. He tried to employ the same strategy for the next presidential period (1944–50), but times had changed and the Salvadoran population was less compliant. In the midst of ongoing Allied victories, democracy became the new buzzword in the Americas. The general's actions leading up to the 1944 election had created discontent among too many sectors of the population, even among professional groups and the upper classes. In a desperate attempt to undermine opposition to his reelection in 1944, Martínez took a populist stance by courting labor, imposing price restrictions, and trying to further regulate markets and trade organizations. However, workers remained unconvinced while the upper classes were further alienated. Younger officers, some of whom were already being trained by U.S. officers, grew tired of what they saw as Martínez's anachronistic governing style. As a result, the 1944 reelection sparked an officer's rebellion on April 2. The revolt was put down, and the government executed many officers, who came to be seen as martyrs for the cause of modernizing military rule. When mass demonstrations hit the streets, the army opened fire, killing more than one hundred civilians. University students began a protest movement that was quickly joined by urban workers and professionals. After a general strike that paralyzed the country Martínez resigned and his minister of defense took over in May 1944. The event was dubbed "*huelga de brazos caídos*" (the strike of the fallen arms).[17]

For five months it appeared as if democracy had triumphed. When the new interim government called for elections, the people who had mobilized against the dictatorship found their hero in a charismatic doctor named Arturo Romero, a presidential candidate who talked about reform and democracy. But the past regime had not been dismantled; the army commanders were the same old generals; the landowners still feared change, and the legislature had the same members that had reelected Martínez. All these groups came to see Arturo Romero as a dangerous reformer who might open the door to communism, if, they suggested, he was not a communist himself. The dictatorship's former chief of police, a conservative colonel named Osmín Aguirre, brought the democratic opening to a halt by toppling the interim government and sending Romero into exile. He then manipulated the electoral process to ensure that the most conservative candidate, another military man, General Castaneda Castro, was victorious.

It was clear that Martínez's main legacy was an institutionalized and politicized army ready and willing to use the levers of power to defend the status quo against threats either real or imagined. Martínez was gone, but military authoritarianism survived and entrenched itself. As a case in point, after four unremarkable years President Castaneda Castro sought to change the constitution to allow himself to be reelected. The tactic failed for him just as it had for his predecessor, although for different reasons. Whereas Martínez was felled by a nascent, albeit unsuccessful democratic movement, Castaneda Castro had broken the unwritten rule of the emergent military authoritarian system; individual generals would not be permitted to perpetuate themselves in office. Instead, power would be exercised by the army as an institution.[18]

Whereas the military did not allow challenges to its institutionalized hold on power, individual military regimes differed from one another in their ideological orientation and governing style. Some of them even emphasized the need to make El Salvador more modern, which could include adopting social reforms. For example, in 1948 Castaneda was overthrown in a military coup that brought to power a new governing junta, the Consejo de Gobierno Revolucionario, which turned toward the populist side of military rule. Comprised of young officers and idealistic civilians, the junta portrayed itself as a renovator of the governing class. It wanted to modernize El Salvador's economy, infrastructure, and society through economic diversification, a revamped educational system, and social reforms. The junta even oversaw the rewriting of the constitution in 1950, giving women the right to vote, advancing worker's protection laws, and granting the state the right to intervene in the economy in the name of the common good.

The new constitutional charter also reinforced the government's right to suppress dissent and to monitor groups or individuals deemed a threat to the state. This type of unrelenting attack on perceived opponents of any ilk became the norm of legislation and governing strategies until the 1992 Peace Accords. Governing officials always interpreted the laws as providing them carte blanche for anticommunist activities. The anticommunism of the Salvadoran Army and the upper classes did not need prodding from the United States, which was in the midst of its McCarthyist witch hunt in the late 1940s and early 1950s. In El Salvador, anticommunism was a durable local-grown product that had more to do with the memory of 1932 than with U.S. fears about the spread of communism throughout the world. In fact, U.S. military aid to El Salvador was minimal until after the Cuban Revolution in 1959.[19]

After passing the 1950 Constitution the situation was ripe for a new presidential election. Not surprisingly, the leader of the junta, Colonel Oscar Osorio, was elected. Fortunately for him, a period of high coffee prices accompanied his election, allowing him to give greater priority to the reform side of the reform/control mix that he and his fellow officers had established as the essence of military rule. Without having to raise taxes the government invested in education, built middle-class and rural housing, created a social security program, built a major dam, and led the movement to create the Central American Common Market (a lowering of trade barriers within the region designed to stimulate trade and encourage industrialization). However, there was a darker underside to these modernization schemes. A state of siege was decreed twice and a stern law, "The Defense of the Democratic and Constitutional Order," limited civil and political liberties. Opposition political parties were allowed to organize but not win elections.

Osorio's chosen successor, Colonel José María Lemus, was ready to continue the modernizing endeavors, but coffee prices took a dive in 1957, less than a year into the new administration. With fewer resources for new programs, the government faced growing social discontent. In response, Lemus began to crack down. By 1960 his regime had violently suppressed demonstrating university students and had become increasingly repressive. A coup d'état, led by officers loyal to former President Osorio, invoked the spirit of the officers' revolt against Martínez in 1944 and toppled Lemus in 1960. The coup plotters hoped to reinvigorate the reformist spirit, but it was one year after the Cuban Revolution and the most conservative sectors of the political system were frightened by the junta's liberalizing tone. After only three months a conservative countercoup returned the government to authoritarianism, where it would remain for many years.[20]

Changes in the international geo-political situation in the early 1960s had important implications for the standard top-down governing approach of El Salvador's military regimes. Castro's success in Cuba changed the balance of power in the Western Hemisphere and brought the cold war to Latin America in new and unprecedented ways.[21] The United States feared Cuba's example, and with good reason, especially after the failure of its Bay of Pigs invasion and the 1961 missile crisis a year later. In a manner of speaking, the United States responded to the new situation with its own version of the Salvadoran reform/control dichotomy, offering economic and social assistance to those it deemed properly "democratic," meaning anti-communist, while at the same time increasing coercive military activities to combat the presumed advance of Soviet-inspired Marxism. As the epitome of this strategy, President John F. Kennedy launched the Alliance for Progress. The idea behind the program was to provide support and resources to advance social evolution in order to stop violent revolution. In addition to monies for education and other social services the alliance also included a military component with training in counterinsurgency and surveillance. President Julio Rivera, the colonel who won the election called by the conservative junta that had taken power in January 1961, understood that the United States was ready to channel unprecedented amounts of money to friendly regimes throughout Latin America. Driven by a combination of personal interest and political ideals, he molded himself into a model Alliance for Progress president. From the perspective of the United States, Rivera was the ideal partner, someone who combined a top-down modernizing vision with unwavering anti-communism. As foreign aid began to flow and as the Salvadoran economy began to turn around, Rivera was able to emphasize reforms once again. His regime promoted the Central American Common Market, industrialization, the expansion of export agriculture, and central planning, all policies favored by the alliance. Landowners begrudgingly tolerated reforms as long as they didn't directly threaten their interests. Rivera's two successors, Colonel Fidel Sánchez Hernández (1967–72) and Colonel Arturo Armando Molina (1972–77), continued similar policies.[22]

After 1969 the cracks in the system became increasingly apparent. One of the flagship projects of the Alliance for Progress in El Salvador, an ambitious educational reform designed to diffuse opposition, backfired. At the center of the reform was a plan to use televisions in the classroom to compensate for poorly trained teachers. Proponents in both El Salvador and the United States saw the use of televisions as an ideal example of employing modern technology to solve social problems at a low cost. But teachers thought differently. Already underpaid and lacking benefits, they saw themselves being transformed into mere teaching assistants to an electronic box. From their point of view, a project that directed millions of dollars to educational technology while teachers could barely make a living was an example of a government with misguided priorities. Massive teacher's strikes in 1968 and 1971 became rallying points for more general opposition to the government. They also radicalized the teacher's union, which would go on to play a prominent role in the leftist insurgency in the 1970s and 1980s. Another major project favored by the alliance, the Central American Common Market, also had unforeseen consequences. The idea behind it was to liberalize trade within the countries of Central America, but freeing trade can lead to unexpected results. El Salvador turned out to be better prepared to take advantage of the new conditions, and it gained larger benefits than did neighboring Honduras. Moreover, the expansion of export agriculture in El Salvador during the 1960s had consolidated landownership even further and pushed tens of thousands of landless peasants into less populated areas of Honduras. This influx irritated the Honduran government, a nationalistic military regime that was predisposed toward opposing El Salvador's growing influence over its economy. The result was a brief war in 1969 that was dubbed the "Soccer War" because its outbreak was preceded by a hard-fought soccer match between the two countries. Although military hostilities lasted only one hundred hours, the war was enough to bring the Common Market to a screeching halt and send thousands of Salvadoran peasants streaming back across the border, exacerbating the already severe social problems in the countryside.[23]

In response to these and other factors, some leftists in El Salvador began to advocate a more militant approach. The Communist Party had been the only radical leftist organization in the country since the party's foundation in 1930. Despite intense repression from police and military units throughout the years, it had survived, albeit in total clandestinity, and it even achieved organizational success among organized laborers and intellectual circles. But after the Cuban Revolution, lines of discord emerged within the party's ranks, between those who advocated a more militant strategy and those "traditionalists" who believed that the country was not ready for armed action. The militants accused the traditionalists of ineffectiveness and wrongheaded interpretations of Salvadoran reality. They pointed to the party's position during the war with Honduras as a case in point, when party leaders succumbed to nationalism and supported the military government's decision to go to war. The party leadership refused to change its strategy of forming electoral coalitions with other political parties and of building support among labor unions. Militants pointed to the increasingly intransigent right to argue that armed response was unavoidable. Groups of militants began splitting away from the party after 1969 to prepare for guerrilla war.[24]

One of the main reasons that the militants insisted that armed action was necessary was the rapid expansion of right-wing rural paramilitary groups. The initial paramilitary organization was Organización Democrática Nacionalista (Nationalist Democratic Organization, ORDEN), founded by National Guard commander General José Alberto "Chele'" Medrano in the mid-1960s. Backed by the government and trained by National Guard units, ORDEN patrols were comprised mainly of *patrullas cantonales*, or rural military reserves. ORDEN members were expected to guard the countryside against communist insurgency. Medrano explained in an interview how to identify the enemy: "You discover the communist by the way he talks.... Generally, he speaks against Yankee imperialism, he speaks against the oligarchy, he speaks against military men. We can spot them easily."[25] Poorly educated peasants were put in charge of spotting communists using those criteria. Scores of people accused of being communists simply disappeared, or their bodies were discovered in ravines or floating down rivers. Some of those who "disappeared" may have been associated with leftist groups, but the overwhelming majority of victims were simply poor people trying to improve conditions for their communities and families, and for that they were defined as enemies of the state, capitalism, and Christianity.

ORDEN was a brutal organization that turned terrorism into policy, but other paramilitary organizations took terror to even higher levels. Commonly known as "death squads," these groups operated surreptitiously and often without centralized coordination, sometimes sponsored by sectors within the government, other times by wealthy citizens. Death squads terrorized the population, torturing and killing anyone who demonstrated support for the armed opposition or even moderate reformism. The intent was to instill fear in the population in hopes of suppressing all forms of popular mobilization. The paramilitaries and their sponsors in the elite and the military pointed to incidents like the kidnapping and murders of young members of the richest families by guerrilla organizations as evidence of the need for a violent suppression of dissent. One of the most renowned death squads would take as its namesake General Martínez. Although their murderous heyday would be in the late 1970s and early 1980s, they had begun to operate as early as the late 1960s and early 1970s.[26]

With the approach of the 1972 presidential election, El Salvador's political climate was already tense. Amidst the reformist efforts of the 1960s new moderate political parties had been allowed to come into existence. One of them, the Christian Democratic Party, had already won the city government of San Salvador. Buoyed by their success and led by a charismatic candidate in José Napoleon Duarte, the Christian Democrats challenged the military government in the 1972 elections. By all accounts, Duarte won, but the army was not ready to relinquish power. It resorted to blatant fraud, cracked down on Christian Democratic supporters, and even arrested and tortured Duarte. The government declared the official candidate, Colonel Arturo Armando Molina, the winner. Although this crackdown thwarted the Christian Democrats, the governing party's legitimacy was also undermined.

During the 1970s, social movements opposed to dictatorship and the intransigence of elites began to expand and diversify. In addition to the growing strength of the Christian Democrats and their centrist ideology, the splinter guerrilla groups from the Communist Party became increasingly active, confronting not only the formal military but also the broad and sprawling paramilitary organizations. Throughout the countryside, the rural poor began to organize themselves into unions and Christian Base Communities. Many of them became adherents of Liberation Theology and interpreted the Gospels from the perspective of creating heaven on earth through social justice, rather than suffering through life and waiting for salvation after death, as the institutionalized church had been preaching. The new approaches to the Scriptures attracted many young clergy and Catholic lay workers, who went to the countryside in hopes of alleviating the misery of the desperately poor peasants. Naturally, they were targeted by the death squads, who followed slogans like "be a patriot, kill a priest."[27]

The growth of opposition movements and the deteriorating social and political situation revived an old debate on the right between reformers and hard-liners. Reformers felt that economic change had to occur to provide opportunities for greater numbers of people and to avoid further social deterioration. Hard-liners insisted that any type of reform was tantamount to communism. Initially, President Molina, with strong support from the United States, sided with the reformers and proposed a modest land reform in 1976 in hopes of alleviating the pressure. The idea behind the land reform was that large landowners would be forced to sell part of their properties to the government, which in turn would distribute small plots to landless peasants. Molina promoted his scheme as an "insurance policy" against social upheaval and swore upon the army's reputation that he would see the plan through to completion. The hopes of the rural poor grew with the prospect of receiving land. Alarmed landowners organized a fierce campaign against the proposed legislation. Death squads even began targeting government officials who worked in the Ministry of Agriculture, which would have overseen the reform. The opposition succeeded and the land reform failed, exacerbating the longstanding frustrations of the rural poor. The defeat also radicalized middle-class reformist intellectuals, who were still angry over the electoral manipulation. In the presidential election of 1977, the army had to rely on even greater levels of fraud and violence to beat back the opposition. A social explosion was looming.[28]

Events around the rest of Central America heightened political tensions in El Salvador. The success of the Nicaraguan Revolution in July 1979 inspired the left and struck fear in the right. Army officers in El Salvador watched in horror as Nicaraguan soldiers and officers were forced into exile, penniless. The Nicaragua National Guard was replaced by a new "people's" army led by former rebels. The far right in El Salvador became all the more convinced that its hard-line defense was correct. But a reformist faction in the Salvadoran Army believed that one final, massive reformist push could keep El Salvador from falling off the edge. In October 1979 these reformist officers orchestrated a coup d'état with the support of progressive civilians. This coup was the last-ditch effort to introduce needed reforms and deflect demands for revolutionary change. Once again, stout resistance from conservative elements in the army doomed the effort.[29]

Disappearances and political assassinations continued unabated. Hopes for a moderate solution dissipated after the murder in March 1980 of Monsignor Oscar Arnulfo Romero (1917–80), the archbishop of San Salvador whose powerful denunciation of human rights violations had enraged the right. In November Ronald Reagan was elected president of the United States after a campaign in which he highlighted anticommunism and criticized his opponent, then-president Jimmy Carter for "losing" Nicaragua to the communists. The U.S. election emboldened Salvadoran conservatives and led the revolutionary movement to believe that it had to take power before Reagan's inauguration.

The civil war started in 1981 when the guerrilla insurgency, a recently formed coalition of the once disparate guerilla factions, the Farabundo Martí Liberation Front (FMLN), launched its "Final Offensive." The offensive failed, but the lines of conflict were set, the guerrillas had united, and the government had an intractable insurgency on its hands. During the first three years of the war, the guerrillas seized control of approximately one-fourth of Salvadoran territory. In these so-called Liberated Zones the government was capable of only a nominal presence. The guerrillas set up popular governments within the areas they controlled, running schools, hospitals, and courts. Never numbering more than five thousand armed combatants, but backed by a massive civilian support network, the guerrillas proved every bit the match of the Salvadoran Army, which swelled in number to more than one hundred thousand soldiers. With superior weaponry and command over the skies, the army could penetrate deep into guerrilla-held territory at will, but it was incapable of establishing permanent control, inevitably retreating to the safety of their own secure areas. As is typical in such civil conflicts, the people who suffered most were noncombatant civilians caught in between, especially because the Salvadoran Army purposefully targeted civilian populations in the countryside in order to eliminate support for the guerrillas. The army perpetrated episodes of mass slaughter of civilians at infamous places like the Sumpul River and El Mozote.[30]

The United States defined the conflict in El Salvador as a new front in the cold war. U.S. policymakers had always placed a primacy on stability in the region, and they preferred governments to be moderate. But when the political center failed, the United States willingly supported military hard-liners in the name of beating back the communist advance. Rarely did any major political figure in the United States conceptualize the insurgency in El Salvador as being fundamentally rooted in long-standing local issues of poverty and mass mobilization rather than international communism. Even the so-called doves, those policymakers who opposed the Reagan administration's support for the military dictatorships, still accepted the central tenets of anticommunism and believed in the need to check the advance of communism throughout the world. During the ensuing eleven years of conflict, the United States would spend more than four billion dollars to prop up friendly regimes in El Salvador, sometimes military, sometimes civilian, who were dedicated to defeating the guerrillas. At one point direct U.S. aid accounted for a higher percentage of the Salvadoran government's budget than its own internal revenues. Many civic organizations in the United States opposed their government's policy in El Salvador. They protested and in varying ways sought to aid the suffering civilian population in El Salvador. During this period, many of them became familiar with the work of Roque Dalton, including *Miguel Mármol* after an English translation appeared in 1987.[31]

By 1989 the civil war had claimed more than fifty thousand victims, the economy was in a shambles, and there was no end in sight to the violence. The Salvadoran Army and the United States were not interested in seeking a negotiated solution to the conflict, yet neither side seemed capable of a military victory. Two things happened in 1989 that changed the dynamic of the war: first, the socialist bloc collapsed; second, a guerrilla offensive focused on the capital city proved the FMLN's ongoing strength and undermined the army's claim that the guerrillas were in decline. During the offensive, the military brought international condemnation upon itself by assassinating six Jesuit priests who throughout the conflict had insisted on the need to understand its root causes and advocated a negotiated solution to the civil war. Even the United States had begun to reevaluate its position. The dissolution of the Soviet threat led a new Republican administration in the United States under George H. W. Bush (1988–92) to reconsider the need to remain so deeply involved in Central America. U.S. officials in the Salvadoran embassy began talking about a negotiated peace. In El Salvador, the army had to face the fact that military victory was beyond its capacity, and the business class had grown weary of the economic costs of civil war. In short, a negotiated solution became possible. Following initiatives from other Central American presidents and with the help of the United Nations, the Salvadoran government and the leaders of the FMLN negotiated an end to the war and signed a peace agreement in Mexico in January 1992. The FMLN became a political party, and the army was reorganized. Political life in El Salvador entered a new stage of free elections and open public debate, but the previous decade of violence left a legacy of trauma and distrust, and economic inequalities continued to define Salvadoran society.[32]

Interestingly, communism has remained a major component of national political debate since the end of the war. ARENA continues to accuse its FMLN opponents of being communists and lackeys of Fidel Castro, even though most of its members either were moderates to begin with, or have since embraced centrist political ideologies. Admittedly, a faction of hard-liners remains prominent within the FMLN, exemplified by the 2004 presidential candidacy of Shafik Handal (1930–2006), former secretary general of the Communist Party and guerilla commander during the war. In part, the ongoing emphasis that Salvadorans place on communism can be explained by the fact that ARENA and the FMLN were antagonists during the war, so its members carry with them the institutional and sometimes deeply personal memories of conflict. But also the ongoing emphasis placed on communism is explained by the legacy of 1932, which continues to affect Salvadoran politics in unique and powerful ways. As the twenty-first-century wave of globalization unfolds, policymakers in El Salvador face a new series of challenges in trying to achieve the long-sought-after goal of bringing the majority of the Salvadoran people out of poverty and into full political participation. In such a climate, memories of 1932 will continue to hold great relevance, even if references to communism diminish in political discourse.

Conclusion

The episode of 1932 was a particularly tragic expression of the longstanding conflicts generated by El Salvador's inequality, political exclusion, and failure to organize an economy capable of providing well-being for all citizens. These issues have profound historical roots and have been a constant presence throughout El Salvador's troubled history. After 1932 these basic conflicts were recast by the state in terms of the struggle against communism. Years before the cold war had began in earnest in the rest of the world, the Salvadoran ruling class had acquired a visceral aversion to all threats to its supremacy, be they from racial subordinates or communists. After 1932 the specter of popular insurrection coalesced with an emerging anticommunism to provide the rationale for maintaining an authoritarian regime that allied the army and economic elites.

CHAPTER THREE

The Life and Writings of Roque Dalton Prior to *Miguel Mármol*

> Memory is not a generic term of analysis, but itself
> an object appropriated and politicized. Or, equally, nationalized,
> medicalized, aestheticized, gendered, bought and sold.
> —Matt Matsuda, *The Memory of the Modern*

The events of 1932 left an indelible mark on the rest of El Salvador's twentieth century. The events themselves were important, but so were the memories of them and the ways in which differing memories informed various peoples' positions. Arguably, no other Salvadoran author influenced the historical memory of 1932 more than Roque Dalton, mainly through the testimonial *Miguel Mármol*. As with many other episodes in Dalton's life, an unassuming personal encounter in a Prague cafe with an old communist became a central part of Salvadoran history. One needs to understand Dalton's life to appreciate how his personal journey became embedded in his nation's history. Dalton's interest in history was no mere academic pursuit. He viewed historical study as a political act, as a precondition for shaping the future. Perhaps this personal identification with history is what gave so much resonance to Dalton's writings.

Roque Dalton was a still a young man, just thirty-one, when he met Miguel Mármol in Prague in 1966. But by that time he had already achieved many things and had lived anything but a mundane life. He was a widely regarded writer who moved comfortably in international circles, a committed leftist with a long track record of political activism in El Salvador, and a historian who had merged his political and intellectual pursuits by writing an alternative version of Salvadoran history that emphasized the events of 1932. In other words, by the time Dalton sat down to convert the handwritten notes of his interviews with Mármol into the seamless testimonial narrative that we have today, his views on politics, history, and art were well established.

Dalton was a brilliant, complex man who lived in dynamic times. He wanted to understand the world and make it better, and he dedicated his mind and eventually sacrificed his life in pursuit of these objectives. An examination of the literary and historiographic generations that guided Dalton's approach to El Salvador's history and that shaped his vision of its future can deepen one's understanding of his life and writings up to his meeting with Mármol. Such an analysis of Dalton's early career also provides the necessary context for understanding his published version of *Miguel Mármol*, particularly as it is compared with Dalton's original notes, which sheds light on his editorial choices.

An Overview of the Life and Death of Roque Dalton

Roque Dalton was born out of wedlock in 1935.[1] His father, Winnal Dalton, was a successful U.S. businessman of Irish descent from Texas who moved to El Salvador in the early twentieth century and married into the Salvadoran elite. Renowned for its small size and considerable wealth, the Salvadoran elite would later be known by the internationally recognized moniker of "the fourteen families," a reference to their status as the nation's ruling oligarchy. Recent research reveals that the number of families comprising the group was actually closer to two hundred, but their namesake still captured the essence of their existence—a small, insular community that protected its ranks and

3–1
Roque Dalton as he appeared on his high school diploma, 1952.

wealth through intermarriage and adherence to a conservative worldview.[2] Even though elite families promoted a strict Catholic moral code, some members engaged in extramarital affairs, often with outsiders from the middle or lower classes. In the latter half of 1934, Winnal Dalton had an affair with María García Medrano, a nurse who cared for him after he was wounded in a brawl with a prominent banker. Roque was born nine months later.

Following the traditions of a conservative Roman Catholic society, the law required that children born out of wedlock be recorded as illegitimate in the public record. Roque had a distant and difficult relationship with his father throughout his life. He lived with his mother and used his maternal name throughout his youth. But Winnal did not reject Roque entirely and provided him some financial assistance, seeing to it that he attended good schools.

With his father's support, Roque enrolled in the elite Jesuit high school, the Externado de San José. Elite families who chose not to send their sons abroad to boarding school enrolled them in the

Externado, which was open only to boys. It was a small institution with graduating classes seldom exceeding fifty students. By attending the Externado, Roque's life resembled that of another famous Latin American revolutionary, Fidel Castro, who also was an illegitimate son who attended an elite Jesuit high school in his native Cuba. The stigma of illegitimacy followed Roque in school and set him apart from his classmates. Whereas all students at the Externado wore the same uniforms and received the same instruction, elite Salvadoran society was proficient at training its members, even its children, in the subtle and not-so-subtle art of social distinction. As the child of a poor, unwed mother, Roque felt alienated from those around him. He commented on his troubling memories of the Externado in an essay that he wrote in Cuba in 1963 during one of his many exiles: "But long years in a Jesuit school, my early development in the womb of the mean-spirited Salvadoran bourgeoisie, my attachment to irresponsible lifestyles, drawn back in holy terror from sacrifice or from the core problems of the epoch, have left their marks on me. The scars of which, even now, are painful."[3] However, Roque possessed an acute intelligence and a natural gift for writing that provided an escape. His teachers at the Externado, especially one of his literature instructors, a gentle Jesuit named Alfonso María Landarech, S.J., noted his talents. He encouraged the young Roque and later called him "the best lyric poet in the country."[4]

Dalton graduated from the Externado in 1952, still politically naïve and religiously conservative. However, a Jesuit scholarship and financial support from his father allowed him to embark on a journey that would transform him and set him on the path to political radicalism. In 1953, he traveled to Santiago, Chile, to enroll in law school. There he absorbed Chilean poetry, especially that of politically active poets like Pablo Neruda. At one point, Dalton attended the Latin American Congress of Culture, where he had the occasion to meet Neruda, as well as the Mexican muralist Diego Rivera. These chance encounters with world-renowned artists did much to inspire Dalton's political and artistic vision. Rivera supposedly told Dalton, "You have arrived to your eighteenth year still an idiot, thanks to not having read about Marxism," which inspired Dalton to immediately read some of Karl Marx's work.⁵ Such influences led Dalton down the path of transforming the Catholicism of his youth into a lasting ideological radicalism and also to merge his art with politics. Dalton would later claim that he became interested in communism through poetry. In one of his first poems, written shortly after his return from Chile, he celebrated the long-ignored 1833 Indian rebellion in El Salvador led by Anastasio Aquino. The metric verse follows a strict Nerudian style:

> Tu pie descalzo ante la dura tierra: barro en el barro.
> Tu rostro unánime ante el pueblo: sangre en la sangre.
> Tu voz viril ante el pueblo: grito en el grito.
>
> Your naked foot hitting the hard soil: clay over clay
> Your unifying gaze over the people: blood over blood
> Your virile voice before the people: scream over scream⁶

The poem's reference to the struggles of peasants and native peoples was appealing to readers of the alternative newspaper in which the poem originally appeared, *El Independiente* (The Independent). The poem characterized the remainder of Dalton's artistic life, in which art and politics became inseparable and mutually reinforcing.

Dalton returned to El Salvador from Chile in 1954 to continue law school at the University of El Salvador, the country's only public university. There he became active in literary and political associations, such as the Círculo Literario Universitario (University Literary Circle), which he cofounded with a young Guatemalan leftist poet, Otto René Castillo, who would eventually die in a Guatemalan prison and who would provide Dalton with a model for the politically engaged artist. Dalton also wrote for student publications, such as *Opinión Estudiantil* (Student Opinion) and *La Jodarria* (The Jokefest). By the end of the 1950s Dalton was already taking on a public persona as his writings appeared in the local press. He was part of a group of young politically active artists who rejected the reigning "regionalist" literary style. Dalton and his cohorts found regionalism to be simplistic and to offer an idealized vision of the countryside and its poor inhabitants for consumption by urban elites. They believed that art had to reject sanitized images and be politically engaged by exposing the harsh realities of Salvadoran society.

In 1957 Dalton traveled to the USSR to represent Salvadoran students in two communist-sponsored events, the Fourth World Festival of Youth and Students for Peace and Friendship. When he returned to El Salvador, he joined the Salvadoran Communist Party. Throughout the remainder of his life, he would insist that his art and his politics were interdependent. In his 1963 Cuban essay, Dalton summarized succinctly the relationship between his art and politics: "I've said that I'm a poet who, in relation to political militancy, works within the ranks of the Communist Party."[7] But Dalton retained a sense of irony and humor that marked his artistic style. He described himself as "a Marxist who bites his nails."[8] Later, in a well-known poem, he compared his early militancy in the party to his childhood religious beliefs: "The militancy in the Communist Party, was like membership in a new Mystical Body, marked by actions *In Majorem Dei Gloriam* [for the greater glory of God] and by faith in the inescapable advent of the Kingdom of Man."[9]

If the popular image of a communist militant living under a repressive authoritarian regime is that of a serene person living an ascetic life, Dalton did not fit the mold. Although his commitment to radical politics was unflappable, Dalton relished social engagements, storytelling, and a good drink. During his international travels, he came to know many of Latin America's leading artists and intellectuals and moved freely in their social circles. Above all, he remained an artist who appreciated the sublime and dared to emphasize the importance of such seemingly idealistic principles as beauty. In his 1963 Cuban essay, once again, he made bold statements about beauty and artistic expression that would come back to haunt him. He contended, "The very essence of poetry [is] beauty," and he insisted that his fellow countrymen, and especially his fellow leftists, not lose sight of the subtle beauty around them: "The poet—above all the communist poet—will have to articulate all of life: the proletarian struggle, the beauty of the cathedrals left us by the Spanish Colony, the wonder of the sexual act, the prophecies of the fruitful future that the great signs of the day proclaim to us."[10] These were not the normal concerns of many of Dalton's radical cohorts who interpreted the world through a strict Marxian economic determinism. But Dalton insisted that it was the obligation of the communist poet to "make sure that the Administrative Secretary of the Central Committee [of the Communist Party], for example, loves St. John of the Cross, Henri Michaux, or St. John Perse."[11] Under certain conditions, like the clandestine life of a guerrilla fighter being hunted by the state's torturous security personnel, such views were risky. They were not likely to be well received by party leaders desperately trying to stay alive and believing in the sanctity of strict discipline. But that was Dalton—a poet and a revolutionary.

Dalton's political activism landed him in jail repeatedly. In December 1959 he was arrested on suspicion of having organized student protests against the government. At that time the government under Coronel José María Lemus was hardening its position against the students of the University of El Salvador whom it considered agitators and the main instigators of social unrest. After he was released in early 1960, Dalton used his knowledge of the law to fight injustice. He organized law students to defend common prisoners held in jail without sentencing. He also served as a private prosecutor against two police commanders who were accused of torture and murder. Dalton's relentless activism did not sit well with the Lemus regime's increasing defensiveness. In September 1960, the military occupied the university after opening fire on a parade of university students on Independence Day, September 15. Dalton was captured in October, after being found hiding with his wife, his bodyguards, and a book by Cuban poet Nicolás Guillén that the army deemed communist propaganda. A reformist coup d'état that toppled President Lemus later that month led to the release of many political prisoners, including Dalton. But a conservative countercoup in January 1961 by the so-called Directorio Cívico Militar led to further reprisals against political activists. Dalton decided he had enough and went into exile in Mexico with his family.

While in Mexico, Dalton published his first collection of poems, *La ventana en el rostro* (The Window in the Face; 1962). A year later he traveled to Cuba, where Fidel Castro's revolution was barely four years old. There he published four books of literature, *El mar* (The Sea; 1962), *El turno del ofendido* (The Turn of the Offended One; 1962),

3–2 Roque Dalton in the arms of supporters upon being released from prison in El Salvador, early 1960s.

César Vallejo (1963), and *Los testimonios* (The Testimonies; 1964), and two books of history, *El Salvador* (1963) and *El Salvador: Monografía* (El Salvador: Monograph; 1965). His poetry gained him recognition as one of the leading revolutionary poets in Latin America, which allowed him to work at the Casa de las Américas (House of the Americas), one of the most prestigious publishing houses in Latin America. Dalton's time in Mexico and Cuba revealed a character trait that would mark the remainder of his life, prodigious artistic production amidst activism, exile, and dislocation. In hindsight, both the quantity and quality of Dalton's writings under such complicated circumstances are remarkable. Dalton later reflected on the challenge of writing amidst political persecution and exile: "For the last few years I always set up to write in a hurry, as if I knew that I would be killed the following day.... It is hauntingly ridiculous to be a Salvadoran writer, yet it may only be out of sloth and national selfishness."[12]

In 1963 Dalton returned to El Salvador in what proved to be a nearly catastrophic mistake. He was a well-known communist wanted by the military government. He lived clandestinely for a while, but eventually he fell into the government's clutches and was jailed once again. He would have remained a prisoner for years, and he might

3-3   Headline the Salvadoran newspaper *Diario de Hoy* from October 30, 1964, announcing Dalton's flight from prison.

well have been executed had it not been for his escape. The manner in which he escaped is still unclear. He immortalized it in the last chapter of his autobiographical novel, *Pobrecito poeta que era yo...* (Poor Little Poet That I Was...) by claiming that a powerful earthquake struck San Salvador and damaged the walls of the jailhouse, thus allowing him to escape. But his escape appears to have been earlier than he claimed in the novel, as evidenced by the newspaper headline in late 1964 announcing his flight. Furthermore, there is no evidence of an earthquake striking the region where was being held (Cojutepeque) during the time of his incarceration. It is likely that he took artistic license with the story as it appears in *Pobrecito*; nevertheless, the details of his escape remain a mystery.

After his escape, Dalton wisely went into exile once again, this time in Prague, Czechoslovakia, where he worked for a leftist magazine, *Revista Internacional* (International Review), from 1966–67. This was a difficult period in his life, marked by money shortages, marital discord, a brutal and mysterious beating by thugs on the streets of Prague, and alienation from the people and land of his home. It was in Prague, on the night before his thirty-first birthday, that he had the chance encounter with Miguel Mármol in a restaurant. Dalton described the encounter as an escape from "what is European" and a return to the country of his youth in which he would recover the "heaven-and-hell where my revolutionary ideals were born."[13] Dalton and Mármol met repeatedly in the next two weeks, during which time Dalton collected the old communist's life story in a series of handwritten notes. After they separated, Dalton knew that Mármol's story had literary and political potential, but he was still unsure how he wanted to present it, whether as a fictional novel, a biography, a testimonial, or something else.

After his return to Havana in 1967, Dalton combined literary work with political activism. His poetry and fiction made him famous, as exemplified by his receipt in 1969 of the Poetry Prize from the Casa de las Américas for *Taberna y otros lugares* (Tavern and Other Places; 1969), which he had written in Prague. Thereafter, Dalton embarked on a period of feverish writing. While completing *Miguel Mármol* in the form of a first-person testimonial (published in 1972), he also wrote a collage book, *Un libro levemente odioso* (A Slightly Hateful Book), his popular *Historias prohibidas del Pulgarcito* (Forbidden Histories of Thom Thumb), and his autobiographical novel *Pobrecito poeta que era yo* ....

This period of intense literary production was also a time of profound political reflection for Dalton. Tired of the official line of the Salvadoran Communist Party that El Salvador was not ready for revolution, Dalton became more radical and began to support the idea of launching an immediate guerrilla insurrection to topple the repressive military regime that had been in power for more than four decades. In this regard, Dalton believed he was following the model of the Cuban Revolution, and especially of its hero Che Guevara, who had left Cuba for Bolivia in 1967 and died trying to spread revolution across the South American continent. Dalton broke ties with the Salvadoran Communist Party in 1974 and joined the ranks of a new splinter guerrilla group, the Ejército Revolucionario del Pueblo (People's Revolutionary Army, ERP) that had broken from the party in 1972 over various ideological issues, but especially over the form and timing of insurrection. The leaders of the ERP embraced the Chinese communist Mao Zedong's belief that "power comes from the barrel of a gun," and they wanted to move forward with armed conflict. As part of his preparation for returning to El Salvador and joining the fight, Dalton visited the same plastic surgeon that had altered Guevara's face prior to his departure for Bolivia. Equipped with a new face and a fighting spirit, Dalton entered El Salvador clandestinely on Christmas day 1974 and began the last stage of his abbreviated life.

Dalton was not much of a soldier. He responded poorly to the physical demands of military training and did not care for the strict discipline demanded of a clandestine rebel. Still, he remained politically committed and well liked by most of his comrades, with the notable exception of certain ERP leaders. A combination of internal ideological disputes within the ERP, accusations of indiscipline against Dalton, and even the suggestion that he was a CIA agent resulted in the leaders of the ERP finding Dalton guilty of treason and executing him in May 1975, just a few days before his fortieth birthday. Shortly before his departure for El Salvador, Dalton had written an eerily prescient poem entitled "Crock Logic." The poem defended the right of a leftist comrade to disagree with his superiors without being accused of treason. Dalton identified two examples of crock logic: "Criticism of the Salvadoran Communist Party can only be made by an agent of the CIA," and "self-criticism is equivalent to suicide."[14] How ironic that Dalton was killed by the group that he joined as a result of his protest against the Communist Party.

Dalton's death became a cause célèbre among Latin American intellectuals. Some were shocked at the thought of a prestigious leftist poet being killed by his fellow revolutionaries. Others highlighted the issue as a means of attacking left-wing political groups as trigger-happy, dangerous organizations that act like modern Saturns and eat their own children. To this day, Dalton's death is shrouded in mystery and his body has never been found. One of the most reliable accounts of Dalton's final days is that of Fermán Cienfuegos, then second in command of the ERP who defended Dalton at the internal trial.[15] He claims that he was unable to break through the irrationality and paranoia of the other three leaders, especially the principal commander at the time, Alejandro Rivas Mira.[16] Frustrated and believing that his comrades had lost all sense of perspective, Cienfuegos and a handful of other ERP members broke away and formed another guerrilla group, the Resistencia Nacional (National Resistance), on May 1, 1975. Cienfuegos claims that he begged Dalton to come with him, that he and his fellow dissenters could spring him from captivity, but Dalton refused to leave, insisting that his comrades in the ERP would find him innocent. A few days later, Dalton was dead. The circumstances of his death have given Dalton a tragic aura. Admiration for his writings has only increased over time, and many consider him to be one of Latin America's most important literary figures. Among all his writings, the product of that legendary interview with Miguel Mármol in Prague in 1966 remains one of the most widely read and influential. It has shaped the collective consciousness of 1932 for generations of Salvadorans.

Dalton and the Generación Comprometida

Dalton's belief that art and politics were mutually dependent had much to do with his membership in a group of young, politically engaged artists that eventually came to be known as the Generación Comprometida (Committed Generation). Most of the members of the group were born between 1930 and 1933, that is, around the time of the Matanza, and they shared the common experience of being reared in a turbulent period in Salvadoran history.[17] In his autobiographical novel *Pobrecito poeta que era yo...*, Dalton has a main character comment on the troubling consciousness that arises from living a country with an event like the Matanza in its history: "A country becomes a different country after thirty thousand people are killed in a couple weeks."[18] Another member of the generation described the group as sharing an "attitude of protest and rebelliousness," which was brought on by living in "a broken country, beaten up by revolts and coups d'état," and being surrounded by "humiliation, demagoguery, political and administrative corruption and disinterest, disgust and indifference to the life of the mind."[19]

Political events in El Salvador and elsewhere in the latter half of the 1940s shaped the consciousness of Dalton's teenage generation. As the threat of the Axis powers waned and democracies triumphed over authoritarian regimes throughout Latin America, the mid-1940s seemed full of promise.[20] In El Salvador, the Martínez regime, which oversaw the Matanza in 1932, collapsed in 1944 due to the opposition of a broad urban coalition. In neighboring Guatemala, the long-standing Ubico dictatorship fell almost simultaneously in what came to be known as the "October Revolution," or "the decade of spring." Ubico's demise and the election of Juan José Arévalo (1944–50) and later of Jacobo Arbenz (1950–54), inspired politically engaged youth throughout Latin America, including none other than Che Guevara, who lived in Guatemala in the early 1950s before heading to Mexico to meet Castro and join the Cuban revolutionaries. Dalton too drew inspiration from Guatemala, as seen in an article he later wrote about his great Guatemalan friend, Otto René Castillo: "The democratic era (the Arévalo and Arbenz governments) fell like an ocean wave over the childhood of the future poet and revolutionary hero, and surrounded the years of his early education and adolescence with sociopolitical stimulation."[21] Dalton might as well have been referring to himself and his fellow members of the Committed Generation in El Salvador because the October Revolution represented a moment of great hope for democracy in all of Central America.

In El Salvador, the political change of 1944 produced more ambivalent results than in neighboring Guatemala. At first the ouster of Martínez offered the promise of a more open political system, but the old forces refused to disappear. A coup in October 1944 dashed the hopes of democratic reformers who were trying to organize free elections. The coup was organized by Martínez's former chief of police, Osmín Aguirre y Salinas, who became president for one year (1944–45). His regime brutally suppressed a democratic countercoup and killed many young men just a few years older than Dalton in a battle in western El Salvador. Fraudulent elections shortly thereafter put another military officer in power, General Salvador Castaneda Castro (1945–48). Castaneda was ousted in yet another coup in 1948 when he tried to have himself reelected. In sum, the four years following Martínez's fall were laden with danger and turbulence.

The regime that came to power in 1948 was the so-called Revolutionary government that portrayed itself as a different type of military rule, one that would defend the common person and modernize El Salvador. To this end, it oversaw the writing of a new constitution in 1950 that contained reformist measures, including enfranchising women and empowering the state to intervene in the economy in defense of the common good. The rhetoric of the Revolutionary regime fell far short of its reality. Instead of breaking with the past, the young officers and civilians who came to power after 1948 updated the governing norm in El Salvador—an informal alliance between the army and the elite that suppressed popular participation. It was in this politically charged environment that the members of the Committed Generation graduated from high school and entered the University of El Salvador. Tirso Canales, one of the members of the generation, reminisced about the memorable "struggle of the working class and university students who organized frequent and big street rallies in front of the facilities of the Constituent Assembly demanding a progressive Constitution that took into account the grievances of the people."[22]

By the time Roque Dalton and his contemporaries finished high school, his generation had lived through a dictatorship, a social movement that toppled it, two coups d'état, two elections, and two constitutions, and they also witnessed the rise of democracy in neighboring Guatemala. As in the case of Dalton's description of Otto René Castillo, their early years were "surrounded with sociopolitical stimulation," which impacted deeply their outlook on the world. They developed a sense of possibility, thought about the problems of their country, and eagerly looked for ways to change it for the better. As high school students, they sought outlets for their ideas and started a variety of literary publications with names like "Young Soul," "Literary Torch," and "Profiles." They considered themselves to be a distinct literary generation with new things to say, and the name Committed Generation, which was given to them years later, reflected their belief that politically engaged intellectuals could shape a nation's future.

Waldo Chávez Velasco, one of the generation's founding members, has written about its beginnings. According to him, a group of ten or twelve young people, about fifteen to seventeen years of age, gathered in 1949 and "identified each other as aspiring poets and writers." On that occasion Chávez met Irma Lanzas, who studied at the Escuela Normal España (Normal School "Spain"), the womens' teachers' college. In his account, this meeting led to the organization of the first group that would eventually become the foundation of the Committed Generation. By Chávez's own admission, the group had tremendous political ideals, but they were also driven by youthful exuberance. As he put it:

> [I] requested a meeting with the principal of the Escuela Normal España to whom I proposed the foundation of a Literary Initiation Group [Cenáculo de Iniciación Literaria], with students interested in writing.... The Principal accepted the idea enthusiastically, with only one condition, that the meetings be held at her school because, as she explained it, [female] students could not leave school grounds. The honorable lady did not have the slightest idea that my main interest was to see Irma, even if only once a week.[23]

Chávez and Lanzas later married.

Roque was a latecomer to the group; he was slightly younger and had been abroad in Chile in law school. When he returned to El Salvador in 1954, the changes in his political consciousness in Chile drew him to the group of rebellious young writers. The original group complemented and somewhat overlapped Dalton's own Círculo Literario Universitario, which he cofounded in 1956.[24] The Círculo became the group's main organizational body at the University of El Salvador. Its members immediately began publishing their writing, mainly in the literary pages of an evening paper, *Diario Latino*.

In 1956 Italo López Vallecillos, who was one of those present at the meeting in 1949 and also belonged to the Círculo Literario Universitario, began publishing *Hoja*, a literary magazine. The first issue included two works by Roque Dalton, a poem and an editorial entitled, "The Committed Generation." That editorial marked the first use of the phrase Committed Generation. It has been said that López Vallecillos coined the term rather than Dalton, but nevertheless, its public unveiling baptized what was already seen by many as an emerging literary movement. In the editorial, Dalton defined the meaning of a politically engaged artist:

> For us literature is, in essence, a social function. Hence we focus our efforts on contributing to the improvement of the society where we live, to establish an order through which man would change his social condition and, at the same time, change his idea of himself.
>
> We understand that our mission is loftier, in these moments of crisis, it is to bring faith and enthusiasm to the intelligentsia. The "Committed Generation" knows that the work of art necessarily has to serve, to be useful to society, to today's man.[25]

Regional political events in the mid- to late 1950s fueled Dalton's call to political activism. In June 1954 the CIA supported a coup that overthrew President Jacobo Arbenz and brought Guatemala's fledging experiment in democracy to a grinding halt. The accusations of communism that the CIA and the coup plotters in Guatemala used against Arbenz worked well in the cold war environment of the day, but even at the time many critics of the coup argued that Arbenz was at most a mild reformer who was trying to modernize Guatemalan capitalism rather than create a socialist state. Recent research shows the coup's critics to have been correct.[26] Nevertheless, El Salvador's president, Oscar Osorio, aided the coup, further exposing the 1948 "Revolution's" paradoxical mix of populism and repression.

The victory of the Cuban Revolution in 1959, and soon after, the failure of the U.S.-sponsored Bay of Pigs invasion in 1961, inspired political activism and intellectual engagement in El Salvador. Supporters of revolutionary change drew inspiration from Cuba and hoped that something similar would happen in El Salvador. Their anticommunist opponents became ever more fearful and drew further into a defensive stance. The fact that the late 1950s was a time of relatively high coffee prices in El Salvador sharpened the lines of debate. Economic prosperity magnified endemic inequalities in Salvadoran society. Many young literary figures responded to these developments with a characteristic sense of mission and a thirst for change. They took the revolutionary messages contained in their writings to the people in factories, construction sites, and labor unions.27

The dramatic events of the late 1950s and early 1960s polarized Salvadoran society and began to draw the lines of battle that would end up in civil war in the 1980s. Literary historians have used the phrase "Committed Generation" as a shortcut to suggest that the members of the group shared a uniform leftist revolutionary stance. This perception is compounded by the fact that the left-leaning members of the group, Roque Dalton and Manlio Argueta, among others, were well known, rendering the right-leaning members of the group less visible. Even Tirso Canales, who tends to portray the Committed Generation as a paradigm of left-wing activism, recognized a spectrum of political positions among its members.28 The members of the Committed Generation shared a belief that artists and intellectuals could change their society, but they responded to the sociopolitical events of the late 1950s and early 1960s in the same fractured manner as the rest of Salvadoran society. At one end of the spectrum were members like Dalton, who committed himself to revolutionary change and lived either clandestinely in El Salvador or in exile and even changed his physical appearance to join a guerrilla war. Other members lived a relatively quiet life in El Salvador, editing literary supplements, acting in plays, or working as journalists. Others emigrated and avoided the spiraling political crisis in El Salvador altogether. One member became president of the University of El Salvador, won the national cultural prize twice, and currently serves on El Salvador's Supreme Court. At the more conservative end of the spectrum was Waldo Chávez Velasco, who accepted a government scholarship to go to Europe in the 1950s and eventually became information minister for one of the military regimes. His wife, Irma Lanzas, one of the participants at the teachers' college meeting in 1949, headed up the controversial Educational Television initiative sponsored by the Alliance for Progress in the late 1960s.29

Most accounts of the Committed Generation insist that its members rejected the work of past Salvadorans and drew inspiration from left-wing writers and artists in other Latin American countries, like the Chilean Pablo Neruda. Dalton reinforced this impression when he credited the influence of "Nazim Hikmet, Miguel Hernández,

Cesar Vallejo... [and] Pablo Neruda."[30] The one Salvadoran who is said to have influenced the Committed Generation was Pedro Geoffroy Rivas (1908–79), who had spent years in exile and often included radical themes in his poetry. One of his poems, for example, was devoted to Farabundo Martí, the leftist leader executed in 1932.[31] In fact, all the members of the Committed Generation drew on El Salvador's literary past, especially those members who leaned to the political right as part of their nationalistic orientation.

The ideological diversity within the Committed Generation underlines the fact that simply being identified as a member hardly explains the corpus of one's work. Roque Dalton was a member, and while he shaped the group's identity, he also transcended it. By the time he was writing *Miguel Mármol*, his idea of being a committed intellectual meant favoring armed insurrection. Dalton expressed this position in his contribution to *El intelectual y la sociedad* (The Intellectual and Society), a book based on a discussion that occurred in Havana in 1969 when Dalton was working on the manuscript for *Miguel Mármol*.[32] He asked himself:

> Should I give more importance to the task of finishing my very important novel or should I accept this dangerous job that the Party assigns to me, the guerrilla, the frontlines, where I could lose not just a precious two months, but all the time that I thought I had left? Should I write sonnets or should I study peasant rebellions? Should my next novel enumerate my real or imagined sexual practices, or should it be an elaborate satire joyfully revealing the mechanisms of imperialist penetration in my country?[33]

Dalton answered these questions by trying to be an artist and a revolutionary simultaneously. As a revolutionary he remained ever literary; as an artist he remained ever committed to radical politics.

Salvadoran Historiography in Dalton's Era

Roque Dalton believed that historical knowledge explained how contemporary conditions came to exist, and therefore any political activist who lacked historical awareness was at a disadvantage. As a writer and activist, Dalton believed in the power of words, and he recognized that the telling of history is an inherently political act. He realized that certain versions of history promote a defense of the status quo, while other versions encourage change. Accordingly, Dalton frequently chose historical subjects as themes for his poems. As a committed communist, Dalton's notion of history leaned toward a Marxist economic determinism, but he didn't allow his embrace of communism to undermine his appreciation of historical contingency and the idea that people have the power to shape the world based on their distinct conceptualizations of their surroundings.

In the late 1950s and early 1960s Dalton began the project of providing an alternative, and in his opinion more accurate, version of the Salvadoran past. Dalton's belief in the necessity of a new history came about by virtue of his having read the available histories and finding them lacking. But without new documentary sources or the benefit of primary research, Dalton remained dependent on the information contained in old books. Therefore, as he began to conceptualize a new history of El Salvador, Dalton would be forced to rely on the existing historiography even though his stated objective was to correct it.

A brief analysis of the books listed in the *Bibliografía histórica de El Salvador* (Historical Bibliography of El Salvador) for the period 1951–65 provides a snapshot of the limited range of studies that Dalton had available to him.[34] About 40 percent of the history titles were published by the government press, the Dirección de Publicaciones (Bureau of Publications), which also meant that they had the widest circulation. Half of the publications from the government press were dedicated to the study of political actors in the independence period (1811–39). The rest consisted mostly of biographies of former presidents and elaborations on various patriotic themes, such as symbols of the fatherland. Some of the publications grew directly out of research inspired by contests promoted by the Ministry of Education, not unlike the contests sponsored by the champions of the Enlightenment in Central America in the late 1700s. For example, as part of the celebration of the sesquicentennial of the first independence movement in 1811, the government offered a prize for the best essay on José Matías Delgado, one of the most well-known leaders of the movement. The two winners saw their work published by the government press. The only exceptions to this traditional government-sponsored historiography were a book on the Indian rebel leader Anastasio Aquino and two books on the independence movement that adopted new approaches; one was a conservative interpretation of the role of the masses, and the other was dedicated to the role of Indians.

One-third of the history books published by the government's Dirección during this period were by a single author, Jorge Lardé y Larín, who spent much of his life teaching history at the army officers' school. Most of his work narrated the deeds of heroic figures or episodes relating to independence and provided historical information about El Salvador's geographic regions. His writings reinforced traditional patriotic values and the standard mythology of the state. He achieved these goals by decontextualizing events, using limited source materials, and carefully selecting his historical actors.

The pattern established by the Dirección de Publicaciones was replicated by the Ministry of Education in its intellectual journal, *Cultura* (Culture). Most of its authors were also published by the Dirección, and they covered similar themes in their writings. Glaringly absent from the publication list of both the Dirección and the Ministry of Education was any study of 1932.

The only real alternative to the government's history was the University of El Salvador. Although publicly funded, the university had legal autonomy and was the natural space for dissenting voices to emerge. Between 1963 and 1967, a new university president, Doctor Fabio Castillo Figueroa, invigorated the intellectual life of the campus by supporting progressive political sectors and giving special attention to library resources and the university's press. The number of historical studies published by the university during this period was small, about one-tenth of the amount published by the government. But the new works coming off the university's press provided a fresh perspective by covering a wider variety of themes and introducing new interpretive approaches. Among the works published at this time were such landmarks as Dagoberto Marroquin's sociological approach to independence and the proceedings of the Seminario de Historia Contemporánea de Centroamérica (Central American

Contemporary History Seminar), an event held at the university in 1963 in which a group of social scientists gathered to discuss historical issues. Remarkably, the events of 1932 were included in the discussion and in the subsequent publication of the proceedings.

Complementing the university's new books were articles appearing in university journals, such as the *Revista Salvadoreña de Ciencias Sociales* (Salvadoran Social Science Review) and *La Universidad* (The University). Collectively, the history materials produced by the University of El Salvador in the mid-1960s initiated a revisionist trend in Salvadoran historiography that Dalton would join. The new books from the University of El Salvador covered many of the same topics as the traditional histories, but they turned them upside down by heralding a different set of heroes or applying a new social history approach to them. Roque Dalton would rely heavily on the titles published by the university in formulating his own revision of El Salvador's past.

Notwithstanding this window of historical reformation at the University of El Salvador in the mid-1960s, analyses of the events of 1932 remained few and far between. When Dalton did eventually turn his attention to writing history, one of his main contributions would be to emphasize the importance of 1932, as exemplified by his work on *Miguel Mármol*. But, once again, without access to new source material, Dalton had to depend on the existing body of scholarship. By the time Dalton began to write history in the early 1960s, barely a half dozen works dealing with 1932 existed. Most were published outside El Salvador, and almost none were formal analyses by professional historians; among them were three novels and two journalistic accounts. Regardless of their limitations, these published works about 1932 performed the important role of keeping the memory of 1932 alive and in the public arena. Furthermore, they laid the foundation for the creation of the communist-causality metanarrative to which *Miguel Mármol* would contribute so profoundly. For these reasons a brief examination of these works is in order.

The Histories of 1932 in Dalton's Era

The first book-length account of 1932 has proven to be one of the most influential. Almost all subsequent analysts have relied on it heavily, including Dalton, who had transcriptions of its pages among his archive of materials used to write *Miguel Mármol*. The book is *Los sucesos comunistas en El Salvador* (The Communist Events in El Salvador), written by Joaquín Méndez and published in San Salvador in March 1932. Méndez was a journalist who toured the western region in late February and early March, barely after the main wave of government repression had subsided. During his tour, Méndez saw the smoldering ruins left by the events, and he visited nearly every municipality involved in the uprising. He took numerous photographs and interviewed a wide range of eyewitnesses and participants, including prisoners still being held in jail. He included transcriptions of many of these interviews. Touring under the auspices of the government and the army, Méndez produced an account friendly to his sponsors. Nevertheless, his book remains the most detailed narrative of the uprising. He pieced together the sequence of events, including the timing and nature of the attacks, the damage caused, the names of people killed and wounded, and the pattern of the military's counterassault.

As demonstrated by the title of his book, Méndez considered the rebellion to be fundamentally communist. Throughout his account, he referred to the rebels as communists and used the terms "rebel" and "communist" interchangeably. He offered numerous descriptions of the rebels shouting "slogans in favor of communism" and marching "under the red flag [of communism]."[35] Almost all of the informants Méndez chose to include called the rebels communists. As just one example, a woman in Nahuizalco who lived through the uprising told him, "The communists came to burn the church.... It's inexplicable.... There are those who think the priests were with the communists, but no one can confirm this."[36] Méndez also reprinted documents supposedly taken off rebels that revealed them to have been communists. One such document was a circular from the Ejecutivo Rojo de Juayúa (Red Executive of Juayúa) directed to "all the Revolutionary Class Organizations," calling on them to follow their local "Comandantes Rojos" (Red Commanders).[37]

Méndez failed to define communism. He apparently considered the term self-explanatory because he did not clarify what being a communist in rural western El Salvador in the early 1930s meant. He did not try to explain how communism originated in El Salvador nor why peasants in the western region supposedly embraced it. Neither did he ask if the rebels were formal members of the Communist Party, or if not, who they were and why they rebelled. The closest Méndez came to providing an explanation was identifying some local leaders and linking them to the Communist Party or to labor unions through documents given to him by the army. In this manner, *Los sucesos comunistas en El Salvador* established the typical pattern of communist-causality arguments—an assumption of communism's central role without defining communism or analyzing the rebels' motives.

Nevertheless, Méndez's detailed narrative allows for interpretive leeway. In particular, his study permitted the counternarrative of ethnicity to survive as an underlying theme. One example is provided by the transcription of an interview that Méndez conducted with a pair of prisoners being held as rebels. He identified them as Indians and asked them if they were communists. They responded by denying affiliation with communism and claiming they were arrested because they spoke Spanish poorly. Méndez did not judge the prisoners' claims, but rather used the interview to reinforce his view that the rebellion and communism were synonymous. He believed that the prisoners either had to be communist and therefore were rebels, or they had to be accused wrongly of being communists and therefore were innocent. What he failed to realize is that if the prisoners were Indians, they potentially complicated his argument about the uprising's communist nature. An astute reader would recognize that the interview revealed that either Indians participated in the uprising and therefore might have been motivated by ethnic issues rather than communism, or the army used ethnicity as a basis for reprisals during the Matanza.[38]

Méndez interviewed mostly rich and powerful local Ladinos, who naturally described the rebellion as communist and therefore supported Méndez's claims about communism. But they too raised the issue of ethnicity in ways that complicated the story. One interviewee, for example, referred to the rebels as "*indígenas comunistas*" (Indian communists), and other interviewees used the word "*indio*" interchangeably with communist, rebel, or peasant. Often times the word indio did not necessarily mean a person of indigenous descent, but rather it was a derogatory term that local elites used to refer to poor people in general. It is no surprise that Méndez's rich Ladino informants would use the term. But, as locals whose lives and livelihoods depended on knowing their social milieu, they were also capable of transcending stereotypes and recognizing the reality of ethnicity in western El Salvador.

For example, one of Méndez's informants in Juayúa was Gabino Mata, a landowner and former municipal official, who described one of the local rebel leaders as "an Indian, an owner of good lands, and a man of some financial means." According to Mata, it was "inexplicable why he became a communist, [but] Timoteo [Lue] did become a communist."³⁹ Mata's reference to Lue as an Indian was not offhanded or derogatory, but rather it recognized Lue as a member of the local indigenous community. Even though Mata defines Lue's participation in the uprising as an act of communism, he nonetheless realized the relevance of ethnicity.

Méndez's account became an invaluable source of information on 1932 for later analysts, especially amidst the long-standing dearth of primary evidence. To the extent that he defined the uprising as communist, but provided recurrent references to ethnicity, *Los sucesos* established the precedent of communist causality and an ethnic counternarrative coexisting in the same source. The presence of that duality created a complex knot that interpreters like Dalton would have to confront years later.

Forty-four years passed before another book on 1932 was published in El Salvador. This long drought offers strong testimony to the public silence surrounding the events of 1932. In the interim, foreign publishing houses provided the sole outlet for interpretive debates on 1932. This shift to foreign publishers had the double disadvantage of limiting Salvadorans' access to the published works and of geographically scattering the dialogue. One such example was *Repertorio Americano*, a literary magazine published in Costa Rica between 1919 and 1958. Although attentive to affairs in Costa Rica, the magazine's editors also took an interest in broader Latin American issues. Roughly a dozen works on 1932 by Salvadorans appeared in the pages of *Repertorio*. Unfortunately, those works remained relatively unknown and had limited impact on later scholarship.

However, publishing houses in Cuba and Guatemala produced two influential books on 1932. The first of these was *Sangre de hermanos* (Blood of Brothers) by Rodolfo Buezo, which was published in Cuba in 1944. Buezo's personal history remains somewhat obscure, but his book's testimonial aspect reveals that he came from a relatively affluent family in El Salvador, attended the University of El Salvador where he developed a radicalized political consciousness, and then joined the Salvadoran Communist Party. He claims to have been involved in producing the party's weekly newspaper, *Estrella Roja* (Red Star), and to know enough about the 1932 uprising to tell the story, although he admits he was merely a cell member and not a party leader. Buezo survived the Matanza and apparently lived for a number of years in Cuba.

Sangre de hermanos strongly promotes communism, the PCS, the SRI, and, in particular, Farabundo Martí in explaining the 1932 uprising. Buezo referred to party leaders as "delegates of the Communist International and the directors of the insurrection."[40] But in contrast to Méndez, who did not try to explain how the rural poor of western El Salvador became communists, Buezo set forth a clear explanatory framework. Buezo recognized that the members of the PCS were from urban areas, but he insists they united urban and rural workers in common cause by physically going to the working masses of the western countryside, organizing them into unions, and then encouraging them to follow the PCS and SRI in armed insurrection. Buezo put it succinctly, "The masses of workers and peasants had united under the red banner."[41] He said this unity was symbolized by the "*hoz y el machete*" (hammer and machete), a local version of the hammer and sickle, the communist icon symbolizing the unity of industrial and agricultural labor. In particular, Buezo portrayed Martí as a popular hero and grassroots organizer who went "from plantation to plantation, village to village, neighborhood to neighborhood, until he created true worker's nuclei."[42] Buezo identified El Salvador's stark social "inequality and reigning misery" as the reason communism had such strong and widespread support among peasants.[43] "In a country where no one suffers from hunger," Buezo wrote, "that lacks in brutal aggressions, where life is respected and the landowner is not a classic master of human life and properties, communism will never take hold."[44]

Buezo did not provide details on the actual uprising, but simply said that its failure could be attributed to chaos in the party's central leadership following the capture of Martí. The subsequent breakdown in communication lines between city and countryside resulted in orders arriving to the rebels inconsistently. Had Martí not been arrested, according to Buezo, "the action would have been more unanimous and victory would have been salvaged."[45]

For what Buezo lacked in extensive details on the insurrection, he made up for in deifying descriptions of Martí during his incarceration and execution. Buezo offered direct quotes from Martí and detailed descriptions of his time in prison, which he claimed to have gained from prison officials, but most likely represented his own imagination. Buezo's obvious goal was to confirm Martí as an unforgettable hero of the masses and as a leader of the insurrection. Two of Martí's compatriots, Alfonso Luna and Mario Zapata, were executed alongside him, and Buezo used their deaths to turn Martí into a veritable Christlike figure.

> Before that feminine figure, Luna and Zapata looked at a smiling Martí, full of a serenity that seemed evangelical: "Teacher," they cried out to him simultaneously, "we are proud to die by your side." "And I," responded the valiant fighter, "am proud of having disciples as heroic and serene as you. We should all die proud of our sacred mission, of our struggle to free an enslaved people. Long live the International Red Aid! Long live the ideal [of communism] and the Communist International!"[46]

This description predicts liberation theology imagery of the 1960s and 1970s, and Buezo's completion of the scene does so even more starkly. Drawing on a theme of resurrection, he said the souls of the three martyred heroes would "continue living in the hearts of all oppressed Salvadorans."[47]

Buezo was a leftist and a loyal adherent of Farabundo Martí, and his work credited Salvadoran communists with organizing and leading the 1932 uprising. In doing so, *Sangre de hermanos* shows how the communist-causality metanarrative emerged out of a combination of arguments from leftists like him and rightists like Méndez. However, Buezo left a complicated argumentative legacy for his communist brethren. He assumed that the PCS and Martí made the proper decision in rebelling. Such an assumption would be both embraced and rejected by leftists in later years, when Roque Dalton entered the fray and when internal party debates encouraged a reevaluation of 1932. Furthermore, Buezo largely ignored the issue of ethnicity, which would prove typical of most leftist interpreters, but less so of their right-wing counterparts, like the next work by Jorge Schlesinger.

The next major publication on 1932 indeed came from a far-right perspective and featured ethnicity prominently. Published in Guatemala in 1946, it was Jorge Schlesinger's *Revolución comunista: ¿Guatemala en peligro?* (Communist Revolution: Guatemala in Danger?). Schlesinger was an anticommunist journalist whose objective in writing *Revolución comunista* was to the use the case of El Salvador to show Guatemalans what would happen if they allowed communism to spread unchecked. Schlesinger based his study on documents provided to him by the Salvadoran government. He reprinted many of them in an extended appendix, along with some grisly photographs of the Matanza.[48]

Based on his materials from El Salvador, Schlesinger cast the uprising as a wholly communist affair. He described El Salvador's Communist Party as playing the decisive role, saying, in an interesting twist, that it was financed and backed by the International Red Aid (SRI). Schlesinger located the center of "communist agitation" in San Salvador and the regional capital cities. In other words, like Buezo before him, he conceived of the potential distance between rural workers in the countryside, who he described as "ignorant," and urban activists of the Communist Party. Schlesinger bridged this gap in the same way that Buezo did, by saying that the party's organizational and propaganda initiatives successfully inspired the rural masses to action.

However, Schlesinger's distinct form of anticommunism had the unintended consequence of encouraging the survival of an ethnic counternarrative. Schlesinger was overtly racist against Indians, which led him to emphasize the ethnic identity of the rebels, assuming their racial category to be sufficient explanation for their embrace of communism. Stressing the rebels as Indians also served his purpose of scaring the Guatemalan elite because their country's racial divide was even sharper than El Salvador's.

In addition to ethnicity, Schlesinger identified injustice and exploitation in the rural areas as inciting rebellion. Such an approach might seem out of character for the anticommunist Schlesinger, but it allowed him to promote an even more radically right-wing solution. He called for a fascist-style corporatist regime that could "harmonize the relations between capital and labor," a classic piece of pseudo-fascist rhetoric. Notwithstanding its fascist overtones, Schlesinger's attention to the misery of the rural masses and his insistence that the behavior of rural landlords needed to be tempered, allowed for an explanatory broadening of the uprising and contributed to the counternarrative. If read carefully, Schlesinger's account could support a political perspective quite contrary to his own. In fact, Dalton claimed that Mármol gave him a copy of Schlesinger's book with comments written in the margins, and Dalton relied heavily on *Revolución comunista* in the writing of *Miguel Mármol*, even reprinting sizeable passages of it. However, Dalton accepted Schlesinger's communist causality and mostly ignored his references to ethnicity.

In the wake of the nonfiction accounts by Méndez, Buezo, and Schlesinger, the main discussion of 1932 shifted to the world of fiction, specifically three novels published between 1944 and 1966. The most influential of them was the last published—Claribel Alegría's *Cenizas de Izalco* (Ashes of Izalco), first published in Spain in 1966 and then reprinted in El Salvador in 1976. But Alegría's book had been preceded by two works published in Nicaragua and Mexico. The first was *El oso ruso: Historia novelada del primer levantamiento comunista en América* (The Russian Bear: A Historical Novel of the First Communist Uprising in the Americas), by the Nicaraguan writer Gustavo Alemán Bolaños, published in Nicaragua in 1944. The second was *Ola roja* (Red Wave) by the Salvadoran author, Francisco Machón Vilanova, published four years later in Mexico.[49] Of the three works, only Alegría's made a significant literary contribution. Furthermore, none of the three works made an apparent impact on Roque Dalton. But for our present purposes, the importance of mentioning them is to illustrate how the argumentative approaches of the nonfiction works of Méndez, Buezo, and Schlesinger were replicated in fictional accounts.

The ideological position of the three authors differs greatly. Alegría approached the events of 1932 from a leftist perspective by expressing sympathy with the masses persecuted during the Matanza. Both Alemán and Machón were fervent anticommunist rightists who described the 1932 uprising as a communist plot and even went so far as to attribute it primarily to Russians and other foreign communists. But all three novels share significant commonalities. Each offers a version of the metanarrative/counternarrative dichotomy by making the issue of communism paramount but also including recurrent references to Indians. Additionally, the plot lines of all three novels revolve around romances and use romantic relationships as metaphors for El Salvador's sociopolitical drama. It was a common trope of novelists in nineteenth- and early twentieth-century Latin America to address sociopolitical issues through romance.[50] But whereas past authors used romances to celebrate national reconciliation, the romances in all three of these novels on 1932 fail miserably, providing a pessimistic view of El Salvador's ability to reconcile its social divisions. It is especially interesting that the authors shared a sense of pessimism, even though they differed in their political views. Right-wing authors like Alemán and Machón believed El Salvador to be under constant threat of communist subversion, whereas left-leaning authors like Alegría saw the elites and the army as power mongers who refused to loosen their control. Either way, the nation was doomed. In light of El Salvador's increasing polarization in the 1960s and 1970s and its descent into civil war in the 1980s, the fictions of Alemán, Machón, and Alegría seem all too prescient and predict the ideological debates that young intellectuals like Roque Dalton would confront between the late 1950s and the early 1970s.

The 1960s represented a decisive moment in El Salvador's deepening political polarization. On both the right and the left, radical militants began to distinguish themselves from their moderate cohorts. These hard-liners were convinced that their enemies were becoming more powerful and that the only solution was increasing violence. Militant right-wing anticommunists wanted to step up counterinsurgency campaigns and rely on terror and death squads to quell the supposed communist subversion. Militant leftists believed that the authoritarian state would never reform peacefully and insisted that violence was the only way to defeat it. Eventually, by the late 1970s, the militants came to dominate their respective movements, hurrying El Salvador down the path to civil war. But in the 1960s, the militants were still in the minority, and the debate between them and their moderate cohorts was a constant feature of political life.

Throughout most of the twentieth century, but especially in the 1960s, factions on both the right and left believed that their respective ideological positions were proven accurate by the story of 1932. In other words, they believed that they knew the true history of 1932, so they marshaled it as evidence in defense of their respective political position. Right-wing and left-wing ideologues debated 1932 with one another and among themselves. Sometimes these conflicts occurred in conversations, speeches, and written works, and other times they became violent and deadly. But in all cases the political implications of historical debates were obvious.

Intraleft debates emerging out of the University of El Salvador in the 1960s influenced heavily Roque Dalton's concept of history. Many of the social science faculty at the UES were either members or sympathizers of the Communist Party, and they embraced the intellectual renaissance at the UES under Fabio Castillo's rectorship (1963–67) as an opportunity to engage in open dialogue, be it in public lectures, debates on campus, or published research. An exemplar of this openness was the Central American Contemporary History Seminar held at the university in 1963.

One of the most divisive issues within the left in the early 1960s was insurrectionary strategy and the question of whether the Communist Party should move forward to immediate armed conflict or adhere to its traditional line that El Salvador was not ready for revolution. The debate caused factions to break away from the PCS in the late 1960s and early 1970s, including the leaders of the ERP in 1971 and later Roque Dalton in 1974. In the midst of such conflict, discussions of past insurrectionary events took on special importance. Inevitably, the events of 1932 assumed center stage.

Those loyal to the PCS's traditional line approached the 1932 uprising from a diversity of perspectives, but always with the same goal of showing that it was not a model to be followed in the contemporary era. They either said the party erred in organizing the uprising, or identified the uprising as a spontaneous movement of the rural poor brought on by relentless military repression in which the party had little or no responsibility. Some even contended that the army incited the uprising purposefully in order to have an excuse to carry out the Matanza and consolidate its hold on power.[51] One participate in this dialogue was Jorge Arias Gómez (1923–2002), a history professor at the UES, a member of the Communist Party, a former student activist in the 1940s, and an intellectual mentor to many young intellectual radicals, including Roque Dalton.[52] Arias advanced his interpretation of 1932 in a variety of publications and presentations, although his most well-known expression was his biography of Farabundo Martí published in Costa Rica in 1972. In that work, Arias credited Martí and the party for organizing the rural masses between 1930 and 1932, but he stopped short of saying that the Communist Party led the insurrection. Instead, Arias claimed that the uprising had a "spontaneous" quality and claimed that party leaders lacked control over the western countryside and joined the rebellion at the last minute only to avoid losing touch with the masses.[53]

Arias had expressed this interpretation of 1932 earlier, at the Contemporary History Seminar at the UES in 1963, where he was joined by David Luna, another left-leaning UES professor. Like Arias, Luna believed that 1932 provided a critical lesson that the emerging militants in the Communist Party had to learn: premature revolution results in disaster. Luna differed from Arias in that he implicated party leaders for organizing the uprising. But he insisted that embarking on insurrection in 1932 had been an erroneous decision and referred to the party leaders who promoted the idea as infantile, sectarian adventurers.[54]

Luna's writings illustrate how complicated the argumentative frameworks surrounding the study of 1932 could be. These debates in the early 1960s formed an important part of the evolving interpretive frameworks on 1932. For instance, traditional, "anti-insurrectionary" communists, like Arias, tended to distance the Communist Party from the 1932 uprising, but they also wanted to teach their contemporary party members a lesson. This led them to reverse themselves and attribute the uprising to the party in order to show young party members the foolhardiness of premature uprisings. The differences between Luna's and Arias's arguments at the UES seminar in 1963 exemplify these differing approaches. But in other writings, Luna followed the opposite approach by distancing the party from the uprising and emphasizing its spontaneous nature. In one writing he even went so far as to advance a counternarrative-type argument by emphasizing the importance of ethnic issues, something most leftist writers of the time were completely ignoring. In a piece written for the newspaper *Tribuna Libre* in 1963, Luna wrote, "One of the most affected zones during the insurrection of 1932 was that which fifty years earlier had seen the expropriation of ejidos and indigenous communities.... The people were becoming for the first time an independent actor in history and were not following any specific group."[55] In short, the political environment that encouraged the retelling of 1932 sometimes produced competing accounts, even in different works by the same author.

The proinsurrectionary radicals in the Communist Party opposed Arias, Luna, and the other traditionalists with their own rendition of 1932. They portrayed the uprising as communist and thus celebrated the party's decision to carry out its role as the vanguard of the suffering masses who tried to fulfill its historical mission by attacking a capitalist government. In this way, the party's decision in 1932 provided a precedent for future revolts. The radicals tended to ignore the issue of ethnicity all together and therefore advanced a singularly communist-causality argument. But they too had to account for the uprising's failure, which they did by distancing the party in a distinct way; they said the party had been correct in deciding to rebel, but then identified the cause of failure as either minor tactical mistakes or the unpredictable sadism of the military. Roque Dalton would emerge as a principal advocate of this proinsurrectionary approach, and his historical writing in *Miguel Mármol* and elsewhere advanced that position. But like his radical cohorts, Dalton's embrace of a proinsurrectionary ideology was a drawn-out process, and he had written on Salvadoran history before he advocated insurrection. In those earlier writings Dalton's position on 1932 agreed with the position of his mentor, Jorge Arias, and the other traditionalists in the Communist Party, who saw 1932 as a debacle and a model that should not be followed. References to the 1963 seminar at the UES and to the writings of Arias and Luna are contained in Dalton's archive.

Dalton's History Prior to Miguel Mármol

Roque Dalton may not have been a proinsurrectionary militant before he wrote *Miguel Mármol*, but he was still a communist and a committed political activist. Thus, his approach to history during his pre-*Miguel Mármol* years reflected his belief in the need for an alternative to the traditional narratives, a politically conscious version of the past that recognized people who had been ignored previously. Prior to *Miguel Mármol* Dalton published two works of history: *El Salvador* and *El Salvador: Monografía* (El Salvador: Monograph).[56] Both were published in Cuba, in 1963 and 1965 respectively, when Dalton was either in exile in Cuba or in jail in El Salvador, but prior to his departure for Prague. The first of the two, *El Salvador*, was a brief forty-nine pages long and had a bibliography consisting of only nine items, four of which were directly linked to the Communist Parties of El Salvador and Cuba.[57] The book's format was that of an almanac and was published in the "Our Countries" series aimed at high school students and general readers. It provides a blueprint of Salvadoran history that Dalton would elaborate on in *Monografía* and later in *Miguel Mármol*. The *Monografía* was four times as long as *El Salvador* and far more detailed with a more extensive bibliography. It too was written in a simple, jargon-free language and published in a series, "Popular Encyclopedia," that targeted lay readers. Other titles in the series included The Renaissance, Marxism and Morality, and Ideas in the Ancient World.

The euphoria of the Cuban Revolution provided the context for both books. In 1956, Dalton had written that intellectuals were supposed to "contribute to the improvement of society [and] ... establish an order through which man would change his social condition."[58] For Dalton, Cuba showed that those goals could be achieved, and in the *Monografía* he referred to the Cuban Revolution as "the most important historical event of the century for Latin America."[59]

The forty-nine-page *El Salvador* consists of two sections. The first is dedicated to the contemporary era and the second provides a historical overview. Dalton reversed this order in the *Monografía* and adhered to a more traditional linear chronology that started in pre-Columbian times and moved forward to the present. Regardless of their organizational differences, the two books cover essentially the same topics. In light of their similarities and the brief time between their publication, it is evident they constitute a common project in differing stages of development.

The historical section of *El Salvador* follows a chronological order but begins a trend that would persist throughout all of Dalton's nonfiction writing: frequent leaps to the present to make political statements. Such a trend was to be expected of a writer like Dalton, who was not trained as a historian and who embarked on the task of writing history in order to satisfy political objectives. One of the more important examples in which he performed this temporal leap was in regard to ethnicity and El Salvador's Indian population. In the section in *El Salvador* dedicated to Indian populations prior to the Conquest, Dalton suddenly jumped to the present, arguing that "the few Indians who survive in El Salvador do not represent a special section within the dispossessed mestizo [mixed blood] peasantry." He then wrote that El Salvador has "no 'Indian problem' per se beyond what is created by the backwardness imposed by the semi-feudal structure [of the country]."[60] In other words, Dalton was subsuming ethnicity to class as a determinant variable of El Salvador's history. He repeated this argument in *Monografía*, after having had the opportunity to read and disagree with Richard Adams's anthropological survey of El Salvador's Indians.

> From an economic standpoint, the few Indians that survive in El Salvador do not represent a special sector within the poverty-stricken mestizo peasantry. Merely for didactic reasons could social anthropology find, as it has [in Adams's work], distinctions in this area. Much as the rest of the rural population, Indians in El Salvador are subject to the harshest exploitation and to identical sub-human living conditions. Thus, there is no specific Indian problem in El Salvador, an Indian group with particular grievances of their own.[61]

This erasure of ethnicity from El Salvador's modern history was part of a broad and complex paradigm known as *mestizaje*, or racial mixing. By accepting the validity of mestizaje, Dalton left himself no option but to ignore the counternarrative of ethnicity and fall squarely into the communist-causality camp when he analyzed the 1932 uprising.

Consistent with his belief that class rather than ethnicity fueled El Salvador's history, Dalton promoted another variable that he believed had been ignored for too long: mass political action. In both *El Salvador* and *Monografía* he depicted history as an ongoing conflict between the popular masses and the local oligarchy, and later the imperialist powers of Britain and the United States. Dalton considered mass struggle to define each phase of Salvadoran history, starting with the Conquest and ending with the most recent events in the 1960s. For example, in his rendering of the Conquest, Dalton wrote in *El Salvador* that history "has been moved by the struggle between those masses and the ruling minorities, struggle carried out, in the end, to determine who will direct history and in whose hands will reside the capacity to make history."62

Dalton applied the same perspective to his interpretation of independence in the early 1800s. Dalton portrayed the first and second independence movements in San Salvador in 1811 and 1814 as widespread popular uprisings. Instead of promoting the traditional pantheon of nationalist heroes in these movements, like José Matías Delgado, Dalton exalted the bravery of a little-known artisan, Pedro Pablo Castillo, who supposedly brought "authentic" and popular leadership to the struggle. Even though Dalton insisted that Castillo's leadership was subverted by the traditional independence leaders, he portrayed the masses as the driving force behind independence, arguing that when independence arrived in 1821 it was because "popular mobilization" had forced the traditional elites to declare it.

Dalton told the tale of independence by using extended quotations from *La Verdad*, the newspaper of the Salvadoran Communist Party. His use of this collage technique of authorship resembles a television documentary in which numerous professorial talking heads make cameo appearances to develop their particular point of expertise within an overall narrative. In this manner, Dalton relied on a style of "authorship by appropriation" that would become a recurrent trend in his nonfiction writings and which he would employ in *Miguel Mármol*.

Inevitably, Dalton emphasized the importance of the 1833 Anastasio Aquino uprising to El Salvador's history. Aquino had captured Dalton's imagination years earlier, when as a student he dedicated one of first poems to the Indian rebel. In both *El Salvador* and *Monografía*, Aquino is featured prominently. But Dalton fit the story of Aquino into his running narrative of class conflict and mass action. Even though he acknowledged that Aquino was an Indian whose uprising was highly ethnic in nature, Dalton insisted that the lesson to be drawn from the 1833 insurrection was that class conflict propelled historical evolution. Characteristically, Dalton jumped forward, in this case to the events of 1932, to underline the class basis of Aquino's movement: "The Aquino uprising was imbued with a clear class foundation. Its proclamations made evident the plan to destroy the oppressive power of the whites.... [Aquino was] a central figure in the revolutionary history of El Salvador and the logical antecedent to the peasant actions one hundred years later, in 1932, when once again the Salvadoran fields would echo the battle cry of 'land and liberty.'"[63]

When Dalton's narrative arrived at the turn of the twentieth century, it introduced British and U.S. imperialism as a key feature of Salvadoran history. Dalton claimed that prior histories had ignored that part of the story; it was a "picture that remains untouched to the present day with regard to the economic dependency of the country."[64] Dalton devoted an entire chapter to imperialism in the *Monografía* with copious quotations from *Prensa Latina*, the official press agency of the Cuban Revolution. Dalton characterized the Salvadoran elite as puppets of foreign imperialists and identified El Salvador as a "semicolonial dependency" in which the United States had "absolute control over El Salvador's national and international politics."[65]

When he turned to an analysis of 1932, Dalton continued to emphasize the role of imperialism. He described the regime of General Maximiliano Hernández Martínez (1931–44) as the consolidation of U.S. imperialism, and he insisted that prior to the 1932 revolt the workers' movement was taking shape and popular sectors were beginning to reemerge as a protagonist in El Salvador's history.

But mass ascent was brutally crushed in the Matanza, "ordered by Yankee imperialism and the Salvadoran oligarchy."[66] For Dalton, the events of 1932 neatly marked "the unification of the oligarchy, the greater dominion of Yankee imperialism in El Salvador and the beginning of the role of army dictatorship as a form of government."[67] Dalton was weaving together all the relevant strands of his historical preoccupations into a seamless cloth.

Dalton's version of the 1932 uprising closely followed the traditional PCS line represented by his mentor Jorge Arias, David Luna, and other noninsurrectionary communist moderates. Recall that one of their common approaches to 1932 was to distance the PCS from the uprising and accuse the army of provoking the masses to violence by relentless acts of repression. Dalton presented a similar version in *Monografía* by once again relying on a collage technique. He included a few paragraphs of a military history of El Salvador by Bustamante Maceo, the son of Antonio Maceo, the martyred black hero of the Cuban independence war. Maceo's book casts the uprising as an unplanned event inspired by the economic collapse of the Great Depression. According to Maceo, the rebellion consisted merely of "hungry day laborers [who] assaulted some stores searching for food." Afterward, "these isolated facts were taken advantage of in order to start a coldly planned massacre. The peasants naturally defended themselves from the attacks and achieved some success in the towns of Tacuba and Juayúa, where local soviets were founded."[68]

According to Dalton, the Salvadoran Communist Party found itself in a difficult situation in 1932. It knew that the uprising was the result of a planned provocation, but it also knew that it lacked the necessary control over the masses. So it had to make the choice of either dying with the masses or rejecting them in the name of self-preservation. Dalton credits them for choosing the former: "Being between a rock and a hard place, the Communists chose the heroic path of the sword, the road of dying with the people, leading the people." According to this version, the Communist Party had not organized the events; the events occurred independently. Agency belonged to the army and the masses, while the party became part of the tragedy only because of its last-second decision. But at least the party separated itself from other less worthy groups who had laid claim to the populist mantle, like the Labor Party that had won the 1931 presidential election, and the followers of the Salvadoran philosopher Alberto Masferrer. Dalton concluded that with the Matanza, "the aim of the oligarchy and the imperialists was more than achieved. The popular organizations were beheaded."[69]

The 1932 uprising became a foundational building block in Dalton's interpretive edifice for the remainder of El Salvador's history. The uprising pitted the popular masses against the tiny Salvadoran elite and their imperialist allies, establishing a precedent for a new round of revolutionary struggle. Dalton described the four decades after 1932 as a rising crescendo of mass mobilization. He presented much of the content for the period after 1932 in collage format by drawing extensive quotations from documents produced by the Frente Unido de Acción Revolucionaria (United Revolutionary Action Front, FUAR), a front organization founded by the Salvadoran Communist Party in 1962. Dalton insisted that the status quo in El Salvador would change and that the masses would follow their historic forefathers in El Salvador and their contemporary brethren in Cuba by attacking the system of imperialist domination and elite exploitation.

Conclusion

By the time he sat down to write *El Salvador* and *El Salvador: Monografía* during his exile in Cuba, Dalton had been thinking about historical issues for many years. He had arrived at the belief that El Salvador needed a new, more accurate version of the past, one that rectified the exclusions of traditional histories and took into account themes he considered essential. Among these themes were the role of the masses and the supremacy of class over ethnicity as a driving force of history. Even though he had very few sources available to him in Cuba, Dalton embarked on the challenging endeavor of writing an alternative history of his country.

When Dalton sat down to interview Miguel Mármol in Prague in 1966, only one year after the publication of the *Monografía*, he recognized Mármol's story as a rich source of historical evidence with great political potential. But Dalton already possessed a fully developed interpretation of Salvadoran history, which shaped the questions he asked Mármol, guided his interpretation of Mármol's story, and affected the way he organized his interview notes into a coherent memoir. Many of the approaches contained in *El Salvador* and *El Salvador: Monografía* reappeared in *Miguel Mármol*. But on a key subject, the uprising and Matanza of 1932, Dalton's views were beginning to change. By the time Dalton interviewed Mármol he was in the midst of adopting a new approach to insurrection. Whereas previously he adhered to the Communist Party's traditional line that insurrection should be delayed until conditions were appropriate, by the time he sat down to complete Mármol's story he had become increasingly militant, and his interpretation of the past was changing. Thus, the *Miguel Mármol* testimonial contains a complex blending of Mármol's words and Dalton's evolving interpretive framework.

CHAPTER FOUR

Dalton, Mármol, and the Notebooks

> Memories don't organize themselves chronologically,
> they're like smoke, changing, ephemeral, and if
> they're not written down they fade into oblivion....
> Memory twists in and out like an
> endless Moebius strip.
> —Isabel Allende, *My Invented Country:
> A Nostalgic Journey Through Chile*

It is no overstatement to say that Miguel Mármol's life story, as contained in the book *Miguel Mármol*, is the single most important contribution to collective memory of the events of 1932 in El Salvador. Many factors account for *Miguel Mármol*'s deep influence, including the timing of its publication, when social revolt was looming in El Salvador, and the fact that both the political right and left agreed broadly with its communist-causality framework. The story's natural drama, as well as its highly colloquial flavor and connection to national culture all contributed to its wide acceptance. For these reasons and many more, *Miguel Mármol* has become not only a piece of canonical literature within El Salvador but also a work of international significance.

The goal of this chapter is to bring the weight of new evidence to bear upon the reading of *Miguel Mármol*. This new evidence consists of Roque Dalton's personal archive, provided to us by the Dalton family, which he used to create the final manuscript. It includes, among other things, the original handwritten notes that Dalton took during his interview sessions with Mármol in Prague in 1966. Also included are letters from Mármol, transcripts of books, and documents relating to the Salvadoran Communist Party. Based on an examination of these materials, we contend that customary interpretations of *Miguel Mármol* as a straightforward, autobiographical testimonial should be amended. Instead, *Miguel Mármol* should be seen as an interpretive history that came about through a process of what we identify as "narrative reconfiguration," in which Roque Dalton turned a few dozen pages of handwritten notes into a published book of more than five hundred pages during a five-year period between 1966 and 1971. In short, Dalton's contribution to shaping *Miguel Mármol* was substantial. Dalton edited Mármol's life story following patterns that he had established in prior historical writings, namely *El Salvador* and *El Salvador: Monografía*. To the extent that *Miguel Mármol* became a master narrative of 1932 and also consolidated the communist-causality interpretation, the contents of its story reflect a broader range of influences than simply a sixty-one-year-old man recalling his youth. We do not analyze *Miguel Mármol* for historical accuracy; rather, we hope to show that its rendition of historical events, like any other depiction, was subject to the constitutive influences of many different memory groups.

Miguel Mármol and Testimonial Literature

Miguel Mármol is commonly described as an example of testimonial literature, a genre that emerged onto the literary scene in the 1970s and 1980s, largely as a result of Latin America's deepening sociopolitical crisis. Other areas of the world experiencing similar turmoil contributed to the testimonial genre, but Latin America was the genre's place of origin. A typical testimonial consists of a disenfranchised or otherwise excluded person telling her or his life story to an intellectual outsider, usually a journalist or academician, who then uses international contacts to distribute the story in published form. One of the most well-known examples of testimonial literature is *I, Rigoberta Menchú*, the story of a young Guatemalan Indian woman growing up in the midst of genocidal civil strife in the 1960s and 1970s. It was first published in Spain, Cuba, and France in 1983 as *Me llamo Rigoberta Menchú* and then was translated into English the following year. Other well-known testimonials include the story of a Honduran peasant woman, *Don't Be Afraid, Gringo* (1989), and the story of a worker in the Bolivian tin mines, *Let Me Speak!* (1978).[1] Testimonials are presented in the first person, and the narrative style often reflects the distinct cultural framework of the storyteller, who typically lacks formal education and narrates in a colloquial manner. The outsider who receives the story remains mostly invisible. S/he might appear on the book jacket or as the author of a brief preface, but the core of any testimonial is the life story of the subject in question. The outsider is presented to the reading audience as a neutral bystander, a mere conduit for the true expression of the testimonial agent. One of these academic outsiders, Thomas Tirado, offered a typical expression of this neutrality in the testimonial of Celsa, a Mexican peasant woman: "Although I did select material and organize her conversations into episodic accounts, which are presented as chapters in this book, as Celsa's biographer I was more a conduit for her story than a storyteller."[2]

Testimonials are heavily politicized, sometimes because they relate the story of activists suffering from political persecution, but mostly because they tell the story of people normally excluded from public forums and from the literary realm of autobiography and memoir. The mere fact that these peoples' stories are told, even if they consist of little more than descriptions of daily life, carries heavy political significance. Although the number of testimonials existing in published form is relatively small, their contents can be read as representations of the lives of millions of other people who continue to suffer poverty and oppression in silence. Rigoberta Menchú made this claim about her own testimonial, reminding her readers repeatedly that in sharing her own experiences she was really telling the story of all Guatemala's Indians.³ Indeed, the publication and distribution of her story played no small part in her receiving the Nobel Peace Prize in 1992 for raising awareness of the genocidal plight facing Guatemala's Indian population. Since its initial publication in 1983, Menchú's testimonial has been translated into multiple languages with more than one million copies in print worldwide.

Miguel Mármol is an example of testimonial literature. It is told in the first person and presents the story of a poor person who lacked formal education, became a political activist, and subsequently endured repression and hardship throughout his life, exemplified by his near-death experience before a government firing squad in 1932. Furthermore, the creation of the text involved the "source," Mármol, telling his story to an educated "outsider," in this case a fellow Salvadoran communist, Dalton, who was a poet and novelist with an established publication record and an international reputation as an intellectual. With its publication date of 1972, *Miguel Mármol* became one of the earliest examples of testimonial literature, helping to define the emerging genre. Indicative of its importance is its embrace by the Uruguayan author Eduardo Galeano, who turned Mármol into a main character in his classic novel *Memoria del fuego* (*Memory of Fire*) published in 1984.⁴ Galeano presented Mármol's life as a symbol of Latin America's history during the preceding eighty years.

Testimonials were widely embraced by academics.⁵ Social scientists used them as a sort of primary evidence, not unlike published interviews or legal depositions in which the person testifying was directly involved in events. In particular, they embraced testimonials because they brought a new type of witness to the stand, the disenfranchised poor whose perspective seemed more "real" and "earnest." A recent book dedicated to studying testimonial literature captured this sentiment with the title, *The Real Thing*.⁶ The events of 1932 offer ample proof of the impact of testimonials on social science research; almost every study of 1932 published after 1972 relies heavily on *Miguel Mármol* for evidence.

Literary scholars also gravitated toward testimonial literature because it advanced an ongoing trend in Latin American literature dating back to the turn of the twentieth century, giving voice to the voiceless. Starting around the turn of the twentieth century, most cutting-edge literary genres in Latin America were defined by the extent to which they told the story of people suffering social, political, or economic exclusion. Not coincidentally, the emergence of this trend coincided with the appearance of newly mobilized political sectors, such as working people, women, and ethnic groups. Now sometimes called the "new nationalism," this political development was characterized by populist leaders redefining the nation in a way that rejected the traditional elitism and racism of nineteenth-century liberalism and advocated for a more inclusive political system. As evidence of the extent to which testimonial literature represented a continuation of this trend, just as it was emerging on the scene in the 1960s and 1970s, its predecessor genre, magical realism, was in the midst of its so-called Boom of international recognition, largely for its representations of previously excluded social groups. Magical realist authors, such as Colombian Gabriel García Márquez and Mexican Carlos Fuentes, garnered Nobel Prizes and sold millions of books worldwide, not only for their daring and highly complex narrative forms but also for making protagonists out of prostitutes, Indians, Africans, and workers.

But academics were not uniform in their interpretation of testimonials. Just as many of them embraced the genre and believed that it was achieving its goal of inclusiveness, others pointed out complexities. Literary critics began to question the supposed neutrality of the intellectual outsiders who received the testimony and put it into published form. They wondered if these outsiders were mere conduits for the testimonial, or if they unavoidably reshaped the contents of the product during the interview and through editing. Furthermore, critics noted that publishers of testimonials inevitably had to take into account sales figures, which created a potential conflict of interest by which market forces might drive the editing process. After all, most of the readers of testimonial literature were in North America and Europe, not in the societies or cultures to which the testimonial agent belonged. A scholar of testimonial literature summarized succinctly the problematic nature of testimonial being created for international readerships: "The editor [intellectual outsider] must...organize the transcripts according to the criterion of verisimilitude acceptable to a reader whose concept of what is and what is not credible might be entirely different to that of the narrator [testimonial agent]."[7]

The recent controversy surrounding Rigoberta Menchú's testimonial provides a clear example of these complexities. North American anthropologist David Stoll argued in a recent study that some of the events that Menchú depicted in her testimonial did not happen. Furthermore, Stoll investigated the process by which Menchú's testimonial was created. He determined that a well-known and widely respected Guatemalan historian, Arturo Taracena, played a critical role in getting Rigoberta to France and getting her in contact with the Venezuelan anthropologist, Elizabeth Burgos-Debray, who "collected" Menchú's story. Taracena was affiliated with the political left during Guatemala's civil war and admitted recently to having played a decisive role in editing Menchú's testimonial for publication. Such revelations have led scholars like Stoll to wonder if political issues did not intrude on the "truth" of Menchú's story. There has also been some debate over the substantial royalties generated by sales of the testimonial. Menchú and Taracena claim that Burgos-Debray has kept the royalties, rather than donating them to organizations dedicated to helping the cause of Guatemala's Indian populations, as initially agreed.[8]

The complexities surrounding Menchú's testimonial have supported the arguments of literary critics who point out the potentially artificial nature of the moment testimonials are "written," the sessions when testimonial subjects relate their stories to interviewing outsiders. These critics argue that the interchange is inherently artificial and that the conditions under which it occurs are potentially decisive. After all, they ask, how have the participating parties decided to meet, and how have they defined the purpose of their meeting to one another? Furthermore, under what conditions does the actual telling of the life story occur, and what determines which questions will be asked?

Anthropologists asked themselves these same difficult questions in recent years as they reevaluated the merits of ethnographic research. Once seen as an objective, scientific study of an alien culture, ethnography was subjected to new anthropological theories that debunked its objectivity. The theories claimed that the mere presence of an ethnographer in an alien culture had the potential to upset the "natural" balance and skew the results that would be received. Also the goals of the ethnography and the disposition of the ethnographer can affect the way informants share information and how the material is collected. As just one interesting example, Rigoberta Menchú famously told Burgos-Debray that she was keeping some of her story secret: "I'm still keeping my Indian identity a secret. I'm still keeping secret what I think no one should know. Not even anthropologists or intellectuals, no matter how many books they have, can find out all our secrets."9

Critical analyses of testimonial literature provide a valuable starting point for reevaluating *Miguel Mármol*. When Dalton and Mármol sat down together in Prague in 1966, they did not have an expressed purpose to their meeting. They encountered one another by accident, and once they decided to a series of interview sessions, the production of a first-person testimonial was not their expressed plan. In a letter written to Dalton immediately after the interview, Mármol downplayed the importance of his life story and specifically suggested that whatever Dalton did with the transcripts, they should serve no more than an inspiration to do more research on Salvadoran history.

> I don't think that the abundance of details that represent the compilation of my lived experiences should be inserted into a document intended to be serious and precise. In my opinion, at most they should promote more research, analysis and criticism.10

In 1966 testimonial literature was still in its infancy, and Mármol had little or no awareness of it at the time. He demonstrated ignorance of the genre twenty years after the interviews during an interchange with a U.S. academician.

> G [Gugelberger, interviewer]: Are you familiar with the genre, testimonial literature, and authors like Rigoberta Menchú from Guatemala?
>
> M [Mármol]: Not really. I have heard of her but I have not read her. I have been asked about Roque and have been told about other authors.11

4–1   A page of Dalton's original notebook (*cuaderno*)

Dalton, by contrast, was aware of the testimonial concept. In the introduction to the final version of Miguel Mármol, he said that he had familiarized himself with "the most noteworthy works of 'documentary literature.'"[12] He had been inspired by Oscar Lewis's pioneering anthropological study on Mexico in the 1950s, *Los hijos de Sánchez* (The Children of Sánchez). Lewis used first-person narratives, and his book was widely read in academic circles in the 1960s and 1970s.[13] Dalton admitted that upon concluding the interviews with Mármol, he did not know how he would use the material. He recognized its richness and potential, but he considered a variety of formats, including a novel or a political essay. Eventually, he settled on a first-person testimonial, or as he called it in his own notes, a "truth-novel." In the notes, Dalton wrote explicitly about his internal debate over plans for the material and his debt to Lewis's study.

> Reading again the material that [erasure] resulted from it [the interview with Mármol]—almost—pages handwritten [erasure] in a tiny clustered script—many times more abbreviations and reminder words concentrate a whole paragraph of the informant—a lot of doubts arose in [erasure] me concerning the method of presenting it to the

reader. Indeed. On one side, the material was for me an unbearable invitation to literary creation. Was it a recreation tending preponderantly towards fiction a priority, disregarding the abundant material of political analysis [erasure] that comrade Mármol constructed alongside the facts? On the other side, the narration concerns world and Salvadoran historical problems [erasure], serious and [erasure] complex whose [erasure] theoretical interpretation is [erasure] makes obligatory, unavoidable. So the way [erasure] would have to have been then to use Mármol's testimonial as [erasure] a factual raw data to build a political essay, charged with giving answers to many of the questions that are raised by the study of Salvadoran revolutionary history of this century? After studying those possibilities, I decided for an ambitious way: to present the Mármol's data as it is and how I collected in the interview: from the literary viewpoint I think it is classified in the genre of truth-novel or novel-truth of which "The Children of Sánchez" by Lewis is a master work. Ultimately, nobody has established that the electric tape recorder is determinant of this genre.[14] [See image 4-1]

It is interesting to note how Dalton differentiates between his notes taken while listening to Mármol, which he refers to as both "Mármol's testimony" and "factual raw data," and the final format of the book, a "truth-novel." This distinction implies that Dalton recognized that he was transforming Mármol's words from their "raw" form into a final publishable narrative. Although, admittedly, Dalton later claimed that the final book presents the "material as it is." Ultimately, Dalton believed that his final manuscript reflected the truth of Mármol's life, but even he seemed to grapple with the contradictions between his notes and the final product.

Also in the above passage Dalton refers to the distinct qualities of his notes. He observes that they were taken by hand and consisted of abbreviations, tiny clustered script, and various reminder words designed to aid his memory later when he reworked the material. He points this out to dispel the idea that his method of data gathering would hinder his ability to achieve accuracy in his "truth-novel." But in doing so, Dalton also reveals that he was aware of the challenge associated with converting his raw evidence into a coherent, readable narrative.

Indeed, Dalton's original notes reveal that he had a highly personalized style for recording testimony. The notes from the interviews are seventy-two pages long. They consist of fifty-four numbered pages, in which each odd page is numbered on the top-right corner, plus an additional eighteen pages without numbers that we have assigned roman numerals (i–xviii). Of the total seventy-two pages, seven are blank and six contain almost no information, which leaves a total of sixty-one full pages of text emerging from the interview sessions. Dalton described the nature of these interviews in his introduction to the published version: "The interview proper lasted almost three weeks, with daily work sessions that varied between six and eight hours in length.... The interview was taken by me directly, writing it down by hand into a big notebook."[15] Interestingly, in his notes, Dalton stated that the interviews lasted only "more than one week."[16] Throughout his notes and in their margins, Dalton used various reminder words, especially *"ojo"* (literally "eye," but meaning "attention" or "look"); so too did he insert various arrows, boxes, and other framing devices designed to organize ideas or group words. Beyond the obvious and glaring question as to how Dalton turned sixty-one pages of handwritten notes into a final book of more than five hundred pages, it is worth noting that his raw data was quite convoluted. His notes resemble the field notes of an anthropologist or the early drafts of a novel rather than the transcript of a recorder or stenographer recording testimony. In light of this, Dalton becomes more of an ethnographer than a neutral recorder.

In addition to the sixty-one pages of notes, Dalton had roughly sixty pages of additional material that he used to create the final manuscript for *Miguel Mármol*. (A list of these materials can be found in the Works Cited section at the end of this study.) Among these materials are some original documents from Mármol, including four unpublished poems, roughly a half dozen letters to Dalton varying in length from one to five pages each, and a twenty-page

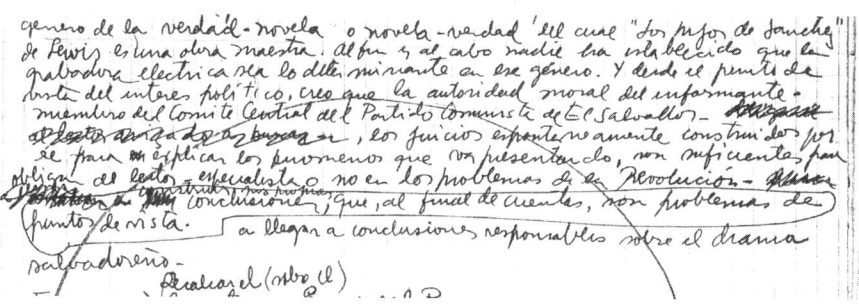

4-2 A page of Dalton's original notebook (cuaderno)

manuscript in which Mármol described his time in Guatemala in the 1940s—a phase of his life not covered in *Miguel Mármol*. Additionally, the package of documents saved by Dalton's family contains a variety of short documents that originated with either the PCS or international communist agencies.

Although Dalton and Mármol did not have a clear agenda when they agreed to their interview sessions in 1966, Dalton clearly appreciated the political implications of Mármol's story. He believed that by publishing it he would raise awareness of key historical events long buried from public consciousness in El Salvador. Furthermore, Dalton believed that the content of the story supported his own political views, namely, an increasingly militant communism. After all, Mármol was a survivor of extreme military repression, a humble man without formal education who dedicated himself to Marxism. From Dalton's perspective, Mármol's communism and his status as a party member granted him the moral authority to represent El Salvador's tragic past and gave his life special significance. Dalton clarified this in the notes:

> And from the viewpoint of the political interest, I believe that the moral authority of the informant—member of Central Committee of the Salvadoran Communist Party—the judgments spontaneously built by him to explain the phenomena he is presenting, are enough for the reader—specialist or not in the problem of Revolution—to arrive [at his own conclusions, that in the end, are problems of points

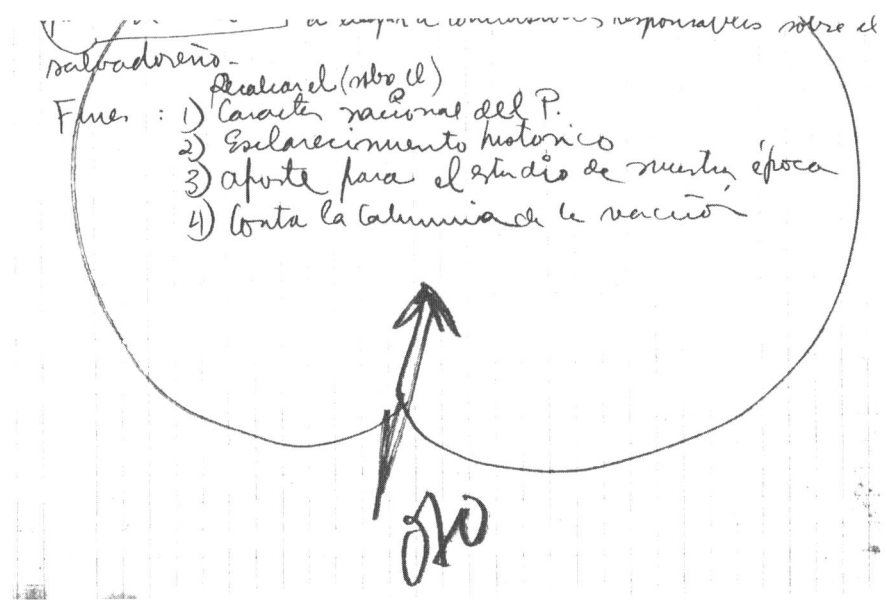

4–3 A page of Dalton's original notebook (cuaderno)

of view] to arrive at responsible conclusions about the Salvadoran drama.[17] [see image 4-2]

In the final published version, Dalton clarified Mármol's identity as a communist to justify the relevance of his life story. He put the issue very simply: "This is the life story…of a Communist from El Salvador."[18] Had Mármol not been a communist, and had his story not lent itself to the promotion of communism and the study of 1932, Dalton likely would not have been interested. As an artist and a Salvadoran, he might have found the life story of a poor laborer from San Salvador to be an interesting piece of folklore, but its merits as a literary exercise and political statement would have been less attractive or compelling.

Dalton made clear in his notes that one of the primary objectives of the interviews with Mármol would be to clarify the contemporary situation of the Salvadoran Communist Party. In his notes, Dalton made this the first of four objectives that he intended to achieve with the eventual by-product of the interviews.

Goals:
1) national character of the P[arty]
2) historical clarification
3) contribution to the study of our times
4) against the calumny of the nation[19] [see image 4-3]

Dalton gave special prominence to these goals by placing them inside a circle with an arrow through its middle and the word "OJO" written in capital letters alongside. In other words, just as he had done in his prior historical writings, *El Salvador* and *El Salvador: Monografía*, Dalton believed that the historical subject matter revealed by Mármol's life story would have direct relevance to contemporary affairs, and particularly to his fellow communists. Given that the events of 1932 became the cornerstone of *Miguel Mármol*, Dalton was more or less admitting that he intended Mármol's testimonial to show contemporary communists the lessons to be learned from the 1932 uprising.

What makes Dalton as the interlocutor of Mármol's life particularly interesting is that in 1966 he and Mármol were on the path to becoming ideological adversaries. It was in Prague that Dalton began to solidify his opposition to the PCS's long-standing view that insurrection should be delayed until social conditions in El Salvador fully matured. When Dalton's mentor and fellow party member at the University of El Salvador, Jorge Arias Gómez, visited Dalton in Prague, he discovered his young protégée's growing ideological discontent.[20] Mármol, by contrast, was a ranking party official and a loyal party member throughout this life. By the time Dalton completed the final manuscript for *Miguel Mármol*, his discontent with the PCS was well advanced and he was beginning to look for alternatives in new militant organizations, like the ERP. Dalton may have embraced Mármol's life as a literary and political opportunity, but he and Mármol disagreed about the party's future in El Salvador. It is logical to assume that they also disagreed about its past, as did other factions in the party at that time. We do not know if Mármol and Dalton recognized their ideological differences during their interview sessions. It is difficult to imagine that a pair of strong-willed comrades whose lives revolved so much around ideology would have been unaware of their differences after so many hours of discussion. Regardless of whether they did, the fact of their differing ideological positions infuses *Miguel Mármol* with great complexity, raising the possibility that the dynamic of personal ideological discord played itself out in their conversations and in the final content of the book. In theory, at least, Mármol and Dalton would have been inclined, however subtlety and unconsciously, if not expressly and overtly, to narrate and interpret the past differently.

Miguel Mármol and 1932

The issue of ideological difference becomes especially important in the context of the version of 1932 contained in *Miguel Mármol*. Both Mármol and Dalton were inclined to emphasize the centrality of 1932 to Mármol's life and to the history of El Salvador, seeing it as an opportunity to expose elite crimes. But again, in theory, Mármol and Dalton would have been inclined to interpret 1932 differently; Mármol would have seen it as proof of correctness of the party's line on delayed insurrection, whereas Dalton would have interpreted it as justification for increased militancy. The possibility of discord between Dalton and Mármol raises the question as to how accurately Dalton recorded Mármol's words, and whether the two comrades disagreed during their conversations about the lessons of 1932. Of course, it is impossible to know if such disagreement occurred because we only have Dalton's notes. Although, in his introduction to the final version, Dalton justified his research method of handwritten notes by claiming that at the end of the process Mármol reviewed the notes and made changes in Dalton's presence.[21] However, the notebooks do not show any evidence of editorial contributions by Mármol. If we assume for the sake of the present argument that Dalton's notes reflect a broadly accurate version of Mármol's spoken words, then comparing them with the final published version can reveal whether Dalton subjected Mármol's narration to a selective process.

The events of 1932 provide the focal point for the entire *Miguel Mármol* narrative. The book's subtitle, *Los sucesos de 1932 en El Salvador* (The Events of 1932 in El Salvador), establishes 1932 as the primary context for reading Mármol's life. References to 1932 are found throughout the text, but the main descriptions of the uprising appear in two sections; the first consists of approximately ten pages in chapter 6 (out of eleven chapters) and provides a detailed description of the final days leading up to the outbreak of revolt. The second consists of roughly thirty-five pages at the end of chapter 7 and defends the party's decision to rebel.[22] In narrative terms, the events of 1932 form the climax of the story, with the remainder of Mármol's life after 1932 serving as the resolution or conclusion. Admittedly, the events of 1932 are so tremendous in scale, and Mármol's narrow escape from the firing squad possesses such a natural drama, that the reason for building a narrative of his life around them is obvious. But it is worth noting that the events of 1932 constitute only a small portion of Mármol's life story, and in fact Mármol did not possess much personal knowledge of the western region where the revolt occurred. He was rarely there in the months prior to January 1932, and during the actual uprising he was in San Salvador, first arrested and then shot. Therefore, Mármol's story has significant limits in its ability to reveal what transpired during the rebellion.

Nevertheless, the final published version of *Miguel Mármol* contains multiple statements, attributed to Mármol, that insist the story of 1932 contains key lessons for contemporary party members and for ongoing party debates. One comment has Mármol saying, "And one thing is certain: that the communist who doesn't have the problem of '32 clear in his mind, its significance and experiences, cannot be a good communist, a good Salvadoran revolutionary." A few pages earlier, Mármol supposedly said, "So long as the events of '32 aren't clear in the minds of Salvadoran workers, the revolutionary vanguard will have a serious ideological obstacle in the way of its work."[23] However, such comments cannot be found in the notebooks, which are mostly silent on the issue. The closest the notebooks come to linking Mármol's rendition of the past to contemporary debates is a comment saying that Mármol's life will "provide us answers that emerge from the study of Salvadoran revolutionary history in this century."[24] In short there is a significant discrepancy between the notebooks and the final version of *Miguel Mármol* as to the role that Mármol's rendition of 1932 should play in shaping contemporary party affairs. This discrepancy suggests that Dalton placed a greater emphasis on the events of 1932 than did Mármol and, furthermore, that Dalton wanted to marshal the story of 1932 in support of his emerging opposition to the party's traditional line on insurrection. In other words, Dalton's views might have given him the incentive, consciously or unconsciously, to construct the narrative of Mármol's life story as an argument in favor of insurrection.

The final text includes a clear defense of communist causality. Mármol's voice puts it succinctly: "In 1932, we made a communist insurrection."[25] Mármol's voice then contends that the PCS was the decisive variable in determining the timing and nature of the revolt and also claims that the PCS achieved its goal of becoming the vanguard of the masses, "given the conditions existing in the country at that time, [the party] could lead the masses and plan the revolution."[26] In addition to its explicit claims about the PCS being the key protagonist in 1932, *Miguel Mármol* advances communist causality through a sort of argumentative inertia. As the story of Mármol's life, the narrative centers on labor activism and the Communist Party. Naturally, the book tells the story of the uprising from the only vantage point Mármol could provide, the internal workings of the Central Committee. This focus leaves the reader with the distinct impression that the decisions being made by the Central Committee determined the nature and course of the uprising. In telling the story of how the insurrection began, Mármol's voice says, "The insurrectional call of the CC [Central Committee] had reached different places in the west and the mass organizations, following orders, had started to go into action."[27]

Miguel Mármol further advances communist causality when Mármol's voice accounts for the uprising's defeat. In an argument almost identical to that of Buezo in *Sangre de hermanos* (1944), *Miguel Mármol* identifies the organizational collapse of the party's Central Committee as the decisive factor leading to failure. Admittedly, Mármol's voice accuses the party of some poor decision making, but it describes the government's attack on the party, and in particular its capture of Martí on January 18 as critical. Martí's arrest exposed the rebellion and gave the government time to prepare, which eliminated the party's one advantage, the element of surprise. Mármol's voice claims that the arrest of Martí threw the PCS's lines of communications into disarray, so that in the critical final days leading up to the revolt, ranking members lost contact with one another and with the masses in the west. Thus, the party's peasant army went into battle leaderless. The implication of this argument is unmistakable; the party had organized the rebellion and established leadership over the western masses, but it failed to fulfill its necessary role at the final critical moment.

Mármol's voice continues this line of reasoning with a sort of conspiracy theory in which the government knew of the revolt and allowed it to proceed in order to expose the rebels and their communist leaders, which allowed the army to wipe out its adversaries in one decisive stroke. According to Mármol's voice, the conspiracy theory provides the only explanation for why regions not under PCS control joined the rebellion—because the government provoked them into action through premeditated violence. Once again, *Miguel Mármol* is reinforcing the notion that outside of any unusual circumstances, the PCS provided the organizational and intellectual inspiration for revolt.

Narrative Reconfiguration

The creation of the book *Miguel Mármol* occurred in three stages: Mármol transmitted his story orally to Dalton; Dalton recorded Mármol's words by hand in sixty-one notebook pages; and then turned his notes into a finished manuscript during the period between 1966 and 1971. We have no way of knowing what Mármol actually said to Dalton during those interview sessions in 1966. We only have what Dalton recorded in his notebooks and then what he produced in the final version. A comparison of those two bodies of evidence reveals much about the complex way in which *Miguel Mármol* came into being. Differences between the notebook and the finished manuscript reveal that *Miguel Mármol* represents a process of what we call "narrative reconfiguration," whereby Roque Dalton reshaped Mármol's story, or at least what Dalton recorded as Mármol's words.

4–4a A page of Dalton's original notebook (cuaderno)

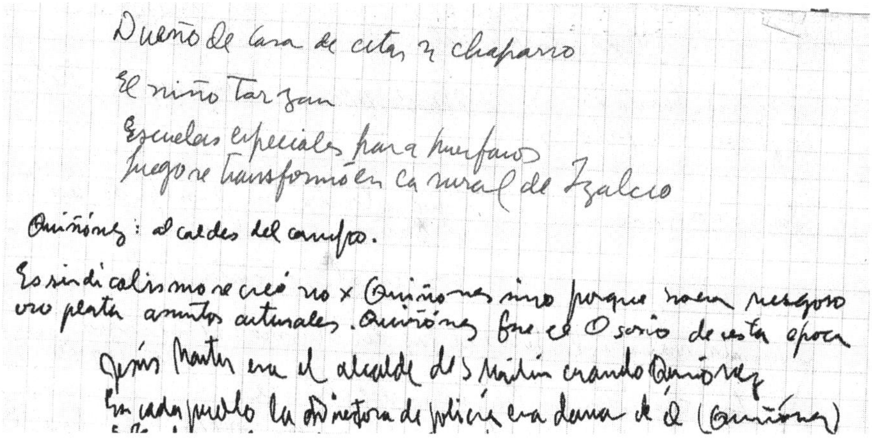
Dueño de casa de citas, y chaparro
El niño Tarzan
Escuelas especiales para huerfanos
luego se transformó en la rural de Izalco
Quiñónez: alcaldes del campo.
El sindicalismo se creó no x Quiñónez sino porque no era negocio
oro plata asuntos actuales. Quiñónez fue el Osorio de esta época
Jesús Martín era el alcalde de S Martín cuando Quiñónez
En cada pueblo la directora de policía era dama de él (Quiñónez)

4–4b A page of Dalton's original notebook (cuaderno)

It has been debated whether Mármol found the final published version of his story to be an accurate reflection of what he remembered having said to Dalton. Evidence on this issue remains unfortunately anecdotal. A local journalist and former guerrilla in El Salvador claims Mármol told him that he read the text and found it so inaccurate that he wanted to write a corrective to it during his exile in Cuba.[28] Ileana Rodríguez, a scholar of testimonial literature working in the United States, wrote that Mármol expressed disappointment with Dalton's exclusion of elements of his personal life from the final version, but she does not provide evidence to support the claim.[29] By contrast, Jorge Arias Gómez, in his 1998 memoir of his relationship with Roque Dalton, specifically challenged critics who claimed that *Miguel Mármol* was "an invention, or at least a product of Roque's imaginative recreation." Arias claimed that Mármol "had the book in his hands, when the ink was still fresh, and never once contradicted a single line. My friendship with Miguel allowed me to know this point, and he, personally, affirmed to me the book contained what he had said in the interview."[30] Arias's claim is compelling, but we know nothing of the context of his supposed conversation with Mármol, and nearly twenty-five years had passed between the conversation and Arias's recording of it. In short, the existence of these contradictory claims and the lack of more definitive evidence mean that Mármol's opinion on *Miguel Mármol* remains unknown.

Dalton's reconfiguration of the text can be broken down into three categories: (1) rearrangement of the narrative to conform to a linear chronology; (2) addition or subtraction of narrative elements, and (3) the use of hidden quotations, that is, the insertion of blocks of text from other sources without carefully citing them, thereby giving them the impression of belonging to Mármol, or at least of joining the narrative evenly. Taken together, these interventions created a coherent narrative with an established plot line that does not always coincide with the content of the original interview notes.

Linear Chronology

Dalton's notes from Mármol's testimony do not adhere to a linear chronology, revealing that Mármol told his story to Dalton with little or no regard to temporal order. A specific example is found on pages 35 and 36 in the notebooks, which contain approximately fifty cryptic lines referring to four episodes in Mármol's life from the years 1927, 1932, 1934, and 1944. But Mármol did not relate the episodes to Dalton in chronological order: he related them in this order, 1932, 1944, 1934, and then 1927.

> (Anecdotes of 1932
>   holy souls} ~~Los amates~~ Cujuapa, Ilopango
>   untie my strings}
>   San Joaquín—the one who remained in the group
>   of executed people
>   The boss saved him
>   Los amates, Santa Tecla—
>   The cow and the bull at the edge of the abysm:
>   the *trisagio!*—
>
> | Year 1944 |
> | The prayer at the tiger's cave |
> | 1) 400 men waiting to bomb a bridge |
> | 2) whip of dogs—fear |

[red box in the original]
"the witch's little duck" Attention: nicknames as fishes
anecdote of the rock fall in the lake
Chigüichón—Guatemala's Cemetery
Move out! the car lost its brakes
"The red Ghost of La Esperanza Neighborhood
It appeared by the bridge
But there he used to meet: in the bridge)

(1934 Terrible rain front   The daughter was "lover of
7 June—Rain   Sagrera"
                                 Consul of Spain

The house in which he was sheltered was strong. He was in the attic (type writer)
his children lived in a weak house. Because of the rain he decided to bring them home. "no little fellow you should not go out I take them. And the rain took away the house. They arrived naked then to refuge in the humble room of the house.
They were not shot during the Martial law. Ms. María: the guards that did not respect anybody

Owner of the brothel and pineapple wine factory
Child Tarzan
Special schools for orphans
Then it was transformed into the Izalco's rural school

Quiñónez: mayors of the countryside
The workers' unions were not created by Quiñónez but because they were not a risk
Gold silver cultural affairs. Quiñónez was the Osorio of his period
Jesus Martín was the major of S Martín during Quiñónez[31]
[see images 4-4a and 4-4b]

This example is typical of the rest of notebook, and especially of the first eighteen pages, which reveal to the reader a temporal jumble. Mármol told his story to Dalton in disjointed pieces, moving freely

*Jopango: sus calles ❧ arboladas: naranjos
Sus fiestas eran ❧ buenas. Alboradas de obreros
y pescadores
Esta belleza y armonía fue destruida a la llegada
de la aviación. Mató el pueblo.
La industria ligación lo revivió. Los de Jopango
van a las fábricas etc.*

4–5a A page of Dalton's original notebook (cuaderno)

between various phases of his life, seemingly not troubled by making vast leaps backward and forward in time. Dalton abandoned Mármol's chronological fluidity and instead chose a rigid linear chronology for the finished version of *Miguel Mármol* by opening with Mármol's childhood and moving straight through to his midthirties.

It is difficult to say with certainty why Dalton reordered Mármol's story chronologically, as he left no insight into his thinking on the matter. But various possibilities exist, not the least of which is that Dalton might simply have preferred narrating the past chronologically. In both his fictional and nonfictional writings prior to *Miguel Mármol*, Dalton exhibited a fairly loyal adherence to linear chronology. Dalton's work in *El Salvador* and *El Salvador: Monografía* is organized chronologically, even if he frequently jumped forward to the present to put history at the service of a contemporary political issue. Dalton's confessed model for framing Mármol's story as a testimonial, Oscar Lewis's *Children of Sanchez*, also employed a linear chronology. Another possible reason for Dalton abandoning Mármol's nonlinear approach is Dalton's training in Marxism and an adherence to Marx's modernist concept of time. Regardless of the reason why he did it, the fact remains that Dalton ignored Mármol's personal narrative style and reordered his life story according to his own preferences.

Addition and Subtraction of Narrative Elements

The discovery of Dalton's original notes allows us to realize for the first time how fragile a scaffold they made for the final version of

4–5b
A page of Dalton's original notebook (cuaderno)

Miguel Mármol. The simple discovery of the fact that the notes are only sixty-one pages long reveals Dalton's substantial influence over the content of Mármol's testimonial. To put it simply, when sixty-one pages of handwritten notes are turned into more than five hundred pages of published text, large amounts of information have to be added. The book's section on Mármol's childhood provides a clear example. Dalton's notes on this subject consist of four abbreviated paragraphs of text spread over four pages.

Ilopango: its tree-lined streets [erasure]: orange trees

Their parties were [erasure] good. Festivities of workers and fishermen.
This beauty and harmony was destroyed by the arrival of aviation. It killed the town.
Industrialization revived it. Ilopango people go to the factories, etc. [see image 4-5a]

I didn't know who my father was–
She told me and the town that it was cap. Carranza.
She was friends with Doña Cresencia–
He appointed him "mayordomo" of the town
And said a bit tipsy that I was his son (8 years)
His daughters stoned him
But he succeeded
Womanizer father. Had many children
He was mayor because of the blows

|
"This boy will make
one of those damned girls bear children"
    both were humiliated
Did not go to court
That curse almost became real
Because of a sister:
He was going to marry her
Not knowing that was elucidated
His mother–
But with a niece
Had children–
His sisters loved him afterwards
But because he was a communist
later turned their back on him[32] [see image 4-5b]

These few lines, along with a five-page letter from Mármol to Dalton dated 1966, was transformed into nearly twenty-eight pages of the published text.[33] The following paragraph from a section of that published text, dealing specifically with Mármol trying to determine the

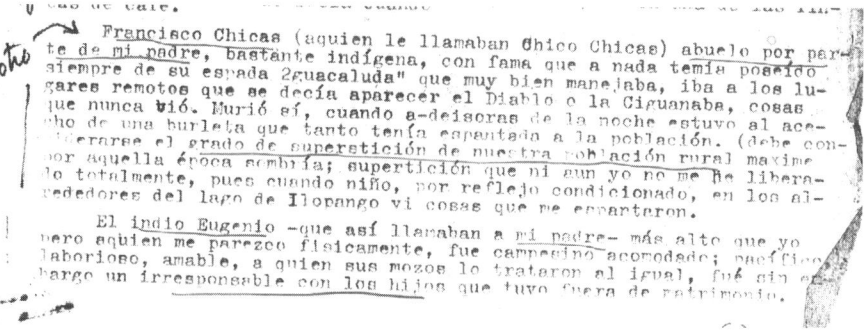

4–6   A page of Dalton's original notebook (cuaderno)

identity of his father, reveals how Dalton transformed a handful of disjointed words into a cohesive 340-word passage, complete with a highly individualized narrative personality.

> I wanted to know who my father was, and I tried to get my mother to tell me. But she considered that a secret between him and her, that not even me, the fruit of that secret, should know. When some well-dressed and good-looking man would go by, I'd run to call her to some see, and I'd say: "Ma, couldn't that man maybe be my father?" She would laugh and I'd show my disappointment since I would have liked that man for my father. Finally, moved by persistence, she told me that my father was Captain Carranza, who lived in San Salvador. I immediately started telling everyone so they'd all know I had a father, too. A name was a big deal for me, and I was as happy as if I had just gotten a new toy or something. But it wasn't true. He was just a name my mother had made up to get me to quit bothering her. My father was then Mayor of Ilopango, Eugenio Chicas, or "Eugenio the Chicken," as they called him. A well-off farmer, he was the son of the famous Francisco Chicas—"Chico" Chicas—who was thought to be invincible with his sword made from the calabash, and who roamed the roads at night looking to do battle with the Devil or with other evil spirits. Chico Chicas had died

> from a heart attack, late at night, on a road near town, caught in the grasp of a ghost that had everybody terrorized. My father didn't inherit my grandfather's combativeness; rather, he was hardworking, quiet, and easy-going. However, he was totally irresponsible when it came to his illegitimate children. And there were plenty of us. My poor mother felt obliged to hide his paternity because he was married and she was good friends with his wife, doña Crescencia. I found out that Eugenio Chicas was my father the same year they killed President Araujo, that's 1913 if I remember correctly, when I was about eight years old.[34]

The basis for the passage is fewer than seventy words from the first two paragraphs of the notebook source above, and the following eight lines about Mármol's father and grandfather contained in one of his letters to Dalton.

> Francisco Chicas (who they called Chico Chicas) was my father's father, very Indian, famous for his fearlessness and carrying his sword, that he handled well, he used to go to remote places, saying that he was looking for the Devil or la Cihuanaba, things he never seen.

> The Indian Eugenio—as they called my father—was taller than me, but looked like me physically. He was a well-off peasant, peaceful, hardworking, friendly, and he treated his workers as equals. But he was irresponsible with his children, having had many outside of wedlock.[35] [see image 4-6]

Although some sections of Dalton's notes are more extensive, this example from Mármol's childhood offers a typical example of the extent of the changes that occurred in transforming the notes into final text.

Given the centrality of the 1932 uprising to the entire *Miguel Mármol* project, the degree to which it reveals an act of narrative reconfiguration is of central importance. Of the two main sections addressing the uprising in *Miguel Mármol*, the first one contained in chapter 6 is approximately three thousand words long. The basis for that section is roughly three pages from the notebooks consisting of twelve hundred words. Both texts provide a fairly detailed look at the internal workings of the Communist Party's Central Committee in San Salvador in early January 1932 as its members debated the party's appropriate response to the surge in militancy among the rural poor in the west. After comparing the contents of these two sources one can conclude that Dalton followed the interview notes quite closely.

However, the second main section on the uprising at the end of chapter 7 reveals broad discrepancies between the notebooks and the final text. It is in those pages where Mármol's voice defends repeatedly the party's decision to rebel in 1932 and attacks critics, both contemporary and historical, who argue that the party erred in taking up arms. The section begins by making sure the reader appreciates the relevance of the debate to contemporary affairs. Mármol's voice says, "I've only wanted to put forth a series of facts for the most part unfamiliar to Salvadorans, so that they can be examined by our youngest comrades and be made use of for an analysis."36 The notebooks contain no evidence that Mármol made this statement during the interviews. The final three pages in chapter 7 analyze the PCS's military plan and offer an explanation for why the uprising failed. They claim that tactical errors in implementing the military plan caused the failure, which left the rebellious masses of the western countryside isolated and leaderless at the critical moment.37 In other words, the ideological premise behind the uprising is not criticized, but rather party leaders are simply accused of failing to implement their own military plan. This claim goes to the heart of the ideological debates taking place within the ranks of the PCS in the 1960s. Those who remained loyal to the party's line of delayed insurrection and who believed that the PCS bore responsibility for organizing it, like Professor David Luna of the UES, defined the decision to rebel as a fundamental ideological error. Those who advocated a more militant ideological line, like Dalton, portrayed the decision to rebel in 1932 as ideologically sound and explained the uprising's failure as a result of minor tactical errors. The three pages at the end of chapter 7 promote the militant argument. They do not correspond to any materials in the notebooks or to any other documents in Dalton's archive, and furthermore, they contradict Mármol's own beliefs on 1932.

At various points throughout the thirty-five pages at the end of chapter 7, the text refutes people who have criticized the party's decision to rebel in 1932. One such figure was Dr. David Luna. At his 1963 presentation at the Seminar on Contemporary History, he harshly criticized the PCS for embarking on armed insurrection. *Miguel Mármol* singles out Dr. Luna for criticism:

> The conditions that established *the existence of a true revolutionary situation* and that demanded the party's call to action to the masses (which is the point that isn't examined often among us nowadays and which is omitted or diminished by, among others, Dr. David Luna in his analysis, but is without doubt a fundamental point) were the following:[38]

It then lays out a ten-point argument against Dr. Luna. The notebooks make no mention of Dr. Luna, nor do they contain any portion of this ten-point attack against him. Instead, the sources for the attack are two handwritten documents contained in Dalton's archive. One is appropriately entitled "anti-Luna." It is difficult to determine who wrote it. The handwriting is clearly not Mármol's, and it is likely Dalton's. The purpose of the document is to refute Dr. Luna's 1963 presentation. Large portions of it appear almost word for word in Mármol's voice in the final version of *Miguel Mármol*. The other document, which we have entitled "OJO" because of the first word that appears on it, is a ten-point analysis of the conditions in El Salvador that led to the 1932 uprising. It appears to be in Mármol's handwriting. The "OJO" document does not offer a strong argument that the PCS was responsible for the uprising. In fact, it identifies the uprising as a "Bourgeois Democratic Revolution," and nine of its ten points have nothing to do with communism or the party, but rather address various social and economic conditions that were causing mass discontent throughout the country. Only the tenth point refers to the Communist Party, and it does so vaguely, without clearly identifying it as the responsible agent. Nevertheless, Dalton freely

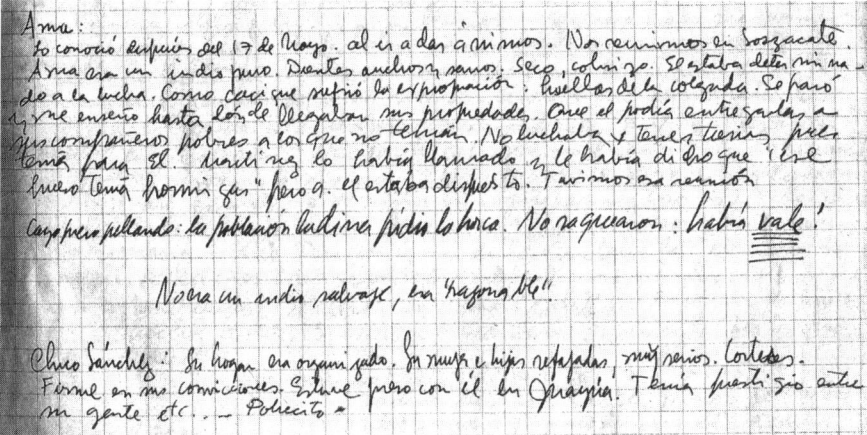

4–7 A page of Dalton's original notebook (cuaderno)

mixed the contents of the "OJO" document with the argument in "anti-Luna" to create a defense of the decision to rebel. Furthermore, the section of *Miguel Mármol* that is based on those two documents claims in no uncertain terms that the PCS was the revolutionary vanguard: "The SCP [PCS] had, two years after its founding, the characteristics of a vanguard nucleus that, given the conditions existing in the country at that time, could lead the masses and plan the revolution."[39] Neither "OJO" nor "anti-Luna" makes this claim.

Another critique of those who opposed the party's decision to rebel is narrated as if Mármol were speaking it to Dalton:

> Okay, in order to give a complete picture of things, the pros and cons, I want to say that those inside the Party who flatly rejected the insurrection, gave, as the basis for their point of view, the following reasons:[40]

This lead is followed by a four-part argument against the decision to rebel. The source is another handwritten document in Dalton's archive identified as "*anti tesis*" (antithesis), this time clearly in Dalton's handwriting. Dalton put its contents into Mármol's voice and then proceeded to have Mármol's voice show the weaknesses of the arguments against the decision to the rebel.

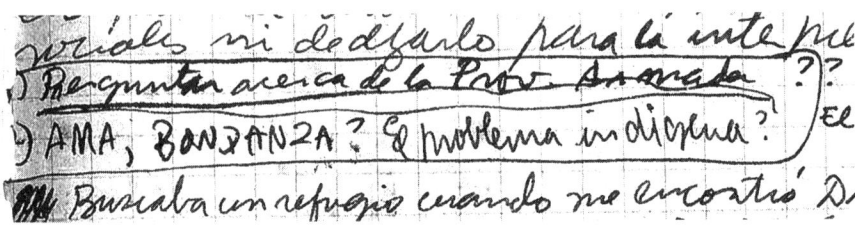

4–8 A page of Dalton's original notebook (cuaderno)

On various occasions through the latter half of chapter 7, *Miguel Mármol* presents Mármol making statements explicitly defending the decision to rebel in 1932. At one point Mármol's voice says, "Our errors were, on the other hand, ones of vacillation in the application of a line that was fundamentally correct."[41] This claim and others like it are not supported by material in the notebooks or any other document that can be attributed to Mármol.

What is particularly interesting about Dalton putting words into Mármol's mouth is that only a few years earlier Dalton's approach to 1932 was the same as Mármol's, or at least that of the traditional party line. In *El Salvador* and *El Salvador: Monografía*, Dalton's interpretation of 1932 accorded with that of David Luna, his mentor, Jorge Arias Gómez, and the PCS leadership in general. But by the time Dalton was creating the final manuscript of *Miguel Mármol*, his interpretation of 1932 had changed in accordance with his different view on the issue of insurrection, from that of a defender of delayed insurrection, to that of a militant radical in support of immediate guerrilla war.

In addition to issues being added to the text, *Miguel Mármol* was reconfigured by subtracting ideas as well. Dalton chose not to include various elements in the final manuscript that were contained in his notebooks. The issue of ethnicity is one of the most glaring examples. *Miguel Mármol* is noteworthy for its failure to provide more than a passing reference to Indians and to the ethnic dimension of the 1932 uprising. But Dalton's notes indicate that Mármol discussed ethnicity more frequently and was willing to acknowledge an ethnic foundation to the rebellion. It was during his discussion of two Indian caciques believed to be rebel leaders,

Feliciano Ama of Izalco and Chico Sánchez of Juayúa, that Mármol ascribed the ethnic character of the uprising. The following lines, drawn from four different pages in the notebook, offer the sum total of Mármol's references to ethnicity.

> Ama:
> He met him after 17 May. When he went to cheer people up. We met in Sonzacate. Ama was a pure Indian. Wide and healthy teeth. Skinny, dark. He was determined to fight. As a cacique he suffered the expropriation: marks of his hanging. He stood up and showed me the limits of his former properties. That he could give them to his poor fellows, to the ones who had no land. He did not fight to own land because he had for himself. [President Hernández Martínez] had called him and had told him "that problem had ants" but he [Ama] was ready. We had that meeting.
> He [Ama] fell prisoner fighting. The Ladino population requested his hanging. They did not loot: they were O.K.! He was not a savage Indian, he was "reasonable."
>
> Chico Sánchez: his home was organized. His wife and daughter wore the traditional Native dress, very serious. Polite. Firm in his convictions. I was in prison with him in Juayúa. Had reputation among his people, etc… Poor. [see image 4-7]
>
> AMA, BONDANZA? The problem of the indigenous population? [see image 4-8]
>
> The reasons behind the insurrection and its failure. Thirty-five-page report. It was read at the meeting in Usulután. A copy was sent to Mexico, one to the [Soviet] Union. But it happens that after he was captured it appeared at the Police [headquarters]. When the P. [Communist Party] grabbed the leadership the reformist and the anarcho-syndicalists had molded the mass with demagogy. Horrible economic conditions. Martínez massacred to make his "revolution."

4–9   A page of Dalton's original notebook (cuaderno)

> Working by blocking, there was a primitive community. The expropriation of land. The Ladino seizure of [local] government away from the Natives. Native Section, Ladino section, with a program of claiming back their land and of their own authorities, it received huge support in Sonsonate, for example. That is why the electoral fraud provoked so big a reaction. [see image 4-9]

> They hang Platero (old man 80 years old)
> they hang Feliciano Ama (They took the school's children)
> Chico Sánchez—
> Names in Mármol's execution—42 [see image 4-10]

These scattered lines demonstrate that Mármol at least recognized the possibility that the uprising had an ethnic component, even though some of his references reflect common prejudices against Indians, such as Ama being "reasonable" despite being an Indian. But in *Miguel Mármol* these references are watered down or eliminated. For example, *Miguel Mármol* explains Ama's motives for rebelling as having to do with class rather than ethnicity, saying that he "hadn't joined the struggle as an Indian, but rather as an exploited man."43 In this single sentence the potential ethnic foundation of the uprising is converted into class conflict. A similar example is found in the discussion of the general motives for the rebellion. What Dalton wrote down in the notebooks as the fight for "the return of the [Indian communal] land," a "Ladino seizure of [local] government," and the subsequent Indian struggle to have their "own authorities" became in the final text, "the first soviet in the America."⁴⁴ Once again, issues that had an unmistakable ethnic component were made to conform to a story of class conflict and communist causality. The notebooks only mention the issue of Soviets once in passing, "*el soviet de Juayúa*" (the soviet of Juayúa), whereas *Miguel Mármol* addressed the issue over the span of six lines.⁴⁵

By eliminating Mármol's references to ethnicity, *Miguel Mármol* followed the pattern Dalton had established in *El Salvador* and *El Salvador: Monografía*. In those works, Dalton dismissed ethnicity's relevance to political affairs in 1960's El Salvador. In *Miguel Mármol* he did the same in regard to 1932. The reasons Dalton eliminated ethnicity from the historical and political narratives are potentially complex and multiple, but we believe they can be narrowed down to two interrelated factors: communism and mestizaje.

Of course, both Dalton and Mármol were communists who agreed with the basic tenets of Marxism-Leninism and dialectical materialism. But with a less doctrinaire and formal conceptualization of Marxism, Mármol remained more open to considering the influence of El Salvador's myriad social identities, including ethnicity. Dalton, by contrast, as a formally educated intellectual whose notions of communist theory remained more rigid, adhered to a more classic Marxist interpretation, claiming that all social relations are based on class. Therefore, when Dalton looked back on the insurrection in the western region in 1932, he was predisposed to ignore the possibility of ethnicity as a causal factor and instead saw class warfare driven purely by economic variables.

Mestizaje is the other factor that explains Dalton's erasure of ethnicity. Mestizaje refers to the complex sociocultural process by which a nation's identity becomes linked to its mestizo or *mulato* (mixed) population and eradicates other ethnic groups, primarily Indians or Africans. This emphasis on the nation as ethnically mixed was a continentwide process that developed in the early twentieth century, when so-called new nationalist political movements began to promote a broader sense of national identity. One of the most famous appeals to mestizaje came from the Mexican

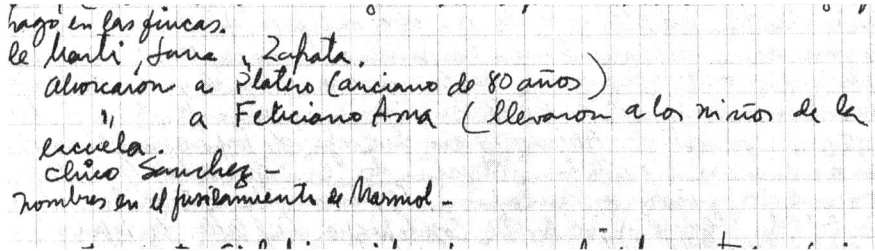

4–10 A page of Dalton's original notebook (cuaderno)

intellectual and minister of education, José Vasconcelos, who in his 1925 book *La raza cósmica* (The Cosmic Race) claimed that the brightest future for human beings would be the elimination of racial difference by interbreeding all the races into one great "cosmic race," the mestizo. New nationalists like Vasconcelos promoted inclusiveness and defended the rights of people previously excluded. Egalitarian in motive, mestizo nationalism had the practical effect of eliminating Indians and Africans (that is, "nonmixed" people) from the national narrative. In his work on Nicaragua, *The Myth of Mestizaje*, North American historian Jeff Gould has shown the complex economic and political reasons for writing Indians out of that country's history in the early 1900s.[46] In Nicaragua and other countries subject to pressures of mestizaje, young Indians began to look, act, and think more like the national "mestizo" and to reject the cultural upbringing that would have identified them as Indian. For the case of El Salvador, Virginia Tilley has shown that by the 1930s and 1940s the Indian population was being written out of public discourse to the point that Indians eventually became invisible to the majority of Salvadorans.[47]

Marxist intellectuals, who emphasized class rather than race or ethnicity as the driving force of politics, did not question the ideology of mestizaje. By the time Dalton was listening to Mármol's testimonial in 1966, these combined pressures had advanced mestizaje in El Salvador significantly to the point that the majority accepted it as an established fact. It was not uncommon by that time to hear Salvadorans describe their nation as "the most mestizo country in Latin America."

A similar example of Dalton reshaping Mármol's testimonial to fit a more doctrinaire radicalism can be seen in the example of religion. The notebooks reveal that Mármol made a few passing references to religious beliefs when telling Dalton about his move to the capital city as a young man and the development of his political consciousness. Mármol described the capital city as a big change from the small town where he was raised, even though his hometown was located near to the capital's eastern edge. He described himself at that time as a sort of naïve rural boy exposed to new things in the city, including atheism and political activism. Mármol told Dalton that when he first arrived to the capital he was religious and believed in folk superstitions like La Cihuanaba, a mythical female spirit who seduced men and left them mentally impaired. In the notebook, Dalton recorded Mármol relating his belief in La Cihuanaba as follows:

> I arrived [at San Salvador to Felipe Angulo's Workshop] with all the prejudices: La Cihuanaba, that I had seen the Devil, God. My shoemaker instructor Gumercindo was an atheist and he liked the Bolshevik struggle. People in the workshop talked against the Meléndez and the Quiñónez [governments] about the Bolshevik revolution, Communism. When I returned to my town, I was a liberal: I passed as an atheist among my simple people.[48] [see image 4-11]

In this description Mármol portrays his early life from the perspective of his later political beliefs in which religion is a "prejudice" and believers are "simple people." But when Dalton edited these few lines for the final manuscript, he expanded them and provided a more doctrinaire critique of religion.

> In my first days working at "La Americana," I swore that I had seen the devil, that "La Cihuanaba" had scared me and not only did I blindly believe in God, but with the pride of any ignorant person I refused to accept the idea that anyone could stop believing in Him. Nonetheless, in the shop I found out that my immediate supervisor,

4–11 A page of Dalton's original notebook (cuaderno)

> Gumercindo Ramírez, was a total atheist, based on convictions powerful for their clarity and evidence. About "La Cihuanaba," for example, I had been conditioned by the social environment, that I sincerely believed that I had seen Her. Although the truth of the matter is that years later I had a very strange experience of which I will talk about later. On returning from the shop to my hometown, my new conversations with old friends caused a certain alarm and I passed myself off as an unbeliever, a person totally liberated from superstitions. The truth is that I was beginning to convert myself into a deeply confused liberal and, of course, I was still filled with all kinds of prejudices. But now I was aware that problems such as those dealing on the existence of God, the Devil or La Cihuanaba herself, were not the fundamental ones, not by a long shot.[49]

In Dalton's rewording, Mármol's view on religion becomes more rigidly modernist and typically Marxist in its critique. Religious belief is associated with blindness and ignorance, and atheism is described as being powerful for its clarity and evidence. Dalton also took the opportunity of Mármol's early politicization to inject a standard Marxist critique of liberalism as being "deeply confused," whereas communism is based on "fundamental" variables. Here again, Dalton's reconfiguration of Mármol's narrative adhered to patterns present in his prior historical works, *El Salvador* and *El Salvador: Monografía*. In those works Dalton singled out the Catholic

Church for special critique for its contributions to El Salvador's social plight.⁵⁰

In an ironic twist, Dalton sometimes took story lines that he had previously disparaged on political grounds and introduced them in the text for dramatic effect. La Cihuanaba provides one example. In the midst of Mármol's description of his flight to the eastern side of the country in hopes of avoiding the police after the Matanza, Dalton inserted an appearance by La Cihuanaba that does not appear in the notes. The notes are as follows:

> I arrived at Sn Miguel to Mr. ~~Miguel~~ ABEL Palacios, Toño's father. The one who requested to go into Sn Miguel, an ex-shoemaker, Silva, was a policeman there, but he did not see me. I had a goal: a small town near Gotera named Delicias. An iron-smith wrote to us from there, he wrote wonderful letters and had an awesome political work. But when we talked to him he did not acknowledge anything, as if the one who spoke was a different person. I thought that it was because the lady was there. I went to ask him to take me out to Honduras. He did not want to: there is no problem, the Governor, etc. I slept in the corridor and at midnight I ~~didn't~~ left. A gentleman found me: do not go to Honduras without papers, that there was a bully, etc. He gave him directions to San Miguel. Passing by a hacienda some workers captured me, but they released me and gave me milk. When I arrived at Sn Miguel they were inspecting people, but I managed to arrive to Mr. Abel's. I decided to return to Usulután via the Sn Miguel Volcano. On the road a big delinquent appeared to me who spoke as a bully and was eating *papaturros*. I was afraid of him and also spoke as a bully. We arrived to a house and we went in to request food. I was shaking, tortillas milk. I have no money. Eat! After eating the guy started throwing the things in his suitcase I protested. Then on the road he became a bully—I stood up of him. Straight ahead, a hut. He was waiting nearby. I told the peasants. That son of a bitch must be bad. Wagon

to Batres. Finally I split from him in Batres. And returned to Usulután.⁵¹ [see image 4-12]

Mármol made no apparent reference to La Cihuanaba during this point in his testimonial, but the final published version has her appearing and repeating the Christian miracle of multiplying fishes. The sentence "he gave him directions to San Miguel" in the middle of the passage marks the point at which Dalton made the following insertion.

> Then a rather pretty girl appeared out of nowhere, asking us the way to a place called Santa Cruz, or something like that. The fishermen came out of the water and stood looking at her, who, with her sad little face in the middle of the night in that dusty countryside, was the picture of abandonment. The men showed her the way and told her to be careful, that it wasn't good for a girl like her to be walking alone around there so late at night. She just said thank you and continued on her way, disappearing from view behind a stone wall silhouetted on top of a rise. Almost immediately we heard a mad-woman's laugh and sort of shriek that made our hair stand on end. The fishermen said, "Holy Mary, it was the Ciguanaba." But then one of them suddenly snapped the terror that had come over everybody saying, "Look at the net it's filled with fish." And it was true...⁵²

The apparent reason for this seeming contradiction is Dalton's attempt to imbue the story with literary value and to provide reference points that his Salvadoran readers would recognize and enjoy, even if some of them opposed Mármol's and Dalton's politics. In chapter 7 of the final version, for example, Mármol is describing his time in Zacatecoluca while fleeing the Matanza. In the middle of his narrative, he supposedly says, "I don't know why in El Salvador the great political problems always happen at the same time as earthquakes, floods and other catastrophes."⁵³ But no reference to this idea appears in the notebook, suggesting that Dalton inserted it as a literary device.

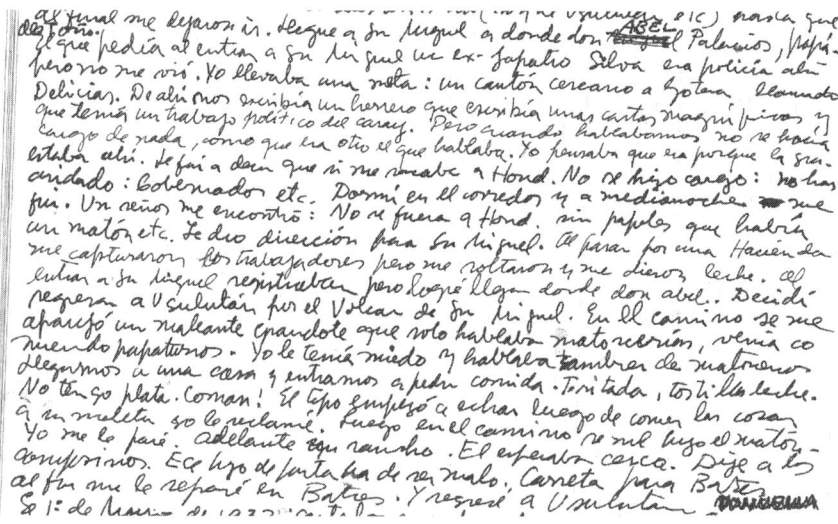

4–12 A page of Dalton's original notebook (cuaderno)

The issue of homosexuality and an apparent homophobic comment by Mármol reveal another example of augmentation by Dalton. During his visit to Russia in 1930, Mármol was supposedly taken to the ballet by his Russian caretakers where he saw male ballet dancers for the first time. The published version portrays Mármol as being offended by them and accusing them of being effeminate.

> The ballet has never really excited me and the Soviet ballet dancers, in spite of everything and though they're Soviets, don't change my mind. For me, to be a ballet dancer means being effeminate and when they come out on stage leaping, shaking their firm little asses, it makes me want to shout out something obscene.[54]

But the notebooks make no mention of this issue. The point at which this issue should have appeared in the notebooks is when Mármol refers to receiving his sixteen-ruble subsidy.

> We went to the Opera. I never missed a meeting, other comrades used to date the soviet girls. It caused me to

appreciate: the Argentine anarchists carried me on their shoulders. There were people being observed: anarchists, etc. We were given 16 rubles every 4 days.⁵⁵ [see image 4-13]

Not only does this quote reveal that Mármol went to the opera rather than the ballet, but also it makes no reference to the issue of effeminate men or remarks about shaking body parts. This part of the text originated entirely with Dalton, which follows examples of other homophobic remarks found in his literary work. One such example is contained in the lengthy poem "Viejuemierda" (Old shit), which Dalton wrote in 1974. It critiques the Salvadoran philosopher of the 1920s and 1930s, Alberto Masferrer, who Dalton considered a nonradical sellout to the bourgeoisie. As part of the critique, Dalton placed Masferrer in the same antiworker camp as the Salvadoran government and its Ministry of Foreign Relations, which he described in oddly homophobic terms:

> ...and the homosexual cults of Foreign Relations
> spew forth into the spiritual depths of our youth
> to squelch their rebellion⁵⁶

Other instances of Dalton adding words to Mármol's voice come in the form of descriptions of scenes that would have required Mármol to be physically present to observe them, when, in fact, he could not possibly have been present. A clear example comes from the disturbing story of the execution of prisoners by the governor of San Miguel Department, General Ochoa. The final published version of *Miguel Mármol* quotes the general directly.

> General Ochoa, who was the governor of San Miguel, forced the arrested men to crawl on their knees up to where he was sitting in a chair, in the courtyard of the barracks, and he'd tell them: "Come here, smell my pistol." The prisoners begged him in the name of God and their children, crying and pleading with him, since before entering the courtyard they had heard intermittent gunshots. But the barbarian general insisted and convinced them: "If you don't sniff the

pistol it's because you're a communist and afraid. The one who has nothing to hide, fears nothing." The peasant sniffed the barrel and right there the general put a bullet in his face. Then he'd say, "Send in the next one."[57]

This story of Ochoa is based on a single sentence in the notebook:

> 5) General Ochoa (Governor of San Miguel). Come smell the pistol. No, general. Smell it, I say, I'm not going to do anything to you.[58] [see image 4-14]

In this example, Dalton not only turned a single sentence into an entire paragraph, adding literary flourish to the text, but also he described the events in San Miguel as if Mármol had been present in the barracks listening to Ochoa speak. But Mármol was not present. Most likely, the story of Ochoa's execution had been passed around and handed down over time. Mármol may have heard it either back in 1932 or at some point afterward and related it to Dalton as an indisputable fact. At least five other examples of narrative reconfiguration of this type are scattered throughout *Miguel Mármol*.[59]

Hidden Quotations

In addition to linear chronology and the addition and subtraction of text, the third form of narrative reconfiguration that Dalton used to create the final version of *Miguel Mármol* is hidden quotations. This refers to the insertion of text from other sources either without citing them or in such a manner that the material weaves naturally into Mármol's narrative. Here again, Dalton was following the pattern he had established in his prior historical writings, *El Salvador* and *El Salvador: Monografía*. By and large, Dalton limited this practice to topics that he considered to be greatly important and that Mármol could not elaborate on sufficiently. One example is the insertion of the infamous "Urgent General Instructions" document into chapter 7 of *Miguel Mármol*. This was a handout that the PCS allegedly produced and distributed in the final days before the uprising to instruct the rebels during the insurrection. It contains an order to be merciless with the bourgeoisie.

4–13 A page of Dalton's original notebook (cuaderno)

4) The revolutionary actions against the bourgeoisie must be as far-reaching as possible with the object, in a short time of merciless terror, of making sure they are reduced to complete impotency, employing against them the appropriate means, that is: immediate execution or death by whatever other means, stopping at nothing.[60]

The notebook makes no mention of this document, but it appears word for word in the final published version, preceded by a short paragraph in Mármol's first-person voice claiming that the document was a fake produced after the insurrection in order to delegitimize the party. The paragraph ends with a smooth transition sentence that makes it seem as if Mármol had the document in his possession in Prague and handed it to Dalton during their interview: "This is that document, down to the last dotted 'I.'"[61] In fact, the "General Instructions" document was first made public in 1946, as a reproduction in Jorge Schlesinger's book *Revolución comunista*. As an anticommunist, Schlesinger used the document to criticize the party and to invoke opposition to the uprising. Recall that most of Schlesinger's documents had been supplied by the Salvadoran military, which supposedly captured them from communists during the Matanza. It is likely that Dalton felt the need to counter Schlesinger by claiming that the "General Instructions" document was an army fabrication. It is possible that Mármol would have agreed with Dalton on this matter, but we do not know. Furthermore, it is possible that Mármol would have known that, in fact, the "General Instructions" document was not a fabrication, as we now know from newly released PCS documents from the Comintern archive in Russia.[62] All we know is Dalton's notes reveal that Mármol mentioned Schlesinger during the interview, and that Dalton claimed Mármol gave him a copy of *Revolución comunista* with his own handwritten notes in the margins. But there is no indication that Mármol expressed an opinion about the "General Instructions" document or that he had it in Prague and was reading it to Dalton.

In addition to reprinting original materials like "General Instructions," Dalton also inserted text from published sources. One of them was Bustamante Maceo's military history of El Salvador, the same book that Dalton had quoted for *El Salvador: Monografía*. Maceo's first edition in 1935 did not mention 1932, but his second edition published in 1951 provided an analysis of the uprising. Dalton included two full pages of text from that second edition in *Miguel Mármol*. Again, the notes offer no indication that Mármol referred to Bustamante or expressed his knowledge of this source. But in *Miguel Mármol*, Dalton has Mármol saying, "There is, for example, one very important official document, among many others that we have, which appears in *The Military History of El Salvador*, by Colonel Gregorio Bustamante Maceo... Colonel Bustamante, referring to the events of '32, says the following." This statement is followed by the long direct quote from the book as if Mármol were reading the passages to Dalton in Prague in 1966.

Conclusion

When Roque Dalton and Miguel Mármol sat down to a series of interviews together in Prague in 1966 they did not have a plan for the outcome of their discussions. They simply recognized Mármol's story as important and potentially useful in promoting their shared commitment to leftist activism. The eventual outcome of that fortuitous meeting was *Miguel Mármol*, a testimonial presented in Mármol's first-person voice. It became a work of great importance: it helped usher in the genre of testimonial literature; it brought the horrors of 1932 to public consciousness like no other work before or after it, and it helped consolidate the communist-causality interpretation of the 1932 uprising. *Miguel Mármol* is a much more complicated text than simply the recollections of a

4–14 A page of Dalton's original notebook (cuaderno)

sixty-one-year-old man looking back on his life in the presence of a transcriber who published his words as a book. In fact, *Miguel Mármol* is more of a collage, reflecting the presence of a wide range of sources and influences. Among these, Dalton was the decisive factor. He subjected Mármol's words (or, at least what he recorded as Mármol's words) to narrative reconfiguration. The process sometimes altered their meaning by adding to them, subtracting from them, and putting them at the service of a plot imbued with political significance. This change in meaning was particularly evident in regard to the interpretation of the 1932 uprising. In theory, Dalton and Mármol did not agree on the lessons that should be drawn from that momentous event, and whether he did it consciously or unconsciously, on purpose or by accident, it seems that Dalton framed Mármol's narrative in a manner conducive to his own emerging militant radicalism and in opposition to Mármol's long-standing support for the party's traditional line.

We do not want our arguments here to be misconstrued. We are not saying that Dalton lied, or that he purposefully misconstrued Mármol's intended meaning, although that remains a possibility. Knee-jerk conservative opponents of Dalton and his politics will likely insist (as they did to us in person during presentations of our initial findings to audiences in El Salvador in 2005) that Dalton was a liar who consciously changed Mármol's story to accord with his own politics. Similar arguments were advanced to diminish support for indigenous peoples' rights in Guatemala during the debate over Rigoberta Menchú's testimonial caused by David Stoll's controversial challenging of her account. Our interest is not to undermine or support Dalton's political positions; in fact, we will show how conservatives also changed their interpretations of 1932 according to their internal ideological debates. Narrative reconfigurations are part and parcel of the social construction of historical memory, particularly in the case of highly charged political topics.

Everything we know about Dalton indicates that he was serious intellectual, who was profoundly political and who considered the study of history to be of major importance. He found himself confronted with material of historical significance, and he passed it along to his audience in a manner that he believed to be compelling. Dalton was trained as a lawyer, and in his own notes to himself, he described his plans for Mármol's story as a "truth-novel," a term that he used to denote "testimonial" before the genre of testimonial literature existed. In hindsight, it appears that Dalton heard what he wanted to hear from Mármol. In this regard, he was no different than any other interlocutor of history; his interpretive framework reflected the constitutive influences of various memory groups. It is just as likely that Mármol's recollection of 1932 had been subjected to a similar process of editing over the decades, and that the story he told Dalton in 1966 was a by-product of this evolving process. But we will likely never know for sure because we do not possess earlier versions of his thoughts on 1932. We only have what Dalton wrote down in 1966 in Prague. When those notes are compared to the final version of *Miguel Mármol*, we are able to see Dalton's transformative process in a tangible fashion. As Dalton's ideological position on El Salvador changed, so too did his understanding of the true meaning of 1932. Dalton's case was not unique.

CHAPTER FIVE

Left-Wing Politics and Memories of 1932

> Los años pasan y son tantas las veces que he contado
> la historia que ya no sé si la recuerdo de veras o si sólo
> recuerdo las palabras con que la cuento.
>
> [The years pass and I've told this story so many times
> I no longer know whether I remember it as it was or
> whether it's only my words I'm remembering.]
> —Jorge Luis Borges, "La Noche de los Dones,"
> *El Libro de Arena*

As Dalton was completing *Miguel Mármol*, political debates within the radical left in El Salvador were intensifying over the issue of armed insurrection. The Communist Party was divided over the question of whether material conditions in El Salvador demanded that the party move to the offensive of armed insurrection or continue along its more defensive path of labor organizing and electoral coalitions. Dalton's considerable rhetorical skills and his prolific writings made him an integral part of the debate, even though he was mostly outside El Salvador in exile. Dalton's work was framed by the contexts of intraleft politics and collective memories of 1932.

The Salvadoran revolutionary left was a heterogeneous group, ranging from moderates to radicals, from armed militants to those who advocated democratic elections, from those who admired the USSR and Stalin to those who abhorred Stalin and drew on rivaling intellectual traditions. But when times were difficult and political confrontations peaked, leftists tried to close ranks and present a unified front. During those unifying moments, the left looked for a common narrative to explain its origins and defend its strategic decisions. But those periods of unity, and therefore the existence of unifying narratives, were the exception to the rule. The civil war (1981–92) was one of those moments, and during that era the left in El Salvador worked diligently, if often unsuccessfully, to downplay its historic factionalism. The guerrilla army that fought the Salvadoran military and its ally the United States during the war, the Farabundo Martí Front for National Liberation (FMLN), consisted of five distinct groups that came together as late as October 1980, barely three months before launching a full-scale armed attack against the government (the first "Final Offensive") in January 1981. In many ways, the formation of the FMLN represented a reunion because it brought back together factions that had split from one another during the 1970s, primarily over the pace and nature of armed insurrection. After the signing of the Peace Accords in 1992, the issue of factionalism continued to plague the FMLN. An older, "orthodox" wing (*ortodoxos*) conflicted constantly with a younger moderate group of "renovators" (*renovadores*).[1] The selection of the late Shafik Handal, a leader of the ortodoxos, as the FMLN's candidate for the 2004 presidential election widened the ongoing divide. Ironically, as secretary general of the Communist Party in the late 1960s and 1970s, Shafik Handal had opposed the militant leftist factions by insisting that the country was not ready for an armed uprising.

At the core of the disputes within the Salvadoran left were interpretations of El Salvador's material conditions and whether they obligated leftists to move to the offensive. The left was divided over the decision to join the uprising in January 1932, and in the next six decades debates over the timing of armed insurrection persisted. In the midst of these debates, the subject of 1932 reappeared constantly as analysts marshaled historical memories of the uprising and the Matanza to defend their respective positions. Political and ideological disputes among leftist revolutionary factions affected the memories of 1932, and those memories in turn shaped the lines of debate for individual interlocutors like Roque Dalton.[2]

The Lines of Debate

"Was there or was there not a genuinely revolutionary situation in El Salvador in 1931–32?" Roque Dalton posed this question in the early 1970s in hopes of determining the lessons that should be drawn from the uprising of 1932. As Dalton's question indicates, the definition of what constituted a revolutionary situation was a constant preoccupation of Marxist groups in El Salvador. Arguably, a core objective of *Miguel Mármol* was to define conditions in El Salvador in the early 1930s in order to analyze the decisions made by the Communist Party in January 1932. Communists believed that defining a society's material conditions, whether in a historic or contemporary context, necessitated an extensive analysis of socioeconomic conditions. The natural reference point was the writings of Marx and Lenin.

Marx's philosophy of history, with its orderly succession of stages, helped revolutionaries visualize a path to a communist utopia. Since prior to advancing to the stages of socialism and communism a society had to pass through preceding stages characterized by class conflict—slavery, feudalism, and capitalism—it was essential to determine where a society was situated on Marx's continuum. The challenge for Marxists was to arrive at a proper understanding of Marx's laws of history and then apply them correctly to their specific case study. However, because Marxism was a basically Eurocentric theoretical model, it did not accord particularly well with the observed reality in places like El Salvador. Subsequently, communists in El Salvador had a difficult time defining their country and deciding on the proper moment to launch the armed revolution. Was El Salvador feudal, semicapitalist, or capitalist? Did it first need to pass through a bourgeois revolution like France in 1789, or was it ready for a socialist revolution like Russia in 1917? The party's official position, that is, the "party line" throughout most of its existence (between its founding in 1930 and its dissolution in 1995) was that El Salvador's material conditions were not ready for armed revolution. This position was supported by the Soviet Union, first through the Third Communist International (1919–43) and then later by Soviet diplomatic agencies. Adherents of the party line both in- and outside El Salvador argued that the country had not advanced sufficiently into the stage of capitalism to justify social revolution, or even if it had advanced enough, the masses had not reached a sufficient level of organization to make armed insurrection plausible. The only moment when this position was changed officially was at the onset of civil war in 1980 when the party argued that material conditions called for revolution. On two other occasions, in 1932 and in the early 1960s, militant factions within the party gained enough support to move a portion of the party toward a more armed stance. But those movements were short-lived failures. Following Lenin's lead, Salvadoran communists defended their varying interpretations of their country with appeals to "objectives conditions," the "objective trends of the historical process," and the "laws of history."[3] But these interpretations left ample room for subjectivity.

As the scientific ambitions of Marxists evolved into debates similar to theological disputes over the supposed true meaning of religious texts, arguments that might have been resolved by persuasion led to acrimonious dispute, factionalism, and even violent clashes. Whose authority should a communist follow? The Communist Party of the Soviet Union? One's own interpretation of Marx or Lenin? Party leaders, who sometimes disagreed among themselves? The Chinese path outlined by Chairman Mao Zedong? The practical example of Che Guevara in Cuba and Bolivia? The situation was compounded by the impatience of some people who thought that the injustices in El Salvador were intolerable and necessitated an immediate response.

In 1965 a Salvadoran communist defended his party's traditional line by dividing the objective conditions of his country into seven categories: Agriculture; Industry; Growth of the Working Class; the Oligarchy; Imperialist Penetration; Economic Integration; and Economic Crisis.[4] After providing copious statistical information under each category, as well as references to the writings of Marx and

Lenin, he concluded that the party's traditional strategy was correct, that the insurrection should be delayed until material conditions in El Salvador were ripe for revolution.[5]

At roughly the same time, another Salvadoran communist, Roque Dalton, argued differently. In an article that he coauthored for *Revista Internacional* in 1967, Dalton quoted Lenin at length and provided a different body of evidence to argue that Latin America was rapidly entering a revolutionary situation, and that revolutionaries must therefore be ready to move to the offensive:

> The circumstance that the revolutionary situation in Latin America has not grown into a series of national revolutions is due not only to objective conditions—and in this sense its duration is not something predetermined. Also factors of a subjective order play an important role. "It is not every revolutionary situation that gives rise to a revolution," Lenin wrote, "revolution arises out of a situation in which the above-mentioned objective changes accompanied by... the ability of the revolutionary class to take revolutionary mass action strong enough to break (or dislocate) the old government, which never, not even in a period of crisis 'falls,' if it is not toppled over." "A revolution may be ripe," Lenin noted in the same connection, "and yet the forces of the revolutionaries may prove insufficient to carry it out, in which case society decays, and this process of decay sometimes drags on for decades."[6]

Many, if not most, conflicts within Marxist revolutionary groups revolved around the analysis and determination of the proper moment to launch a revolution. For the Salvadoran left the study of 1932 became an inevitable point of departure for the discussion.

Factional Disputes Before, During, and Immediately After the Events of 1932

El Salvador's Communist Party was born out of a factional dispute. Its founders were part of a group of young activists in El Salvador's main labor union, the FRTS, who came to believe that the union was insufficiently radical in its ideological orientation. The FRTS was formed in 1924, and by the late 1920s it had roughly thirty constituent unions. With as many as four thousand members, it was by far the largest and most important labor organization in the country. Its main source of membership was workers in small factories and artisans' shops, located mostly in the capital city of San Salvador and the main departmental capitals. As embodied by its leadership, the FRTS was reformist, meaning that it believed that El Salvador's socioeconomic structures had to change to better benefit workers, but it did not believe that capitalism was inherently flawed or that socialism was necessary or inevitable.

By the time of the union's Fifth Annual Congress in May 1929, a group of radical members formed a subcommittee within the FRTS called the Congress of Workers and Peasants. The congress's inaugural charter, heralding its opposition to the official FRTS reformist stand, declared the new group's opposition to all forms of "bourgeois politics" and its advocacy of social revolution. The congress, which became the kernel of the Communist Party in El Salvador, sought to suppress factionalism from the outset. Failure to conform to the organization's stated Marxist-Leninist views was cause for sanction. Before the end of the year, numerous members had been accused of ideological lapses, and many were expelled, including at least two members of the original executive council.

The congress established contact with the Comintern in Moscow, Russia, which responded by sending three operatives to El Salvador to aid the radicals in their nascent organizational endeavors. All three operatives were Latin American, and one of them, a Mexican named Jorge Fernández Anaya, would go on to play a major role in the organization of the Salvadoran Communist Party.[7]

Under Anaya's leadership, the members of the Congress of Workers and Peasants focused their attentions on gaining control over the FRTS. By virtue of diligent campaigning and effective organizing, Anaya and the radicals won control of the union's executive council in the VI Congress in February 1930. One of the new council members was Miguel Mármol and another was Ismael Hernández, who, like Mármol, would go on to hold prominent positions in the Communist Party. Almost immediately, the new leadership began expelling members who opposed the turn to the left. Among those expelled was Luis Felipe Recinos, one of the union's cofounders.

Inspired by their victory in the FRTS, Anaya and the radicals formed the Communist Party in March 1930. During its first few months of existence, the party worked diligently to create cells and recruit members. It established cells in San Salvador, Santa Tecla, Sonsonate, Ahuachapán, and Santa Ana. It located its Central Committee in San Salvador, and within a few months its membership topped one hundred. Most members were recruited from the ranks of the FRTS.

The fact that the radical movement grew directly out of a reformist trade union organization left a debilitating imprint on the Communist Party and made internal ideological issues a priority for its leaders. The concern with ideological purity was reinforced by directives from Moscow. Between 1928 and 1934, during its so-called Third Period, the Moscow-based Comintern ordered all communist parties throughout the world to break ties with nonradical organizations and purify their ranks by eliminating members with suspect ideological views. During its first year of existence the PCS invested a disproportionate amount of time, energy, and resources on internal ideological affairs, or as one member called it, in a "campaign of purification."[8] The campaign lasted until March or April 1931 and involved the monitoring, sanctioning, training, and even expulsion of members. Even after party leaders decided at the end of the year that their members' ideological orientations were sufficiently correct to end the campaign, they remained highly concerned about possible nonradical influences and ideological deviations.

A variation on the conflict over reformism within the PCS was the emergence of an ideological dispute with its sister organization, the International Red Aid (Socorro Rojo Internacional, SRI) and its leader Farabundo Martí. The SRI was another radical internationalist worker's organization with headquarters in Moscow. The Salvadoran branch appears to have been founded shortly after the PCS in 1930. The SRI operated parallel to and in alliance with the PCS, but it had a distinct bureaucratic organization and a slightly different mission. Whereas the PCS saw itself as the organizational backbone of the revolution, the SRI had a more moderate, public face.

Its declared mission was to serve as a sort of communist Red Cross, providing aid to workers who suffered from job losses, wage cuts, and, especially, police repression. Martí took the leadership position of the SRI in El Salvador at the behest of his internationalist superiors in New York, just as he had done in the late 1920s when he went to Nicaragua to serve as secretary to Augusto Sandino during the guerrilla campaign against the U.S. occupation. Like the PCS, the SRI grew steadily in its early months of existence, due in no small part to Martí's mass popularity. Reports from leaders of both the PCS and the SRI reveal that by late 1930, the SRI had twelve locales and three thousand people who promised to purchase membership cards. But the organization's growth was checked by government repression. The same report claims that the SRI went through an organizational nadir between December 1930 and March 1931, when most chapters became nonfunctional due to the government's "intense wave of terror against revolutionary organizations."[9] The report also indicates that the SRI experienced a long period of ideological purification similar to that of the PCS.[10]

Although the PCS and the SRI were allies working toward a common revolutionary goal, they had important differences that operated like a factional split. Much of the dispute centered on the issue of revolution and arguments about whether El Salvador's objective conditions mandated that the radical organizations prepare for armed insurrection. Anaya and the other leaders of the PCS argued emphatically that El Salvador was not ready for revolution. They established a policy of "delayed insurrection," meaning that while armed revolt was inevitable, its day of arrival was somewhere in the unknown future. They were supported in this argument by the Caribbean Bureau in New York and Comintern headquarters in Moscow.

Martí and other members of the SRI disagreed, believing that conditions in El Salvador were ripe for revolution and that the radical organizations should prepare to move to the offensive. Martí's contrarian views served as the basis for repeated criticisms by Anaya, sometimes in direct correspondence with Martí, other times in reports to his superiors. For example in late 1930 Anaya wrote a letter to Martí in which he accused him of ignoring the proper chain of command and adhering to a variety or fallacious ideological positions, particularly regarding the timing of insurrection. In the letter, Anaya repeatedly cited Marx and Lenin to show Martí the error of his ways. In subsequent reports to his superiors, Anaya accused Martí of being an "opportunist." Even at the end of his life Anaya maintained his critique of Martí. In an interview with a Mexican periodical in the 1980s, the aged Anaya looked back on his time in El Salvador and said, "The problem with Farabundo Martí was his impulsiveness. At times I think that was one of the gravest problems we faced."[11]

Unfortunately, the historical record does not offer Martí's personal responses to the accusations against him, but reports from other SRI leaders reveal that such charges did not go unanswered. In one such report to his superiors in New York, Gregorio Ramírez, another SRI leader, expressed his disregard for the PCS, saying its leaders "act like dictators in which what they say is law and nothing else is permitted." He went on to credit the SRI for organizational gains among the working masses, and then he accused "ill prepared communists" of destroying that progress. In elaborating on this critique, Ramírez brought into focus the ideological difference between the PCS and the SRI. He said the SRI understood the goal of organizing to be the creation of a "Bolshevik" party, which could only be achieved by actually organizing the masses into specific unions. In short, Ramírez was accusing the PCS of inaction and failing to take a proactive stance toward organizing the working masses for revolution.[12]

The apparent fact that Farabundo Martí and the leadership of the SRI advocated insurrection in contrast to the PCS does not mean that they organized or led the uprising of 1932. The debates between the SRI and the PCS reflected differences at the leadership level over theory, strategy, and tactics. Neither Martí nor any other leaders of the SRI had a greater ability than their PCS counterparts to lead the western masses in armed insurrection in January 1932. In fact, during the insurrection, the SRI and PCS worked closely together, and Martí was present in San Salvador with the Central Committee of the PCS during the final two weeks leading up to the outbreak of revolt. By all indications, Martí did not bring anything distinct to the planning of the insurrection, neither well-established contacts with the western masses nor an organizational infrastructure that could have served as a template for a military plan.

If the clash between the PCS and the SRI was not over the actual capacity to organize the insurrection of 1932, it nonetheless contained all the elements of an intraleft factional dispute. Each side accused the other of improperly interpreting the writings of Marx and Lenin, incorrectly evaluating the objective realities of El Salvador, and adhering to a flawed strategy. The clash also illustrates the lasting impact of the campaign against reformism that both organizations experienced during their first year of existence. The PCS and Anaya used the same language to criticize the SRI and Martí as they had earlier to attack reformists, such as "bourgeois opportunism" and "adventurism."

The decision as to whether to join the insurrection in January 1932 provided another source of intraleft dispute with potentially long-term consequences. When the leaders of the PCS and SRI learned in late 1931 that an insurrection of potentially massive proportions was going to occur among the western peasantry, they found themselves divided over how to respond. Some leaders welcomed the insurrection and advocated supporting it out of a belief that its existence proved that El Salvador was ready for revolution. Other leaders believed that the uprising was doomed, but insisted that the PCS and SRI had no alternative but to join because they could not be perceived as letting the masses engage the class enemy in combat alone. Still other leaders said that joining the revolt was suicidal because it was not in accordance with Marxist-Leninist principles and the country was not ready. Those who supported joining won the debate in a vote held on January 10. As a result the PCS and the SRI contributed what they could to the insurrection, although significant disagreement remained.

"Comrade H," the surviving member of the Central Committee of the PCS who testified before the Caribbean Bureau in late 1932, commented on the constant disagreement among party leaders before and after the decision on January 10.[13] Miguel Mármol also commented on this issue in his interview with Roque Dalton in 1966. According to Dalton's interview notes, Mármol claimed that various leaders refused to abide by the vote and decided to go into hiding rather than participate in the uprising. Mármol used the term "intellectuals" to refer to these holdouts.[14] The term "intellectual" was a loaded one in radical parlance. It would reappear constantly as a way for one faction to classify and discredit another. Supposedly working-class members of the party labeled ideological antagonists as "intellectuals" or as belonging to the "professional class" in order to undermine their credibility and therefore the validity of their arguments. Thus, the disagreements over the 1932 insurrection established lines of debate that would reappear constantly in the next seven decades.

Comrade H's testimony before the investigative committee of the Caribbean Bureau in late 1932 further consolidated the lines of debate. Based on Comrade H's report and his extensive oral testimony, the investigative committee determined that at the time of the insurrection, El Salvador was not ready for revolution. In the words of "Comrade R," one of the committee's members:

> The CC [Central Committee] had to try to establish a clear understanding of the objective factors and ask the question "is the objective situation, as it is prevailed them, mature for the revolution, for armed struggle for power?" I am certain that if the CC had posed this question before itself and had undertaken to analyze all the various factors which must be analyzed in order to establish whether or not the objective situation in Salvador was mature for a revolution, their answer would have been "no, it is not yet mature."[15]

Among the many factors that went into R's and the committee's conclusion was the fact that Comrade H could not offer evidence that the Communist Party or the SRI had made substantive organizational inroads among the western peasantry. Even when asked specifically to comment on the issue, H did not provide evidence on the existence of rural labor unions or peasant leagues under the party's influence. Instead, H's testimony portrayed the party as desperately trying to insert itself into a leadership role only after the insurrection had become an unavoidable reality, which suggests that the main organizational impetus for the rebellion originated with the western peasants themselves.

By concluding that conditions in El Salvador were not ready for revolution, the investigation committee decided that the party had erred in joining the rebellion. In the words of Comrade R, the decision to join proved that the party was "petty-bourgeois" and "putchist." He also said that the party failed to employ "a Leninist approach and Leninist methods of organizing and leading the mass revolutionary struggles."[16] These are roughly the same terms that the PCS used to attack reformists during its purification campaign and also to criticize Martí and the SRI for their contrary ideological views. Now, in an ironic twist, the Caribbean Bureau was directing the same criticisms back at the PCS for failing to establish an effective leadership over the rural masses so that it could have convinced them not to rebel.

Remembering 1932 in the Aftermath

The repression of 1932 devastated labor and radical organizing in El Salvador. Although peasants in the western countryside were the primary targets of the counterinsurgency, the army also pursued members of the Communist Party and labor unions. Many members of the FRTS, PCS, and SRI were killed. The precise number is not known, but a safe estimate would put the figure at many dozens, if not hundreds. The scattered reports from survivors are chilling. For example, Carlos Castillo, secretary general of the FRTS, escaped to Honduras and sent a letter to New York in May 1932 describing the devastation.

> As you know, El Salvador has seen a most horrendous massacre, some 10,000 campesinos and workers killed in one week. Between the dates January 21 and February 21, some 15,800 have been killed; all family members of those people known as more or less militant revolutionaries have been killed. They have been burning piles of 200 to 400 killed and wounded.

Castillo described his flight to Honduras, during which he was arrested twice. One time he escaped; the other time he was let go by mistake. For three months he waited in Honduras, alone, afraid of being rearrested, and unaware of what was happening back in El Salvador. Finally, he decided to return to El Salvador in May, hoping the Caribbean Bureau had heard from other survivors. He wrote,

"Mail is unsafe, I will make my way back to El Salvador to see what is happening.... Tell me if you have received any information from militants in El Salvador."[17]

After the uprising El Salvador became a veritable police state. Having proven its willingness to employ terror on a mass scale, the government had little opposition to its ongoing clamp down. Although the army had ended its widespread executions in early February, it continued to arrest anyone suspected of political activism. Supplementing its own police, military, and intelligence forces, the Martínez regime had a vast network of informants, or *orejas* (literally "ears") that made organizing next to impossible. Even mainstream political figures were subjected to round-the-clock police surveillance, and some of them were forced into exile, such as the aged former president and advocate of democracy, Pío Romero Bosque, who died in Costa Rica in 1934.[18]

Surviving members of the FRTS, PCS, and SRI went into hiding. Miguel Mármol's story provides an example. According to the version published in *Miguel Mármol*, which corresponds closely to Dalton's handwritten notes, Mármol was arrested in San Salvador shortly after the uprising broke out. He was imprisoned briefly then taken to a roadside on the eastern outskirts of San Salvador and shot, along with a dozen other prisoners. The soldiers assumed him to be dead and left him, but he survived despite being shot four times. Bleeding and disoriented, he made his way home. He nursed his wounds for two months and then headed to the eastern part of the country. He avoided capture for two years by changing hiding places constantly, but eventually a police informant identified him in 1934. He spent the next two years in prison, where he found an array of political prisoners, including military officers whom President Martínez suspected of plotting against his government.[19]

Even for activists trained in clandestine life, the surviving members of leftist organizations found the months and years after 1932 debilitating. The SRI more or less dissolved, never to reappear in the country, and the PCS suffered major reductions in membership and organization. Party cells reemerged, but in isolation from one another and marked by factionalism. Different cells advanced distinct ideological perspectives that often reflected past disputes.

5–1   Miguel Mármol at an unknown location and date, although sometime later in his life, ca. 1960s or 1970s.

Various cells claimed to be the nucleus of the national party and identified other cells as rivals. Correspondence with the Caribbean Bureau and Moscow fell to a trickle, and the letters that did arrive often consisted of cells requesting recognition as the party's leader over other cells. One of the few letters that arrived to New York came from a group of comrades in Santa Ana in 1936 who described the chaotic nature of the situation:

> Shortly after the massacre, small groups of workers and peasants appeared in villages and neighborhoods in the center and western regions of the country; all were autonomous, disorganized and lacking in ideological orientation. They distrusted one another, looked upon one another with suspicion and fought amongst themselves. For example, here [in Santa Ana] four or five groups with communist tendencies exist, but with their own outlooks and initiatives. We have struggled to unite them, but they have refused the

fusion, and we all remain separate and suffering from a terrible passivity.[20]

The party's recovery after 1932 was long, slow, and painful. El Salvador remained under the control of right-wing military dictatorships until 1979, beginning with the thirteen-year reign of General Hernández Martínez (1931–44). The onset of the cold war after WWII exacerbated anticommunist hysteria, and communism remained illegal in El Salvador. Even mildly reformist political parties found it difficult to gain a public profile amidst the steady consolidation of military authoritarianism. In the midst of such circumstances, the Communist Party had no alternative but to remain a modest, underground organization that could try to influence events where possible and hope to avoid a major military crackdown. The party began to recentralize in the late 1930s and early 1940s, and according to some reports, it participated in the mass protest that led to General Martínez's downfall in 1944. The party also had success in gaining an organizational foothold among labor unions in the late 1940s and early 1950s.[21] Indeed, by recognizing its limits and avoiding overextension, the party survived the remainder of the 1930s, 1940s, and 1950s relatively intact. It grew slowly in size, remained a poignant symbol of opposition, and had influence in some labor, political, and intellectual circles. By the late 1950s, the University of El Salvador emerged as a place where party members or sympathizers expressed themselves publicly, which explains why the regime of President Lemus attacked students and occupied the university in September 1960 during a crackdown on opponents.

It seems that little ideological factionalism existed within the PCS during its rebuilding years. By all indications, most party members between 1932 and 1959 agreed that El Salvador's objective conditions were not ready for revolution and that launching an insurrection would have been an error and a betrayal of Marxist-Leninist doctrine. Moreover, most members seem to have realized that the party did not possess the personnel, resources, or organizational capacity to challenge the Salvadoran Army. The Soviet Union and other international communist agencies agreed with this view and encouraged the Salvadoran communists to focus on labor organizing instead of insurrection and even to form electoral coalitions with nonradical political parties in hopes of weakening the military's monopoly on government.

Throughout the rebuilding years, the memory of 1932 remained painful and complicated, and there were good reasons to forget the events. It was not an easy task to turn a failed uprising and thousands of massacred noncombatants by the army into a motivational narrative. Roque Dalton believed that party leaders preferred to ignore 1932 because of its complicated legacy, which resulted in party members having a limited knowledge of 1932 prior to the publication of *Miguel Mármol*.[22] But countervailing pressures existed that encouraged the remembrance of 1932. After all, every communist believed that El Salvador would inevitably pass into the stage of socialism through a violent revolution led by the Communist Party, and regardless of the failure in 1932, the uprising had still been a valiant assault on the elites and the military.

Unfortunately, very few documents exist that illustrate how communists remembered the events of 1932 during their rebuilding years between 1932 and 1959. Luckily, we have found three documents: the report by the Santa Ana comrades in 1936; Rodolfo Buezo's memoir, *Sangre de hermanos* (Blood of Brothers), published in Cuba in 1944, and a document written by Miguel Mármol in 1948 while in exile in Guatemala. Given that the party's strategy remained consistently opposed to armed insurrection during the rebuilding years, one might expect that these three documents would find that the party in 1932 had either not been involved in the uprising or had made a major mistake by inciting the insurrection. But the three documents offer an alternative perspective by crediting the party for its capacity and courage. It would be reasonable to assume that other interpretations of 1932 also existed at the time, but we remain unaware of them. Nevertheless, these three documents illustrate the convoluted nature of the memory of 1932 by showing how distinct contemporary pressures affected historical interpretation.

Analyzing the documents in chronological order, we begin with the 1936 report from the Santa Ana comrades.[23] The goal of their report was to discuss contemporary conditions and the activities of their cell, but its authors insisted that "to analyze the current state of affairs... it is necessary to provide a brief historical overview." They began with the arrival of Anaya to El Salvador in 1929 and dedicated extensive space to the events of 1932.

The authors of the report produced a new narrative of 1932 that differed significantly from Comrade H's testimony before the Caribbean Bureau in late 1932. The authors criticized relentlessly Anaya and the Central Committee of the Communist Party and held them accountable for the terrible failure of the uprising. One of the report's main accusations against party leaders was that they allowed nonradical, petty-bourgeois activists to participate in decision making, especially in the crucial days leading up to the insurrection. The report singled out Luis Felipe Recinos, the FRTS leader who had been expelled for his reformist views back in 1929, as one of these interlopers. According to the report, "The responsibility for the horrendous massacre of 1932 rests, in part, with Luis Felipe Recinos and... Fernández Anaya." The report accused Anaya of promoting "leftist tactics," which meant that he was overly exuberant about armed insurrection and was willing to circumvent the administrative hierarchy in New York and Moscow.

In contrast to Anaya and the PCS leadership, the Santa Ana comrades hailed Farabundo Martí. The report credited him with turning the FRTS in a more radical direction in 1930 and called him, "the most capable of the all the Marxist intellectuals." Martí's only fault, according to the report, was failing to "better analyze the prevailing class consciousness of the comrades that comprised the Central Committees of the P.C. [Communist Party] and FRTS—comrades of inferior capacities—and impose himself on them as their leader in an effective manner." In the eyes of the report's authors, the problem with the rebellion was not the idea of revolt, or the determination of the fighters, but party leaders: "The principal cause of the massacre was the tactical errors of the Central Committee [of the Communist Party]." The implication was clear; had comrades like Martí and the other "true and loyal red soldiers" been in charge, the rebellion might have ended differently.

It would be safe to assume that the Santa Ana comrades were former SRI members who were trying to salvage their defunct organization's ideological stance by recasting it as Communist Party history.

It also seems apparent that the motivation behind the writing of the report was to discredit the claims of other factions throughout the country to the mantel of party leadership. Such an approach involved making outrageously inaccurate claims about Anaya (that he was a "leftist" and cavorted with reformists like Luis Felipe Recinos) and crediting Martí with the organizational work that Anaya had done for the party during its formative stage. It is also possible that the authors of the 1936 report were boldfaced liars who manipulated the past on purpose to achieve their ideological objectives. But it is also possible that they believed every word they wrote in their report. After all, if they had been members of the SRI in 1932 they would have interpreted the uprising in a particular way, one that might have looked very similar to their description in 1936. In the four years after the uprising, they had little contact with other leftist groups and developed their memory of 1932 in isolation. It remains entirely possible that what they wrote in 1936 reflected their genuine beliefs and their conviction that they harbored the accurate version of the party's past and thus were the rightful heirs to the party's leadership positions. Regardless of whether they were lying, the report by the Santa Ana comrades shows that distinct groups of survivors advanced different versions of 1932, which left a convoluted narrative legacy for future generations.

Less than a decade after the Santa Ana comrades sent their report to New York, another leftist activist who survived the massacre of 1932, Rodolfo Buezo, published his version of events in *Sangre de hermanos* in 1944. We want to stress the point that Buezo identifies himself as a former member of the Communist Party from San Salvador, and therefore we might expect that his book would offer an alternative version to that of the Santa Ana comrades, one that rehabilitated Anaya, critiqued Martí, and questioned the decision to rebel in 1932. But instead Buezo advanced a strong communist-causality interpretation that hailed Martí as a party leader. In an interesting contrast to the 1936 report, he ignored internal divisions and celebrated the Communist Party and the SRI equally for having organized the rural masses and instigated the uprising.

In 1948 none other than Miguel Mármol offered yet another version of events. Mármol had taken refuge in Guatemala under the regime of Juan José Arévalo (1944–50), and he was working with the Confederación de Trabajadores de Guatemala (Guatemalan Workers' Confederation, CTG), Guatemala's main labor union. But Mármol's primary concern remained El Salvador, and in 1948 he wrote a detailed overview of labor organizing in El Salvador entitled, "A Brief Historic Overview of the Union Movement in El Salvador." This document was captured in 1954 during the U.S.-supported coup against Arévalo's successor, Jacobo Arbenz, and was sent to Washington, DC, where it remains in the National Archive.[24]

Mármol identified his motive for writing the 1948 document as generational conflicts over the leadership of the PCS. More specifically, Mármol referred to the emergence of a new cohort of party members from "intellectual and professional" circles that were challenging the old working-class militants like himself. Mármol did not identify the precise nature of the disagreement between the two groups, but he said that the new cohort was trying to rewrite the party's history as a failure, as exemplified by 1932, and to hold the old militants accountable for past debacles.

The 1948 document was Mármol's response. In it, he defended the party's past activities and referred to the criticisms against older leaders as "false theories and wrong interpretations." He lauded past radicals' accomplishments, including their ability to successfully organize the western masses in the years leading up to the 1932 rebellion. Mármol's description of the insurrection remained vague, and he did not credit the party for having led it. Without mentioning internal debates, he ignored Anaya, hailed Farabundo Martí, and cited the machinations of the Martínez government as the main cause of the uprising's failure. In other words, Mármol's version of events was similar to that of Rodolfo Buezo in 1944. Later in life Mármol became a consistent supporter of the party's strategy of delayed insurrection, which did not necessarily accord with the arguments he was advancing in 1948. But Mármol found himself in the position of having to defend the historic capacity of the party and its old comrades before a group of young "intellectual" upstarts who were criticizing the party's older leadership. Thus, Mármol advocated an interpretation of 1932 that looked more like the proinsurrectionary line than the official "delayed insurrection" line.

For two decades after the horrendous massacre of 1932, the shell-shocked survivors of the Communist Party approached the events from a perspective that did not question the wisdom of the party's actions and placed the blame for the disastrous results elsewhere, primarily on the brutality of the army and the oligarchy. Largely absent from this approach were questions about whether the situation in 1932 was truly revolutionary. Not coincidentally, the party was not asking itself this question about its contemporary situation and therefore saw no need to ask such a question of 1932. But after 1959, contemporary conditions changed, and some party members began to believe that a revolutionary situation was coalescing in El Salvador. At that point their retelling of 1932 began to include similar revolutionary conditions.

Intraparty Debates in the 1960s and 1970s, and the Consolidation of Delayed Insurrection

Despite the apparent existence of generational divisions within the party over issues of leadership in the late 1940s, no evidence exists to suggest that party members disagreed sharply with one another over the strategy of delayed insurrection. However, the ideological unity of the party was about to be challenged. Castro's victory in the Cuban Revolution in 1959 energized militants who became eager to follow the Cuban example. Suddenly, interpretations of 1932 became highly politicized as debates over the wisdom of pursuing a militant strategy after 1959 became intertwined with analyses of the party's actions back in 1932.

According to various sources, the coming splits within the party over the issues of militancy and armed insurrection followed generational lines, with younger comrades being more anxious to move to the offensive and older comrades believing that El Salvador was not ready for armed revolt. One source is Dalton's homage to Otto René Castillo, his Guatemalan friend and militant communist poet who joined a guerrilla column in Guatemala and was captured and died in prison in 1967. In his homage to Castillo, Dalton portrayed him as a role model for his own party's insurrectionary youth, which should be no surprise given that Dalton wrote his homage to Castillo in 1969 when he was in the process of embracing armed revolt. Another source is the historical overview written by the PCS's Central Committee in honor of its forty-fifth anniversary in 1975. In that overview, the authors criticized their militant youth by identifying them as "petty-bourgeois" intellectuals who lacked a proper understanding of both Marxism-Leninism and El Salvador's material reality.[25] The defenders of the party's strategy of delayed insurrection defined themselves as older party members whose origins lay in the peasantry and working class.

The late 1950s and early 1960s was an inspiring era for leftists of all generations in El Salvador. They had witnessed many dramatic events across the globe in recent years, including the downfall of democracy in neighboring Guatemala at the hands of the CIA, the defeat of the French in Vietnam in 1954, the corresponding increase in U.S. involvement in Southeast Asia, the victory of the Cuban Revolution, and the subsequent Cuban missile crisis, the beginnings of decolonization across Africa and Asia, the consolidation of socialism in China, and the Soviet Union beating its Western rivals into space. Closer to home, the military remained in power in El Salvador and the populism of the 1948 "revolution" was proving vacuous. Many party members in El Salvador started to believe that the Cuban Revolution marked the beginning of a new era of activism in Latin America. The number of militants in the party grew rapidly, and they wanted to follow the Cuban lead and deliver another blow to U.S. imperialism by joining the ranks of the world's socialist states. The fact that most of the militants were young, urban intellectuals lacking military training, weapons, money, or organizational contacts in the rural areas meant little to them. They reasoned that Castro had started with fewer than a dozen men on a remote mountain in eastern Cuba and had marched victoriously into Havana less than two years later.

Shortly after Castro's victory in Cuba, the PCS began to take a more activist stance. The party first organized a front organization, the Frente Nacional de Orientación Cívica (National Front for Civic Organization, FNOC), which allowed party members to be active in mass mobilization. The FNOC participated in the movement that led to the downfall of the Lemus regime on October 26, 1960. Also in 1960, it organized its first military wing since the 1932 uprising, the

Grupos de Acción Revolucionaria (Revolutionary Action Groups, GAR). The following year the party created a second military wing, the Frente Unido de Acción Revolucionaria (United Front for Revolution Action, FUAR), which incorporated the members of the GAR. The creation of the FUAR reveals a growing belief within the party that the combination of the Cuban Revolution abroad and the increased repression by the military at home meant that a potentially revolutionary situation was emerging.[26] One party leader later claimed that party membership doubled in a six-month period in 1962.[27] Nevertheless, the revolutionary wave never coalesced, and FUAR was defunct by the end of 1963.

The fact that the GAR and FUAR came into existence reveals the growing influence of the militant wing of the party and the fact that some party leaders considered armed action plausible. However, the demise of the GAR and FUAR reveals that traditionalists who opposed armed insurrection remained in control of the party. The traditionalists defended the line of delayed insurrection, and they used the memory of the 1932 uprising as a key element to support their argument.

The Central American Contemporary History Seminar at the University of El Salvador in 1963 represented a public moment in the traditionalists' critique of the younger militants. Two of the speakers in the panel that revolved around the event of 1932, Jorge Arias-Gómez and David Luna, defended the party's traditional line. Both Arias and Luna argued that El Salvador's material conditions in 1932 were not ripe for revolution, although they advanced their arguments distinctly. Arias argued that the party lacked the capacity to organize such a massive movement, which challenged the militants' belief that the 1932 uprising provided a precedent for contemporary armed action. Luna took Arias's argument a step further by insisting that even if the party had not been capable of organizing and leading the insurrection, the party nevertheless made the fateful decision to participate. He called that decision a grave error in judgment because conditions were not ready for revolt, so the uprising could only have ended as it did, in failure and massacre. Luna said that the failure of 1932 showed what happens when rebellions occur prematurely, and he took the opportunity to deliver a stinging critique to the young militants: "study more and talk less."²⁸ He closed his talk by citing a personal interview with Jorge Fernández Anaya, the original proponent of the party's line of delayed insurrection, as a main source of information.²⁹

Although Arias was a party member and Luna was sympathetic to the party, neither of them portrayed their presentations at the 1963 seminar as official party positions. Instead, they presented themselves simply as professors at the university with a vested interest in historical subjects. As Luna put it, "I did this study as an impartial observer and I have tried to set aside all subjectivism.... This is very hard because... my sympathy lay with the revolutionary cause, but a historian's work is separate."³⁰ However, traditionalists within the party consolidated their position against the militants with arguments identical to those of Arias and Luna.

The rise of Salvador Cayetano Carpio to the party's highest post of secretary general in 1964 signified the resurgence of the traditional line. Ironically, Carpio had promoted the creation of the military wings in the early 1960s, but he had come into the party through the union movement and believed in the need for widespread mass organizing before embarking on armed action.³¹ Furthermore, he had traveled to the Soviet Union in the early 1960s and returned from there with a renewed opposition to "ultraleftism" and premature insurrections.³² Even more ironic is the fact that five years later, Carpio would lead the first defection from the party over the issue of insurrectionary strategy, leaving Shafik Handal as the party's leader and defender of the traditional position. But when Carpio became party leader in 1964, he represented the traditionalist faction, and it was at the party's Fifth Congress in 1964 that he and the other traditionalists reestablished delayed insurrection as the party's official line.³³ The proceedings of the congress were recorded in *Revista Internacional*, the magazine that Dalton was working for in Prague in 1966 when he met Miguel Mármol.³⁴ Although the proceedings of the Fifth Congress did not mention specifically the 1932 uprising, anyone familiar with Salvadoran history understood what its authors' meant when they wrote, "Experience has proven in El Salvador that premature or adventurous actions can damage the revolutionary movement."³⁵

Another article appearing in *Revista Internacional* in 1965 provided a more specific defense of the party's position at the Fifth Congress. The article was written in celebration of the party's thirty-fifth anniversary, and the author was a major party leader who used the pseudonym Alberto Gualán, a communist who had been killed in the 1932 Matanza. Presumably the author was either Cayetano Carpio or Shafik Handal.[36] The article celebrated the party for its bravery during its thirty-five-year history and especially for enduring constant repression by the military regimes. But the author noted that the party's history had been marked by factionalism and ideological deficiencies.

> The party has been characterized by factionalism because of its extremely small size caused by the Matanza [in 1932], constant attacks by our enemy, insufficient revolutionary experience [among members], and an enormous deficiency in theory. Ideological currents like "workerism" and "intellectualism" have flourished, reducing our unity and fueling factionalism.[37]

The author moved quickly from 1932 to the present day and insisted that the decision to prepare for armed insurrection in the early 1960s represented a moment when poor theory led to wrong policy. The author admitted that conditions in the country were changing and mass activism was on the rise. But he insisted that it was erroneous to interpret those changes as evidence of El Salvador entering into a revolutionary phase. "Party tactics," he said, "were caught up in a leftist fever between 1961 and 1962."[38] He continued:

> Especially prejudicial against our movement was the leftist direction of the line of preparing for popular insurrection, which had been sketched out. Insurrection was being spoken about in the public plaza and in our written propaganda. This created the idea among the masses that the decisive battles for the taking of state power were pending shortly. This was not the objective reality. The decisive actions had not yet transpired.... Also lacking

was a vanguard Party, organically prepared, capable to performing the complex tasks of leading the proletariat and the people in general.[39]

From the author's perspective, party leaders came to their senses by the Fifth Party Congress in time to leave behind the "romantic leftism" and return to "scientific Leninism."[40] The party abandoned armed insurrection and refocused on mass organizing and uniting urban and rural labor in a common cause.[41]

Ten years later, in 1975, the party celebrated its forty-fifth anniversary, and once again its leaders wrote a lengthy historical overview that justified the party's current ideological position. During the ten-year interlude, the party's commitment to the ideology of delayed insurrection had not changed; if anything, it had only grown stronger in the face of serious challenges by militant factions. Just as in the early 1960s, party traditionalists were confronted by internal dissension from militants who believed that El Salvador was ready for armed action. But whereas the debates of the early 1960s had not split the party, the disagreements between 1965 and 1975 became bitter, causing significant organizational realignments. Starting in 1969, factions broke away from the PCS, primarily over the issue of insurrection and the party's refusal to move toward an armed offensive. The fissuring began with no less prominent a figure than the party's general secretary between 1964 and 1969, Salvador Cayetano Carpio, who left the party in 1969 to found the appropriately named, Fuerzas Populares de Liberación Farabundo Martí (Farabundo Martí Popular Liberation Forces, FPL), in April 1970. Successively over the next five years militants severed ties with the party, leaving behind organizational confusion and personal animosity. Eventually, five different radical organizations competed with one another for support, membership, money, weapons, and international recognition.

By the time of the party's forty-fifth anniversary in 1975, its leaders had grown even less tolerant of proinsurrectionary arguments, either contemporary or historic. Whereas in 1965 they had made limited references to 1932, their 1975 overview focused on episodes of past militancy in order to critique them harshly. They said that the comrades in 1932 had led the uprising, but they lacked "preparation, experience and political acumen" and fell victim to an "infantile leftism."[42] Yet, although they believed their forefathers had erred in 1932, they insisted that their courage should not go unrecognized: "Now, 43 years after the 1932 uprising, when the Party has a clear understanding of the errors, deficiencies and weaknesses committed at that time, we nevertheless must offer a fervent tribute to those comrades and true revolutionaries who tried, for the first time, to take power on behalf of workers and peasants."[43] In regard to the period 1961–63, the party leaders in 1975 were less forgiving of the militants, perhaps because many of them were the same people who broke with the party starting in 1969.[44]

Once they had doled out their array of criticisms against militants, the party leaders in 1975 reaffirmed their commitment to delayed insurrection and defended such tactics as forming electoral alliances with nonradical political parties. As just one example of such tactics, the party supported the National Opposition Union (UNO) in the 1972 presidential election. The army's ruling party won that election by resorting to blatant fraud and widespread repression, including the torture and exile of the opposition candidate, José Napoleon Duarte. Notwithstanding such harsh repression, the party remained committed to nonmilitant tactics, and it did so by using carefully selected terms to define El Salvador's objective conditions. They said the country was characterized by "dependent and deformed capitalism," which meant that it was not in the advanced stage of capitalism that would provide the proper environment for launching an armed revolution.[45]

Roque Dalton and the Militant Reaction

Militants in the party bemoaned the results of the Fifth Party Congress and their leaders' increasing intransigence toward the idea of armed action. Eventually, the militants' frustration grew to such a level that they began breaking away to form guerrilla columns. The first to break was the FPL, followed by the Ejército Revolucionario del Pueblo (People's Revolutionary Army, ERP) in 1972. Further splits within those factions led to the formation of the Resistencia Nacional (National Resistance, RN) and the Partido Revolucionario de Trabajadores Centroamericanos (Revolutionary Party of Central American Workers, PRTC), both in 1975.

In their arguments in favor of insurrection in the latter 1960s and early 1970s, the militants included analyses of historic events, especially the 1932 uprising and the turn toward militancy between 1961 and 1963. Roque Dalton defended the militant position. Of course, Dalton had written about the events of 1932 before he broke away from the official party line. He wrote nonfiction analyses of 1932 in *El Salvador* (1963) and *El Salvador: Monografía* (1965). Additionally, he made various references to 1932 and its iconic figures, like Farabundo Martí, in his poetry and prose. And of course there was *Miguel Mármol*. His analyses of 1932 prior to *Miguel Mármol* echoed the interpretations of his mentor Jorge Arias and other party traditionalists. But soon his analyses of 1932 would change.

In 1966 Dalton was in Prague, growing dissatisfied with the party's opposition to militancy. It was in that year that Dalton sat down to interview Mármol. In the next five years he became increasingly committed to the revolutionary option as he completed the manuscript for *Miguel Mármol*. It was this change in ideological position that established the context for Dalton's interpretation of Mármol's story. Dalton the militant interviewed Mármol the lifelong party loyalist about a historic event that presumably stood outside contemporary debates, but in fact had become a central point in an intense intra-party disputes over insurrectionary strategy. *Miguel Mármol*'s promotion of communist causality and its defense of the party's decision to rebel in 1932 were more consistent with Dalton's militancy than with Mármol's oral testimony. Mármol's voice in *Miguel Mármol* deflects criticism of the revolt by saying, "I don't think we should be accused of petty-bourgeois adventurism for having done it [led the rebellion].... I believe these aspects of Salvadoran reality at the time are enough to prove that we were facing a typical revolutionary situation."[46] The notebooks offer no evidence that Mármol made such a claim. Furthermore, the terminology of that claim bears a strong resemblance to how militant party members in the late 1960s defended their growing radicalism against party traditionalists.

One of the most revealing sources that defended the militants' radicalism in the late 1960s and early 1970s is also one of the least known. It is a roughly one-hundred-page, typed, unpublished manuscript of the history of El Salvador's Communist Party that Roque Dalton wrote in Cuba in 1972. The manuscript was a part of Dalton's personal archive provided to us by his family. Presumably, Dalton intended to publish the work or distribute it to his comrades, but his untimely death prevented him from doing so. As an unknown piece of nonfiction writing by Dalton, its value as a historic document is immeasurable. But for our immediate purposes, it provides a strong defense of armed militancy with an elaborate historical analysis. Dalton's analysis bears a strong resemblance to the historic overview written by the party's Central Committee on its forty-fifth anniversary in 1975. Both documents used many of the same examples and defended their interpretations of Salvadoran "reality" with copious references to Marx and Lenin. But Dalton simply interpreted things differently than party leaders, and also differently than he had in his own writings roughly one decade earlier. Whereas party leaders concluded that El Salvador was not ready for armed revolt, Dalton argued that it was time to move to the offensive.

Dalton opened his history with an examination of El Salvador in 1931 and 1932 and insisted that conditions at the time were ripe for revolution. It was, he wrote, "a typical revolutionary situation according to a Leninist definition."[47] Dalton credited the party for having achieved wide and deep organizational ties with the western masses, saying the party "was the indisputable vanguard of the Salvadoran workers; it had sufficient contacts with them to lead them in insurrection."[48] Dalton did not hold back criticisms of the party for devising a flawed plan and for trying to do too much in too little time. But he delivered those criticisms in the context of arguing that the party's main failure was having not capitalized on a genuinely revolutionary situation.

The discussion of 1932 infused Dalton's entire history of the party, so it is difficult to say where it ended and analyses of later periods began. But, in a manner not atypical of his past historical writings, Dalton moved quickly from 1932 to the contemporary era, making it clear that he believed the study of 1932 provided lessons for contemporary debates. Dalton said that throughout the 1930s, 1940s, and 1950s, the party suffered from organizational malaise and was

5–2
Roque Dalton during his exile in Cuba with the poet Roberto Fernández Retamar, ca. early 1960s.

infested with nonradical, "petty-bourgeois" ideological values that hindered its ability to organize the masses. He called this weakness the "*viejo mal*" (old malaise) and even agreed with party leaders in 1965 who argued that the party had erred in going on the offensive between 1961 and 1963 because this "viejo mal" had still been present at the time.[49]

But when Dalton examined the late 1960s and early 1970s, his agreement with party leaders evaporated. He said that it was time for the PCS to become a "party of combat."[50] Dalton based his argument on Lenin's writings, insisting that a revolutionary situation existed in El Salvador and that by not going on the offensive the leaders of the Communist Party were failing to fulfill their historic mission. He commented on the factions that had broken away from the party, including the former secretary general, who "renounced his position accusing party leaders of being too conservative."[51] Dalton closed his history by citing the work of Lissagaray (1838–1901), a participant of the Paris Commune of 1871 who wrote about its bloody defeat by the French state. Dalton quoted Lissagaray's preface that said, "Children have a right to know their forefathers failures," and that the person who "tells false revolutionary legends...is as criminal as the geographer who provides false maps to navigators."[52]

Civil War and Unification

Throughout the remainder of the 1970s, the PCS leadership continued to disagree with its militant rivals that conditions in El Salvador were mature for revolution. As late as 1978 the party's secretary general, Shafik Handal, cited Lenin to explain the party's strategy of participating in electoral coalitions with nonradical political parties: "Lenin wrote: 'One should know how to *combine* the struggle for democracy and the struggle for the socialist revolution, *subordinating* the first to the second. In this lies the whole difficulty; in this is the whole essence.'"[53]

Under Handal's leadership, the party continued to define its primary mission as mass organizing, and it believed that electoral politics and coalition building were appropriate tactics. Accordingly, the party followed up its participation in the UNO coalition for the 1972 election by joining UNO again for the next presidential contest in 1977. Once again, the military won the contest by resorting to widespread fraud and even more extreme repression than it had in 1972. Still, party leaders believed that electoral politics had the chance to succeed, which garnered them the label of "electionists" and "revisionists" by their militant adversaries. The militants pointed to the two presidential elections as proof that peaceful solutions were moribund.[54] Handal later admitted that it was hard to stay the course, "to follow Lenin's wise advice," amidst such savage repression and a growing belief among the masses that the militants were correct.[55] During the funeral of an assassinated member of the party's Central Committee, who was also a deputy in the National Assembly, Rafael Aguiñada Carranza, Handal proclaimed that the party continued to believe, as Rafael Aguiñada did, "that this broad democratic front should be centered on the unity of the working-class movement, on its alliance with the peasants and the more active and organized middle strata."⁵⁶ Even as late as October 1979, the party lent its support to a reformist military coup that deposed the regime of General Romero amid promises of social and economic reform.

But the reformist junta of 1979 proved unable to control the paramilitaries and the army, and social conflict escalated. Popular support for the leftist militants rose, and international conditions, especially the victory of the Sandinistas in Nicaragua in July 1979, suggested the viability of armed conflict. Even the PCS began moving toward armed action in 1979. At its Seventh Congress in March 1979, the party outlined a military plan, and throughout the remainder of the year militants within the party engaged in minor armed actions, mostly around San Salvador, with the intent of accumulating weapons. At the end of 1979, they increased the scale of their operations by destroying a National Guard post and killing ten guardsmen in the town of Santo Domingo in San Vicente Department.

In late 1979 and early 1980, leftist factions explored the possibility of reuniting. The first major step toward what would become the united guerrilla army of the FMLN occurred on January 10, 1980, when most of the factions, including the Communist Party, formed the Coordinadora Revolucionaria de Masas (Revolutionary Coordinating Committee of the Masses, CRM).⁵⁷ They announced its formation at a press conference at the auditorium of the law school of the University of El Salvador. They said they were preparing for a frontal confrontation and they were stronger united than divided. Two months after the formation of the CRM, the Communist Party officially founded its military wing, the Fuerzas Armadas de Liberación (Armed Forces of Liberation, FAL), marking a growing belief within the party that armed conflict was becoming inevitable. Coincidentally, on the same day Archbishop Oscar Romero was assassinated by a paramilitary death squad while saying mass in San Salvador, elevating the level of social conflict to unprecedented heights. Finally, in October 1980, all five of the left-wing factions united for combat by forming the FMLN (named after 1932 communist leader Farabundo Martí) and declaring themselves to be a singular guerrilla army under collective leadership. Shortly thereafter, Shafik Handal reversed fifty years Communist Party policy by saying "a revolutionary situation exists in El Salvador."⁵⁸

Amid the surge in armed mobilization, 1932 became a key symbol. Shortly after the formation of the CRM, the popular movements organized a mass demonstration on January 22, the forty-eighth anniversary of the 1932 uprising. It was later described as "one of the largest popular demonstrations in the country's modern history."[59] When the marchers reached San Salvador's central square, military units opened fire. El Salvador's human rights commission estimated the number of dead at sixty-seven and the wounded at two hundred fifty.[60]

As the PCS began to believe that El Salvador was ready for revolution, so too did it change its interpretation of 1932. No longer was the 1932 insurrection a failure and a lesson, but rather a model of revolutionary determination. After 1979, PCS leaders began describing the uprising in ways familiar to Roque Dalton's portrayal in his 1972 history of the Communist Party. In fact, PCS leaders were even less critical of the party's actions in the uprising than Dalton had been. For example, in a 1980 article explaining the party's decision to join the FMLN and embark on armed action, Handal referred to 1932 as simply "headed by the Communist Party." He provided none of the usual caveats that the comrades had been foolhardy and wrong. Ten years later, in 1990, Handal provided another example on the occasion of the party's sixtieth anniversary in the customary historic overview. Therein, Handal again referred to the uprising of 1932 in uncritical terms, citing the comrades who led it as embodying "the revolutionary character of our Party."[61]

Conclusion

It is no surprise that a strong leftist movement emerged in El Salvador, a country ruled by economic elites and an army willing to use mass terror to defend wealth and privilege. Some of the people who became leftists in El Salvador were poor workers and peasants, often with minimal education, who may or may not have read Marx and Lenin and understood their writings, but nevertheless perceived in socialism or communism the possibility of a better future and freedom from fear. Even Miguel Mármol, a lifelong member of the Communist Party, admitted to Dalton in his interview, "I too read Marx, but what was I going to understand of it?"[62] Other communists were members of the middle and upper classes who were driven to the left not by hunger but rather by a belief that Marxism in its various iterations provided a road map to create a more just society. Still other leftists were not at all Marxists or Marxist-Leninists but still believed that the power and economic structures in El Salvador were unjust and in need of profound change. For those who used a Marxist theoretical framework, arguably the majority of Salvadoran leftist intellectuals at the time, the study of the socioeconomic conditions and the history of the country were preconditions for political activism. The events of 1932 rapidly emerged as one of the most important themes in their historical inquiries.

Contemporary ideological debates inevitably affected readings of history. Historians from the left believed they were engaging in an objective exercise, but, in fact, they belonged to subjectively constituted memory groups that had vested interests in how the past was told. For some memory groups, 1932 provided a model to be followed; for others, it was a lesson in what not to do. The story changed from group to group and from decade to decade. Sometimes the observed shifts occurred in the writings of individuals, as with Dalton between the early 1960s and the early 1970s, and with Shafik Handal between 1975 and 1980. Other times the shifts occurred at an institutional level, such with the intellectual leadership of the Communist Party and its changing approach from Comrade H in 1932, to the Santa Ana comrades in 1936, to Miguel Mármol in 1948, to Jorge Arias and David Luna in the early 1960s, to Shafik Handal in 1980 when the party joined the FMLN. None of these changing interpretations were accompanied by the discovery of vast amounts of new documents or historic evidence. The only thing that changed was the contemporary political position of the authors and the groups to which they belonged. Memory groups sought to legitimize contemporary political positions with socially sanctioned interpretations of the past. Thus, memory was inherently political and politics was based on historical memory.

CHAPTER SIX

Right-Wing Politics and Memories of 1932

> I know not who paints the pictures on memory's canvas;
> but whoever he may be, what he is painting are pictures;
> by which I mean that he is not there with his brush
> simply to make a faithful copy of all that is happening.
> He takes in and leaves out according to his taste.
> He makes many a big thing small and small thing big.
> He has no compunction in putting into the background
> that which was to the fore, or bringing to the front
> that which was behind. In short, he is painting pictures,
> and not writing history.
> —Rabindranath Tagore, *My Reminiscences*

Compared to the left, the Salvadoran right exhibited more ideological and political unity throughout the years. Various right-wing groups may have vied with one another for the spoils of office, but they typically agreed on some core issues, such as elite control and anticommunism. When confronted by a threat from the left, whether real or perceived, they tended to set aside their differences and rally around those basic points of agreement. This unity diminished the need to employ historical references to undermine one another's ideological position. Another important characteristic of the right was its unbroken hold on government power after 1932. Since the fact that thousands of innocent people were killed during the Matanza was hardly something to be proud of, the right was inclined to remain silent on 1932, finding it difficult to reconcile a discourse of modernization with a history of mass murder. The events of 1932 were seldom taught in schools, and before the presidential election of 1967, they were rarely mentioned in political debates or speeches. If right-wing groups were not talking about 1932, they had fewer opportunities to disagree with one another about its meaning and memory.

Notwithstanding this proclivity toward silence, the right also had many reasons to tell the story of 1932. Some on the right felt proud of the events and believed the government had to take a strong stance to defend the fatherland against the threat of destruction. Even rightists who found it difficult to justify the Matanza were not above using the story of 1932 to advance their political and ideological agendas. Furthermore, the right did suffer from internal disputes, despite its tendency toward unity. Rivaling groups tended to recall the past differently. The main reason for disagreement within the right was differing views on whether reform or repression should be the main governing strategy. Advocates of repression believed that any challenge to their ideas or authority must be suppressed, violently if necessary. In contrast, reformers believed that challenges must be met with moderation, even accommodation, because failure to do so only made the problem worse. Naturally, these countervailing tendencies led to differing interpretations of 1932. Hard-liners tended to celebrate Martínez's firm hand, whereas reformers tended to criticize it.

Interestingly, it took longer for a communist-causality approach to 1932 to take hold as a cohesive metanarrative among right-wing memory groups, even among the rabid hard-liners, then it did among leftists. The right had many alternative narratives at its disposal to explain uprisings. Long before 1932, before Karl Marx had even been born, rich conservative Salvadorans had been confronted by mass rebellions and the prevailing social inequality in their society. They had constructed explanations rooted in discriminatory ideas about race, class, nation, and religion to account for rebellious masses and inequalities in wealth. In 1932 the right had these older narratives at its disposal to explain the rebellion and justify their harsh response. Even though conservative society believed communism to be a serious threat in the 1930s, the right found it easy to merge communism with its older explanations. It was not until after the Cuban Revolution in 1959 and the increasing social polarization in El Salvador in the 1960s and 1970s that the right began to unify around communist causality, turning the 1932 uprising into a pivotal moment in the nation's history. But the old narratives did not disappear, and one unintended consequence of their durability was the existence of counternarrative explanations for 1932, especially those that stressed the importance of ethnicity.

In the following pages we analyze three categories of right-wing accounts of 1932: official, semiofficial, and unofficial. Official accounts originated directly from people in power, either in the military or in government. Semiofficial accounts came from individuals who were either previously in government, or were at least closely tied to it. We tend to include newspapers in this second group because even though they were owned independently, the military governments practiced censorship, and more often than not, the newspaper owners were themselves prominent members of the economic elite. Unofficial accounts reflected the perspective of private, nongovernmental persons or organizations that adhered to conservative viewpoints.

Before, During, and Immediately After January 1932

The uprising of January 1932 was preceded by weeks of rising social unrest in the western countryside. Rumors circulated about a looming rebellion, and conservative spokespersons tried to prepare their society for a coming onslaught. They created an atmosphere of fear by describing the events in terms that would scare their constituents. The term "communism" appeared ubiquitously in their descriptions. By early January, San Salvador's daily newspapers provided daily reports on the surge in conflicts between "communists" and the authorities.[1] Once the revolt began, references to

6–1 Headline of the Salvadoran newspaper *El Día* from January 21, 1932, describing the uprising as a "Communist Plot."

communism continued to pour out of conservative channels. The first published reports on the uprising in daily newspapers described the rebellion as communist. Typical examples included the coverage by *La Prensa*, which used phrases like "the communist movement," "red groups," the "red danger," and "the one hundred-headed hydra of communism." Another newspaper, *El Día*, had headlines that read, "The Horrible Crimes of the Communist Hordes" and "The Communist Hordes Were Going to Set Cities on Fire." If there was any definition of communism underlying such accounts it was extremely lax. Instead, their authors used the term communism as a convenient way to incite fears of lawlessness and the mass challenge to elite power. Newspapers appealed to their main readers, middle-class urbanites, by expressing horror at the brutality of the rural people who had taken up arms. A group of policemen in Sonsonate were reportedly killed by "communists [who] took their eyes out of their sockets and placed cigar stubs in the bloody holes."[2] *El Día* published a story entitled "In Tacuba the Victims' Heads Were Thrown to the Hogs."[3]

But the right's use of the term communist revealed some mixed ideas about what communism meant. Many members of conservative society were aware that the difficulties were caused by injustices toward workers in the workshops and on the plantations, and they defined the threat to their society as more material and domestic rather than ideological and foreign-sponsored. For example, on the eve of the rebellion the conservative-leaning archbishop of San Salvador wrote a public letter to capitalists and landowners, warning them that the communist danger would only be averted if they started treating their workers more fairly:

> Workers have not only duties, but also rights that ought to be recognized out of fairness. It is precisely because these rights have been impaired, at the expense of the charity and justice that ought to regulate the relations between bosses [*patronos*] and laborers, that we experience now, with deplorable consequences, the social animosity that alters public peace and threatens the life and interests of the capitalist class.[4]

Furthermore, the right mixed their references to communism with their old narratives, especially those based on race. Once the rebellion had begun, newspaper accounts used terms like "drunken Indians" amidst graphic descriptions of the supposed savagery of the rebels. Such descriptions appealed to traditional Ladino views of Indians as impulsive, untrustworthy brutes. A prominent coffee planter in the western countryside described the rebellion in highly racialized terms in early February 1932:

> Other than one or two [men] who engaged in communist propaganda, I never saw a meeting. But then, to see them the day of the assault perfectly organized, enraged against us, it is something that I consider to be latent in the blood of these people; something that with very little [encouragement] catches fire.[5]

Another example that blended race and communism was an editorial that explained the uprising in terms of a lack of religious instruction. The author argued that the Spanish conquistadors had given the gift of Christian religion to the natives, but then something went wrong by 1932:

What happened to those healthy doctrines, so absent in this horrible struggle where we found ourselves? Who erased the idea of a healing and just God from the spirit of gentle and suffering peasants and workers?[6]

By linking the rebels to the Conquest, the author was labeling them as Indians. He argued that the failure to reinforce religious instruction among them created a moral and ideological vacuum that communists were able to exploit.

Initial coverage of the rebellion exhibited the classic hallmarks of racist and xenophobic tactics in which the rebels were turned into an amorphous "other." The coverage deprived the rebels of individuality and portrayed them as an indistinguishable mass capable of committing heinous acts against virtuous property owners. Every destructive act of the rebels received intense journalistic scrutiny, and victims of the rebels were turned into martyrs, especially if they belonged to the local elite. In comparison, the brutal massacre by the government that followed the uprising was glossed over and described in antiseptic and generalized terms. Stories about it commonly used impersonal sentences or the passive voice. As one newspaper put it, "A great number of communist's cadavers were incinerated in all the places where the movements were repressed."[7] On February 15 *La Prensa* announced blandly, "Peace has been fully restored thanks to the energy of General Martínez's government." Another newspaper described the killings simply as the "restoration of the peace" and limited coverage to concerns over public hygiene: "In order to avoid epidemics the General Health Directorate has ordered the incineration of the cadavers of the communists who died in the confrontations that took place throughout the Republic."[8]

However, newspapers also published more complex descriptions of the events, even though the country was under a state of siege and the press had limited freedoms. The existence of these alternative descriptions suggests a lack of consensus among conservative circles at the time of the uprising. For example, on January 28, with the mass killings in the western countryside still occurring, the newspaper *El Día* published a piece entitled "Is there a Communist Party?" which questioned if "a five-year-old group that had never presented a coherent ideological program for action could be called communist." The author claimed further that "not even the communist speakers could agree among themselves [during the recent elections] as to their collective mission."[9] In fact, the party was only two years old, which makes the editorialist's point all the more valid. A similar perspective was offered by another mainstream newspaper, *Diario Latino*. It questioned the depth of communist influence in the country and suggested that communism was a minor factor in causing the rebellion. The more relevant cause was "the disorientation of the masses, the encouragement of caudillo-type leaders, joblessness, and the fierce selfishness of those who out of nothing try to improvise a position or a fortune."[10]

Such divergent renditions of the uprising emerged from official sources as well. A communiqué from the army on January 27 blamed the rebellion on "communist hordes" and accused them of "murder, arson, assault, the ransacking of defenseless homes, the violation of the honor of women, destruction and theft, in a merciless attack on military and civilian authority."[11] But a few days later, President Martínez offered an alternative description in his speech before the opening of the National Assembly on February 4, less than two weeks after the rebellion had started.[12] He repeatedly used the word "communist" in his speech to refer to the uprising and the rebels. But he was quick to separate the masses of impoverished peasants from the so-called communist conspirators. He condemned the communist "terrorists" for having taken advantage of the simplicity and humility of the rural working poor by offering them "radical" and untenable solutions to their lives of misery. He said the government had done everything in its power to prevent the "terrorist plan," but unfortunately the situation was too far advanced by the time he came to power. Given the "destruction, arson, murder of both honorable and humble people, of civilian and military authorities, the furious attack of garrisons [and] the looting of shops" carried out by "out-of-control mobs," the government had no choice but to react strongly. Martínez said it was "painful" to have had to use "severe measures of military repression," but it was indispensable to protect "society, property, and family." Interestingly, Martínez ignored the issue of ethnicity.

By distinguishing between campesinos and communists and by ignoring ethnicity, Martínez fit the military's actions during the Matanza into a populist program. He portrayed his government as defending the rule of law and protecting all Salvadorans, rich and poor, Indian and Ladino alike. Martínez repeatedly identified the cause of the rebellion as the crisis in "relations between capital and labor," a classic example of fascist rhetoric. Benito Mussolini in Italy and other architects of fascism described the authoritarian state as the only entity strong enough to force capital and labor to collaborate with one another for the betterment of the nation and thereby avoid a dangerous class struggle. Following that model, Martínez said that a strong and interventionist state in El Salvador would "harmonize" relations between class antagonists and solve the problem of communist insurrection. During his speech, Martínez said that the government would respond to the uprising by creating a reform program to benefit the working poor, thereby countering communist organizing and their ability to employ violent solutions. Although Martínez did not detail the plans for reforms in his speech, over the coming months his government unveiled Mejoramiento Social, a program designed to provide social services to poor people. Regardless of the program's modest scale, the government touted it as a great step toward easing social tensions. Even the Communist Party admitted in its internal memos to the Caribbean Bureau that the government's populist tone was well received by the masses.

Martínez's speech was a major contribution to right-wing interpretations of 1932 and demonstrates the complex turns that the intraright debates over 1932 took. Martínez ignored ethnicity, set limits on who could be identified as a communist, and called for social reforms, all of which clashed with other right-wing arguments, both at the time and later. But the fact that the government had responded initially to the uprising with mass killings meant that its credentials as an agent of hard-line repression were incontestable. By referring to campesinos as "ignorant" and "humble," Martínez reinforced long-standing conservative narratives about Indians and poor people, and by labeling the conspirators as "communists," he laid the foundation for the right's embrace of the communist-causality approach to 1932.

Nationalism was another component of Martínez's speech that would contribute to long-standing intraright debates over the meaning and memory of 1932. Martínez promoted himself as a strong nationalist, but strangely in his speech before the Assembly he did not describe the rebellion as being foreign-inspired, nor did he refer to the rebels as agents of Moscow. In failing to do this, it might seem that he missed out on an ideal opportunity to promote his nationalistic credentials. But in fact, Martínez had another, more immediate adversary to his nationalism: the United States. After the coup that had brought him to power, Martínez rejected U.S. demands that he step down. During the uprising, he stoutly refused U.S. offers of military assistance, saying that the Salvadoran Army had the situation under control. In his speech, Martínez continued his hard-line stance against the United States, saying that his regime was legitimate and would not accede to U.S. pressure. He presented his government as a defender against lawlessness and portrayed himself as a proud Salvadoran defying arrogant Americans who presumed to know what was best for his country. A few weeks after Martínez's speech, a group of citizens led by some of the nation's largest landowners and business leaders, signed a letter supporting the president and asking him to cancel efforts to seek diplomatic recognition from the United States.[13] As would be the case half a century later, elites were using nationalism toward the United States to defend their right to impose their will on the rest of the Salvadoran population without international monitoring. But in 1932, the cold war had not yet begun, and the right did not necessarily consider communism to be its most immediate threat, compared to rebellious Indians or a U.S. invasion.

At roughly the same time that Martínez was delivering his speech to the Assembly and the elites were writing their letter in support of him, another major contribution to right-wing interpretations of 1932 appeared. It was Joaquín Méndez's *Los sucesos comunistas en El Salvador* (The Communist Events in El Salvador). Ostensibly, an independent journalistic description of the events, *Los sucesos* is as close to being an official account as it could be without coming directly from the government printing press. Its publication was made possible by direct aid from government agents who granted Méndez access to the region and allowed him to interview whomever he desired.

Los sucesos did not describe the rebellion as having a singular cause, but rather embodied the dichotomy of communist causality and the ethnic "counternarrative." It emphasized the centrality of communism, but it also made constant references to race, exemplifying the diversity of right-wing interpretations of 1932. His informants ranged from deeply racist landowners and anticommunist hard-liners to reformists who considered the cause of the rebellion to be social inequity and even expressed an inkling of shame over the Matanza.[14]

Méndez's local elite witnesses expressed a pervasive fear of losing control over their society. One of his witnesses, the head of a civil guard unit, described a band of "about five hundred individuals screaming, swinging machetes and threatening the town dwellers. They shouted long life to Red Relief International and to Communism and said that the country belonged to them."[15] Following the lead of his witnesses, Méndez's descriptions of the rebels ranged from well-organized communists to bloodthirsty Indian mobs, depending on the witness or even on different portions of the same testimony. One witness put it succinctly, "There is no Indian that is not affiliated with communism"; it was "the nature of Indians to be fanatical."[16] Many of Méndez's witnesses justified the harsh response of the Matanza with long-evolved stereotypes of Indians as ignorant fanatical creatures, at once meek and savage, and always lusting after Ladino women. In fact, Méndez's witnesses often used the image of Ladino women being threatened by dark-skinned, lascivious Indian mobs to mobilize support. We mentioned earlier that one of the most widely circulated rumors in conservative circles was that the rebels had chosen January 25 as the day for a mass rape of the elite women. Conveniently, the date for the alleged plan was the same day when the military regained control of all the occupied towns. Therefore the story had the effect of casting the military as saviors of Ladino women. One of Méndez's informants talked about a fixed date "to choose among the best *señoritas* of the town."[17] "This girl," an army commander told Méndez, pointing at the daughter of a landlord, "was selected to be [Indian leader] Chico Sánchez's wife, she was one of the girls who appeared on the list." More credible reports described the extent of rebel abuses against elite women as forcing them to make tortillas for rebel troops. But in either case, the people who believed the stories of the planned rapes supported exemplary punishments for the rebels, providing an after-the-fact justification for the Matanza.

But in the same way that Martínez's February 1932 speech had reflected the possibility of differing approaches to the uprising within right-wing circles, some of Méndez's government and elite informants described the rebellion in more moderate terms. Without necessarily challenging the open contempt for Indians displayed by most local elites, they suggested that the cause of the uprising had been the deteriorating social and economic conditions in the countryside. Although this approach did not preclude them from arguing that the ignorance of the masses made them vulnerable to communism, it allowed them to equate the social crisis with the need for reform. One of Méndez's informants used an agricultural metaphor to defend the idea of reform, saying that communism was like a seed falling on fertile soil, to end the problem it was necessary to make the land sterile by educating the masses. The governor of the Santa Ana Department went even further by arguing that it was necessary to improve the conditions of the workers. And a former National Assembly deputy argued that it was necessary to "legislate in order to protect the campesino and the worker from the injustices perpetrated by those who have more power."[18]

In sum, before, during, and immediately after the events of 1932, official and semiofficial sources explained the uprising and massacre from a variety of perspectives. Instead of a singular, unified narrative of a heroic army running triumphant over an organized communist insurgency, as would be the widely accepted view in later years, their descriptions included a diversity of issues, including anticommunism, racism, nationalism, the diplomatic crisis with the United States, the Great Depression, the lack of religious instruction, and abuses by local landowners. As later interpretations became more homogenous in accordance with the prevailing political and ideological views of the day, this initial diversity of explanations would make it possible for alternative explanations to survive as counternarratives. However, one consistent by-product of the right's initial descriptions of 1932 was a climate of fear and a rich repertoire of terrifying images that all future right-wing interpreters would rely on in the renditions of 1932.

Military Reformism 1948–1972

The initial flurry of attention that conservative circles gave to 1932 came to a quick end. With each passing year, public discussion of the events became more infrequent and monuments were not erected, either to celebrate or to denigrate the terror. Instead 1932 was left to the silent realm of personal memory and stories shared among family and friends. Under General Martínez, open criticism of the government was dangerous, but, interestingly, praise for his actions after the uprising was also absent. Palace flatterers, potential appointment seekers, and obsequious journalists did not find it advantageous to tell the story of 1932, even in a way that would have portrayed General Martínez as a heroic savior of the republic. A newspaper editor closely associated with official circles during the early period of the dictatorship attributed this silence to shame and to a guilt complex caused by the dimension of the tragedy.[19] But 1932 certainly had not been forgotten, and under proper conditions its memory was invoked as a mobilizing force. One such moment occurred when the Martínez regime fell in 1944.

President Martínez was overthrown by a mostly urban and middle-class coalition after he tried to amend the constitution and allow himself to be reelected to a third term in office. Times had changed, and peoples' willingness to tolerate dictatorship was diminishing as the Allies advanced in Europe and Asia. The demise of Martínez coincided with a similar movement toward democracy in Guatemala, where the Ubico dictatorship crumbled and the exiled reformist, Dr. Juan José Arevalo, was elected in his place. The nearly simultaneous demise of two long-standing dictatorships gave the supporters of democracy hope for a political realignment throughout the region. The prospect of change triggered memories of 1932 throughout all political circles.

Opponents of the Martínez dictatorship pointed to the Matanza as an example of what happens when power is unchecked. A two-part article published in the Costa Rica-based literary and political magazine *Repertorio Americano* expressed this sentiment. The first part appeared in March 1944, when Martínez was still in power, suggesting that the author and/or editors were trying to mobilize opposition to the ailing dictatorship. The two articles amounted to an alternative explanation of 1932, different from Méndez's *Los sucesos comunistas*. The article in *Repertorio* was also based on interviews, but it portrayed the rebels sympathetically.[20] Written under a pseudonym by someone who supported the Communist Party, perhaps a member, the account goes out of its way to describe the motivations of the rebels and humanize the victims of the government. In the description of the mass executions that took place in central square of Nahuizalco, the author wrote:

> The Nahuizalco commander decided that the Indians gathered in the square were threatening to rise up in arms, even though no Indian carried even a needle. Anyhow, he gave the order to put the machine guns to work and without compassion they executed men, women and children. The blood of every age mixed together; the limbs, separated from their bodies, scattered around. One could see the faces of the dead still showing the expression of horror or pain. What is more horrifying, no one could offer even a glass of water to those in agony. In that square compassion was a fault to be punished by death.[21]

As with its predecessors, the account in *Repertorio Americano* used the terms Indian and communist interchangeably. Here, however, the rebels were portrayed sympathetically as the long-suffering victims of a crime, whereas the perpetrators of the massacre were nameless criminals.

If the demise of the Salvadoran and Guatemalan dictators encouraged leftist expressions of sympathy for the rebels in 1932, it also inspired conservative voices that considered social reform and democracy as tantamount to communism. Arguably no work in the entire history of the study of 1932 was more explicit in this regard than Jorge Schlesinger's *Revolución comunista: ¿Guatemala en peligro?* (Communist Revolution: Guatemala in Danger?), published in Guatemala in 1946.[22] Schlesinger used the events of 1932 in El Salvador as a warning to the Guatemalan elite, already incensed by the mild social reforms of the new Arévalo regime.[23] It was a constituency ripe for a retelling of the story of 1932. The author played up the ethnic dimension; it was logical for him to do so since Guatemala was defined by stark ethnic divisions. Schlesinger argued that communists in El Salvador had taken advantage of the political openings under Presidents Pío Romero Bosque (1927–31) and Arturo Araujo (March to December 1931) to organize the ignorant masses, especially the Indians of western El Salvador, whom he described as having a natural tendency to embrace destructive doctrines like communism. Schlesinger's lesson was clear: reformist governments were unable to suppress "anarchist tendencies."[24]

Schlesinger included thirty pages of photographs that supposedly depicted victims of the rebels and bore captions suggesting that the rebels had engaged in widespread killings. Photos of the army's massacre were also shown, but they were described in more neutral or even positive terms. Echoing Méndez's depiction of the alleged plan for mass rapes in Juayúa, Schlesinger embellished the story with images of the "reds" inducing the excesses of the rebel masses. The intent of Schlesinger's book and imagery was to leave his readers afraid about what happens when communists and Indians are not curtailed.

During the four years after the demise of the Martínez dictatorship, the political situation in El Salvador remained much the same. The brief rise of Dr. Arturo Romero as a presidential candidate in mid-1944 provided a glimmer of hope to supporters of democracy, but the conservative coup by Martínez's chief of police, Osmín Aguirre, late in the year ensured that conservative militarism remained the governing norm. But the coup d'état that occurred later in 1948 brought the so-called Revolutionary military regime to power and kept the rhetoric of social reform alive. It also created an opening in which the memory of 1932 could be invoked to support the new rulers and their policies since criticism of Martínez helped to highlight the differences between him and the new regime.

The twentieth anniversary of the Matanza in 1952 provided critics of the Martínez dictatorship with an opportunity to voice their opinions. By that time the leaders of the "Revolution" had consolidated their identity as a new, more moderate variation of military rule. The

Martínez dictatorship was a bitter memory, and the regional tumult associated with the U.S. anticommunist campaign against President Arbenz in neighboring Guatemala had not yet occurred.[25] In the midst of the relatively populist atmosphere in El Salvador, the editorialist of the moderate newspaper *La Tribuna* commemorated the anniversary with a remarkable series of editorials that characterized the events of 1932 as the consequence of an economic crisis. In an even more extraordinary assertion, he noted the indifference of the wealthy classes who lived opulent lives that including travel to Paris, the Côte d'Azur, and Monte Carlo.[26] By identifying elite indifference as a primary cause of the rebellion, the editorialist sympathized with the plight of the Indians and their historic grievances:

> Among us, the communist growth was not the root, it was rather the bloom of a malaise that had been sown much earlier. Just as the Indio Aquino's movement in the past century, it was nothing but a strident protest against the remnants of the period of Spanish colonial domination that still burdened the Indians, in a country that considered itself a democratic republic and had erased from its legislation the word SLAVERY.[27]

The objective of the editorial was to draw parallels between 1932 and the economic conditions of 1952 in order to express support for the spirit of change embodied by the new regime. The editorialist was turning the Matanza into a cautionary tale to advocate social reform.

A pair of examples illustrate that the editorialist in *La Tribuna* was not alone, and that even people closely tied to the military shared his views. The first one is the *Historia militar de El Salvador* (Military history of El Salvador) by Gregorio Bustamante Maceo. The first edition of the book was published in 1935 in El Salvador and did not mention the events of 1932. However, the second edition, printed by the official government press in 1951, ended with a narration of 1932 in which Maceo characterized the uprising as a peasant movement against the Martínez regime, which had dashed their hopes to obtain the land promised to them by President Araujo. The subsequent instability was then "taken advantage of by naive followers of communism to propel the masses to a daring and dangerous adventure." Bustamante then depicted the military's massacres in frank terms. He mentioned summary executions, the lack of due process, the thousands of innocent people who were killed, and the truckloads of cadavers leaving the police stations in which "not even the names of the martyrs were registered by the barbarous executioners."[28]

The second example is a work by Osmín Aguirre Cardona, the son of Martínez's chief of police, Osmín Aguirre y Salinas, leader of the conservative coup in late 1944. Aguirre Cardona studied law in Chile and in 1954 published his graduation thesis on the constitutional history of El Salvador. He dedicated his work to his parents, but he did not mince words in describing his father's former employer as a brutal dictator. His work also provided a fairly sympathetic description of the rebels, but in a way that supported the "Revolutionary" military's rhetoric of reformism. Aguirre described the rebels as trying to "conquer by force the welfare that the state had always denied them."[29] The implication of the statement is clear; if the state provides, then the revolutionary incentive will disappear.

A history textbook used by most of the elite high schools during the era of the 1948 Revolutionary regime (including the Externado de San José, the Jesuit high school that Roque Dalton attended) portrayed Martínez as a ruthless dictator.[30] The author of the textbook informed his readers that the Martínez regime was a "Nazilike dictatorship" and that his government "consolidated itself when he [General Martínez] ordered the execution of 20,000 Indian peasants who had carried out an insurrection that was characterized as 'communist.'"[31]

One reason such frank criticisms of Martínez were allowed after 1948 was the populism of the new military regime. But it is conceivable that the leaders of the new regime could have hailed Martínez as a model populist. They could have defended his Social Betterment program, however limited it might have been, as the inspiration for their own reforms. But the memory of Martínez was too complicated, even among some staunch conservatives. The right might have cared little about the lives of thousands of peasants in the western countryside, but they were less willing to ignore Martínez's repression of hundreds of middle-class protesters in 1944. Even more troubling for them was Martínez's willingness to execute officers after the failed military revolt in March 1944. A clear example of a critique of Martínez coming from the right was written by Jorge Lardé y Larín, the longtime teacher in the military school and the most published historian of the era. Almost all of Lardé y Larín's works were published by the government press, and one of his studies even called the noise of machine-gun discharges against the peasants in 1932, "a balsam of consolation" for honest landlords who had seen their families victimized by pillage and terror. Nevertheless, Lardé y Larín portrayed Martínez as a dictator whose regime was toppled thanks to the sacrifice of the "blood of the heroes and martyrs of April and May of 1944."[32] According to Lardé y Larín, Martínez was not a hero, but his sins were other than the Matanza.

Another reason that highly critical portrayals of Martínez could appear during the era of military reformism after 1948 is that no consensus had yet formed among conservative circles as to whether 1932 constituted a turning point in the nation's history. Conservatives were inclined to emphasize other events when they narrated the country's history, like independence from Spain and the rise of the coffee economy. A lingering sense of shame over the brutality of the Matanza might well have contributed to their willingness to overlook 1932. An example of the lack of consensus can be seen in work of Alberto De Mestas, a conservative Spanish diplomat who represented Franco's government in El Salvador. In the late 1940s he set out to write a book that would offer a general perspective on El Salvador based on substantial research, including conversations with his Salvadoran acquaintances, that is, the kind of Salvadorans who socialize with conservative Spanish diplomats. His perceptions were also shaped by his status as an employee of a firmly anticommunist regime back in Spain. His section on 1932 acknowledges that the uprising had a substantial ethnic dimension, but ultimately he painted the Matanza as an attempt to halt the advance of communism. In his words, "The government forces succeeded in frustrating the Communist plans for El Salvador. Had the latter been accomplished, it would have created a very serious situation throughout Hispanic America."[33] In De Mestas's narrative, the events 1932 are presented as one minor incident among many events in El Salvador's past. He did not consider 1932 to be a decisive nor a foundational moment of the Salvadoran state.[34]

Throughout the 1950s, official sources continued to remain silent on 1932, referring to the events only in euphemisms and veiled language, which suggests that the shame of the Matanza had not dissipated. The memory of 1932 still caused discomfort, and official spokespersons found it difficult to fit them into their descriptions of El Salvador as a modernizing country moving ahead with hydroelectric power, airports, and television and being run by a government sensitive to its peoples' needs. A semiofficial propaganda book published in 1952 to celebrate President Osorio provides a clear example of how the events of 1932 were described tangentially:

> Demagoguery had nurtured a sense of unease, but the problem was deep and old. The tragic, terrible crisis had to happen; the communist masses, naive, ignorant, fanaticized tried to conquer what was not conquerable, even if they had reached their objectives. The consequences did not wait, and the country still tremors at the memory of the sterile, immense sacrifice.[35]

The larger goal of the text was to show that reform and modernization are desirable goals that have to be carried out from above by enlightened rulers.

After the Cuban Revolution in 1959 references to the events of 1932 in right-wing circles became more commonplace and increasingly uniform. Castro's victory caused conservatives to demonize communism and to look for ways to rally the population around its anticommunist program. A remarkable example of this occurred during the political campaign leading up to the 1967 presidential elections, which coincided with the thirty-fifth anniversary of 1932. The elections were held in March, and throughout the preceding weeks the ruling party declared constantly that the country was on the brink of a communist revolt. Not coincidentally, the conservative newspaper *El Diario de Hoy* dedicated one full-page every day between mid-January and mid-February to a sensationalized and gore-filled account of 1932. The first installments were written by Gustavo Pineda, who based his rendition on personal memories and on the work of Jorge Schlesinger. Later installments reprinted original coverage of the events in newspapers and various personal accounts.36 In case any of their readers failed to understand the objective of the stories, the editors of *El Diario de Hoy* explained themselves:

> *El Diario de Hoy* considers it more than appropriate and beneficial to publish writer Pineda's contributions that take the reader, step by step, to see how initial propaganda that could be considered inconsequential at first, can lead to a terrible and painful tragedy, capable of sinking a country like ours into the worst abyss.
>
> We recommend the reading of this series of articles to the Salvadoran public at large, and particularly to sectors of the government, the army, the Church, professionals and students, as well as those who are naive enough to believe in "peaceful revolutions" and in innocent changes to the social and economic structure of a country.37

The newspaper had a precise agenda: to use the proverbial "slippery slope" argument to oppose any social reforms that might be promised in the heat of an electoral campaign. Its reference to "peaceful revolutions" was a direct critique of those members of the ruling military party who supported President Kennedy's Alliance for Progress and were inspired by his famous sentence: "Those who make peaceful evolution impossible will make violent revolution inevitable." *El Diario de Hoy* was playing the 1932-as-cautionary-tale plot by insisting that any deviation from the status quo would lead to disaster.

In addition to *El Diario de Hoy*'s daily dose of 1932, the Salvadoran public was subjected to similar arguments by editorial writers, the Catholic Church, and campaign advertisements. Editorialists warned that the communists wanted to turn all of Central America into another Cuba, and op-ed pages included such titles as "Constitution Yes; Communism No" and "Writing About 1932 Is Relevant Today."38 The bishop of San Vicente, a diocese in central El Salvador, excommunicated in advance anyone who voted for a

6–2   One of the Installments of the series "Tragedia Comunista de 1932" that appeared in the conservative Salvadoran newspaper *Diario de Hoy* as prelude to the 1967 presidential election.

political party that was alleged to have communist influence.[39] To put this fearmongering in perspective, a 1968 CIA document assessing security risks in the region in preparation for a visit by President Johnson described El Salvador's Communist Party as "small, illegal, intimidated and generally ineffective."[40]

In contrast to the election of 1967, the next presidential campaign in 1972 started with a cautious approach to 1932. Daily newspapers did not mention the fortieth anniversary of the uprising, and even the "Today in History" column published in the editorial section of *El Diario de Hoy* failed to mention the events. This is not to say that the characteristic anticommunism of the Salvadoran elite had weakened. By the early 1970s conservative writers had been warning the populace on an almost daily basis about the horrors of Allende's Chile and communist Cuba. A typical example of their approach was a headline in early January that read, "Christmas Without God in Cuba."[41] References to 1932 during the first weeks of the year were mostly tangential.[42] The reason behind the apparent soft-pedaling of the anniversary of the Matanza is that conservative newspapers were saving their most damaging weapons for the last stage of the presidential campaign. Exactly nine days before the election *El Diario de Hoy* began to publish a series of three full-page articles. The series began February 11 under the heading "Forty years ago the communists called to arms and murdered thousands of innocents." Just below the heading, with bold letters, the newspaper implied that a statement made by Napoleón Duarte, the opposition candidate, was a comparable call to arms: "Today Duarte says 'The time for the machetes has arrived...' Will our country live a new 1932?"[43] To answer its own question, the newspaper compared Napoleón Duarte's statement to the "General Instructions" issued by the Communist Party in 1932. Four days later, the second part, entitled "I lived through the 1932 events," included personal accounts of witnesses of crimes committed by the rebels during the uprising. The article illustrated what can happen to law abiding Salvadorans when the peasantry rises up with machetes: "My brother, Samuel Recinos, was castrated and killed with multiple machete blows." The most inflammatory tale was reserved for the last installment published four days before the election. The story began with a witness of 1932 stating that Duarte and his followers were "the same [people] that I heard in 1932, my brother Samuel was killed because of them." Then the witness continued with the detailed description of an alleged collective rape of three hundred white and Ladino girls, some of them as young as four years old. The narrative includes references to the rebels as "wild dogs" and "the vile laughter of the red rapists." The culmination of the event was the moment when "Sánchez, the communist leader of that horde, raped a boy until he killed him."

Differing interpretations of 1932 between the mid-1940s and the early 1970s illustrate that a single elite or state-sanctioned version of the events did not exist. Varying right-wing authors characterized the repression as either barbarous or justified, and the causes of the rebellion to be communism, poverty, or ethnicity. Their solution to such problems ranged from reform to repression. Conservatives neither universally praised nor universally condemned Martínez. The new faction in the military that emerged victorious after Martínez's downfall was more inclined to appeal to the events of 1944 rather than the massacre of thousands of peasants in 1932 as a turning point in the nation's history.[44] The middle-class movement of 1944 seemed more quotable and heroic, and more consistent with the modernizing image of the new regimes, especially the "Revolutionary" government of 1948.[45] Arguably, the massacre of 1932 had eliminated any credible threat of a popular uprising, thus allowing the military to tolerate dissenting views, so long as they stayed within the limits.[46] Yet, images of the uprising were brought out of storage, as heavy pieces of artillery, whenever the ruling elite perceived a serious threat to their hold of power.

Skeptical readers, perhaps those with personal experience living under the military regimes in El Salvador, might dismiss the liberalization during the period 1948–72 as mere window dressing for authoritarianism. However, the fact remains that moderate opposition was tolerated. State-sponsored repression continued, sometimes fiercely, but it was intermittent and selective, directed toward the most radical challenges to the regime.[47] The story of wholesale massacres in 1932 was less useful under these circumstances, and regimes after 1948 were particularly inclined to highlight their dissimilarities with the Martínez era. President General Osorio (1950–54) glorified the 1948 coup d'état each year with public celebrations, and one year he commissioned a large monument based on imagery borrowed from the mural art of the Mexican Revolution. The state's new image was not that of a praetorian guard for landowners, but rather a modernizing group of middle-class officers that had defeated an austere and backward dictator of Indian origins who was influenced by Eastern religions and who had hindered the nation's progress.

However, when the state found it necessary to raise the specter of communism, references to 1932 were always available as a cautionary tale. Nonofficial right-wing circles demonstrated how 1932 could be used to lobby against even moderate reforms. By the early 1970s most of the population had not been alive in 1932, and the "communist threat" had taken on new meaning in the wake of the Cuban Revolution. These new circumstances would encourage right-wing interpreters to close ranks around a more uniform narrative of 1932.

The Hardening of Elite Views, the 1970s

Changing political conditions in the 1960s and 1970s created the impetus for conservatives to gather around a version of 1932 that ignored ethnicity and emphasized communism. The social and political situation was becoming increasingly conflictive. The consciousness of the masses was rising, the left was becoming more vocal and organized, and the international situation after Castro's victory in 1959 seemed threatening. In the early 1970s, the Salvadoran elite's sense of security began to erode with the organization of guerrilla groups after 1970, the failed governmental attempt at land reform in 1976, and increasingly frequent kidnappings and murders of wealthy young businessmen. The elites began to characterize every threat and source of opposition, whether real or imagined, as part of an overarching and carefully orchestrated communist conspiracy. In an official communiqué, the National Association of Private Enterprise (ANEP) portrayed various student organizations and other associations as a conspiracy that wanted to kill "public security agents, assault banks, kidnap to extort and profit, and commit cowardly assassinations." The authors of the communiqué defined such actions as evidence of the activities of "communist fronts at the local, national and international levels." The communiqué closed by urging the government to "put an end to all hesitation and accommodation!"[48] In the same vein, an even more conservative landowners' group, the Frente Agrario de la Región Oriental (Agrarian Front of the Eastern Region, FARO), published a document in the newspapers claiming that there was no difference between Liberation Theology and Marxism, or between Christian peasant organizations, the Jesuits at the UCA (a Jesuit University in San Salvador), and guerrilla organizations.[49]

In their propaganda campaign against the left, rightist spokespersons painted the opposition as savage and inhumane. After a confrontation between government forces and a Christian peasant union in March 1977, the communications office of the presidency fed the newspapers a story falsely claiming that members of the union first "murdered [people] and then forced the relatives of the victims to bite their corpses." The story variously described union members as "beastly subversives," "bandits," and "mobs of men and women."[50] Days later the progressive-leaning archbishop's office, outraged by the salacious nature of the coverage, published the results of its own investigation, showing that the conflict had been provoked by groups sponsored by the government.[51]

The association of coffee processors (ABECAFE is its Spanish acronym) brought their reading of the political moment to its logical conclusion by making a veiled reference to the need for a response similar to that of General Martínez in 1932. In a public statement, the ABECAFE argued, "We believe the time has arrived to understand that internal security has priority over any eventual pressure against the destiny of our fatherland. This was understood many years ago by a government that established the security, peace and internal order of the Republic as primary conditions for the development and prosperity of our country."[52] A respected newspaper columnist felt no need to veil his comments. Sidney Mazzini stated boldly in 1977 that the situation was worse than in 1932 and that El Salvador was facing the prospect of an even greater conflict if nothing was done. After comparing El Salvador to Chile under Allende and to the civil war in Lebanon, he asked the government to abandon scruples and ignore external pressures to respect human rights. Implicit in his message was the idea that authorities needed to repeat the actions of 1932. He believed Soviet imperialism was waiting around the corner, and El Salvador was about to become a Soviet satellite, like Cuba or Angola.[53] If this unveiled praise for mass murder suggests that Mr. Mazzini belonged to an embarrassing fringe of the radical right, he was far from it. A respected lawyer and columnist, he was chosen by President Romero to be the permanent representative of El Salvador to the Organization of American States shortly after he wrote his inflammatory article.[54]

A common thread in conservative arguments in the late 1970s was strong resentment toward the United States for raising the issue of the human rights violations. One well-known conservative columnist in 1977 called President Carter, "the number one accomplice to world communist subversion."[55] The elites considered pressure from the State Department and various human rights organizations to be a violation of Salvadoran sovereignty, just as elites back in 1932 had argued that Martínez should ignore U.S. demands that he resign. In fact, President Martínez's image was being rehabilitated in the late

1970s. He was increasingly remembered as a warrior against communism and as a prime example of an honest military man who defended the status quo. In November 1977 the Military Fraternity of El Salvador held a public homage to Martínez in the Officer's Club. Even today, Martínez appears in the Salvadoran Army's Webpage as one of the nation's most important military heroes.56

In this polarizing atmosphere, both left- and right-wing activists found it advantageous to remind the population of 1932. In July 1977, the FPL, one of the guerrilla organizations, murdered Osmín Aguirre y Salinas, the army officer who had been Martínez's chief of police at the time of the Matanza. Without referring to 1932, *El Diario de Hoy* took the opportunity of Aguirre's obituary to rewrite history and send a message about the political crisis. The newspaper hailed Aguirre y Salinas as a man who had saved the country in 1944 from a totalitarian despotism inspired by Marxism-Leninism. The newspaper was referring to Aguirre y Salinas's coup d'état to stop the election of Dr. Arturo Romero, a moderate reformist politician who represented the spirit of the pro-democracy movement that had toppled Martínez. The obituary had a thinly veiled message: moderate politicians who advocate reforms to avoid revolution actually sell the nation out to communism.57

In the 1950s and 1960s, differing right-wing and establishment versions of 1932 coexisted in textbooks, official publications, and newspapers. But by the 1970s, after the political situation had worsened and an epic confrontation seemed to be looming, conservative versions of 1932 united around the singular narrative of communist causality. As the state felt threatened, any form of opposition was defined as a communist conspiracy, and the solution to the problem was a military reaction similar to that of 1932.

During the War

In 1979 El Salvador was spinning out of control, and events elsewhere in Central America exacerbated the crisis. The triumph of the Sandinista Revolution in Nicaragua in July 1979 inspired the guerrilla movements in El Salvador and sounded a warning to the government, the elites, and the United States. The coup d'état of October 1979, orchestrated by reformist military officers with the support of progressive civilians, represented a last-ditch effort to stop the descent into war by introducing changes in the economic system and trying to stop human rights violations. But the persistence of disappearances and political assassinations proved that the army and paramilitaries were beyond the reach of the reform-oriented junta. After the murder of Archbishop Romero and the victory of Ronald Reagan in the 1980 election, guerrilla groups organized themselves for a frontal attack, and the army responded in kind.

By January 1981, when the civil war began in earnest, the conservative view of 1932 had become devoid of ambiguity. It turned 1932 into an exportable sound bite, ready to be used in national and international debates. One of the most prominent right-wing death squads called itself the Maximiliano Hernández Martínez Brigade, after the president who oversaw the Matanza. On the left, the disparate rebel groups banded together under the name Frente Farabundo Martí para la Liberación Nacional, after Farabundo Martí, the communist leader executed during the Matanza. The secretary general of the newly formed right-wing political party, the Alianza Republicana Nacionalista (Republican Nationalist Alliance, ARENA), was Mario Redaelli, the son of Emilio Redaelli, the prominent citizen of Juayúa killed by the rebels in 1932.[58] These references to 1932 made it seem as though the same enemies were fighting one another again, but according to a new and distorted script that eliminated any of the complexities that had defined earlier narratives.

The few works produced during the war that discussed the events of 1932 emphasized its central role in Salvadoran history. A book by Mariano Castro Morán, a colonel who had been part of the junta that took power in January 1961, provides a good example.[59] He devoted an entire chapter in his historical study of the army to the events of 1932. The chapter is based on well-known secondary sources (although *Miguel Mármol* is not in the bibliography), and it includes twelve photographs. The manner in which Castro Morán structured his story reinforced his argument. The first section is devoted to profiles of seven communist leaders, which the author justified by saying that "their labors represent the beginning of the tragedy that culminated with the bloody events of 1932."[60] The chapter ends with a second section describing the uprising and Matanza, using the traditional style of military historians. Castro Morán related the story as a series of confrontations between government forces and communist rebels. In so doing the narrative presents a stark picture of a state attacked by communist subversion in the form of murder, pillage, and rape. Absent are references to drunk Indians or any mention of ethnicity. Castro Morán justified the repression as a logical consequence of the crimes committed by the rebels and the casualties suffered by the army.[61] When the book was published in 1983, confrontations between the government and guerrilla forces were occurring daily, death squads were killing intellectuals and union leaders, villages were being destroyed by the army, bombs exploded frequently in the capital city, and the country's economic infrastructure was being sabotaged by left-wing rebels. The average reader might have found it unnecessary for the author to draw a direct link between 1932 and contemporary events, but the author wanted to make sure that his objective was clear: "The murders of peaceful and unarmed citizens, the rape and pillaging, the vandalism in the destruction of property, will figure in Salvadoran history as an example of what would have happened throughout the Republic had the subversive communist movement triumphed."[62]

In the United States, the political debate over the war in El Salvador turned bitter. The Reagan administration provided steady support to the Salvadoran Army and described El Salvador as the "line in the sand" against international communism. Critics accused the administration of oversimplifying the nature of the conflict and ignoring human rights violations. Jeane Kirkpatrick, Reagan's ambassador to the UN, helped to formulate the administration's position through references to 1932. One of her many influential writings was a working paper published by the American Enterprise Institute, a Washington, DC-based think tank dedicated to conservative causes. In the working paper, Kirkpatrick used the events of 1932 to illustrate the need for a firm hand to stop communist subversion. The paper portrays El Salvador's political culture as based on machismo and a sense of "competition, courage, honor, shrewdness, assertiveness, a capacity for risk and recklessness, and a certain 'manly' disregard for safety."[63] In such a context, Kirkpatrick described General Hernández Martínez as an "assertive" hero in a

Hobbesian confrontation, the manly champion capable of providing the order "necessary to provide public goods." Kirkpatrick echoed statements made by the coffee processor's association that considered "security, peace and internal order of the Republic as primary conditions for the development and prosperity of our country." "To many Salvadorans," wrote Kirkpatrick on the subject of the Matanza, "the violence of this repression seems less important than the fact of restored peace and the thirteen years of civil peace that ensued."[64] Kirkpatrick continued by describing the "traditionalist death squads" called the "Hernández Martínez Brigades...as seeking to place themselves in El Salvador's political tradition and communicate their purposes." Once again, a highly simplified version of the Matanza dictated a future course of political action. It helped to articulate a conservative position that ruled out the possibility of negotiation. In both the United States and in El Salvador, the new conservative narrative of the Matanza was seen as a metaphor for the current fight.

Postwar Narratives

Once the war ended in 1992, prominent members of the Salvadoran intelligentsia felt free to write memoirs covering 1932 in ways that previously would have been dangerous. One of the most compelling examples is a memoir by Reynaldo Galindo Pohl, who was born and raised in western El Salvador and was the youngest member of the reformist junta in 1948 that toppled General Castaneda Castro. He had a distinguished career that included serving as minister of culture for a short time and as ambassador to the UN for many years. His memoir, entitled *Recuerdos de Sonsonate: Crónica de 1932* (Remembrances of Sonsonate: A Chronicle of 1932), offers a lengthy description of the uprising and Matanza. He portrayed the Matanza as having been incited by collective hysteria rather than by an actual threat to the state. He described the Indian leader Feliciano Ama as being uninvolved in the uprising, and thus his execution was a mob lynching rooted in ethnic tensions. Galindo Pohl's narrative suggests that the alleged cruelty of the rebels depicted in works like Méndez and Schlesinger was inspired by elites trying to justify their actions during the massacre.[65]

More traditional conservative viewpoints were also available after the war, as seen in the competition between the two leading newspapers to produce a history book. In 1994, the two major daily newspapers, both conservative, launched parallel ventures to produce illustrated history books of El Salvador. One of them, *Centuria*, was produced by *El Diario de Hoy*, the long-standing defender of the far right. Its section on the Martínez dictatorship was constructed as a collage that included such descriptions of the uprising as "the communist conspiracy" and the "thousands of peasants who [were]... incited by communist leaders, some armed with machetes, others with Mauser rifles given to them by [former President] Araujo to organize the defense of his faltering regime." *Centuria*'s depiction of the uprising revived the role of the Indians in a manner similar to the blatant racism of Jorge Schlesinger in *Revolución comunista*. *Centuria* described the murder of Emilio Redaelli as having been done "with unspeakable brutality after the gang rape of his wife and the arson of his home by Francisco Sanchez's Indian mob." *Centuria* then referred to the Matanza as a "cleansing" process and described the mass slaughter without indictment: "As the common graves filled up in the western provinces affected by the 'red wave' the communists who appeared in the voting registries were captured in San Salvador and taken to the margins of the Acelhuate River where firing squads of six soldiers executed groups of up to fifty people."66

It seems inconceivable that in a postwar environment one of the leading newspapers could produce a work of such raw viciousness. But the story line of 1932 as a cautionary tale was not losing its political relevance. One of the last sections in *Centuria* mentioned that Miguel Mármol had been one of the survivors of the executions in 1932 and became the first official member of the FMLN when it became a political party after 1992. The link between the past and the present could not have been more explicit. In the next ten years, the issue of communism and the memory of 1932 remained a central component of right-wing political circles. The conservative ARENA party opened each of its national elections in Izalco, a center of the events of 1932. During the 2004 presidential election, ARENA based its attack on the FMLN candidate Shafik

Handal on the idea that he was an unreformed communist fanatic who would link the future of the country to socialist Cuba. Not surprisingly, *El Diario de Hoy* led the charge against Handal. In 2004, the Webpage of the Salvadoran embassy in Washington, DC, stated bluntly, "In the year 1932 he [President Hernández Martínez] represses the first Marxist-Leninist uprising which was supported and financed by the Soviet Union."[67] In January 2005, Izalco witnessed two different commemorations of the seventy-third anniversary of the Matanza. One was held by the FMLN and was geared toward remembering the events in a manner consistent with its traditional narrative about poor masses struggling to create a better life for themselves. The other commemoration was by an Indian activist group trying to draw attention to the long-standing plight of Indian peoples by portraying the events of 1932 from an ethnic perspective. In particular, it cast the Matanza as an attempt at ethnocide, or the elimination of an entire ethnicity. In short, in postwar El Salvador, 1932 remained as vibrant a symbol as ever.

A final example of postwar narratives illustrates that a debate within the right between nationalism and neoliberalism has the potential to affect historical memory. Although established originally on a foundation of stout nationalism, the ruling ARENA party has become an unabashed supporter of neoliberalism and of harboring close ties to the United States, especially during the Bush administrations (2000–2008). But arguably ARENA's traditional nationalism is at odds with such openness to the international economy. The way in which this debate is being played out in historical memory can be seen in the 2005 memoir by David Ernesto Panamá Sandoval, a founding member of ARENA and a close personal friend of the party's founder and archetype, Roberto D'Aubuisson. Panamá is also the descendent of a coffee-planting family from western El Salvador. He describes himself in his book as a "freedom fighter," which refers to his and ARENA's anticommunism.

Panamá opens his book with a description of the 1932 uprising that begins predictably by referring to it as "the first communist uprising in the American continent." But Panamá also revives the "duped Indian" narrative, which reinserts the issue of ethnicity and the ethnic counternarrative back into the explanation:

> Extremist lawyer Farabundo Martí took advantage of the inconformity of the Indians who were being deprived of their lands and were weighed down by the dire economic conditions (the decline of indigo and coffee prices), and on January 22, 1932, he steered them against humble landowners in different municipalities in the western and central regions of the country. On January 23, the supreme government recruited all those willing to fight communism.... The events resulted in a cruel blood bath.[68]

Panamá's description of his social group, western coffee growers, as "humble landowners" would have been unthinkable in the 1960s when coffee planters were at the height of their power. Even more surprising is his reference to the Matanza as a "cruel bloodbath." When he turned to the "lessons of history" that he believed should be drawn from 1932, Panamá's description contains even more surprises.

> This lesson of history and its internal causes have been kept hidden, and those who held the levers of economic power at the time of the events [in 1932] were the great beneficiaries. At the end of the conflict, they said that responsibility for the conflict was externally caused: communism.
>
> The Salvadoran historical evidence shows that, among other things, many of the [country's] great family fortunes originated with ancestors who had held the presidency of the Republic, or with people who had served their [the presidents'] interests. Wealthy people [*el gran capital*] used the armed forces to guarantee that they would enjoy privileges, monopolies and oligopolies, and, as a result of that, myopia lead Salvadorans, thirty-eight years later, to a new, cruel, and useless confrontation between brothers.[69]

This version of 1932 and the description of the civil war in the 1980s as "useless" would be unremarkable if it came from a social democrat or was part of an academic debate. But instead it comes from a founding member of ARENA and an unabashed anticommunist.

These seemingly strange descriptions reflect Panamá's social group uncertainty over ARENA's rapid embrace of neoliberal policies promoted by the United States, such as lowering of import and export taxes, the elimination of subsidies, and even the abandonment of the national currency, the colón, in favor of the U.S. dollar. Coffee growers such as Panamá and his family have watched coffee prices decline steadily, largely due to the rapid growth of production in countries like Viet Nam that have been subsidized by the World Bank. Coffee no longer serves as El Salvador's main source of hard currency. Instead remittance money sent back to the country by Salvadorans living and working abroad holds that honor. Panamá sees this new globalized environment as altering the balance of power in the country. The traditional conservative groups whose wealth was based on export agriculture have been pushed aside by financiers and bankers. The coffee growers are portraying themselves as victims of "el gran capital." They believe that they fought a fierce fight against revolutionary forces in the 1980s and are not reaping the rewards. It is for this reason that Panamá refers to coffee growers as "humble landowners" in both historical and contemporary eras. As he describes it, the contemporary conflict is between "humble landowners in different municipalities in the western and central regions of the country" and "the super rich whose origins are to be found in ancestors who held the presidency of the Republic." Once again 1932 is retold from a contemporary perspective, and this time coffee growers and landowners seem hardly different from the peasants who rose up and were mercilessly crushed by the power-wielding elites and their military allies.

Conclusion

Even though conservatives sometimes found it difficult to justify mass slaughter as a governing model, they nonetheless believed that their vision for El Salvador's future was legitimated by historical truths. At times they found it advantageous to overlook the massacre of 1932 in their historical narratives, but when they did address it, they believed it justified their political ideology. Even though the Salvadoran right has demonstrated a remarkable degree of cohesiveness during the past seventy years, different groups of rightists nevertheless disagreed with one another about the lessons of 1932. Some insisted that the events of 1932 justified a hard-line policy of repression, while others believed it demonstrated the need for reform. In either case, the claims of all the interlocutors of 1932 illustrate the inexorable link between politics and memory. Conservatives used their memories of 1932 to justify their political programs at the same time that unexpected political developments altered those memories without their conscious awareness. They told the stories of the past that they believed to be true, but once again, the question becomes why do people accept one version as true and reject others as false? And the answer, once again, is that politics is based on memory and memory is inherently politicized.

The uprising and the Matanza of 1932 were seminal events that constituted a tragic foundation of the modern state in El Salvador. The story of the events became a basic metaphor that was used by Salvadorans of all political persuasions to understand their society and justify their plans for its future. The Matanza became the ultimate trope, a capacious and highly malleable container, with shifting walls, at times rigid, at times flexible, but always loaded with meaning. As early as 1932 a writer recognized that the events would serve as a potent political symbol for future generations:

> The wicked legend will grow and for these ignorant peoples there will always be a voice that in the moments of danger will blame communism for all the disgraces that afflict them. It is worth reflecting deeply about what happened in El Salvador, because it makes of the word "communist" an instrument of human superstition.[70]

CONCLUSION

> We do not grow absolutely, chronologically. We grow sometimes in one dimension, and not in another; unevenly. We grow partially. We are relative. We are mature in one realm, childish in another. The past, present and future mingle and pull us backward, forward, or fix us in the present.
> We are made up of layers, cells, constellations.
> —Anais Nin, *The Diary of Anais Nin, 1944–47*

More than a century ago, Ernest Renan realized the importance of historical memory to group identity. In a speech delivered at the Sorbonne in Paris in 1882 entitled, "What Is a Nation?" the French historian said that "the essence of a nation is that all individuals have many things in common, and also that they have forgotten many things."[1] Renan believed that the members of a nation were bound together by a shared "soul or spiritual principle." But he also understood that nation building invariably required acts of coercion and violence, which contradicted the high moral principles that the members of a nation touted. Thus, the making of national identity required collective amnesia.

> Forgetting, I would even go so far as to say historical error, is a crucial factor in the creation of a nation, which is why progress in historical studies often constitutes a danger [for the principle] of nationality. Indeed, historical inquiry brings to light deeds of violence which took place at the

origin of all political formations, even of those whose consequences have been altogether beneficial. Unity is always effected by means of brutality.[2]

Renan appreciated the irony that remembering and forgetting are mutually dependent, or that remembering one thing often requires that something else is forgotten. Seldom can the memory of mercy be reconciled with the memory of repressive violence. Furthermore, Renan understood that in the case of group identity, remembering and forgetting are done collectively. In other words, we as individuals forget certain things because the group to which we belong has remembered selectively.

Evidenced by the recent outpourings of studies on collective historical memory, professional historians are embracing the implications of Renan's ideas to an unprecedented degree.[3] Although ranging widely in topics and approaches, these studies have a common argumentative thread running through them: what people *think* happened in the past can be just as important as what *actually* happened. Historians are showing that people often base their contemporary actions on conceptualizations of history in the form of memories. The more distant a person gets from any particular event, the more layered the memories become. Some scholars have even employed the term "postmemories" to refer to ideas about history that are held by people two or more generations removed from actual events.[4] Historians are coming to appreciate that when we study what people think about the past we are often studying "memories of memories."[5] As a result, they have focused increasing attention on the mechanisms, processes, and institutions through which people as both individuals and groups come to possess their memories about the past, and also how people put them at the service of contemporary concerns. As one historian put it, "Memories are like snapshots that capture remembrances at a specific moment and that when the moment changes, these memories also change."[6]

Often, but not exclusively, studies of historical memory focus on collective traumas, such as the Holocaust, the enslavement of Africans in the Americas, the Stalinist collectivization in Russia, the "Dirty War" in Argentina, or the Vietnam war.[7] As Renan understood more than a century ago, the more emotionally and politically charged an event, the more likely it is to have contested meanings and thus serve as a lightning rod for contemporary debates. The present book has been about collective memories of a trauma, the uprising and subsequent massacre in western El Salvador in January and February 1932. Indeed, the 1932 Matanza was one of the single worst episodes of mass killing in modern Latin American history, a dubious distinction given the number of repressive acts that have occurred in the region over the past two centuries.

Whether tragic or joyous, the collective memories of certain events can become so central to a group's identity that they evolve into something akin to a creation myth, a story of origin, or even an original sin. In other words, sometimes a historical subject can become so intertwined with a group's sense of self that none of its members dare ignore it if they hope to maintain legitimacy among their compatriots. Arguably, the story of 1932 has that quality in El Salvador. Despite the strong pressures on people to forget the events or remain silent on them during the early years of the military regimes, references to 1932 steadily become ubiquitous. Now historians of El Salvador cannot ignore 1932 and almost uniformly define it as a turning point in the nation's history. Politicians and political organizations are obligated to stake out positions on 1932 and incorporate them into their public imagery. In the past seventy years the uprising and Matanza provided the vocabulary and the parables for political confrontations, especially during the civil war of 1981–92. Each time a reference to 1932 enters into the public discourse, the idea becomes more solidified that it is the decisive event in El Salvador's recent past.

Not every group or nation has a memory as essential to its members as 1932 is to Salvadorans. In Nicaragua, perhaps it is the story of Sandino and his insurgency against the U.S. Marines, or in socialist Cuba it is the life of Che Guevara. But in the case of El Salvador, to be Salvadoran means knowing that something tremendous happened in late January 1932 in the western countryside. Because the story of 1932 has been so dominated by the argument of communist causality, whenever the memory of 1932 was invoked, the issue of communism arose simultaneously. Conversely, whenever the topic of communism was brought up, the memory of 1932 provided a ready-set bundle of images and passions to frame the discussion. The story is so powerful that throughout the twentieth century different narratives of the events enabled and even spurred political action, either as cautionary tales or as scripts for confrontation. Arguably, one reason communism remains such a focal point of political debate in contemporary El Salvador, even though the cold war is over and most of the rest of the world has left the fight between communism and capitalism behind, is that the memory of 1932 has emerged as a sort of creation myth for the twentieth century. The autonomous and malleable memory of the Matanza has not been exhausted.

Our goal in this book has been to explore how 1932 was remembered by subsequent generations and how these memories intermixed with political and ideological disputes. We have analyzed how different groups in El Salvador constructed narratives of the past that seemed true to them at a certain moment. Our intention has not been to reinterpret the events of 1932 but rather to show why varying groups of people have preferred to remember some aspects and forget others, even though all groups tended to have access to the same body of evidence and sources.

We have shown that the right and left in El Salvador tended to converge on an argument of communist causality, even though we have shown that there were times when many of their members found good reasons to question communism's relevance to the uprising and massacre. The path by which the right and left came to agree on the story of 1932 was far from linear or predetermined. In the immediate aftermath of the events, right-wing interpretations varied. Older narratives of race and class competed with anticommunism to explain the uprising and justify the massacre. Furthermore, differences between repression-oriented rightists and their more reform-oriented rivals resulted in differing interpretations of 1932. Only after 1959, when all rightists began to share the belief that their nation was being threatened by communism, did they coalesce around a common narrative of 1932, one in which the rebels were communists and the Martínez regime (1931–44) had defeated a communist insurgency honorably. Until that time, many right-wing groups found it more convenient to forget Martínez, or at least remember him negatively.

As for the left, the events of 1932 were an ever-present source of factional dispute, right up to the beginning of the civil war in 1981. At the center of intraleft conflict was the need to determine if and when El Salvador was ready for social revolution. Following the models of Marx and Lenin, communists believed that extensive historical analyses were essential to arriving at such determinations. As the most significant rebellion in modern memory, the uprising of 1932 emerged as a focal point of their studies. Even before the 1932 uprising began, the left was divided over whether El Salvador was ready for revolution. The divisions remained when the revolt began. Those who favored joining the rebellion won a close vote over those who opposed, and even after the party decided to join, some members refused to participate because they believed the party lacked the capacity to win. After the uprising, as the left struggled to recover from the devastation of the Matanza, differing memories of the events emerged. One version distanced the party from the events, whereas another one tended to credit the party with leading the uprising. Around 1959, these rivaling approaches to 1932 became increasingly differentiated. Ironically, at that same moment rightists were converging on a shared interpretation of communist causality. Inspired by the Cuban Revolution, leftist militants who believed the time for taking up arms was drawing near celebrated the 1932 uprising and defined it as proof that revolutionary conditions existed at one time and that the party had responded properly by leading the masses in armed revolt. Even if the military crushed the rebellion mercilessly, the militants argued that the failure was the result of poor planning rather than incorrect analyses. Nonmilitant reformists on the left interpreted 1932 differently, either as proof that the party had not been involved, or that the party was responsible for the rebellion but had joined it on the basis of erroneous analyses that could only have ended in failure. As these intraleft divisions grew more pronounced in the 1960s, so too did the different memories of 1932. Not until the left reunited in 1980, after having broken apart in the early 1970s, did it find a consensus to 1932 in the argument of communist causality. The newly united left portrayed their conflict with the right in the

1980s as a reenactment of 1932, in which poor masses in the countryside followed the leftist vanguard into battle against the class enemy and international imperialists. Conveniently, the issue of ethnicity was left by the wayside.

Amidst all these rivaling pressures of interpretation, many alternative approaches to 1932 became plausible in the ensuing decades. Differing accounts emphasized the role of the Communist Party, International Red Aid, long-standing ethnic conflicts in western El Salvador, or more specific indigenous grievances against Ladinos over the loss of land or sexual predations against indigenous women. As suggested by the existence of these diverse and rivaling narratives, influential events like 1932 have complex origins. But attention to complexity blunts raw emotions, and nuanced arguments soften the hard edges of confrontation. Any interpretation of 1932 that weighed multiple causations did not prove useful to those people who needed simple "historical lessons" that they could pass on to a mass constituency in the form of sound bites and emotional appeals. Good slogans, invigorating political shouting matches, powerful speeches at rallies, and effective electoral campaigns demand simplicity. The political usefulness of the Matanza has always worked against the adoption of complex interpretations.

Academic interpreters of 1932, despite their claims of impartiality and being above the fray, were no less vulnerable to the influence of the times in which they were writing. Studies of 1932 have been influenced by the cold war, discussions of modes of production and class conflict in the Marxist tradition, conceptualizations of agrarian mobilization and land tenure following American sociological schools, and, lately, ethnic and gender studies.

If writings about the Matanza have been affected by their historical context for three-quarters of a century, it would be presumptuous to think that the present book and its authors are immune to their times. Just as Roque Dalton's personal history affected his memories of 1932, our personal histories have affected our memories. Our motivation to write about 1932 can be traced directly or indirectly to experiences with the wrenching pain and polarization of Central American politics and warfare in the 1980s. Each of us has had a conflicted relationship with our times and with the story told in this book. Héctor Lindo-Fuentes and Rafael Lara-Martínez were classmates at the same Jesuit high school that Dalton attended, the Externado de San José. Members of their families, friends, and acquaintances became polarized by the war, with some turning to the left, others to the right, and still others trying to remain in the middle. Some went into exile, some were killed, some disappeared, and others thrived as members of the conservative ARENA party. Their Jesuit teachers at the Externado went on to teach at the Jesuit University (the UCA) and were brutally murdered by the army in 1989. Many of the people discussed in the present book were personal acquaintances, and memories of 1932 were often present in family discussions. Erik Ching grew up in the U.S. Midwest, far away from the tragic reality of El Salvador's civil war. But he became interested in Central America as a result of U.S. involvement in the region, and he turned his political interests to academic pursuits. He became versed in the historiography of 1932, and then as part of his dissertation research he went to Moscow after the fall of the Berlin Wall to see if Soviet archives held anything of relevance to El Salvador. There he found the documents of El Salvador's Communist Party, which suggested to him the need to reconsider existing interpretations of the uprising. Further research in El Salvador's archives suggested the need to subject the Matanza to similar scrutiny. Even as the three of us try to evaluate ourselves and take into account what led us to the interpretations contained in this book, we ultimately can't know. We too belong to memory communities; we too are caught up in narrative flows; we too are living with memories of memories; we too try our best to present our arguments and evidence as rigorously as possible.

As revealed by this self-evaluation, the challenge with studying historical memory is determining which factors influence a person's memories at any given moment. We belong simultaneously to numerous memory groups, all of which compete for influence over our ideas about the past. Are we most affected by our families, our peer groups, our political parties, our religious affiliations, our reading communities, our nations, or some other groups? And if we are able to isolate one or more of these groups and demonstrate their impact on us at a given moment, that influence will likely shift to another group or factor shortly thereafter. Susana Kaiser, a historian of collective memory, found this same challenge in studying the memories of the "Dirty War" in Argentina among second-generation youth who didn't live through the events. She asked, "What is more influential on a teenager, his family's insistence on how terrible this period was, or his peers' encouragement to be apolitical and stop thinking about what happened?"[8]

Take the case of Roque Dalton as an example. We suggested that his personal history played a role in pushing him toward the political left and thus toward particular memory groups of 1932. But isn't it just as possible that the sting of rejection he felt from the Salvadoran elites for being one of their illegitimate sons could have turned him to the far right and led him to adopt an extremist conservatism in hopes of convincing the elites of his worthiness of inclusion? Our study of Dalton and his writings has caused us to be all the more fascinated by this individual. He was a pioneer of his generation in terms of his all-embracing sense of Salvadoran history and his passion to shape his nation's future with words and action. He was a committed intellectual who was driven by a pursuit of historic truth and the desire to apply that knowledge to political programs. Dalton established a precedent of serious inquiry that has been enormously influential in Salvadoran history. His collaboration with Miguel Mármol is the main manifestation of his influence, and a comparison of his original notes from 1966 and the final manuscript in 1972 has allowed us to see how his changing approach to the issue of insurrection affected the shape of Mármol's testimonial. Dalton's shadow follows Miguel Mármol throughout the pages of the famous testimonial, whispering suggestions, signaling directions, at once opening and closing doors of inquiry.

Skeptical readers might argue that changes in historical memory are done consciously, purposefully, by people who seek to put the past at the immediate service of their political interests. In short, skeptics might insist that people lie about the past to achieve their conscious desires in the present. We found this was a common point of inquiry from Salvadorans during a series of lectures and seminars that we presented in the country during the summer of 2005. Salvadorans, in particular, have good reason to approach historical memory from this perspective of intentionality. They lived through a civil war in which propaganda was a central element of the conflict. They saw opposing sides purposefully manipulate the truth in order to mobilize public opinion in their favor. They are right to recognize that people often do manipulate stories of the past for the purposeful intent of promoting a current position. But the analyses in the present book have shown that people tend not to lie. Instead they pursue the "truth" and make earnest efforts to understand the evidence available to them as best as they can. Most people do not want to kill other people or sacrifice their own lives for lies and fabrications. They want to defend righteousness and base their lives on a foundation of accuracy. So the central concern is not why a few people might lie, but rather most people in the form of memory groups accept certain stories as true and reject others as false?

Once again skeptical readers might emphasize the determinant role of elites, political leaders, and intellectuals who control the creation and dissemination of stories in the form of books, articles, speeches, editorials, movies, photographs, art, literature, and so on. But here again, the analyses in the present book have shown clearly that although the narratives of 1932 have been affected by changing dynamics of memory groups and the individuals who lead them, narratives are decidedly not the sole product of authors' conscious intentions, however earnest or deceptive they might be. Instead, memories and the narrative forms they assume have resilient, autonomous characteristics. As discourses, they can shape the way authors, politicians, and intellectuals approach the interpretive exercise, superseding their conscious intentions. This resilience was clearly demonstrated with the survival of the counternarrative of ethnicity. Present from the inception of interpretations of 1932, it was eventually overwhelmed by the communist-causality metanarrative. But it never went away, and it showed up in surprising ways and in unexpected places—like Schlesinger's right-wing anticommunist analysis in 1946, and in David Luna's leftist but anti-insurrectionary approach in 1963.[9]

If we take Schelsinger as an example, we can see clearly how narratives have autonomy. Schlesinger, a devout anticommunist, but also an unrepentant racist, emphasized the role of Indians in the 1932 uprising on the assumption that their essentialized racial natures explained their proclivity toward destructive ideologies like communism. A few decades later his ideological progeny on the right, in the midst of the cold war and a desperate attempt to justify a harsh counterinsurgency campaign, preferred to ignore the issue of ethnicity and focus instead on communism. In short, they had no use for Schlesinger's inclusion of Indians in the narrative of 1932, even if they may have shared his racism. Furthermore, Schlesinger's study would actually be used by emergent Indian groups in El Salvador as a tool in their demand for greater political recognition. They simply rejected Schlesinger's racism and borrowed the remainder of his arguments to write themselves back into the history of the nation and portray the Matanza as an attempt at ethnocide.[10]

What we are trying to show here is that historic narratives are like streams that interlocutors enter and leave, both as individuals and as groups. While in the stream they advance its flow through writings and argumentation, but the stream also sweeps the interlocutors along to places they never intended to go. It is impossible for them to know the myriad influences that went into shaping their interpretive frameworks. Also, it is impossible for them to know how their arguments might be interpreted differently under unpredictable future conditions in the hands of alternative readers. Nor are they able to predict that their own views might change, as we saw with Roque Dalton's interpretations of 1932 between the early 1960s and the early 1970s. Old narratives do not disappear suddenly. They remain alive in the form of written works and personal memory, as latent history, as the historian Jan Assmann put it.[11]

In contemporary El Salvador, the cold war and the civil war are rapidly becoming memories, even "memories of memories" for an increasingly greater number of Salvadorans. As politicians and the media in El Salvador shift their attentions from the threat of communism to the threat of gangs, from singing the praises of export agriculture to promoting free trade, as the local currency is replaced by American dollars, and as the remittances sent by Salvadorans in Los Angeles and Washington, DC, replace land cultivation as the main source of wealth, the memory of 1932 is being subjected to transformative pressures once again.

In the second semester of 2005 the authors of the present book presented advances of their research to Salvadoran audiences. What would have been a dangerous topic only a decade earlier generated widespread interest among audiences as diverse as students of the public university, members of the Salvadoran Academy of History, and people watching historic-oriented programs on public television. The question-and-answer sessions in all these events were lively, yet not confrontational. Neither the members of the communist party nor traditional landowners felt insulted or threatened by the topic. People from all walks of life, some born of Indian families in the areas where the massacres took place, relatives of General Martínez and of Miguel Mármol, made an effort to contact the authors and express their interest. A few months later, the ARENA Party went to Izalco to launch their latest political campaign for midterm elections in March 2006, and an indigenous rights organization announced its plans to commemorate the seventy-fourth anniversary of the Matanza in Izalco in January 2007.[12] As these two examples reveal, the memory of 1932 remains as pertinent today as it ever did, and the debates over the contents of those memories are as contested as they ever were.

Both Renan and Santayana recognize the relevance of historical memory to group identity, although one stresses the importance of forgetting and the other remembering. Neither the issue of remembering nor of forgetting fully explains the way 1932 has been understood. Forgetting the events would have been immoral; remembering them was no guarantee against repetition. On the contrary, *how* they were remembered was an important ingredient in the polarization of the 1980s. We can be certain that as time passes, memories of 1932 and the massacres of the recent civil war will be rearranged in various narratives. How Salvadoran society remembers these events will help to either avoid similar confrontations in the future or guarantee their return.

APPENDIX

DOCUMENT 3-1

Roque Dalton, "Testimony of the Committed Generation,"
La Prensa Gráfica, April 28, 1957

EXCERPT

The following document shows Dalton's early decision to put his art at the service of a larger cause. The writer, not yet twenty-two, was about to enter the Communist Party when he wrote this piece for the cultural section of one of El Salvador's most important morning papers, La Prensa Gráfica. *He wrote it as a response to criticisms and also as a way of explaining the intellectual posture of the literary group to which he belonged.*

... This brings to mind the words of the Spanish poet Eugenio de Nora, which illustrate our position quite well: "There is much argument these days about social poetry. This is ridiculous, ALL POETRY IS SOCIAL. It is produced, or rather, it is written by a man (who, when he is a great poet, relies on and is nourished by an entire people) and it is destined for other men (if the poet is great, to his entire people and even to all mankind). Poetry is something as inevitably social as labor or Law.... Man, regardless of the individual, which is to say Mankind, he is the destination of poetry."

As we have repeated on many occasions in articles, lectures, seminars, etc., the following argument is sufficient to prove the social element in all poetry: Man is a social animal ("It so happens that man, whatever may be the ability with which he cultivates his I, continues to be on all occasions a social unit and not a cosmic unit, similar to plants."—Maxim Gorki). Poetry being an act of man directed to man (in this sense it is communication, even if it could then be argued whether it is not more exact to define poetry as a configuration), it follows logically that it is, then, eminently social. And it is not the case that this is just what certain sectors may believe. It is not that, concretely, we new poets may believe that this is how it is: it is that THIS IS HOW IT IS, even if all those who raise their voice, never clearly defined, in supposed defense of subjectivity and egotistical and nirvanic ivory towerism may not want it to be so or cannot comprehend it.

Let us take a somewhat different tack on the problem and the argument, not out of a desire to keep repeating the same thing until we are blue in the face, but rather out of the desire to get us to understand as clearly as possible.

Art is the creation of man. Animals do not make Art nor do any of the other organisms in the hierarchy of life forms. But man, since taking his place precisely as a social entity, as we have already mentioned, has been born to an "existence based on those of his kind," or rather, to that way of being in which he subordinates his vital method and action to coexistence, understanding that the only possibility for integral survival arises from the mutual and connected subordination of lives.

From this, follows the fundamental basis for considering Art (and therefore Poetry) as creation with ends, as existence in terms of something, as an accessory apparition in all that is.

On this scale, the highest value is the existence of man, whose only possibility for living a full life is to do so socially. To this end, man subordinates the external world (when he makes use of the energy from a waterfall, for example), his ego as an individual (he obeys a judicial order) and his creation (he makes poetry).

All human creation, then, has to exist in terms of man, and man being, for Aristotle, for Marx, for Jesus Christ, and for all of us, a social creature, Art (and poetry) as an eminently human creation has to exist in social terms.

From there then, even those who swear that they are making "pure art" absolutely clean of any social vitality are making in reality, creation in collective terms although in the negative sense. Authentic poetry, we used to say, connects the poet to the man, to Mankind: it sings his struggles, his joys, his sorrows; it denounces his ills, his obvious stumbling blocks. "Pure" poetry, ivory tower-like, subjective and unblemished, silences all of this and because of that it performs a social function: social-lie, social-treason, or, in the best of cases, simple and restrictive social-silence.

Poetry as a social entity is a communication. Its endpoints (production-reception) are two social entities: the poet and the man who reads, the people. Poetry should exist insofar as it fulfills its communication function, and this will be possible for it only so long as it responds to the needs of these endpoints, poet and people, which needs are determined by the existential state of the endpoints. What is the state of man, in the abstract, the concept to which, in the long run, the two endpoints in the relationship set forth can be reduced? One does not have to dig deep to find out: man in the present is completely circumscribed by pain. Ninety-nine percent of Mankind sees that its pain serves as the basis of the ignoble happiness of the remaining few.

Well, then, in our way of thinking, and this is not just another literary phrase, but rather the expression of a concrete attitude, EVERYTHING that exists must be put at the service of the great cause of definitively expelling that pain from man's flank.

And for that reason, Poetry must be there, on the militant front lines.

DOCUMENT 3-2

Roque Dalton, *El intelectual y la sociedad*, 1969

EXCERPT

Twelve years after Dalton wrote the previous piece, he participated in a discussion in Havana, Cuba, on the role of intellectuals in society. By this time he had embraced a militant stance and had become convinced that El Salvador's Communist Party was unwilling to take the necessary step of armed action to liberate the people of El Salvador. The comparison of this text and the prior document shows Dalton's evolution from a young poet struggling to harmonize his artistic inclinations and his political beliefs, and the mature intellectual who had written acclaimed poetry, who had been in prison repeatedly, and who was getting ready to join a guerrilla front. At the time he wrote this, Dalton was working on the manuscript for Miguel Mármol.[1]

... We do not mean to say that a writer is good for the revolution only if he goes to the mountains or kills the Director General of Police, but we do believe that a good writer in a guerrilla army is closer to everything that the struggle for the future means, the advent of hope, etc., meaning the coarse and positive content that so many rhetorical loops have hidden for so long, than one who limits himself, determined to be at the most, the critic of his society who eats three meals a day. Isn't that why, in the Cultural Congress in Havana, we place Che Guevara as our ideal? The way I understand it is that someone who consciously and responsibly states that Che Guevara is his ideal cannot then come around telling tales without ending up being a scoundrel. That is to say, when we talk here of intellectuals, Latin Americans, we are interested in adopting a high level of perspective: that of their responsibilities in the face of the gargantuan task of the Latin American Revolution. Once the principal perspective is accepted (which commits us directly or indirectly to the only viable means of struggle for taking political power in Latin America, that is, armed struggle), then, I repeat, may we analyze concrete cases. And consider, even, how we are going to help those *compañeros* and friends (ourselves, many times) when they intend, or we intend, to follow the course of our Dantesque contemporary history with the criteria peculiar to our old spinster aunts, who insist on repairing old umbrellas, who sin daily by drinking a second little glass of port, and who believed that Fidel Castro couldn't be communist, couldn't possibly be a Marxist-Leninist, because "he is the living visage of Our Lord."

DOCUMENT 3-3
Roque Dalton, *El Salvador*, 1963
EXCERPT

When he wrote this text in 1963 Dalton had already developed a view of the significance of 1932 for the history of El Salvador. In a little more than two pages, Dalton links the forces of imperialism, his country's dependent economic system, an oligarchic political system control, the massacre of 1932, and the inevitability of revolution. The interpretation is fully consistent with the narrative that he would construct in the following eight years in the book Miguel Mármol.²

At the end of the last century and the beginning of this one, capitalism moved into the imperialist stage in its development. The United States, England, and other great powers threw themselves into the conquest of markets and bases for the penetration of their capital.

El Salvador did not escape this phenomenon. First, British, then North American imperialism invaded the country. The first concessions were for the railroads. Little by little, North American imperialism displaced the other powers in the Central American area until it alone remained as the exclusive and dominant foreign factor. In El Salvador, this dependence became definitive through North American control over foreign trade. El Salvador became increasingly dependant on the export of just one product, coffee, to just one market, that of the United States of America.

This factor consolidated the monoculturist deformation of the Salvadoran economy and set the stage for the definitive consolidation of the semifeudal oligarchy.

Imperialism, owing to this economic control, began to have absolute control over El Salvador's national and international policy. This state of affairs crystallized during the government of General Maximiliano Hernández Martínez, following the worker-peasant massacre of 1932, and would be reinforced even further in the aftermath of World War II.

Having clarified the situation of the dominant classes, it is important to point out the shape of the new consciousness of the popular masses with regard to the role that they should take in the new society. Starting in 1910, trade organizations began to appear (Society of Commercial Employees). The Confederation of Workers of El Salvador was founded in 1914 and the Typographical Alliance in 1923, which took the lead in the new proletarian movement. The first peasant organizations emerged in the late 1920s, and in 1929 the Communist Party of El Salvador was founded.

So the ideological struggle changed to a new course, completely removed from old conservative-liberal alienation. The Twenties turned El Salvador into a battleground for new ideas: anarchism, syndicalism, Marxism, Masferrerism (utopian doctrine of the Salvadoran writer Alberto Masferrer), etc. blazed with new flames among the multitudes.

This revolutionary ascent of the people would be cut short by the great massacre of 1932—ordered by North American imperialism and the semifeudal oligarchy—in which tens of thousands of workers and peasants died and democratic organizations were destroyed for many years to come. This bloody event sharply marks—as was pointed out earlier—the unification of the oligarchy, the much greater dominance of North American imperialism in El Salvador, and the investiture of the military dictatorship as the form of government.

The conditions provided by the semifeudalism and semicolonialism that characterized the economic base of the country remained immutable during the thirteen long years of the Martínez dictatorship. With its overthrow from the pressure of the popular forces, several governments followed that had no other end than to consolidate the military dictatorship once again for the sake of maintaining the prevailing social-economic structure.

It would not be until 1950, with the Constitution that would serve as the basis for the government of Colonel Oscar Osorio, that there would be talk of democratic-bourgeois reforms: new labor legislation, social security benefits, the social function of property, etc., which, as in the case of the liberal reforms of the last century, ended up being merely hollow formulaic pronouncements.

With the arrival of the Cuban Revolution, the Salvadoran popular movement started to regain its strength. New organizations emerged, and when all peaceful alternatives were exhausted due to the dictatorial pigheadedness of the oligarchy and imperialism, the flag of armed popular insurrection was raised. In the country, the most prominent democratic Salvadoran organizations are now striving toward this objective, such as the United Front for Revolutionary Action (FUAR), the Salvadoran Communist Party, the April and May Revolutionary Party, the General Confederation of Workers and the organizations of students, youth, women, etc.

In the face of this situation, imperialism, in turn, took power directly on January 25, 1961, installing the Army in a political, executive, and administrative role. Since then, the interests of the oligarchy have been relegated to the background.

The economic crisis is worsening, unemployment is growing, desperation and hunger are gnawing away at the popular masses. And the doors are opening on the second independence—the definitive independence—of El Salvador.

DOCUMENT 3-4
Roque Dalton, *El Salvador: Monografía*, 1965
EXCERPT FROM THE INTRODUCTION

In the introduction to El Salvador: Monografía, Dalton outlined his critique of traditional historiography and the need to write a new history. For him the real El Salvador had always been kept hidden by propagandistic renditions that painted the country in a quaint image and hid the reality of poor people being subjected to control by a ruthless oligarchy. The real heroes of the country were individuals who had fought for the common people. Dalton set out to show how the history of El Salvador was about the efforts of the common people to shape their own future by defying unjust social and political structures. Their heroic struggles, despite obstacles and false starts, had one inevitable outcome: a liberating revolution. The Cuban Revolution showed the way.[3]

The Republic of El Salvador, one of the smallest countries in the world in terms of size, has for centuries been the stage for a social drama of colossal proportions. However, the Salvadoran drama continues to be in large part a drama ignored. The economic powers that exploit and bleed the people of El Salvador have cloaked the true face of the country in a dense veil, trying to hide from the world the backwardness in which nearly three million dispossessed and despoiled men struggle, where the most basic of human rights and the latest advancements of civilization and culture are beyond their reach.

Deceptive advertising has positioned El Salvador before the nations using a showy touristy, picturesque approach, as "a paradise where no one dies from hunger or thirst, nor from cold or heat," when in reality even the most conservative figures show truly frightful mortality rates from malnutrition, lack of medical care, and generalized subhuman conditions in work, housing, and health in general across the country. The bourgeois writers who coined the ridiculous term "the Tom Thumb of America" for El Salvador refuse to talk about problems such as those that for a country with an extremely small territory and underdeveloped economy are inherent in a high population density that is increasing at an awesome rate. Successive Salvadoran heads of state, who are always talking of freedom and democracy, of Christian civilization and continental solidarity, omit from their speeches and reports any mention of the jails stuffed with political prisoners, of the murders in the torture chambers or in the night streets, of the hundreds of people persecuted and exiled. Professors of history and historians take good care not to include reliable references about the true heroes of the Salvadoran people in their seminars or in their textbooks, such as the great nineteenth-century indigenous leader Anastasio Aquino, or about events that are quite revealing because of their tremendous historical impact, such as the terrible massacre of 1932, in which more than thirty thousand Salvadoran peasants and workers were murdered by the repressive government forces in less than a month.

The success of this constant and prolonged labor of concealment and distortion of Salvadoran reality—both of its historical development and with regard to the current concrete situation—is undeniable. The Salvadoran people have been the primary victims and for decades have suffered from gravely warped minds that have kept them from awakening to resolve their basic problems caused by backwardness and submission.

Furthermore, there is almost absolute ignorance in the sphere of international relations and among the peoples of the world about El Salvador's problems, and this even extends to facts about geographical location, customs, and traditions.

Salvadoran revolutionaries understand that the time has come to fight in new ways against this bleak panorama. They understand that

El Salvador is currently a country in a revolutionary situation that increasingly needs the solidarity of all the peoples of the world in order to be able to arrive completely successfully to the end of its struggle for national liberation; they also point out that it is extremely damaging for the interests of all progressive mankind that the valuable experiences—of triumphs and defeats—of the Salvadoran people, accumulated over centuries of oppression, continue to be unknown to the people, who for their part are struggling today against the same enemies and in search of identical ends.

It is around these sorts of ideas that the following pages have been drafted. Throughout them, an attempt will be made to give a concise overview of the historical development of Salvadoran society—in particular, from the point of view of the people's struggle, for taking into their hands the capacity to make their own history and of the specific conditions in which the country's great popular masses currently live and struggle.

DOCUMENT 3-5
Roque Dalton, *El Salvador: Monografía*, 1965
EXCERPT ON THE ISSUE OF ANASTASIO AQUINO

One of the recurrent themes in Dalton's work was the image of the indigenous leader Anastasio Aquino, who led a rebellion in 1833. He presented Aquino as a leader of the masses driven by class interests who sought to guarantee that people had access to property. Aquino symbolized the age-old struggle of the masses to be protagonists of their own history. The one hundred years separating the Aquino rebellion and the Matanza endowed the events with even greater symbolism. Consciously or unconsciously, Dalton and Jorge Arias, the main leftist historian of his era, told the Aquino story in a way that drew parallels with the communist-causality version of 1932, which highlighted economic grievances and minimized the role of ethnicity.[4]

As was previously mentioned, the internal struggles, the financial chaos, sustaining the troops necessary for defending the postures of shaky governments, the taxes of the new state, etc., etc., convinced the Indian with proof positive that Independence had not been meant for him. The indigenous masses very soon realized that the only thing that had changed were the faces of the masters. The problems of Independence, in addition, had been sorted out in the "big cities" such as Guatemala City and neither the agrarian population nor the miners had had the opportunity to loudly voice their demands outside the palace.

In El Salvador this event was not accepted with the attitude that the ruling classes tend to expect from the sadly celebrated "public character" of the Indian. In El Salvador the indigenous cry of protest arose suddenly, it organized masses, and got them up in arms. The Nonualco peoples (Pipiles from central El Salvador), led by Anastasio Aquino, opposed the forced recruitment of their men for the army of the "white man's government" and the increase in taxes on indigo, which they grew.

The Salvadoran government sent its troops to wipe out the opposition (it was 1832 and Dr. Mariano Prado was at the head of the local government), but Anastasio Aquino, at the head of three thousand men armed with lances of *huiscoyol* wood and with several cannon they had made themselves, defeated these forces several times in a row. Dr. Prado turned power over to the vice chief, Joaquín San Martín. Aquino took the towns of Zacatecoluca and San Vicente.

The Aquino uprising was imbued with a clear class-consciousness. Their proclamations demonstrated their intentions to destroy the oppressive power of the whites and restore all that had been stolen from the Indians: land, means of production, freedom. "Because all that there is—all across this land—belongs to my brothers—who live in misery," were words attributed to Aquino in a popular ballad of the time.

In the village of Tepetitán, the great indigenous chief issued a celebrated decree calling himself the commander general of the liberating arms of Santiago Nonualco (previously he had crowned himself king of the Nonualcos, with the crown from the statue of Saint Joseph that was venerated in the Pilar Church in San Vicente). In this decree, Aquino set severe penalties for robbery, pillage, rape, etc., which shows that he was not the highway bandit, raper of women that the bourgeois history of El Salvador had painted him to be. Likewise,

Aquino decreed a ban on collecting taxes and debts, all with very severe penalties. He also banned the making and consumption of liquor, a means for sedation and degradation used by Salvadoran governments against the large masses in the countryside.

All available means were put to use in trying to check the momentum of the indigenous rebellion, which in addition—to the thinking of several modern scholars—had the potential for turning into a great indigenous uprising on a Central American scale. Catholic priests played a large role in appeasing large sectors of the countryside that otherwise might have supported Aquino's heroic deeds. Priests sent by the enemy went to the Nonualco leader's side in an attempt to destroy him.

The Salvadoran government was eventually able to rally its forces and launched a great joint offensive against the Nonualco forces, which ended in the Nonualcos' defeat in February 1833. In April of that year, as the result of a betrayal, Anastasio Aquino was captured. He was executed in the town of San Vicente and his head was cut off to be publicly displayed as an "example to rebels."

Aquino is a central figure in the revolutionary history of El Salvador and is the logical predecessor to the peasant actions of one hundred years later, in 1932, when once again the Salvadoran countryside would resound with the vindicating cries of "land and liberty." On this historic event, the young Salvadoran writer, Jorge Arias Gómez, has written a monograph of particular importance, entitled "Anastasio Aquino: His Memory, Significance and Presence," which was published in an underground edition by the United Front for Revolutionary Action (FUAR) of El Salvador in 1962.

DOCUMENT 3-6

Roque Dalton, *Historias prohibidas del Pulgarcito*, 1974

EXCERPTS FROM "PEOPLE, PLACES, AND EVENTS OF 1932"

At the same time that Dalton was writing Miguel Mármol *he was working on* Historias prohibidas del Pulgarcito, *an entertaining and original collage of his own work, stories, laws, anecdotes, poems, newspaper clippings, and bits of gossip that sought to strip the official picture of El Salvador from the gloss of tourism-propaganda and to expose in a caustically humorous fashion the distortions and fabrications coming from officially sanctioned authors. In the following text, Dalton uses a disjointed, seemingly haphazard mishmash of texts to deal with exactly the same set of historical preoccupations found in a highly organized fashion in* Miguel Mármol.5

I.

Close Up: Arturo Araujo was elected President in the only free elections of this century in El Salvador.

Araujo issued a call to elections for Congressmen and Mayors.

Close Up: General Maximiliano H. Martínez, Araujo's Minister of War, then overthrew the Constitutional President.

Long Shot: Despite all the pressure, jailings, persecution, provocation and murders in a basically fascistized election, the Salvadoran Communist Party achieved resounding success at the polls.

Military repression began in western El Salvador.

Medium Shot: The Salvadoran Communist Party proposes discussing the situation with President Martínez in order to stop the massacre. Representatives from the Party's Central Committee arrive at the Presidential Palace but Martínez refuses to receive them. The Minister of War tells the communist leaders that he is not authorized to parley.

Close Up: The main communist leaders, headed by Farabundo Martí, are arrested.

American Shot: Mass executions by gunfire of communists and "punitive operations" in the countryside begin.

	The Salvadoran Communist Party called for popular armed insurrection.
Long Shot:	The nationwide massacre reached monstrous proportions. The sheer volume would not drop off until after there were thirty thousand murdered.
Close Up:	Martínez began, over those thousands of dead bodies, his slow reign of 13 years.

II. Sovereignty

The Nicaraguan guerrilla
Augusto César Sandino
said to the Yankee soldiers
who had invaded Nicaragua:
"The sovereignty of a people is not open to discussion:
it is defended with arms in hand."

At the time of the worker-peasant uprising in El Salvador
    in 1932
the Yankees and the British proposed
to General Maximiliano Hernández Martínez
landing troops in La Libertad Port
to aid him in putting down the rebellion.

General Martínez said that that was no good for
    national sovereignty
and he sent the admirals a telegram
which he in turn had received from General
    José Tomás Calderón,
better known as "Short Jacket,"
Chief of Operations of the Punitive Forces of the
Government
    of El Salvador
at work on Pacification in the Western Zone of the
    Republic.

The telegram read as follows:
Saluting honorable commanders we declare situation absolutely dominated El Salvador government forces. Guaranteed lives properties citizens foreigners protected and respectful laws of the republic. Peace is established in El Salvador. Communist offensive dissolved its formidable nuclei dispersed. As of today fourth day of operations four thousand eight hundred communists liquidated. Martínez spent thirteen years defending thus
national sovereignty.
In the last 40 years
12 new governments have passed this tremendous responsibility from hand to hand.

III. An Official Testimony

"Thus it was that in December of 1931 large popular uprisings took place in the Western Departments of the Republic, organized by the principal leaders Farabundo Martí, and the students Mario Zapata and Alfonso Luna, who had their headquarters in the suburbs of San Salvador, where they were captured and executed immediately, without any kind of trial, and as several lists of followers had been seized, which contained the names of workers residing in the capital, they were all pursued and executed as soon as they were caught, including innocent workers who were reported to the authorities out of personal grudges, for any old biddy's word was enough for many upstanding men with families to be led to their deaths. Every night trucks full of victims would leave the Directorate General of Police heading for the Acelhuate River, where they were shot and buried in large trenches dug beforehand. The barbarous executioners did not even take the names of those martyrs. General Martínez mobilized forces in order to send them to combat the uprisings, giving extremely far-reaching orders, without any restrictions at all on the commanders who were leading those troops. The machine guns began to sow panic and death in the regions of Juayúa, Izalco, Nahuizalco, Colón, Santa Tecla, the Santa Ana Volcano, and all the shorefront villages from Jiquilisco to Acajutla. There were villages that were completely razed and the workers from the capital were barbarously decimated and a group of naive men who presented themselves voluntarily to the authorities offering their services were taken inside the National Guard Quarters, where they were lined up and every last one was mowed down. The panic spread. Several foreign merchants asked for aid from their respective nations, and the British government sent warships to the Port of Acajutla, where they requested permission from President Martínez to land troops in aid of their fellow citizens, but the tyrant did not grant said permission, alleging that his authority was sufficient for controlling the situation, and as proof of this he forwarded them a telegraphic message datelined from the city of Santa Ana, sent by General Don José Tomás Calderón, which said, "So far I count more than 4 thousand communists liquidated." The slaughter was horrendous, neither children nor old people nor women escaped. In Juayúa the order was given for all upstanding men who were not communists to report to the Town Hall, where they would be given a safe-conduct pass, and when the public plaza was packed with men, women, and children they blocked off the streets and machine-gunned the innocent multitude; not even the poor dogs that faithfully follow their indigenous masters were left alive. Just days later, in the parks and promenades of San Salvador, the commander who led that terrible massacre would be referring in great detail to that macabre event, bragging of being the hero of said action. The killings continued meticulously, carried out by the famous "Civic Guard" organized by General Martínez in every village, made up of depraved men who committed unspeakable abuses against the life [of the people], property, and the honor of innocent girls. They would report daily to the Chief Executive on the number of victims from the previous twenty-four hours and the looting of goods was such that even the fowl ran out. Chronicles published by different people affirmed that the number of dead amounted to more than thirty thousand, and in truth the murdered were no fewer than twenty-four thousand. Those ill-fated months of December of 1931 and January, February, and March of 1932 will never be able to be forgotten."

Colonel Gregorio Bustamante Maceo, Military History of El Salvador, *2nd edition, Publication of the Ministry of the Interior, National Press, San Salvador, 1951.*

IV. Vox populi

"In 1932 no one was tortured. At what time, sir? Just with shooting those loads of people we had more work than we could seriously attend to. Therefore, I'm not surprised that there were survivors among the executed. The case of Mr. Miguel Mármol is known, but there must be other ones out there, who don't speak for fear that they'll be shot again at the first chance."

"Nobody would eat pork. In the first place because of course those animals would have taken it upon themselves, together with the vultures and the insects, to devour the cadavers of the peasants who had fallen among the brush and secondly because more than one person assured that unscrupulous vendors had been selling human meat in western regions particularly hard hit by hunger, passing it off as pork."

"The Civic Guard had carte blanche to kill anyone. The judicial and military authorities, on the contrary, were encouraging the members of those corps to take as few prisoners as possible and to mete out direct justice forthwith, guns ablaze. The Civic Guard groups competed among themselves to see who could kill or locate the most communists in one day. These Guard units went to work and killed people even in places where there had never been communist activity or communists."

"From several pulpits in San Salvador, priests absolved aforehand whatever sin of excess might be committed by the members of the Civic Guard in the performance of their anticommunist duties."

"That there was no torture? That is not true. Torturing was done constantly on a daily basis. Every person who was captured was killed following horrible beatings, machete-blows, taking out of eyes, hangings. The National Guard killed many people by blows with their rifle butts alone; the army distinguished itself in the use of the bayonet. When a peasant who might have resisted was captured, he was grabbed by his arms and legs by four men; he was thrown into the air and hooked with their bayonets as he fell. The only assurance against being tortured was to be killed from afar."

"All the hospitals had orders to notify The Guard or The Police of the wounded who came in seeking treatment. In this way, many who had survived the machine-gunning in the rural areas were captured and killed."

"In Izalco the elementary school children were taken to witness the hanging of the indigenous leader Feliciano Ama."

"A detachment of The Guard in San Salvador raided a well-known brothel and liquor store. Threatening that they would accuse the women of being communists and kill them if they did not agree to oblige them, they forced the prostitutes to participate in an orgy that lasted a week, until the liquor supplies ran out. One of the prostitutes was beaten to death by the Civic Guardsmen in the middle of the binge."

"Don Miguel Mármol says that, in Armenia, a general named Pinto personally killed more than seven hundred peasants who had been captured by the army. The soldiers forced the prisoners to dig their graves and then the general would come along and kill them with his pistol."

"According to the population at the time, there were more than one and a half deaths per square kilometer in El Salvador in January of 1932."

"Among the executions committed with great publicity in Izalco, one that caused immense grief was that of the poor peasant Francisco Sánchez, known by the inhabitants and among the Indians as Chico Sánchez, who had joined the communist movement, and it was precisely because of the affection he enjoyed that had been followed by many people into the ranks of the Communist Party, the peasant unions, and International Red Aid. A series of photographs of the execution of Chico Sánchez was circulated in Central American anticommunist publications. In them, the peasant leader can be seen posing between Colonel Juan Ortiz and the priest who offered him the "last rights," or then kneeling before this same priest at the moment of his Catholic confession. The final photo in the series shows Sánchez dead, with his mouth and eyes open, gazing at infinity, as the Izalco Volcano begins a violent eruption. A poet of the time, a leftist who with the passage of time turned into a rabid rightist, was able to capture in several defective but heartfelt lines what the people thought of the figure of Francisco Chico Sánchez:

Francisco Sánchez, Francisco,
Indian of faraway gaze,
a hardened, craggy face
and a Franciscan heart...

"The .45 pistol gained high esteem in the army of El Salvador during the events of '32. From then on, it became the personal weapon par excellence of officers on campaign. The thing is, it was undoubtedly notable how rifle bullets, let's say from a 30.06, and even heavy machine-gun fire of that caliber, were unable to restrain the peasants who charged the troops with their machetes bared. The inflamed communists would end up dying, but they would manage to reach the machine-gun nest and on occasion even wounded the army soldiers. The impact of a .45 bullet, which, as is known, has the force of a five-hundred-pound blow on a surface eleven millimeters in diameter, would immediately paralyze whoever was hit by it on the spot. It seems that this is due to the shock or something like that. What is certain is that no officer carrying a .45 pistol had the slightest difficulty during the acts of war of that year. The North American invading forces in the Philippines had previously had the same experience."

V. On the Agrarian Law Reformed at that Time

"Art. 69. The agents of the National Guard shall constantly pursue in the fields, roads, cattle ranches, plantations, estates, hamlets and settlements where there is no Municipal Authority the day workers, lawbreakers, players of banned games, common drunkards, vagrants of all types, classified as such by the laws of the police, giving, in each case, report of such to the competent authority for the imposition of the respective penalties.

Art. 71. The agents of the National Guard, at the first request by any plantation owner or farmer, shall take into their custody the person or persons whom the other shall indicate to them as suspects...

Art. 72. The inhabitants of the countryside who belong to the class of day workers shall be summoned in order to present their passes that accredit them as working on some farm or estate; those who do not present said passes shall be taken to the nearest Town Hall in order to be given work from among the public or private jobs, in the town or outside it.

Art. 74. In accordance with the respective Municipal Mayor and through confidential data that he shall collect, huts or shanties in the wilds shall be destroyed if they serve as cover for evildoers or if their owners are notorious indulgers of thieves or receivers of stolen goods and they will be confined to town, electing themselves the town that is most suitable to them, without prejudice to any illicit act being proven against them, in which case they shall be arrested and turned over to the competent authority for their punishment.

Art. 75. All persons who in the wilds shall be encountered at night by the authorities' agents shall be requested, if they are suspect, to show what they are transporting, and if they have beasts of burden or other animals with them, they will be asked to whom the livestock and the effects that they are transporting belong, if they were loaded or pulling vehicles, the same if they shall be automobiles of dubious origin, destination or load, and if in effect they are suspect according to the explanations, they may be detained for further investigation of the livestock, load and vehicles..."

Articles such as these, still in effect, have, since 1932, provided a legal cloak over the worsening violent repression in the countryside, the unlimited dictatorship of the local landowners and caciques, the expulsion of small landowners from their plots of land, the submission of the rural proletariat to slavelike working conditions, etc. On the contrary, "not one single labor law that would grant social benefits was decreed in the thirteen years of the Martínez regime, which began in December 1931 and consolidated itself with the Matanza."

VI. Martínezkampf

The United States recognized the Martínez government in 1933. In 1934, Martínez enacts a discriminatory law against Arabic, Asian Indian, and Chinese minorities. Blacks are denied entry into the country. In 1936, Martínez recognizes the Franco regime, ahead of

Hitler and Mussolini. Martínez also recognizes Manchukuo, the imperialist Japanese puppet state in Manchuria.

A Prussian colonel, Von Bonster, serves as Director of the Military Academy.

President Martínez sends the German Joint Chiefs of Staff a tactical plan for landing troops on the coast of the United States.

In Mizata, the natural Salvadoran harbor, Japanese submarines provision themselves.

In late 1941, El Salvador declares war on Japan, Germany, and Italy. The Martínez Government seizes the property of citizens from those countries living in El Salvador.

VII. Primary School Morals Curriculum (1940)

"Theme for the month of August: Strengthening the spirit in adversity. f) Teaches that death is only a change in form; that civilized peoples pay their respects to this change; that this transformation causes grief in the family members and that our duty is to:

1) Respect these laws of transformation.
2) Help those who are suffering.
3) Pay our fellow men the ultimate tribute of love, and teach them that these duties are fulfilled by burying the dead and consoling the mourners."

VIII. Philosophy for Governing El Salvador for Terms No Greater (or Lesser) than Thirteen Years.

[Thoughts from general Maximiliano Hernández Martínez, Master Theosophist and President of the Republic—from 1932 to 1944— Q.D.E.S.G.L.T.]

"It is good for children to go barefoot. That way they better receive the beneficial effluvia of the planet, the vibrations of the Earth. Plants and animals do not wear shoes."

(With regard to an offer made by Mr. Winall A. Dalton, on behalf of the North American colony living in El Salvador, to give rubber sandals to the barefoot children in the public schools.)

"The biologists have only discovered five senses. But in reality there are ten. Hunger, thirst, procreation, urination and bowel movement are the senses not included on the biologists' list."

"Why does a man smile to himself when he is walking down the street? Because of the power of the spirit over matter."

"It is a greater crime to kill an ant than a man because when the man dies he is reincarnated, while the ant dies definitively."

"If water is heated, vapor results. What then would supervapor be like? Even though we have not seen it, in reality it exists."

"The lower forms of democracy put emphasis on rights; the higher forms on duties."

"Democracy is love."

(From his weekly lectures on theosophical topics, delivered in the Auditorium of the National University and broadcast by radio link to the entire country. Quotations from William Krehm.)

"I am God in El Salvador."

(Response to the Archbishop of San Salvador, when he asked him in the name of God to cease the executions of the revolutionaries of April 1944.)

"On the occasion of an epidemic outbreak of smallpox in El Salvador, General Maximiliano Hernández Martínez absolutely refused to put modern antiepidemic measures into practice or to accept the aid of international health agencies. He simply ordered the street lights covered with colored cellophane, alleging that the rays of light tinged this way would be sufficient to purify the environment, killing the bacteria causing the pestilence."

"General Martínez's son, the youngest, the most beloved, came down with appendicitis. The General refused to place him in the hands of a surgeon and began treating him personally with 'Blue Waters' (which were natural waters put out to sun in large colored bottles in the patio of the Presidential Palace). The course of the appendicitis worsened, peritonitis came on, and the boy died in horrifying pain. General Martínez said that the only thing to do was to resign himself, that if 'the invisible physicians' had not wanted to save his son, he must not intervene in the impenetrable designs of nature."

DOCUMENT 4-1
Roque Dalton/Miguel Mármol, *Miguel Mármol*, 1972

EXCERPTS

The following except consists of roughly six uninterrupted pages from Miguel Mármol where Dalton/Mármol offer an executive summary of the 1932 uprising. Its overarching message is that of communist causality. The careful reader might note the presence of Dalton's and Mármol's conflicting ideological interpretations. Whereas credit for the uprising is generally given to the PCS, the cause of the revolt's failure is attributed to various causes, ranging from poor planning by the party, to improper ideology, to a government conspiracy. Like other communist-causality authors, such as Méndez, Buezo, and Schlesinger, this excerpt portrays the PCS as the active agent of the insurrection and the mobilizing force behind peasant mobilization. Nevertheless, the careful reader will observe that the descriptions of the critical link between the urban PCS and the rural insurgents remain vague, and also that they allow for the issue of peasant autonomy to be read into the story. The criticism of "intellectuals" who abandoned the party at the critical revolutionary moment is foreshadowed in an earlier document that Mármol wrote in 1948 on the issue of party factionalism, which is reproduced as a later document.[6]

In that same informational meeting, and in a very firm way, I proposed that we immediately call the Salvadoran masses to armed popular insurrection, led by the Communist Party. I enumerated the favorable conditions, which, in my judgment, existed for the triumph and for the seizing of political power for the later realization of a bourgeois-democratic revolution. The meeting at that point was being held with Farabundo Martí as Internal Secretary General, in the absence of the actual Secretary General, Narciso Ruíz, a baker who was at that time doing urgent organizing tasks in Sonsonate. Max Ricardo Cuenca and other intellectuals left the meeting for different reasons and, according to what we later discovered, they had gone looking for a safe place to ride out the storm that was approaching. The discussion was intense and heated. Farabundo Martí finally agreed with my proposal, accepting that the duty of the Party was to take its place as the vanguard of the masses. In order to avoid the greater, imminent danger and disgrace for us of an insurrection that was out of control, spontaneous, or provoked by the actions of the government in which the masses would go alone and without leadership onto the battlefield. The meeting lasted all through the night between the 7th and 8th of January, 1932. The carrying out of armed popular insurrection was unanimously accepted (I mean by those present, not the leaders who left). It wasn't a matter of making a hasty, irresponsible decision; within the dizzy whirl of events it was well thought out and planned. I proposed that, given the ripeness of the revolutionary situation, all preparations be taken care of in eight days, at the end of which time we should open fire and attack: that was enough time to prepare all the work, and it would allow us to maintain the element of surprise that Lenin required in this case. Thinking over the exact timing of things, that Lenin also demanded, I said that the insurrection should begin not on the 15th of January nor the 17th, but precisely on the 16th, at zero hour. My proposal was accepted in principle, and it was resolved that the Central Committee would be the organism responsible for all military matters. Farabundo Martí and other comrades were in charge of finding operatives among friendly officers in the Army, getting arms, preparation of war materials such as explosives, etc., setting up communications with different regions of the country, incorporation of different social and political sectors into the struggle (for example, democratic political personalities, the student movement, etc.), raising money, etc. These same comrades were also responsible for preparing the insurrection's manifesto that would be addressed to the people. Next, the country was divided into zones of operation, and each comrade on the Directorate was assigned to one of them. The CC proceeded to name the Red Commanders who would be responsible for the military commissions in the subzones, in the work places, in the regiments, in the mass organizations, etc. and who would report back to the CC about their activities. In the actions of the raging insurrection, the Red Commanders would fulfill the military functions of a captain leading his company. But the military commissions had, moreover, as nucleuses of military direction, other duties that went beyond mere combat. These commissions were going to be in charge of doing all the revolutionary organizing within the army, dividing units into platoons of ten men, getting arms and storing them in distribution centers and distributing them when the CC gave the go ahead, sabotaging lines of communication, pinpointing the public and secret itineraries of the bourgeoisie's Army, forming details of trench diggers (they were actually formed in San Miguel, Usulután Santa Cruz Michapa, but they never went to work), controlling the railways and other means of transportation, etc. In our calculations, we counted on the barracks in Sonsonate and Ahuachapán, where our penetration was significant, being incorporated into our ranks, and on the support of at least the relatively large number of nucleuses in the barracks in Santa Tecla. We also had in the capital the support of two companies from the Sixth Regiment of the Machine Gunners, which was a regiment with a great democratic tradition, that of the two cavalry companies, a small cell of soldiers in Zapote (the Artillery Regiment) and all the soldiers from the Air Force garrison in Ilopango. At the last minute, we found out that we also had the support of two companies of soldiers from the Regiment of San Miguel, in the east, and that around them waiting for a joint action more than seven hundred citizens from San Miguel were gathered in the local cemetery, ready to begin military operations. We also had nucleuses of officers in several other barracks, but these contacts were being handled solely and exclusively by Farabundo Martí. In short, we had more than enough strength in the Army, together with the active support of the insurrectionist masses in the countryside and cities, to smash the bourgeois state apparatus. On another front, the unions in the countryside were in the midst of organizing a general strike. From a practical point of view, they were working under conditions favorable to creating a situation in which the agricultural and rural proletariat could lead the peasantry in a revolutionary insurrection.

Sectors of the revolutionary petty-bourgeoisie—and these were other contacts that Martí, almost single-handedly, was going to incite—were going to be used to set up the Government; I'm referring to cadre like Dr. Merlos, Dreyfus, radical professionals, etc. In general, the initial unfolding and development of the organization was very effective. Up to that point the repression hadn't undermined the apparatus upon which the insurrection depended, not even putting a dent in its efforts to organize and strengthen itself. The instructions at that point were for each one to take his place and wait for the order to go. However, when we met again with the CC on the 14th of January to discuss the final details, we were greeted with very bad news: It was proposed to put off the insurrection until the 19th. No one present liked that dangerous idea, but Farabundo Martí calmed us down saying that the postponement was necessary in light of the very real possibility of incorporating the officers and troops from the First Infantry Regiment into the revolutionary movement. Already by this time Farabundo was more than an Internal Secretary General; through the force of events and because of his leadership, supreme leadership—as much within the Party as within the organization for the insurrection—remained in his hands. The irreplaceability of *el negro* was surely one of our biggest weaknesses. Which makes the position of various intellectual comrades even more serious, intellectual comrades who found in Martí's hegemony the pretext for getting angry, for withdrawing from doing revolutionary work, and refusing to make any contribution whatsoever. Martí, himself an intellectual, but very proletarianized, said that they were just vacillators worm-eaten by petty-bourgeois ideology. I proposed on behalf of the Young Communist League that the Supreme Military Committee (a new organism that was proposed, based in the membership of the CC) should be organized strictly with workers as a way to get rid of so much vacillation. After the meeting, we dispersed to communicate the proposal to the immediate leadership in the areas of operation to which we had been assigned: no one liked the news. And on returning to San Salvador after this task, we encountered something even worse, another proposal: postponing the start of actions until the 22nd of January. Taking this new plan to the masses was truly a sad, difficult job. With all this, the enemy already had obtained a large amount of intelligence about our intentions and each day, each hour that passed, they were closing in on us more and more. And this in spite of the fact that the enemy's intelligence and counterintelligence operations were very deficient. Our intelligence operations were worse, and we didn't have any counterintelligence. Above all, the enemy aimed to destroy right off our political and military leaders, our highest-level nucleuses. My older sister had a friend who was an undercover agent with the police and who passed her information, since he was one of our sympathizers. Through her we were able to learn that the police had El Negro Martí, Luna, and Zapata under surveillance, that they knew the location of the safe house where they were staying, and that they were going to arrest them at any moment. I went to see them immediately to warn them and tell them about the reports coming in from Santa Ana that there was talk of an imminent uprising of Araujistas, for which, they said, huge amounts of arms had come in Guatemala. Martí, in light of the alarming news, just started laughing, and he told me that I shouldn't be afraid—he refused to take seriously the danger of being arrested—and he gave me a package of bombs they had been making in the backyard of the house. He even tried to calm down the owners of the place, who grew alarmed with my news. This was a family friendly to the party who lived near María Auxiliadora Academy. Martí told me I should go to San Miguel and place myself at the front of the actions in the eastern zone, but I told him that I had already been assigned to direct the actions, which were the responsibility of the Air Force garrison in Ilopango, and that that was too important a mission to drop just like that. Martí agreed. So I left, and in spite of my persistence they gave no importance to what I had to say. That very night they were all arrested. My sister came to my place crying to tell me, and I sought refuge in the house of master José Enrique Cañas, since I figured the next one arrested was going to be me. Immediately a full plenum of the CC was convened to consider the situation. This meeting was called by Max Cuenca, who came out of hiding for it and who was the leading voice at the Plenum. He angrily called for the immediate suspension of the insurrectional work since many comrades had already been taken prisoner, among them the leaders of the movement who had concentrated in their hands our most important military contacts. I opposed that idea and said that the workers of the Republic were now morally up in arms, that we had deceived and misled them a lot, and that at this point we couldn't stop them even if we wanted to and even if we made a most desperate effort. Max Cuenca insisted on suspending the insurrection: he said it wasn't possible to go stupidly into armed uprising about which the

Government knew practically everything and knowing damn well that the Army was just waiting for our first move to spring the trap with blood and bullets on the whole nationwide revolutionary and democratic movement. He reported something that we didn't know yet, that the Government had already taken the first steps to institutionalize the repression and had decreed a state of siege throughout the central region of the country, a state of siege that would surely extend to other areas in no time. The majority of us insisted that to vacillate meant the premature death of the insurrection, that it was already too late, that if we put on the brakes now we were going to lose even the ability to defend ourselves against the terrible governmental repression which was going to come down on us, insurrection or no insurrection. We weren't wrong about that. We carried the motion, and it was agreed to go all out and step up the insurrectional work, and to make various adjustments and changes in our plan of action. Max Cuenca, despite his opinions, was assigned to reestablish those contacts Farabundo had been working with, and, generally speaking, we decided to fall in line with the call for a nationwide general strike in order to begin mobilizing our forces toward insurrection. We agreed not to attack the Army detachments unless it was unavoidable, and we prepared guidelines and teams of cadre to fraternize with the troops who were called out of their barracks. At the same time, we decided to put up roadblocks to stop the flow of government trucks, to cut them off from lines of communication, to try to pin down the enemy in the cities, isolating them there and stopping the flow of supplies from the countryside into the city. An Information and Coordination Commission was set up within the CC, which would be responsible for making sure that the dispositions of the Revolutionary Command were circulating at every level of the movement. The CC, however, after the downfall of Martí, Luna, and Zapata, found itself lacking information regarding many vital details that were needed to correctly direct the insurrection. It was now the 20th of January, and there wasn't one complete report on the material and human resources we had to count on: we didn't know very much about the number and kinds of arms our forces had, we were ignorant of the exact number of red battalions formed, and there was hardly any data on the consolidation of commands at every level, on the assigning of concrete responsibilities, etc. We were basically ignorant of the displacement and movements of enemy forces nationwide, and we had only scattered information that had no relation to the overall picture. The little reliable information on which we depended was jealously guarded by a limited number of comrades on the CC and it didn't filter down to whoever among us needed it in order to get results. At the same time, it was a fact that the CC of the Party, due to the arrest of those comrades I just named, had remained very badly integrated from the standpoint of internal unity, the majority being comrades who held opposing points of view, who were immature and more or less sectarian. I believe at that point our Central Committee wasn't capable, in practice, of turning itself into an efficient and indisputable coordinating and directive force for all the revolutionary work. Within the CC, an incredible ignorance of the importance of intelligence and its revolutionary use, as well as a tremendous underestimation of insurrectional military tactics and strategy, abounded. Up to the very end the Party managed the insurrection simply as a mass political event, without developing a specific military conception of the problem. It simply never saw that the military problems would become the fundamental ones once it has been decided to carry out the insurrection, and that the military problems are solved with a special technique and science, which has its own laws, etc. We were working with the masses as if the nationwide uprising was simply a more elevated form of work on the trade union front, on the mass front of the Party. The central military plan almost wasn't a military plan at all, as we'll see later on. As if that wasn't enough, we were relying on next to nothing in material resources: we had no means of transportation and no money, nor were we able to get them. The 22nd, the date fixed for the beginning of the insurrection, I was going around coordinating cells in San Salvador (work prior to the operations with the garrison in Ilopango), on foot, and without even a penknife in my pocket. And what hurts most is that the revolutionary spirit of the masses was incredibly high: a very serious spectacle not just for sociologists to study thirty years later, but that should have been the North of the insurrectional compass of the Party. Already by that awful 22nd of January, the enemy had seized the initiative from us: instead of a party that was on the point of initiating a big insurrection, at least that's how all the cadre in San Salvador talked about it, we had the appearance of a group of desperate, persecuted, and harassed revolutionaries. From one moment to the next, the work was in practice abandoned, and everyone tried to save themselves from the unrestrained repression. The enemy didn't wait for our famous Zero Hour to begin their counterrevolutionary military actions. Reports about the start of fighting in different places began to reach us few comrades who, in San Salvador, maintained contacts close to the Directorate. When the reports referred to places that weren't considered by us as zones of operation, it was obvious that there had been provocation by the Army, which had forced the masses to react with violence, providing an excuse to move ahead and wipe them out completely. Despite the disorganized state of the communications, the insurrectional call of the CC had reached different places in the west and the mass organizations, following orders had started to go into action. Reports to this effect started coming into San Salvador, especially from the Department of Sonsonate, where the government in retaliation sent in a heavy column commanded by General José Tomás Calderón, a sinister murderer, nicknamed "Short Jacket." From the first moment, it was clear that rivers of blood were flowing, that the fighting was completely lopsided and the people were losing, due to the better organization and total superiority of firepower of the government forces.

DOCUMENT 4–2
Roque Dalton/Miguel Mármol, Dalton's Handwritten Notes on the 1932 Uprising

SELECTION

The following document is a direct transcription of three pages of Dalton's notebooks in which Mármol was describing the final few days leading up to the outbreak of revolt in January 1932. As mentioned above, these notes correspond directly to seven pages in the final published version of Miguel Mármol *(Document 4–1). These two documents provide an extended example of narrative reconfiguration. The reader is invited to compare them to see how twelve hundred words of notes were transformed into three thousand words of text. In this example one can see how Dalton took schematic interview notes, reordered and rephrased them, linked the different topics with transitions, and produced a final text that was a smooth and polished narrative that recaptured the drama of the moment. We also include this here to show how, despite our insistence that Dalton altered much of the meaning of Miguel Mármol's testimony as it related to the ideological lessons of 1932, here we see more of an example of simple rewriting and editing than changing meaning. The reader is invited to ask whether the following material would have lent itself to supporting an ideological position of radical militancy in the late 1960s and early 1970s. If not, that might help to explain the latter half of chapter 7 in the final version of* Miguel Mármol, *where Dalton's intrusive influence was much greater and the argument being put forward explicitly supports the decision to have rebelled in 1932.*[7]

Then I proposed the popular armed insurrection led by the P[arty]. I listed the conditions favorable to its triumph and for achieving the Demo Bourgeois revolution. Max Cuenca and other intellectuals had withdrawn, according to Martí's report. [erasure] (*insert Mármol's documents here*). This meeting was held in the absence of the Cc Sec'y Gen because he was in Sonsonate (Narciso Ruiz)—A baker. Martí took command of the CC temporarily. Finally Martí accepted *in order to prevent the imminent and greater danger of an uncontrolled insurrection.* The meeting lasted all night: the insurrection was accepted (night of 7 January 1932): These were not hurried decisions within the dizzy whirl of events it was thought out and planned. I proposed that the insurrection be planned in 8 days everything was at a point where that was enough to do it well and maintain the surprise that Lenin required. The 24th too soon, the 26th too late. The 25th. I said not the 15th not the 17th: the 16th of JANUARY: At 0 hour. [erasure] It was resolved that the CC would take charge of military matters. Martí and others from SRI took charge of seeking contacts with officers, friends in army, search for arms, preparation of war materials, incorporation of other sectors into the struggle (personalities, connections), seeking money, drafting a manifesto to the people. Each compañero was assigned to a zone of operation. The C. Committee named Red

Commanders who were in charge of the military Commission of their zone and would report back to the CC. These commissions would contact the army, organize platoons (platoons of 10 men) get arms and distribute them, sabotage lines of communication public and secret pathways for troops (details of shoemakers organized in San Miguel, Usulutan and Santa Cruz Michapa, Modesto in Santa Cruz—quickly fell prisoner—stop the military trains) We were counting on [erasure] the barracks in Sonsonate and Ahuachapán and nucleuses in the barracks of Santa Tecla, 2 companies of the 6th regiment of machine gunners (democratic tradition), 2 Cavalry Companies, a small [end of page 27] (2 companies in San Miguel: we also found this out last. 700 men in Cemetery) cell of soldiers in El Zapote and the soldiers from the Air Force Garrison. We had officers in Ahuachapan. Martí had. In short, we had more than enough strength in the army that with the support of the insurrectionist hands to smash the bourgeois operative—Since they were communists: unions in the countryside, Youth work, etc.—An insurrection of the proletariat (rural and agricultural) together with the peasants. The proletariat had 16 proposed in entire west organizing a general strike—The sectors of the revolutionary petty-bourgeoisie (that were Marti's contacts, they were going to be used to make the Government: the Merlos', Dreyfus, etc.) The organization was developed with full efficacy, the repression hadn't managed to undermine the apparatus upon which the insurrection depended nor stop the organization. The instructions were now to take their places and wait for the order to go. When on the 14th we went back to discuss the bad news: it was proposed for the 19th. We did not like it but Martí calmed us down because he told us that he had offer from officers to hand over the 1st Infantry. Martí, himself an intellectual, said that the intellectuals were bastards they did not approach to cooperate. The [erasure] Youth proposed that a military committee be organized composed strictly [erasure] of the workers since we were afraid of new postponements. We returned to inform the countryside of the postponement: didn't like it. Then we returned to S. Salvador and the CC once Again postponed from 19th to the 22nd! Taking this to the masses that were furious was difficult. With all this the enemy had already obtained a lot of information. A police inspector friend (Elias

Guevara) was informing my sister. He was just a sympathizer. My sister: go tell Negro that they already have him under surveillance. Today they arrest him. He did not leave me the source. I received a delegation from Santa Ana. They reported that the Araujo supporters were moving for a coup that arms had come in near Santa Ana. They had bomb [erasure] to me [erasure] it turned out to be Joaquín Rivas (candidate) and I told him that there was alarm. I went to where Martí, Luna and Zapata were. They were in a little house across from María Auxiliadora belonging to a family. They were working. Report. And you're afraid over that, said Martí. Negro's courage made Luna and Zapata brave. He gave me a bag of bombs.—Thus he arranged for me to go to San Miguel, but I had the more important work with the Air Force with Camilo. They did not give it any importance. In the early morning hours they were arrested. My sister crying. I went to take refuge in the house of Cañas the shoemaker. But I had to leave to work since the thing was heating up. A plenum of the CC of the P. was convened. Called by Max Cuenca; he came out of hiding and was the leading voice. He called for us to urgently suspend the insurrectional work that there were many prisoners among them C. Martí, Luna and Zapata. I objected: the workers were morally up in arms that they had been deceived a lot that it couldn't be stopped. Cuenca that the coup was revealed that the government knew everything that the state of siege had already begun in one Department in the central region Chalatenango? I don't remember which. Max was in charge of doing Martí's work bureaucratic contacts. We changed some arrangements no attacking the army detachments fall in with the line of the national general strike; prepare measures to fraternize with the troops in case they were to leave their barracks, dig up the roads

Change of inf. and coordination and delegate coordination commission Santa Tecla (Luis López) in case the War machinery moved out, to not recognize the red flag in order to prevent ambushes by the squadrons, [erasure] isolate the

not drop of milk not a faggot of firewood not a grain of cereal to the cities enemy, cut communications [erasure] The Central C. had all run to report (ON 20 JANUARY) the information. He had then knowledge of the means available for the insurrection that is arms, number of battalions formed, their commanders, etc. Neither about

HIGHLIGHT PRIOR UNIONIST movement: years '20, '21. Until fall of Estrada Cabrera! In the Guat. police force to the fall of E. Cabrera (Herrera) they were Salvadoran. All of us Cs. were unionists.

the displacement and the movement of the enemy. That information was centralized by the CC. Mistaken makeup of the leadership of the insurrection

And lack of coordination. Incredible ignorance of the importance of information and the military technique of an insurrection. [erasure] I remained in S. Salvador coordinating. We did not have vehicles going about in full repression without arms. Mármol was moving about for example in S. Salvador on the 22nd \: The spectacle of the masses in insurrection is difficult. It's awful it is not the stuff of social psychologists nor leaving it to be interpreted 10 years later—/ [an arrow connects both sentences]

|————————————————|
| 1) Question about the Squadron Provision? | The Schlésinger book 700 copies.
                                                            guat.
| 2) AMA, BONDANZA? The indigenous problem? |

DOCUMENT 5-1
Jorge Fernández Anaya's Report on El Salvador, September 1930

Jorge Fernández Anaya, the Mexican agent of the Comintern sent to El Salvador in 1929 to assist the nascent radicals in their organizing, became the de facto leader of the radical left in El Salvador during his roughly one-year tenure in the country. He left El Salvador for Guatemala in August or September 1930 due to police persecution.

Immediately after arriving in Guatemala, he wrote a series of lengthy reports on conditions in El Salvador. Among his recipients were fellow comrades back in El Salvador, Comintern officials in the Caribbean Bureau in New York City, and the Colonial Department of the Communist Party USA. In his reports Anaya expressed his belief that the Communist Party in El Salvador was facing a critical moment of development, in large part because of internal ideological factionalism. In writing these reports, Anaya hoped not only to clarify conditions for his superiors, but also to support those comrades in El Salvador whom he believed held the proper ideological perspective. The following selection is drawn from his letter to the Communist Party USA. In it Anaya argues that the PCS is facing ideological challenges from the nonradical reformists on the right and the militant "opportunists" on the left. Among the latter he includes Farabundo Martí. He details his attempts to show Martí and the other militants the error of their ways. In the process, Anaya then emphasizes the party's official line on insurrection that El Salvador is not yet ready. [Editor's note: The original was typed by someone working with a machine that did not allow for accents. We have left some of the original spelling errors and missing accents. Some others, like Martí, we have rectified.][8]

> Guatemala, 8 September 1930
> Compañero Alberto Moreau
> Secretariat General of the Colonial Department
> of the CPUSA
> Dear Comrade:
> This letter, written following the accompanying one, is for the purpose of explaining to the Secretariat two questions of great transcendence and it is to them that I turn forthwith. As you will remember, from El Salvador I set out well in advance the need that upon my leaving another compañero prepared, active and disposed to walking day and night would go there. Three days following my departure from that country and being in this one we have received a letter where it talks of a "compromise" with the fascist national government of Pío Romero Bosque. Two days later I have received a private letter from another compañero

where he informed me of another tendency that violently emerged in the compañeros who are directing the work nationally. This is that of going to insurrection.

The first tendency is a contemptible, traitorous tendency and under separate cover I am sending you a letter that I wrote to the P.C. [Communist Party] and to the J.C. [Communist Youth] of El Salvador. How I would like to be able to apply every single epithet there is to this class of people who are opportunistic, traitorous, and allied with the bourgeoisie, consciously or unconsciously. I wrote the following to them on this point concretely: "All the compromises that you intend to make or are making at the present, those who calling themselves revolutionaries, seek mercy, compassion, attempting to restrain the growth of fascism, are sirens of the bourgeoisie who are attempting to soothe the working masses, with your pacts and compromises that only benefit the fascist semifeudal bourgeoisie in the concrete case of El Salvador. We are not willing to come to compromises with capitalism; our line is the struggle unto death, irreconcilable class struggle. Whatever the compromise may be, it is something odious, contemptible, that all of us as conscious workers must repudiate. No compromises, mass struggle is what the revolutionary movement must engage in now."

In a personal letter to comrade Martí of which I am sending you a copy I tell him the following: The struggle against opportunism, against revisionism, inevitably takes on new characteristics in El Salvador. Therefore, the struggle against all rightist and leftist deviations is the central question; it is the fundamental basis for giving our movement true revolutionary effectiveness. [Editor's note: All following text in quotation marks indicates Anaya's inclusion of text from other sources.]

"Surely the cowed, the unconscious would speak of new tactics, a thing that is absolutely impossible. In a letter to the SRI [International Red Aid] I have set forth in general terms the characteristics that the revolutionary movement should have in that country.

The fact of having established a compromise is something simply wicked and humiliating for the working class, for the international revolutionary movement. It may well be true that you will accuse me of not knowing the content of that compromise (Martí was here with me during those days), but whatever it may be, it is nothing other than something shameful that should never have been accepted, at any price, for any motive."

"That is only due to fear, to lack of consciousness, and to incomprehension of what mass movements are and what they mean, and the absolute incomprehension that against fascism there is only one struggle, organizing on the basis of production and mass demonstrations. It seems impossible, incredible that after having said it ten thousand times we could be in the same place, or possible worse off.

"We have talked about temporary organs of masses, we have explained their functioning, and in the struggle against national fascism we have forgotten it all in the flight that our valiant compañeros have taken, to a "compromise." You have committed the greatest absurdity. The temporary organs should have been initiated at that time, enlisting all the working masses in the defense of the FRT [Regional Federation of Salvadoran Workers], of the SRI, of the PC and of the JC, adding to this the fundamental demands for which we are fighting. In exchange for having abandoned actions by the great masses, we have seen one thing: "A COMPROMISE." Clearly and concretely a betrayal.

As you shall see both in the letter that I address to c. [comrade] Martí who in those days was with me, as in the one I address to the P.C. and to the J.C., I have set forth very clearly the character of the compromise.

On the one hand, the last night, speaking with the secretary general of the J.C. and with the secretary general of the P.C., I indicated to them the necessity of putting the masses into action in defense of our organizations. I indicated to them the importance, "although we talked about this a long time" of creating committees to fight in defense of the revolutionary workers' organizations. I indicated to them the necessity of unmasking the current government as an agent of Yankee imperialism, which is proved by the fact that in less than one year Pan American Airways and Tropical Radio have been introduced, permits have been given for "scientific" research and for treasure hunters in the bay [sic] of Fonseca, the concession of fields and part of Llotango [Ilopango] lake for an airport for Pan American Airways. All this, like the purchase of the majority of the shares of the Banco Agrícola Comercial by National City Bank, like the events that are being reported that everyone is asking for the resignation of the auditor general of the republic, because he requests collaboration, help from the English firm Laiton, Bennett, Chiene & Tait, the upcoming opening of the branch office, the savage repression, the jailing en masse of our comrades. I indicated to them that this could not stay this way, that it was necessary to unmask them. With this, add our demands and study them for the purpose of being able to fully mobilize our compañeros.

That is to say the comrades knew perfectly what line should be followed. The other tendency is the ideological consequence of which I have already spoken, that is, the one that wants to carry out the insurrection now.

Compañeros who are incapable of tolerating persecution from fighting against national fascism on a daily basis, from continuing to organize the masses, in light of the idea that a commitment is one to the end. I must be very clear. Martí has this tendency. He did not tell me this personally because I would have explained it to him and severely rebuked him. Vazquez told me. Then I wrote him a personal letter of which I have made mention in several paragraphs. I do not openly tell him you have the tendency because it is not the right time, but instead I very clearly point out the character of this tendency in several letters.

"The idea, let's more clearly call it the leftist insurrectional tendency, is due to the unconsciousness prevailing in some comrades. Such a tendency is negative; I do not mean to say that we might not have to get there soon; but, at the present time, this covers cowardice, lack of consciousness, the panic caused by the beginning of national fascism as the ally of Yankee imperialism: Pío Romero Bosque; something even more, these comrades intend to cover their opportunism with leftist phrases, since that is what they are.

To not consider the enormous responsibility that exists with regard to our class in these times is almost like betraying it. The everyday struggle, the daily struggle, is one of the preliminary conditions through which we will reeducate ourselves, we will perfect our leadership and militant ranks.

In the letter to Martí I told him:

"Instead, we see impatience for getting to the final struggles; the compañeros consider somewhat slight acts that are so important, so fundamental in the life of our class. Because of that I remember some of the teachings of our teachers Marx and Lenin. For them, and the same for us, insurrection is an art quite as much as war." Lenin on 8 October 1917 wrote in his historical article "Advice of an Onlooker" the following: "But insurrection is a special form of political struggle, one subject to special laws to which attentive thought must be given."9

"The rules that Marx has given for this purpose are chief in all these actions. And there is no exception for any country, they are the following: 1- Never play with insurrection, but when beginning it realize firmly that you must go all the way.

2nd—Concentrate a great superiority of forces at the decisive point and at the decisive moment, otherwise the enemy, who has the advantage of better preparation and organization, will destroy the insurgents. 3rd—Once the insurrection has begun, you must act with the greatest determination, and by all means, without fail, take the OFFENSIVE. "The defensive is the death of the insurrection" (My underlining). 4th—You must try to take the enemy by surprise and seize the moment when his forces are scattered. 5th—You must strive for DAILY successes, however small (one might say hourly, if it is the case of one town), and at all costs retain MORAL SUPERIORITY.

"Marx summed up his words in the words of Danton, the greatest master of revolutionary tactics yet known: de l'audace, de l'audace, encore de l'audace."

"Lenin always expressed the following fundamental question: The task of the Bolshevik Party consists of attracting millions of men to the politics of our Party. Only when millions of working masses join the movement, can one speak of true politics." Therefore he considered the insurrection in April–June of 1917 as negative. In October he himself said, waiting means death. This is necessary for the impatient comrades to have in mind."

Further on in my personal letter to Martí I indicated to him the following, which in my opinion is of great importance for the entire movement:

"In addition, the success of the Party in the revolutionary movement depends on the extent to which our PC and JC show themselves to be suitable and capable of winning over the majority of our class and leading it as their guide, their chief, fulfilling their vanguard functions. Only when the PC and the JC have finished their radical change, begun in February of this year, will we then be able to truly say to ourselves, the vanguard capable of any revolutionary action."

Later, in the same letter I indicated to them what my conclusions, my observations were about this transcendental problem. Before explaining this, two fundamental reasons must be explained that I observe will inevitably develop.

The Salvadoran (excuse the nationalism) is an impulsive, impatient kind, very given to doing everything immediately; but very little given to studying everything and looking and thinking before acting. If one says the slightest thing to the compañeros, they are immediately ready to comply, it doesn't matter if it's day or night, they comply, they make an effort to do the best possible. I would say they are dynamic types, that what they need is greater revolutionary consistency (theoretical and practical). I have observed that successive defeats discourage them, they violently disappoint them. This is a side that to my way of seeing things is very dangerous, which is why I have written said letter. This is due to the fact that there is no revolutionary tradition and if there is one it is only a few months old.

The revolution in El Salvador will be inevitably bloody. All the concentrated hate, which will build up more and more, will inevitably have to give it, in addition to everything else, a bloody nature. Don't think that I am against such a thing. I feel that this nature is the fundamental basis of the insurrection; something even more, I feel that only a hate to the death against capitalism will be capable of resolving some of the fickleness of the working masses.

Today we cannot consider that true revolutionary conditions exist, what exists is a severe aggravation of the crisis that will end in a true revolutionary situation.

DOCUMENT 5-2
Report by Comrade H Before Caribbean Bureau of Investigation, late 1932

This first selection consists of the report written by Comrade H, the surviving member of the PCS's central committee who went to New York in late 1932 to testify before an investigative committee of the Caribbean Bureau on the party's actions during the January uprising. The selection opens with a portion of H's original written report and concludes with transcripts from the verbal exchange between Comrade H and the committee members. Included in H's report is a description of the western region during the Matanza provided by a fellow comrade who traveled there to gather intelligence for the party. Comrade H credits the PCS and his fellow comrades for their commitment to the general cause of communism, but his precise details of the party's activities leading up the uprising suggests its limited influence over the events.[10]

At the end of 1930 the workers, not finding any orientation toward their revolutionary demands sided with those bourgeois groups that satisfied their demands personally, such as the demand for the suspension of the law of taxation. At the same time, the masses were informed by the propaganda of the leaders of Araujo, that at the close of the elections, the land would be distributed among them (the workers).

After December 21, after the massacre of Santa Ana, Comrade Martí was definitely deported from Salvador. The illegality of the leaders of the revolutionary movement of El Salvador was an accomplished fact. The lack of leadership during this period, the lack of concrete line for the workers during this period, brought about a condition of receding of the movement, which dates since December 21st up to March, 1931. During the period leaders were in jail. This was responsible for the receding of the movement. During this period the conditions of the crisis were aggravated. The contradictions in the capitalist camp also were noticed and the class struggle took on more of a militant character.

The presidential election took place in 1931. Araujo obtained 100,000 votes; Zárate, 60,000, Córdova———, Martínez, 2,000. The result of the elections proves also that the majority of the workers, who at the end of 1930 were controlled by the revolutionary organizations, supported Araujo and contributed in his election.

February 27, 1931, Martí came back to the country, and since then he devoted all his time to work for the reorganization of the revolutionary forces, that is, the reorganization of the FRT[S], the CP, the controlling of the independent forces of the ILD. These three organizations, together with the YCL [Communist Youth League] constituted the only revolutionary organizations of the country. On March 1st of that year Araujo took the presidency. This day was celebrated throughout the country by the workers. The workers thought it would be the beginning of the materialization of the promises made to them, especially that promise of the distribution of land. On March 15th there took place in San Salvador the first conference of the FRT which was held with the presence of seventy-four delegates, who were not the representatives of the various workers organizations in the departments of the country, but were the representatives of groups which remained loyal to the tactic which was then adopted by the Party of no intervention in the elections. In spite of the short time that transpired since the election of the President the workers understood pretty well that the promise of the distribution of the land and the other propaganda carried on by the propagandists of Araujo was nothing else but a means of fooling the masses to vote for Araujo. This was an opportunity for the reorganization of the trade unions, especially the agricultural union, which constitute the majority of the working classes in the Occident. Also, the opportunity of exposing the monopolizing of the land which left landless many workers.

Before the FRT conference, the movement attempted to concentrate in the cities without taking into consideration the basic industry of the country, which was agricultural production. It was necessary to work in the hacienda where the workers constituted the majority. The movement decided reorganization was to be among the agricultural workers.

From the period of March 15 to the 20th it was possible to proceed with the reorganization of the leadership of the CP in Salvador. Also attempts were made to direct the Party in accordance with the instructions received by them; for the transformation of the T.U. [trade union] committees into CP factions and for the effective work of the Party committee. It was also noticed that the lack of a clear form of organization was responsible for the lack of militants, of revolutionary spirit in the provinces.

During this critical period in the country it was easy for the workers to retrace their steps and come back to the trade unions and C.P. This movement was helped because of the discontent of the masses and on the March 20th the FRT organized a National Unemployment Council which called for demonstrations against unemployment and stopping of work. Demonstrations which were held in San Salvador and other cities. The demonstration in San Salvador was the most important. This proved to the leading organizations that the masses were coming back under the control of the revolutionary organizations....

It was the policy of the revolutionary organizations during this period between March, October–November of 1931 to work among the masses in order that when the time for the harvest and export of coffee came, which usually lasts from Oct. to March, there would be an opportunity to carry on an effective mass struggle in the coming period. The time of the municipal elections coincided with the harvest and the masses began to incorporate themselves into the revolutionary organizations to struggle for the economic demands. This disposition of the masses was very clearly seen and this was manifested undoubtedly by the great enthusiasm with which the masses greeted the decision of the C.P. to participate in the municipal elections....

At the end of the year [1931], that is from the 1st to the 10th, we made a balance as to the results of the recruiting campaign of the Party and revolutionary organizations. In San Salvador, Party had 40 members in March, 68 in September, and 280 at end of year which were organized in 7 street nuclei. And besides we had organized fractions in the motormen's union, construction workers union, and bakers union.

In Santa Ana we had 53 members organized in 4 street nuclei. In Sonsonate, at the beginning of the campaign we had 12 members, in middle we had 15 and at the end of the campaign, 18. In Ahuachapán we had 7 at the beginning and 70 at the end. In Santa Tecla we had 30 members. They were in the capitals of the states, not in the interior....

Q[uestion]: Did Party have any members in haciendas, plantations?

A[nswer]: Not certain as to number but Party did have nuclei in plantations....

Q: At a meeting of the CC when the election question was taken up [as to whether the Central Committee of the Party wanted to delay the insurrection] you invited a Party member that had come from Argentina. Was this Comrade called for advice?

A: Was not called because he was not a member of the CC. But I spoke to him in the morning, and he was in full agreement with my proposal. Following this decision I asked the comrades what was to be done, and they decided to meet the following day, and that some comrades should be instructed to go to the neighboring organizations in the town of Soyopango and that we await the developments of the events in that town. They did not manifest anything of what was to be done in Salvador itself which, as I have already stated, was under siege and it was impossible to do anything.

On the 21st it was impossible to meet because the house we were to meet in had already been raided. The comrades who owned the house had been candidate for mayor of city of Salvador. He and his family were placed in jail. That morning I was informed that Comrades Maraki Mármol, Morales had been detained. Rest had disappeared. I remained in Salvador until the 5th of February. On the 2nd Comrade M... secured a pass from the Minister of the Interior and went to Ahuachapán. She returned on the 3rd of February and gave me the following report:

At midnight of January 22, all villages of the West were taken by our comrades, that is La Libertad, Ahuachapán, Santa Tecla, Sonsonate, and Santa Ana. In Santa Ana all the villages were taken by our forces with the exception of Metapan. In Sonsonate the central armory was occupied for three hours by our forces. The cities of the state of Sonsonate for 7 hours. At midnight of January 22nd martial law was declared throughout the country. Special trains of troops were sent to Sonsonate. These troops took back the villages and repulsed our comrades from the armories. It must be stated that in Sonsonate our comrades attacked the city with 5,000, in Ahuachapán approximately 5,000 comrades attacked the capital. The attack against the capital by our forces was not directly supported by all the organizations due to the fact that everyone of them has special assignments, one for instance was to proclaim Soviets, and other had other tasks.

The government was occupying the cities in the surroundings of Santa Ana and Ahuachapán. Strong detachments were advancing toward the Eastern region. The National Guards were also mobilized. This advance was undertaken after the government assured itself of the capital in which martial law had been in effect, ordering anyone on the streets after 5 p.m. captured. Mass arrests took place. In the evening the jails were vacated, the prisoners taken in the surrounds of the city, mass shootings took place. The bodies were left exposed on the streets.

The government troops occupied Ahuachapán and Sonsonate, occupying villages that were being abandoned one after the other by our comrades after the most heroic resistance. On the 26th of January special report made by the expeditionary forces stated that in Sonsonate 800,000 [probably 800 or 8,000] comrades were killed. The entire villages abandoned by our comrades were reduced to ashes by the government troops. The comrades were going toward Guatemala.

On January 29th the government troops occupied our last stronghold, Tacuba. [Note: this actually occurred on January 25.] Our last revolutionary forces were in Tacuba, unable to get to Guatemala because [t]his field was occupied by troops under General Odiga of Guatemala. We must say very few were able to pass, only those comrades who knew the roads and were fortunate in getting to the other side. But we have no concrete data as to the number. About 200 were killed. Our comrades were hanged by the tens, and their bodies remained hanging for a few days. Suspicious elements were arrested. Emergency degrees were put into effect by government. Bourgeoisie, which was armed from the very beginning, undertook to carry out these executions. No village was left. No finca, no plantation. Executions took place of all suspicious elements, not sparing women and children. Amount killed estimated to be from 19,000 to 21,000....

When the woman comrade came back to San Salvador she told me that she thought I had died in the Western region; but that the authorities knew my whereabouts and were looking for me in the capital. I attempted, therefore, to get a passport in the Guatemala Legation. The passport was given me, but the stipulation was that I had to present myself to the police headquarters for a visa. I did not want to do this. Through a friend of mine I was able to get a pass through the National Guard, in his own name. This enabled me to get to the Zaculinta and from there take the train to L'Ing.... There I found Costillo who I thought was in San Salvador. Got word to him that he must leave and go to the orient near Honduras frontier....

Q: Do you know whether this actually took place, or are you assuming that they followed instructions?

A: This the report given me by this woman comrade who went to Ahuachapán. She got in touch with the people wherever she went and she was told this actually happened....

I estimate that the insurrection in El Salvador was in reality the conclusion of a series of events of class struggle, which events entered fully into display with the terrific crisis since the beginning of March 1931. These events could only end with the events of January. If the insurrection had, for one reason or another, been postponed by the CC, the impulse of the masses was such, and this from the very beginning, for struggle, that at any rate, this could only end as it did. [...]

DOCUMENT 5-3
Reply by Comrade R to Comrade H, Caribbean Bureau of Investigation, late 1932

Comrade H's initial report is followed here by the response from Comrade R, the main spokesperson for the Caribbean Bureau's investigative committee. He criticizes harshly the PCS, accusing it of committing a major error in judgment by joining the uprising. He also argues that the party's willingness to consider insurrection as a viable option reveals that too many party members adhered to improper "sectarian" or "putchist" ideological views. But perhaps even more revealing, R accuses the party of ineffectiveness and of having had limited organizational ties with the rebellious masses. Thus, the party was neither able to prevent the masses from embarking on a doomed insurrection, or of properly leading them in such an event.[11]

On the report itself, I want at this time to make only a few preliminary observations.... The first and most important one, in my opinion, is that the January uprising in Salvador was a genuine mass revolutionary movement of peasants and agricultural workers. That the uprising has historical significance for the revolutionary movement of the whole of Latin America and that it constitutes the beginning of a rising surge of revolutionary mass struggle throughout Latin America, which will be led by the Communist Parties of those countries. The January struggles in Salvador, in my opinion, are not the end of a pervious period....

The present situation in Salvador arises primarily from this fact. A powerful revolutionary upsurge of the masses and a small and weak Communist Party, which was very strongly, especially in its top leadership, dominated by putchist, sectarian ideology. And I will undertake to show by a more concrete examination of the events in Salvador that this is the key to an understanding of what happened in Salvador.

I think it is pretty well established that during the months from approximately March 1931 to the beginning of 1932, the mass revolutionary upsurge in Salvador was constantly rising. This is demonstrated very clearly in the last vote and the wide mass support given to the communists in the municipal elections. It is also shown in the numerous and wide agricultural and peasant struggles, especially in the Occident, although there were also various struggles of agricultural masses in the Orient with which our comrades, unfortunately, had no contact. And finally it has shown itself in the January uprising itself, which would have embraced considerable masses also in the Orient of Salvador if the Communist Party had carried on any revolutionary activities in that part of the country. Thus there can be no doubt that from the spring of 1931, and on, we were dealing with a rapidly rising revolutionary mass upsurge, due primarily to the catastrophic crisis, the white terror, the disillusionment of wide sections of workers and peasants with the Araujo government; to the activities of the Communist Party and the other revolutionary organizations. The sharpening contradictions between bourgeoisie landlord groups and within the bourgeois landlord Imperialist camp, generally has also contributed toward undermining the stability of the Araujo government. Thus forcing the masses to press forward with the revolutionary struggle against the existing conditions.

This is one side of the picture. Then let us examine the strength and organization of the Communist Party, the revolutionary union, the Young Communist League, the peasant leagues, etc. At the highest point in 1931 the membership of the Party in Salvador did not amount to more than about two hundred people, or thereabouts, according to the reporter himself. The membership of the revolutionary unions, the reporter did not give us. He only indicated that there were a large number of unions, including unions among the agricultural workers, but in view of the entire information at our disposal it is safe to assume that these unions were weak unions. They were not really entrenched with large membership in the big Occident plantations, factories, railroads, etc. Peasant Leagues, the reporter did not mention a single word about peasant leagues. Obviously there were none, and incidentally I must make note here of the fact that the reporter spoke as though there are no peasants at all in Salvador, when as a matter of fact there are large numbers, undoubtedly the bulk of the agricultural population in Salvador are landless peasants. And even the agricultural workers, in large numbers, are semipeasants themselves. But there were no peasant leagues. The Young Communist League was undoubtedly even weaker than the Party from the point of view of membership and organization. And when you inquire how the Party itself was organized, how its units were functioning, you must come to the conclusion, on the basis of the report itself, that at the time of the uprising the Party was making its first steps—I emphasize—its first steps to organize itself on the basis of nuclei, on the basis of a stable membership carrying on activities among the masses. And this, contrasted with the rapidly growing mass revolutionary upsurge, gives us the key to an understanding of the chief weaknesses of our movement and its shows what the 11th Plenum of the Ecci already emphasized—the danger of the lagging behind of the Communist Party. And it also leads us into another question. The question of the correct methods of revolutionary mass work, to which also the 11th Plenum has drawn the special attention of all Communist Parties and which I will deal with later on.

I think we ought to devote our main attention to an estimation of the methods of mass work. What was the approach of the Salvador Communists to the masses? How did they visualize the task of winning the masses, winning the majority of the working class, of the peasantry, for the revolution? And how did they go about fulfilling this task of winning the masses and organizing them for the revolution? With this question, which in my opinion, is the decisive one before us, we cannot undertake to deal with before we get the report, that is, we could deal with this question only sporadically but not thoroughly enough....

The fact that there can have been so many serious weaknesses in the military preparations we see by the fact that the government was on the very eve of the insurrection able to locate and arrest what they called the general staff. I am not in a position, as I said, to more concretely discuss it except to indicate what is so obvious, that when the government is able so easily to attack and seize the general staff in the headquarters there must have been something basically wrong in the preparations for military activities. I attach great importance to military preparations. Also, the fact that the government was able to arrest practically all our groups in the army. The comrade reported we have Communists or revolutionary groups in the machine-gun regiment, in the infantry regiment, which were to play a decisive part in the revolution. Now the government is able to seize not only the general staff but pick out from the regiments the revolutionary groups....

The third point I want to raise in the connection is this. How did it happen that our forces were merely concentrated on the plantations in the coffee regions? These forces, having started out to seize the provinces, found no response in the cities themselves. An army of insurgents marched from the surroundings to Sonsonate. But what happened in Sonsonate itself? This is a political question, the organization of city workers, city petty-bourgeoisie. This is a political question but also a military question. The concentration was in the villages, separate from the masses, cannot link up both forces.

Another outstanding fact is that the CC, as such, was practically out of commission during the uprising. No CC to lead the masses, the revolutionary military committee consisted of three; one was arrested, the other two did nothing, therefore the committee as such, did not exist. No central leadership, no national leadership, just a series of local insurrections....

It is also impossible to deal at present with the lessons of the uprising itself. This is impossible because we know practically nothing of how the uprising developed in various localities, how the fight took place.

DOCUMENT 5-4
Response by Comrade H, Caribbean Bureau of Investigation, late 1932

H more or less agreed with the central premises of R's criticisms. It might be possible to read H's response as being driven by fear of the Comintern and his unwillingness to challenge its spokespersons. Suggestive of this possibility are the moments when H says that he didn't realize the party's errors or deviations at the time. But this response does not vary significantly from H's initial report, suggesting the party's limits over the uprising.[12]

I stated in my report that what we did in Salvador was what we thought correct. It has been established that it was absolutely incorrect.

When there is participation in events, and when part is taken in all its preparations, the tendency of the participants may express itself in not finding the opportunity for self-criticism, because the mistakes are of a general nature. Because of lack of examination, it is considered correct at a given moment. And what appears correct at a given moment needs the experience and criticism of a comrade, or comrades, better prepared, to analyze all the mistakes and deviations that took place. Our case in Salvador is such a case.

We proceeded from the point of view that the line laid down by us was a correct one. We thought that our tactic was a correct tactic, but it is clear that the events have proven that we have been mistaken. But it is not enough to draw the experiences from the events. It was necessary to criticize, clarify our point of view, and all the mistakes and errors made.

We cannot deny that the putchist, sectarian, and left-opportunist tendency, pointed out by Comrade R was unquestionably the one that prevailed in the thoughts of every member of the CC of Salvador and all the members of the Party who participated in the appreciation of the situation and the decisions and resolutions that were to be adopted in accordance with the situation.

Thus, until I arrived in Tegu[cigalpa] and read the appreciations of the El Salvador events I realized the existence of those tendencies in the CP, without succeeding in learning the real significance of the tendencies. I learned immediately that we had suffered from these tendencies and deviations. But even today I am not in a position yet to know in what these deviations consisted. I believe that all the comrades who have read the appreciation in El Communists find themselves in the same situation I find myself.

Nevertheless, I consider that if our tendencies in El Salvador were the same as those of the bourgeois parties, at the same time our Party suffering of chieftain (*caudillo*) tendencies, then the name given is correct when it is applied to our case. Those tendencies which Comrade R referred to are predominant in all Caribbean Parties and it is not the result of the lack of training of Party policy. Caudillian tendencies were inoculated in our Communist Parties by the wrong activities of the comrades of the left over from the parties of the bourgeoisie. The comrades are giving up these old tendencies, they are getting closer to the Communist Party but they do not come into it clean but with all these remnants, which manifest themselves at the first opportunity....

In our case, all the comrades are guilty of these mistakes. There was not one single comrade who could foresee the repercussions of the events, not only completely, but not even superficially, and to bring it forward in a manner which could be discussed.

We estimated good things, we were mistaken, and the most militant of our movement paid with their lives, faithful (no one can doubt) to the cause of the revolution. But it is clear they would be Communists if after receiving such a lesson, in their own flesh, they would be capable of bringing forward lessons from the depth where they find themselves.

The misery of the masses in this period increased daily because of the crisis, and in those countries where agricultural is the dominating economy, we felt the crisis in one single stroke and then it is logical that the masses demand to solve their situation through the means they consider most correct. But there is, undoubtedly, the danger of not counting with the Communist Party, which, without having developed the rhythm, the capacity to lead the masses in the development of the different stages that take place in the course of the daily struggles. If we do not count with the Communist Party being in such a position, nothing can be begun.

Our case in Salvador is the typical question of the situation prevailing in the Caribbean countries. On the one hand, the masses in the months of the crop, even those in the course of the year, that suffer hunger and misery when the crop comes, it makes them feel their own situation so badly and so suddenly that they endeavor to break off once and for all the load imposed on them by the native exploiters and Imperialism. On the one hand, we had the masses very anxious to liberate themselves, and on the other hand, a Communist Party, weak, but which had influence among the masses, a Communist Party carried away by the impulse of the masses and contaminated by them instead of training them and without the Party itself being trained in the constant struggle of immediate demands, and as the last resort, having the determination to put itself at the head of them in the struggle, which ended with the results which we all know.

It is clear that it is easier now, that we know the results, to analyze the objective and subjective factors existing then in Salvador. And it is easy to say, in such circumstances, that everything that was done was bad....

When referring to the membership of the Communist Party in Salvador Comrade R mentioned that there were only 250, approximately, in the country. There were about 520 members. Of course the estimate of the membership of the Communist Party is an essential point, but I do not believe that we should give this much importance as to establish a given amount of inhabitants a given number of members of the Communist Party in order to be able to carry on struggle. For example, for 100 population if we need 100 Party members to be able to carry on a decisive struggle with effective results against the bourgeoisie and Imperialism and for the agrarian anti-imperialist revolution, we would be reducing the revolution to a simple arithmetic question. If the Communist Party of El Salvador was able to mobilize with its 520 members from 45 to 50,000 workers in the coffee plantations, it is clear that it did not consist in the number of Party members but, as he himself later states, in the forms of organizations. On the other hand, if we rely only on the number, that is to say the subjective factors, without counting the fact that there might be enormous objective conditions, it becomes more obvious that the comrades in the Caribbean countries must intensify their campaign of recruiting. That until they increase the number of members they are incapable to act. We must make this question clear for them and make them see that each one of the members that come into the Party must be recruited as militants of daily struggles influenced by the Party.

DOCUMENT 5-5

Report on El Salvador from Santa Ana Comrades, 1936

The issue of internal party factionalism over ideological issues, and especially over historical interpretations of 1932, is clearly demonstrated in the following excerpt. It is drawn from a document written in

1936 by a faction of the PCS in Santa Ana. They refer specifically to the existence of varying party factions throughout the country in the aftermath of the Matanza. But they also reveal that these factions have their roots in the pre-1932 era. They then proceed to explain how and why the events of 1932 transpired as they did. They hail Martí, disparage the Mexican Comintern agent Francisco Anaya, and subtly shift the description of the uprising to one that promotes a proinsurrectionary stance.[13]

In order to be able to analyze the current status of the social movement in El Salvador, an historical overview of this movement is necessary first....

Although Fernández Anaya had the intention of organizing the Salvadoran P.C. with legal status, that year we saw nothing apart from the formation of the S.R.I., which was practically a transformation of the FRTS. With the economic base of the movement thus converted into an organ of defense with combative functions, Martí was the standard bearer who gave his all to the movement with his propaganda and sacrifices, and the Salvadoran P.C. began to form with members who were the most distinguished of the era and the most experienced in organizing matters, and one of their objectives was, first, to try to extract the masses from the influence of the bourgeois electoral parties, which was not achieved as shown by the overwhelming victory of the Araujo laborists in 1930. The masses, deceived by laborist demagoguery, began to be enlightened by the massacres of workers perpetrated in Zaragoza and Sonsonate (1931), and with this, the P.C. and the S.R.I. gained strength, taking advantage of the moment to demonstrate the treachery of the laborist leaders and to win over proletarian sympathies. With the movement fortified by the laborist desertion, with a portion constituted by peasant masses enthused about winning their immediate betterment, a series of agrarian strikes began, of which the majority were successful. A well-conceived movement that collapsed with the massacres of Atiquizaya (December 1931).

The bourgeoisie, and therefore the state, in considering the dimensions that the demands of the P.C. were taking on and its degree of development promised electoral freedom, an action that served to prove the magnitude of the movement when proletarian candidates ran in the municipal elections (January 1932) per P.C. resolution. With the civic action of the proletariat quashed by government repression, the masses, heroic in their political and social rights, and in good part in substance seeking economic and Party improvement with the very untimely fall from Power of their caudillo Araujo, were fertile ground for the rapid dissemination of Communist propaganda toward to the taking of political power by the proletariat, which culminated on January 22, 1932.

As can be seen from the account of the events, the ideological state of the trade unions in the departments was poor and of a markedly collaborationist bent, and despite the fact that the FRTS was already affiliated with the Third International, outside of the Capital the fundamental revolutionary watchwords of the I.C. [Communist International] were unknown, which led the trade unions, in their demands, to lamentably confuse their economic watchwords with those of the political struggle. It was not until the arrival of the Guatemalan Antonio Obando Sánchez, who organized the first autonomous local of the P.C. here (with no other instructions that the organizational format) that we half understood the political end that was being sought. And due to our ignorance, at that time we were not capable of analyzing the political ideology of C[omrade] Obando, it wasn't until afterward that we understood that the C. in mention suffered from leftist failings.

Given such a disorderly beginning to the social situation, Communist cells sprung up everywhere, which were lacking in revolutionary discipline and which were almost completely ignorant of Marxist-Leninist tactics and theory, and lacking in cohesion and full of prejudices, leading to dissension and rivalries among the leaders of the departmental cells. The centralism that the C.E. [Executive Committee] of the P.C.S. tried to exercise among the departmental committees, instead of preventing this, laid them open to biting criticisms, some of an opportunistic nature and others of leftism, and it happened that, when a sincere compañero tried to correct all these anomalies, the leaders who had taken offense and were recognized by the C.C. [Central Committee] complained to it, and the C.C., faithful to its discipline, considered that compañero expelled, without meeting him, without hearing him, and without even addressing the reason for his criticism; hundreds of good comrades were expelled and disowned in this way, who shortly afterward would also fall victim to the brutal repression of bourgeois militarism.

Among the Marxist intellectuals that we knew, C. Martí was the only capable one, because of his sincerity, upon whom we truly counted in the struggle and who, despite his knowledge made his mistakes, such as developing revolutionary propaganda that was too vast and for an imperialist country, which did not fit in a colonial framework such as ours, of relative, transitory liberty, and furthermore he did not analyze the class consciousness that existed among the compañeros in the C.E. of the P.C. and from the FRTS, compañeros of inferior ability, to whose discipline he submitted, without intelligently imposing his position as leader beforehand, since the above-mentioned councils were still influenced by the leftist tactics of Fernández Anaya.

The P.C.S., composed as we said, of heroic, self-sacrificing, but intellectually handicapped, compañeros, after centralizing the executive power, but still influenced by a dangerous extremism that did not enable them to be politicians, fell into the electionist trap set by Martínez, and impoliticly abandoning the series of strikes that were breaking out every day on the large estates and which had already reached alarming proportions, changed the course of the situation and threw themselves into the electoral campaign for the municipalities, disorganized, without a defined battle plan, without studying the social and political conditions of the time, simply following an urge to compete with the opposing parties of the bourgeoisie and make a show of force. Numerically and out of discipline, the proletariat that supported our candidates made a grandiose showing of solidarity to our P.C., which greatly alarmed the bourgeoisie and gave the militarist government the opportunity to win the servile support of this bourgeoisie. This showing gave the class enemies the opportunity to verify the numerical capacity of the movement and the regions that were the best organized, thus giving them the ability to plan its extermination, first inciting the masses to a revolutionary strike, and then unleashing terror and persecution against the most distinguished fighters, while closing down the union halls. And since this measure affected all the parties in opposition to Martínez and the discontent was general, in a plenum of the P.C. the possibility was raised of taking advantage of the discontent of the masses in order to attempt the taking of political power by the proletariat. This plenum lacked responsibility, insofar as there were connections in it between members of the bourgeoisie and several leaders in charge of the P.C., even in the Revolutionary Council that was formed to direct the action petty-bourgeois individuals were included who never had contact with the masses and who dedicated themselves, in several villages, to inciting the masses to commit outrages instead of reaching revolutionary objectives, for the purpose of diverting the attention of the true and loyal red soldiers. Several of these same individuals later denounced our compañeros who had managed to save themselves from the massacre, before the military councils, or instead persecuted them personally, invested with authority as Civic Guards. In summary: the responsibility for this horrendous massacre in 1932 is due, in part, to Luis Felipe Recinos and to the leftist tactics of Fernández Anaya, and in part to C. Martí's submission to the discipline of the C.E. of the P.C.S.

As will be understood from the explanation, the principal cause of the massacre were the tactical errors of the C.C.E. [Central Executive Committee], first for sending delegations to the departments made up of members drunk on leaderism, who in the face of the insistence of the C.C. that was demanding the rapid training of cadres, and feeling threatened in their position as militants if they did not comply with the pressing job, turned to deceit, informing the departmental Committees and the C.C. of having organized cadres in the cantons, which in reality did not go beyond being simple informational meetings, which were attended more by curiosity seekers than by the true followers, of whom they made lists and then sent them to the P.C. as affiliated cadre, and with these false statistics, the C.C. believed it had been strengthened. (Evidence of this maneuver came principally from this region.) With regard to the regions where there were organized cadres, the work of those delegates was more opportunistic, inasmuch as they exploited the good faith of the peasants, living for a long time at their expense, several of them going to the extreme of trying to force themselves on the daughters of the aforementioned comrades. In those regions, in order to not be criticized for their disgraceful actions, they replaced the Cs that made up the committees with honorable compañeros, this is true, but lacking revolutionary preparation they didn't dare inform on them. For this reason, the organizations in the country were in the hands of irresponsible leaders, who were lacking in solid political preparation, and who at the same time were nothing more than instruments subjected to the command of the C.C. of the P.C.S., and at the same time, who would plan the revolution without previously having even organized any departmental socialist council, soviets or military councils, which would be what would take over the economic and military administration at the necessary time. When the military councils were appointed, primarily in this (January 1932) several compañeros who were appointed for it, some were already being persecuted while others had already fallen into the hands of the authorities, and despite those anomalies of great political importance, on that extremely false basis that clearly demonstrated that there was no organization here at all, the action still went on deliberately, resulting in a horrifying slaughter that had the outcome of spiritually smashing the masses because of the terror spread by the bourgeoisie and the military caste, leaving us, as the only gain, the demarcation of classes. This of course marked a shift to action that we judge as being favorable for illegal struggle.

Shortly after the massacre, small groups of organized workers and peasants appeared in villages and hamlets in the center and west of the Republic, all autonomous, ideologically separate and disoriented, mistrusting each other, eyeing each other with suspicion and fighting amongst themselves. For example here, there are four or five groups with communist tendencies, each with its own watchwords and tasks and which we have struggled to unite, but they have refused to merge, and we all live separately and in a terrible passivity. (I will give details of this merging below.) In the Capital, leaders of the old school who suffered the brutality of the repression have also organized and rebuilt the political leadership of the P.C. (which in fact exists nowhere but in the Capital), who believing no doubt they are reaping results, have put methods into practice that are typical of legality, such as posters and manifestos, probably with the good intention of sabotaging bourgeois politics, but with negative results for our cause because the known militant compañeros who are ignorant of the maneuvers in the capital section are the ones who suffer the vexations of the reaction, while at the same time, with this, sympathizers of the I.C. who could possibly be organized become fearful and move away from us. We judge these acts to be exhibitionist and opportunistic, contrary to the cause because of the resulting effects on the spirits of the masses who are still frightened by the terror, and what makes us doubt the sincerity of the compañeros in the capital is how they have set themselves up as the head office of the Salvadoran movement dependent on the National Council of the P.C.S. residing in Tegucigalpa, we feel that there they do not know that this section is made up of members among whom there are several of dubious conduct, and if we say this it is because of statements made by compañeros imprisoned since '33 until the present, who say that the work done by this section is reduced to forming revolutionary groups, that then, quite easily, are picked up by the police, with the Salvadoran section limiting itself to reporting to the C.N. [National Council] of the P.C. of Tegucigalpa about their work, and using this trick to justify spending the money that they send. This, of course, we have not been able to prove; it has been impossible, but we inform you as information that we demand be communicated to the Caribbean Bureau so that a detailed investigation can be conducted.

DOCUMENT 5-6
Miguel Mármol, Brief Historical Notes on the Labor Movement in El Salvador, 1948

During his tenure in Guatemala in the 1940s, after fleeing persecution by the military government in El Salvador, Mármol wrote the following historical summary of the labor movement in El Salvador. In many ways, this brief but substantive document is a precursor to Mármol's narrative to Dalton in 1966. One of the main elements that emerges from this document is Mármol's frank discussion of the factions within the communist movement; in particular, he argues that new "intellectual" communists are trying to pin past party failures on old cadres. Inherent in this accusation of failure is a historical interpretation, which suggests that the factional split is being played out in rival renditions of the past. Mármol is coming to the defense of his fellow "old cadres" by insisting that they made many strides in the organizational work in the late 1920s and early 1930s. But he remains vague on any specifics relating to the 1932 uprising.[14]

Union Work in the Countryside

As fruits of the experience and enthusiasm obtained in Mexico by our delegates who attended one of the Congresses of the Mexican Regional Labor Confederation (C.R.O.A.), held in 1927, union activities were taken to the countryside, to the strongest coffee-growing regions—center and West—as well as among the urban workers in Santa Ana, Sonsonate, Ahuachapán, and Santa Tecla. And it was after the return from Uruguay of the delegation that attended the first Congress of the Union Confederation of Latin America (C.S.L.A.) held in Montevideo in '28 that labor work began in earnest among the workers in the factories and other enterprises located in the Capital, with this work being done more intensively among the agricultural workers and peasantry in the Central and Western zones of the country....

Red Aid Back in Action

Because of the Red Aid meeting, Farabundo Martí went to prison once more and responded again with a hunger strike, which lasted actively for 27 days—27 days that were also days of hard struggle for the workers of San Salvador, Santa Ana, Sonsonate, and rural workers. This time the peasants from Sonsonate were massacred, primarily indigenous people from Izalco; this was on May 17 in '31 by the Santa Ana Cavalry, which acted on orders from the Field Commander of Sonsonate, Colonel Juan Ortiz. Many were killed, among them compañero Crespín, an outstanding peasant fighter; tens of wounded and hundreds of prisoners. It also needs to be remembered with indignation that days before this murder, peasant compañeros from Azuehillo, Zaragoza, who were meeting peaceably and unarmed, were massacred.

This time Martí, with the support of the masses and with the public's flattering opinion clearly on his side, came out with flying colors and carried on the struggle with greater ardor and enthusiasm, in response to the tenacious persecution set off by Araujo, whose strength and hegemony was being reduced across the country by the day....

Considerations

If the tragic events of '32 had not occurred, so fatefully arranged by Martínez and his clique, in order to, according to him, finish off the union movement once and for all, murdering tens of thousands of workers to this end in the most horrendous, cowardly fashion, making them dig their own graves, burying them like locusts, machine-gunning settlements on farms and in villages without taking any risk, and mercilessly shooting into the depths of the ravines in search of new victims, subjecting the workers from the central and western zones to three months of persecution with a phobia and great cruelty never before seen, making abundant use of the law of flight [shot while "trying to escape"] and, as a specialty, playing bayonet with the worker leaders, and hanging indigenous leaders in public view: it should be added and emphasized that in this horrifying slaughter masses [indecipherable] juveniles and even developing adolescents, since the composition of the organizations was 40 percent prepubescent youth and women of all ages.

If this despotism had not been suffered, the F.R.T.S. would have been able to fulfill its historical mission, bringing together all the wage workers of the country and the peasantry until a better life was won; since the peasants, desperate from their growing poverty and the threat of having 90 percent of their lands expropriated, which they had mortgaged to the farm owners, would have squeezed all the revolutionary fervor they were overcome with into that titanic struggle for liberation....

Prejudice from False or Misinterpreted Theories

The trade union movement in El Salvador has been suffering since 1936, time and again, from false theoretical and scientific appreciations;

this has happened each time new activists emerge, meaning younger ones. We attribute these errors, then, to a great extent to the failings in the actions of 1946 recorded lately. A movement, if the truth be told, which lacked a true direction, since they did not know how to bring the unions into the struggle from the beginning. There was no true unity in the struggle, in tactical action, the reason why the railroad workers instead acted independently and when the initial push was already over. In addition, there were other errors of a political nature.

Because of those marked theoretical errors, an inequality has been seen in workers' consciousness in El Salvador. It is not that remote that there would still be those in El Salvador who believe that it is fair that unions that we would call elite, superior unions, exist, around which the "inferior" unions revolve.

Ever since Marxist currents penetrated El Salvador, among members with no militancy among the masses, there has been discrimination against and underestimation of the union camp, arguing that the guilds are masses of artisans and for that reason they cannot unionize, placing importance only on factory workers and special attention, from their desks or small circles, on organizing the railroad workers, electricians, and the coffee, sugar, and cotton workers, as if it hadn't been done before....

These theorizing members coming from the intellectual and professional camp have never been sufficiently consequent; who instead of accepting the responsibility of improving the practical capacity of the old militants, have tried to invalidate them, holding them responsible for all the guilt in the aforementioned failures. They have never taken it upon themselves to conduct a careful, in-depth study to clarify for certain what the Martínez period truly was and to stimulate what was worthwhile in the efforts made in the past and the successes peremptorily won. And also because they have been ignorant of the conditions that existed in those years of tough international struggle in the 1914–18 postwar period, of its third phase of grave economic crisis sharpened by the Stock Market crash in the United States that was for 7.5 billion dollars that deeply shook the world economy, this period followed by the prewar period from 1932–39. The third 1914–18 postwar period culminated with the Matanza of '32 in our country, and the prewar period of 193[?]–39, began with the ascent of Nazism in Germany that murdered the revolution in that country, with the murder of Sandino, the invasion of Ethiopia by the Italian fascists, the invasion of Republican Spain by the Italian-German fascists, and the civil war in China (the Italian invasion in Abyssinia).

It is true that they have tried to train new worker and artisan members, but instead of linking these to the old cadres, it has turned out that there has been maliciousness by these new ones toward the old ones, and in reaction, from the old ones toward the new ones, since there have been sharp differences in judgment and bad accounting. They have tried to humiliate the old cadres by saying they are incompetent, but they have been and especially during their time, incapable of combating with better energy the demagogic acts of Martínez, who made a farce of "land distribution," the construction of "inexpensive houses," his road policy, the Sports "plebiscites," the enlistment of huge numbers of workers for the Panama Canal.

It is advisable, then, to rectify these negative attitudes and carefully review union development from its beginnings; this on the one hand; on the other, study the history of our society's development, the country's economic picture from an international viewpoint and assimilate union theory more and better, from a completely Marxist point of view. Then, disseminate this knowledge better without exception among the members, meaning among all the militants, and among the workers in workshops, in factories, in electrical enterprises, railroad workers, and agricultural workers. And to observe a completely revolutionary ethic with the rest of the compañeros that encourages each and every one of the compañeros.

The preceding report is a bare outline that would be immediately strengthened with input from the rest of the militants. It merits particular information on the role of the Popular University, on Red Aid, and an explanation of the electoral question when dealing with informing from a political point of view. This effort is still vague, given that it is necessary to specify dates, details, and names of magnificent fighters who gave their lives, their youth, and their childhood for the sake of the struggle.

DOCUMENT 5-7
David Luna, *Tribuna Libre*, "The Uprising of 1932," 1963

EXCERPT

David Luna was a leftist scholar at the University of El Salvador who participated in the 1963 Central American History Seminar held at the UES. At that seminar both he and his colleague, Jorge Arias Gómez, analyzed the events of 1932 from the perspective of the party's traditional adherence of delayed insurrection. Jorge Arias said the party had not been the leader of events in 1932. Instead he looked to the western masses themselves for responsibility, whereas Luna accused the communists of having had responsibility for the uprising in order to harshly criticize them for deciding to rebel. The following excerpt is derived from a piece Dr. Luna wrote for the newspaper Tribuna Libre *in 1963, the same year as the history seminar. His argument in the following piece is more consistent with Jorge Arias in that he distances the party from the rebellion and gives agency to the western masses. He even focuses on the issue of ethnicity. He analyzes El Salvador from a Marxist perspective in order to say that an armed revolution was not an option in 1932 because the country had not yet passed into a stage of mature capitalism. He identifies Jorge Fernández Anaya as an important figure in the Communist Party—a reference rarely made by leftist interpreters who advocated for guerrilla warfare because Anaya had been the founder of the party's strategy of delayed insurrection. The following excerpt shows the complicated nature of leftist interpretations of 1932 in that Luna could offer two different approaches of the uprising on differing occasions but with the common result of promoting his support for the party's contemporary strategy of delayed insurrection. Nevertheless, Luna offers in the following document some of the strong critiques of the communists in 1932 that he also said publicly at the history seminar. It was this type of argument by Luna that Roque Dalton attacked so vociferously in both the* Miguel Mármol *testimonial and his 1972 history of the communist party, which appears as the next document.*[15]

Those who are known as "*obreros*" [unskilled laborers] were not the European-style industrial proletariat that had served as the basis for founding the socialist and later communist parties. They were artisans, of a petty-bourgeois composition, and closer to anarchistic rather than socialistic political manifestations.

The agricultural *jornaleros* [day workers] were better qualified, which in the end turned out to be explosive:

1) They were proletariatized peasants stripped of their lands by the voracious large landholders and coffee growers. The Law on the Termination of Ejidos and Indigenous Communities of 1882 and other additional provisions (for example, the Agrarian Law) were the legal testament of this usurpation that sooner or later would be answered with arms in hand.

Feliciano Ama, indigenous cacique from Izalco, justified his affiliation to the revolutionary movement, saying that the Regalado family had usurped the lands that had been left to him by his ascendants (for that purpose he would show injuries on his fingers that represented the violence he had suffered) for the granting of land titles.

2) The semipeasants and jornaleros of the Western Region were to a great extent remains of the indigenous nationality oppressed over the centuries. In addition to the economic-social conflict that was assumed by their condition as agricultural obreros, they felt ancestral racial hatred toward the white exploiter....

A point that is also known by all history scholars is that our independence did not generate a capitalist revolution as it did in the United States. Any step toward a socialist revolution must take into account the aforementioned supposition....

A group of anti-imperialists, along with anarcho-syndicalist laborers and artisans founded, as we have explained, an organization [the Communist Party] that had in its sights the destruction of the nation's economic and social structure. It was, then, a profoundly revolutionary party, which was assisted and advised from the outside by the Mexican Marxist political organizations. Jorge Fernández Anaya, a communist since the age of fourteen, an organizer of Aztec agricultural worker unions, hardened in this type of struggle, was detailed in order to provide advice and collaboration to the Salvadoran revolutionary movement. This important person, together with a hundred activists, devoted himself in the early months of 1930 to organizing unions of agricultural workers in the center-west region of the country....

[Note: In the following sentence/paragraph, Luna is referring to the policies of the Martínez government after the overthrow of Araujo in early December 1931.] The Martínez government initiated a series of provocations in order to inflame the peasant masses even more, with the objective of propelling them into a fight in which he knew he would dominate them without ceremony....

With regard to the question asked by many as to whether this insurrection was a socialist proletarian revolution, I have to answer in the negative. The insurgents issued no decree nationalizing the land, a necessary and immediate supposition for a revolution of this type. They limited themselves to conducting military operations that did not have the success expected. The insurrection was only seeking to take Power by a party that believed itself to be backed by broad strata of the population in order to carry out a bourgeois democratic revolution. The fact that the participation was for the most part peasant does not take away from this idea, since the same phenomenon had occurred in Mexico twenty years earlier. The difference with the Mexican Revolution is that the masses in Mexico were led by the bourgeoisie, while in our country, the people were, for the first time, an actor in history and were not following any other class.

This is the only positive thing to come out of the insurrection of '32. The people, in a childlike and heroic way, wanted to make history with their own hands and with their own feet. This is one of the principal reasons why they were massacred mercilessly, since it was not the present enemy being liquidated, but the future one.

Causes of the Insurrection:
1st Economic crisis of 1929 (Drop in coffee prices).
2nd Political crisis caused by the overthrow of civil power in the Republic.
3rd Lack of political play in the electoral parties of the bourgeoisie.
4th Political frustration of the masses because of the demagoguery of the parties of the bourgeoisie.
5th Infantilism in the groups leading the revolution.

6th Sectarianism in organizing the masses by the Party of the revolution.
7th Adventurism by the revolutionary groups.
8th Irresponsibility of the de facto dictatorship in provoking and accentuating the hate of the masses.

Conclusions:
1st In El Salvador demagoguery should not be practiced, since this is a country with a low political level in the masses and, at the same time, with an enormous longing for freedom and social and economic well-being.
2nd The ruling classes have to plan a serious solution to the social problem, still solvable, and now, tending to intensify because of the intense population pressure.
3rd The parties of the bourgeoisie should have sufficiently elastic political play.
4th The "persecution of ideas" needs to be totally abandoned, since this is completely infantile and aggravates the problem.
5th The Army must receive conscious and serious political education about the social problems affecting the country.
6th The agrarian problem must be addressed through comprehensive, revolutionary, and efficient reform.
7th The revolutionary sectors have to study more and talk less. They need to have responsible and scientifically serious knowledge of our social reality.

DOCUMENT 5-8

Roque Dalton, Unpublished 1972 Manuscript on the History of the Communist Party of El Salvador

EXCERPT

The following excerpt is drawn from Roque Dalton's unpublished 1972 history of the Salvadoran Communist Party that was found in his archival collective given to us by the Dalton family. Following a common pattern of communist spokespersons, Dalton provides an extensive historical overview to explain his current view on El Salvador and his strategic position. By the time Dalton wrote this overview, he had become increasingly convinced in the necessity of guerrilla warfare, and, thus, he was growing further alienated from the Communist Party's leadership for its insistence that armed insurrection was an incorrect strategy. In this document, Dalton invested an inordinate amount of time analyzing the 1932 insurrection. He contended that a revolutionary situation existed in 1932 and that the party was in position to take advantage of the opportunity and lead the masses in armed action. But he argued that the party failed to fulfill its obligation owing to variety of leadership failures, an argument that sounds strikingly similar to Dalton's assessment of party leaders in 1972. Dalton says the party in 1932 failed to become a "party of combat," which characterized the party over the next four decades. He believes that by 1972 conditions had become revolutionary once again and that the proper strategy was to embark on guerrilla warfare. In short, this document is a classic example of a change in historical memory in an individual interpreter. Whereas in his earlier writings, Dalton agreed with party leaders on 1932 and the merits of delayed insurrection, by 1972 Dalton's position had changed and so had his interpretation/memory of 1932. Interestingly, Dalton refers directly to the Miguel Mármol *testimonial as a factual document that provides evidence to justify his position.*[16]

In 1931–32 a typical revolutionary situation arose and developed in El Salvador along the lines of the Leninist description. (The quotation from Lenin in this regard is almost superfluous, since it is so famous: "What," asks 'The Collapse of the Second International,' "generally speaking, are the symptoms of a revolutionary situation? We shall certainly not be mistaken if we indicate the following three major symptoms: [1] when it is impossible for the ruling classes to maintain their rule without any change; when there is a crisis, in one form or another, among the 'upper classes,' a crisis in the policy of the ruling class, leading to a fissure through which the discontent and indignation of the oppressed classes burst forth. For a revolution to take place, it is usually insufficient for 'the lower classes not to want' to live in the old way; it is also necessary that 'the upper classes should be unable' to live in the old way; [2] when the suffering and want of the oppressed classes have grown more acute than usual; [3] when, as a consequence of the above causes, there is a considerable increase in the activity of the masses, who uncomplainingly allow themselves to be robbed in 'peace time,' but, in turbulent times, are drawn both by all the circumstances of the crisis and by the 'upper classes' themselves into independent historical action.") Few revolutionary situations in our country have fulfilled so exactly the embodiment of the distinctive symptoms of Lenin's fitting description. The Salvadoran revolutionary situation of that time further intensified with events such as the fall of the Araujo government, the electoral fraud against the Communist Party (closing off the last legal means on the road to power for the people), and the worsening of the government's repression and crimes around the country.

In 1930–32 a developing Marxist-Leninist party existed in El Salvador and not a factionalist germ [sic] of one (a party in development with the above-mentioned characteristics) as a 'panorama of achievements': it was—I said—the organized political-vindictive and indisputable vanguard of the Salvadoran workers movement; it had sufficient contacts, for the purpose of not going into an insurrection in isolation, with the middle strata of the population and with the army (after having worked out to a significant extent, for the only time in our history, the worker-peasant alliance for revolutionary action), and it had an organization at the national-territorial level. Its capacity as the vanguard had been won in the political practice of the masses of which Arismendi speaks, and it maintained although at basic levels, continuous political and ideological discussion and theoretical preparation at the average level of the time in the bosom of the Latin American communist movement. This party was capable of guiding the masses within the current courses of the class struggle being carried out in the frameworks of the oligarchic-dependent society (that even involves diverse instances of partisan violence) managing to put the Salvadoran people in the condition of legally winning basic positions in the State apparatus—which could have in turn opened the road to power through a prolonged democratic process—through triumph in municipal and parliamentary elections. Only through fraud and sheer force, the Olympian suspension of elections and the greatest of arbitrary actions and crimes (which cross the line into the realm of pure and simple provocations) could the Martínez government prevent the triumph of the people led by the Communist Party and the labor movement in the elections of January 1932. This proves that the PCS was an efficacious political agency for mobilizing the masses in an appropriate manner in order to orchestrate the class struggle within the limits (although the most extreme ones) of bourgeois legality (or normality). [pp. 267–69] ...

How did the national armed insurrection arise in El Salvador in 1932? Without going into overly broad considerations in this regard and corresponding to the introductory and provisional point of view with regard to the problem that we have already stated in these lines, I would say that the following facts can be gleaned from the narration of Miguel Mármol (which have been able to be checked by the examination of the sparse literature existing on this matter, with the documents I have at hand, etc.): ...

2) There were EIGHT DAYS to prepare all the organizational and politico-military aspects of the insurrection (plan, policy on alliances, military organization of the insurrection, or rather essentially organizing the revolutionary armed forces, the popular army; gathering arms, dissemination of the insurrectional instructions within the party apparatus around the country in order to mobilize it as an operative vanguard; international aspects, etc.), in conditions in which the broadest masses of the country were, it is true, enflamed by the deepening of the economic crisis and by the criminal actions of the regimen, but to whom the insurrectional option had not been concretely posed, and they had been called until then to actions that were unarmed, electoral, union-based, strike-based, etc. The extreme brevity of time implied the impossibility of the creation and development of a revolutionary army to crush the armed forces of the bourgeoisie, which assumes a process that is always complex and not the simple distribution of arms to citizens full of valor and hopefulness.

3) The vacillations, the ignorance of the most elemental norms of conspiratorial security, the lack of information and coordination in the preparatory work, marked the "putting into practice of the organizational work for the insurrection" from the beginning. The starting time for the insurrection was set three times with days difference between each date. The preparatory details and the objectives of the insurrection, its general strategy, were therefore able to be learned

with sufficient lead time by the enemy, which dismantled its fundamental aspects and was capable of crushing the insurrectional outbreaks that did occur, responding to the original instructions of the Party leadership....

5) But the main thing was the lack of resolving the organizational-military aspects of the insurrection, the lack of creating the revolutionary armed forces, the inexistence at all times of the insurrectional process of a popular revolutionary army. [pp. 273–76]...

What I can guarantee is that my work on the preparation of Mármol's testimony made evident to me, more than any other phenomenon, the urgent need to learn creatorly [sic] the lessons of '32. On that occasion the spiritual conditions of the class were set: their spirit and their combativeness. But the spiritual conditions are not all the subjective conditions of a class. On the contrary, the fundamental subjective condition of a class in order to revolutionarily resolve the revolutionary situation is organization. But throughout this report I have been saying that it was precisely in that era when the Salvadoran workers had a party, a union movement, etc. What failed was, paradoxically, the best that they had. What failed was the Party. And it failed because with the PCS being a Marxist-Leninist party in development in 1932 it could not end up being, because of the above-mentioned conditions, a party of combat, a combat organization, a politico-military organization, indispensable for leading the tasks of a revolutionary process that takes place through the armed route that leads to a national insurrection.... That is the essence of the failure of '32, and that deficiency continues being the fundamental deficiency of the Salvadoran people in their revolutionary struggle. From that, the decades-long silence about these problems. [p. 292]...

[I] wrote in my book "Revolution in the Revolution and the Rightwing Critique": "We believe that we need new communist parties, new Marxist-Leninist vanguards. We are convinced that those parties can only arise from revolutionary action, from the process of armed anti-imperialist struggle, and at present Latin America is on the verge of the definitive beginning of this struggle. We believe that revolutionary guerrilla forces, acting from a correct strategic perspective are, in fact and by conviction, the new party in gestation. Do the current communist parties want or not, or can they cope with or not, the new revolutionary vanguards? Life shall tell." Without keeping this generalizing tone as a current cause ... I would say that in our country, in the current conditions in El Salvador this position is not only valid, it is not only a position that gains concrete relevance every day, but it is also a unitary position, a position that involves the necessity for the union of all revolutionary Salvadorans against the common enemy. That position has been presiding over all of my work on the testimonial of Miguel Mármol and in these lines. Mármol's testimonial and these lines are written as they are, attending first and foremost to establishing the fitting revolutionary truth. [pp. 296–97]

DOCUMENT 6-1
"A Landowner's Account," 1932

The following excerpt is an article written by a landowner shortly after the uprising and published in Diario de Santa Ana, *a regional newspaper in the west. It illustrates the fears and racist attitudes of prosperous Ladinos and the mentality behind the massacres. The visceral terror and the desire for vengeance that emerge from this article illustrate the kinds of emotions that gave force to the Matanza as a cautionary tale.*[17]

An honorable resident of Juayúa, with whom I had the opportunity to converse, offered me a newspaper clipping, which contained the account that one of the hacienda owners from that region gave of the activities of the communists in those days. This account was published in the Diario de Santa Ana, in the edition of Monday, February 1, 1932.

It reads as follows:

"I never imagined, not even for a second, what communism could be capable of in our popular masses, which constitute some ninety-five percent of the inhabitants here.

"Neither you, nor anyone who lives in the towns, in the cities, and feels defended by the agents of order, can have even a slight idea of how we have felt here, in decisive moments, upon finding ourselves alone, absolutely alone, in the hands and at the mercy of the masses, of the kind that was no more than a horde of enraged savages, with demonic impulses, who were loudly jeering the Ladino, jeering the boss and brandishing their machetes, thirsting for robbery, thirsting for any thievery imaginable.

They Say They Did Not Get Involved...

"Fortunately for those of us who live in the countryside, the horde set off first for the villages, and while there enjoyed themselves by engaging in ignominy, true pillage, shameful acts, robberies, outrages and every sort of thievery; the armed forces came and were able to repel the barbarous movement a little, in order to later combat it efficaciously. Otherwise, at this hour when I am writing to you, I would be in the ground, and with me so many others who have committed no other crime than living here, engaged in cultivating the land. There is not a single Indian who is not an affiliate of devastating communism. One or another who stayed at home, was waiting for the final notice in order to join the ranks. Good farmhands whom I had considered loyal and whom we had treated as part of the family here, were the first to join up and lend their contingent to the dark cause. And these people have such nerve that now that they seem rather vanquished by the activities of the government, which ended up annihilating them, those same ones who just a short time ago were making attempts on our lives and on all we possess, are the ones who are now seeking protection and swearing that they belonged to us and that they did not get involved.

They want to dodge the danger. But that punishment is being exacted! And it should continue as it has begun, with a strong hand, forcefully, executing the leaders and every participant, in order to see if they manage to finish off the plague.

They Wanted to Make 'Mincemeat' of Him...

"They passed by here with the great mob, on the night of Saturday the 23rd, those who attacked Nahuizalco, and with no time to make mincemeat of me, since their presence was urgently required in Nahuizalco; they made do with shouting blasphemies and pointing me out as one of the first who should fall into their hands. In the mob, in the immense confused multitude, they were all there: close to two hundred farmhands of mine, of my neighbors and of my brothers. Those men whom we had thought to be humble, honorable, who have been receiving favors of every kind on our part, to whom we grant land for their crops without charging them any ground rent; whom we have paid with religious punctuality. Their wage, which, although small, as is always paid in this country, is a wage in conformity with their abilities, since they are incapable of earning more; some of them barely able to do their job, and others who have to be led about by the hand, in order to teach them to do basic chores, because of the idlers they are, they do not take pains to become efficient nor to better themselves at anything. And they, who carry the germ of roguish blood, who are of a constitution inferior to ours, who are of a conquered race, it only takes a little to inflame their infernal passions against the Ladino, at whom they point, because they hate us and they will always latently hate us. An extremely grave, extremely dangerous error was made with them in granting them citizens' rights. This was enormously bad for the country. They were told that they were free, that the nation also belonged to them, and that they had the full right to elect their leaders and to rule. And they understand that to say leaders and to rule is exactly the same as engaging in robbery, theft, scandal, the destruction of property, etcetera, and killing their employers.

Depicting Scenes of Juayúa

"The example is there in Juayúa. None of you has the slightest idea of what occurred there in my hometown. It was shameful, horrifying, it sets one's nerves on end, and I do not want to bring it all up. Society girls were grinding corn and making tortillas for the bandits, and afterward... they committed upon them all that a barbarian, an assassin, or a villain might harbor in his poisoned breast against a Ladino girl, an honorable young lady. They broke down doors with machetes and then lit off rockets and bombs, just for the fun of it. They dragged, they beat. They cruelly and barbarously killed, mutilating him alive, he who had a big heart, a heart of progress and civilization for Juayúa. I am referring to the unfortunate Emilio Redaelli. And if they did not kill more of the 'bourgeois' people, as they say, it was because that would come last, turning themselves first to robbery and then to killing the rich, in order to take over their houses and live in them: such was one of the most salient points in their plan for governing.

They Were on the Brink of Dying

"Once the town of Nahuizalco was sacked, on the night of Saturday the 25th, they came toward Tajcuilujlán on Sunday morning, two-hundred strong, and from there they headed to El Canelo and neighboring estates, to have their way with our lives and our property. They jeered us and unsheathed their knives.

"I, who always felt I could dispose of ten Indians in a row, they with their machetes and I with my revolver and fifty bullets; I, who have not trembled before these wicked men, because I saw them as humble little lambs when they were looking good, and I felt I had the rogues under the might of my arm if our might be measured; when I made out that throng, the mob of two hundred that was coming after me, I had to mount my horse and I broke into a dizzying race over rocky ground and precipices, tearing apart fences, until I joined up with a brother of mine on his hacienda....

"Luckily, before getting to my property, the mob was turned back in order to reinforce Nahuizalco since in those instants the government troops were arriving and they wanted to repel the force that had been constituted. That saved us. Although a few still did come and made off with many things of personal use that they found on their way.

"You Should Have Seen Them in Action...!"

"We want the plague exterminated at the roots; otherwise, it will sprout forth with greater determination, now experts and less foolish, because in new attempts they will pitch themselves against the lives of everyone, first, and finally slit our throats. We need the strong hand of the government, without asking advice from anybody, because there are pious people who preach forgiveness because they have not yet had their lives hanging by a thread. They did well in North America to do away with them; by shooting them first, before they impeded the development of progress in that nation; first they killed the Indians because the Indians will never have good sentiments toward anything. We, here, have been treating them as family, with every consideration, and now you have seen them in action! They have ferocious instincts.

The Only Cry: Silence...!

"A nephew of mine tells that he saw from the window of his house when one of those gentle farmhands who was so awfully good before, shouted, 'Silence!' at the poor widow of Colonel Vaquero, who upon identifying the body of her ill-fated husband, killed by machete blows, the night of the event, broke into tears out of the natural grief of her lacerated heart. 'Silence!' the gentle farmhand shouted at her, unsheathing his machete, and ordering the widow to remove herself, and to not even sob, while they put the body of the commander of Juayúa cut down in his prime, in a coffin in order to go bury him. 'Silence!' another one of these gentle ones screamed at Mrs. María de Math, because upon seeing that they were dragging Mr. Emilio Redaelli, already moribund, she shouted from her window, 'Poor Mr. Emilio!' 'Silence!' the gentle one shouted, and grabbing her by the hand led her to the jail, and many entreaties and implorations were needed in order to get them to give her back her freedom."

DOCUMENT 6–2
MESSAGE
of the Distinguished President of the Republic, General Maximiliano Hernández Martínez Read before the National Assembly, in the opening ceremony of its period of ordinary sessions, the 4th of February of 1932

EXCERPT

The following text is an address delivered by General Maximiliano Hernández Martínez to the National Assembly less than two weeks after the insurrection. It is a rare instance of the president trying to explain publicly the nature of the insurrection and the reasons behind the government's reaction. In his speech he made the first official effort to shape the public's perception of the Matanza.[18]

The Government, disposed to initiate the implementation of its broad program of reconstruction in all the administrative spheres and promote national progress by all the means at its disposal, became aware, with deep sorrow, that only a few days following the issuance of the decree that lifted the state of siege and when it had all its forces engaged in averting to the extent possible the effects of the economic situation that is pulling the country down, the communists, enemies of peace and of their homeland, were secretly making moves, attempting to sink the Republic into the greatest disarray. With supposed ideals of betterment to the benefit of the peasants and the workers in general, they abused their simplicity and took advantage of their meager culture in order to throw them unbridled against the constituted authorities and the other classes of society, promising them a radical change in the institutions that live under the protection of the laws in force.

The plans and activities of the communists were discovered by the Government, which acted with the promptness and energy that the circumstances demanded, effecting the arrest of the principal leaders and the seizure of great quantities of war materiel, documentation, proclamations and instructions for the general attack.

Anyone who has seen all that material of destruction and read the concepts contained in said instructions for initiating the fight planned by those men without restraint or conscience, must have felt the greatest of horrors and the most anguished of worries.

Imposed as a preliminary measure, the state of siege was introduced in the Departments of the Western Region of the territory, where threatening events provoked by the affiliates of communism had already been recorded, and later on it was necessary to extend the effects of said decree to the entire country, prudently anticipating that the communist action might grow to greater proportions.

However, the precautionary measures taken by the Executive in order to contain the criminal objectives of the rebels were not sufficient, and from threats the rebels went on to violence on the previously appointed day and hour. In Sonsonate, Santa Tecla, Izalco, Nahuizalco, Juayúa, Sonzacate, Colón, Ahuachapán, Tacuba, and many other towns, as well as along the roads and fields of the same territorial division, they carried out their terrorist plan to a great extent. The destruction, the burning, the murder of honorable or humble persons, of military and civilian authorities; the raging attack on the military quarters; the looting of commercial establishments and other similar outrages, were the measures to which the unbridled hordes resorted in order to sow desolation and panic everywhere. One's heart is saddened by the details recorded in the official reports received by the Government immediately following the events, and it is difficult to even conceive of the extent this wave of unprecedented crimes could have reached, if it had not been headed off by the vigorous, resolute and efficacious posture of the Army, of the National Guard and of the Police, guided by expert commanders, who are known to go as far as sacrifice in the discharge of their duties.

It was painful for my Government to have to have used severe measures of military repression under the jurisdiction of the War Councils, but they became indispensable to the protection of society, property, and the family, in view of the fierceness and contumaciousness of the criminals.

The great majority of the members of society in the capital, in the Department seats, and in the other towns gave the Government valuable aid and all their moral support in this grave emergency, offering it their personal services in order to defend public safety with arms, as well as contributions of money, provisions, medicines, etc., intended for the forces of attack and vigilance, distributed in the places of danger. It is also fitting that I mention the patriotic attitude of the banking institutions, of the commercial outfits, companies and other entities, Salvadoran and foreign, which in these difficult hours for the Nation, have demonstrated their affection and their desire to see it free from greater hardships.

We extend to all the most sincere displays of gratitude from this people and from your Government, as well as the best words of encouragement on my behalf that your longings for peace and prosperity may be fulfilled.

I am able to say with satisfaction that the greatest danger has been averted; that the authorities are maintaining the most efficacious control of the entire Republic and are occupying themselves now with executing the measures agreed upon, in order to keep the lamentable occurrences of these days from being repeated.

The work imposed by what has occurred should not end here. Needed still is for the Government and the ruling classes of society, united before the imperative need to ensure the country a tranquil and successful future for all, to study and resolve without delay the problems posed by the relationship between capital and labor. These affairs have at present a global character; but nevertheless, it is possible to find here amongst ourselves the means that the environs may suggest to us for securing the harmony of clashing interests, recurring to the dictates of a stricter justice in such a way that all are protected by its umbrella. For this noble purpose I make a formal call to those to whom it may concern to make their contribution in this task that will have as ideals the harmony, peace and prosperity of El Salvador.

DOCUMENT 6-3
Joaquín Méndez, *Los sucesos comunistas*, 1932
EXCERPTS

These excerpts from Joaquín Méndez's Los sucesos comunistas de 1932 en El Salvador *illustrate the manner in which his account identifies the rebels as communists, and therein lays the foundation for the eventual communist-causality metanarrative. Both Méndez and his informants use the term communist to refer to the rebels, but the nature of their communism is never explained or contextualized. The following sections also show the rebels being referred to as Indians, which kept the counternarrative alive. A typical cross-section of Méndez's informants from three different municipalities is represented—an unnamed market woman, a military officer, and a local elite.*[19]

[Sonsonate: Méndez is interviewing an unnamed market woman who witnessed the rebel attack on the city.]

"When we heard the first shots," she said, "we thought that our last moment had come. People had already been talking for several days about the assault on the city by the communists, and when we realized that they had come, we thought that they would make good on their threat, leaving no one over the age of seven alive. They would only respect the children. They would kill us, and then they would burn down our houses. And dying isn't the problem, but not the way they kill, like they did with the poor customs policemen.... But, despite it all, there was barely a family that was not ready to defend itself. In every home, the fathers, the mothers, and even the sons and daughters, were waiting for the moment they would hear the machetes first strike the doors. The families were armed, with pistols, clubs, knives, and other things. There was no alternative but to fight hard for our lives, if they stormed the houses."...

How the Barracks Were Attacked

"It was a few minutes after midnight on January 23rd," says Major Castillo, "when a telegram was called in from the neighboring town of Izalco, indicating that they were being threatened by the communists. In light of this, Colonel Ernesto Bará, departmental commander, ordered Major Mariano Molina to organize an aid brigade, in order to go to the place indicated.

"It has been shown," he continued, "that this was a stratagem of the reds, that they had the intention of making forces leave this plaza, luring them to others of less importance, so they would find the barracks debilitated when they attacked. You'll see—just like they ordered him, Major Molina proceeded to organize the expedition, which would go out in automobiles. The troops were formed in the barracks' outside yard, while one of the cars went in search of other vehicles. That's what we were doing, when groups of communists started showing up that had come from the surrounding areas and had gathered in the avenue (the road out of town toward the port and other places). The car belonging to our men had been intercepted by the reds, and some of them were riding in it, at the head of their followers. And at the precise moment when the commission was going to leave, the communists burst upon the regiment.

"The forces that were awaiting the automobiles found themselves enveloped by the communist elements, and the first shots were exchanged. Then, in order to offer proper resistance, they went inside the barracks; but there was such confusion in the moment, that together with the commission, seventeen reds managed to penetrate, who were discovered later. The barricade was closed, but right then the rest of the communist contingent attempted to penetrate the barracks, being stopped by fire from our rifles and machine guns. They fled in disorder, leaving two dead, and then they headed off by two different routes—some went back the way they came, and others, through the northwest gate of the regiment.

"The seventeen individuals who managed to enter were executed.

"At the same time as the assault on the barracks, they attacked the customs house, which is why we could not defend it. You must already know that the reds killed the police force that had mounted guard there, taking several arms and ammunition, after having torn open several bundles of merchandise, which they stole. When the bodies of the customs guards were picked up, they were notably disfigured, giving an idea of the torment to which they were subjected. Some of their heads were completely destroyed and their bodies unbelievably wounded. The murders were committed with machetes and axes, with a savage ferocity, as shown by the preceding details."

[Juayúa]

In the dining room there is nothing. In a room that appears to have been a bedroom, some furniture completely destroyed. The mirrored wardrobes, with the doors broken. On a small commode, "*Long live the Juayúa communists*" is written in chalk. As they say, the trademark....

There is as much elegance in these large residences in Juayúa as there is in the best of the capital.

They were reserving it for the Chief.

The house of Doctor Jerez [a local elite] is richly furnished, with the exquisite taste of a person who has traveled widely.

"So you can see how they did not touch my house," says Doctor Jerez, "even though it is so close to the telegraph office, which is the first place the Indians went to. It seems to me that this was due to the fact that one of their leaders was thinking of installing himself here or reserving it for the wife that he would take. Because you must know that they already had a date picked out for choosing amongst the young ladies of the locality. Well then, this was not the only house to escape the communist frenzy. There are some others, in which there is also a great deal of luxury, objects of value, in short, everything necessary to attract the attention of the Indians, and they were also respected by the enraged masses. I heard perfectly when they were approaching in order to break down my doors, and I also heard when one of them said to his companions: 'No, not there. That is for the chief.' To be sure, in my house they did not touch a thing.".…

[Nahuizalco]
They wounded Merino, the guard.

"Since the place where the communist automobile was, which was moving forward, is closed in, they gunned the motor, thinking they could save themselves through speed. From the moving automobile, they opened fire on our troops, almost at pointblank range, wounding the guard, Timoteo Merino, in the left frontal, who was taken to the Sonsonate hospital later.

"In that encounter, the communist ranks suffered many casualties, which could not be seen at the moment due to the darkness."

Arriving in town.

"Finishing the encounter, we continued the march toward Nahuizalco. Along the sides of the road there were many communists who were throwing rocks and then blocking our way, brandishing their machetes.

"Finally we arrived in town, where we saw that some of the houses had been burned and others looted.

"It was completely dark; on top of that, it was raining. For that reason, and knowing the rebellious spirit of the Indians, I abstained from appointing commissions. We could hear, clearly, bugle calls that came from the nearby hills, seeming to us to be signals.

"The next morning, I sent out commissions from the forces at my command, advising them with Ladino guides, who knew all the communist indigenous people. Those commissions managed to capture some, seizing what they had stolen in the looting of the town and the red insignia that they carried. They clearly confessed their identity, and were executed forthwith."

DOCUMENT 6-4
Jorge Schlesinger, *Revolución comunista: ¿Guatemala en peligro?*, 1946
EXCERPTS

Schlesinger's renowned study of the events of 1932, Revolución comunista: ¿Guatemala en peligro?, *offers an example of communist causality from an anticommunist perspective. Similar to his right-wing predecessor, Joaquín Méndez, Schlesinger uses the term communist unproblematically to refer to the rebels. But he also describes the Indians as rebels with much greater purpose than Méndez. In this selection from the introduction to his book, Schlesinger shows that the purpose of his book is to draw parallels between El Salvador in 1932 and Guatemala in 1946. He gives a clear indication that his work will depict the terror of the insurrection, the enormous dangers of communist propaganda, and the need to respond firmly to any attempt to disseminate it. This work was as much about the Guatemalan political situation as about 1932 in El Salvador. Following the introduction, we offer two additional selections: a general description of El Salvador and a brief reference to the specific case of Juayúa. In these selections Schlesinger refers explicitly to the rebels as Indians. The reason for this is Schlesinger's overt racism and his belief that Indian racial traits made them susceptible to communism. While his intended objective in such an argument is to categorize the uprising as communist, his racism has the ironic and unintended consequence of suggesting the uprising's noncommunist, ethnic foundation.*[20]

Introduction

The history of our peoples has left out one of its bloodiest chapters: the COMMUNIST REVOLUTION IN EL SALVADOR.

In the present, full of social and economic movements, of anxiety and uncertainty, I consider it necessary and pressing to make those events known; the causes that gave rise to them and their bloody outcome, a consequence of the propaganda spread at that time by national and foreign agents of the Third International.

Under the pretext of redeeming the oppressed and exploited masses, the dangerous agitation propaganda of that era has been brought back to life with new determination but identical artifices. Now, as before, suspect agents are traveling around our countryside; they are invading our workshops and factories causing new outbreaks of quiescent race and class hate, inconformity and all-out struggle between capital and labor. Among them figure men with baneful backgrounds, guilty of the tragedy that fifteen years ago would stain the ground of Cuscatlán with blood. They preach anarcho-terrorist doctrines without realizing that this does not fit in our society, where the lack of large industrial centers, the excess of fertile land, the lack of farmhands, the low population density, the lack of capital and of the problem of unemployment, together with benign climatic conditions, lend themselves to an easy, peaceful solution to worker-management conflicts, with a minimum of social justice and dispassionate comprehension by governments, capitalists, workers and peasants.

General Maximiliano H. Martínez, despot for twelve years, following a military coup led by a "Military Directory" ('Council of soldiers, workers and peasants'), became president of the republic. In order to ingratiate himself with the masses and consolidate his illegitimate government, he expressly authorized communist propaganda and recognized the Communist Party as a political association, formed and financed by International Red Aid; arousing with this the distrust of the neighboring countries, governed by the generals Jorge Ubico and Tiburcio Carías Andino, and the manifest ill will of the United States.

At the eleventh hour he was obliged to drown in blood the communist movement that had taken on uncommonly violent characteristics, and he took advantage of the circumstances to liquidate, at the same time, the party of the ex-president, Arturo Araujo, an engineer.

Just a few days of indescribable terror took a tragic toll on the Salvadoran people: twenty-five thousand persons—workers, peasants, capitalists, professionals, ministers of religion, women, the elderly, and children—succumbed, killed in the cities and in the countryside. Firing squads discharged—day and night—their bloody duty, while the birds of prey devoured those fallen in the fratricidal fight.

That—and not improvement of the conditions of the proletariat—was the result of the lack of foresight and political integrity of the de facto head of state, who, propelled by unbridled ambition, ominously began his long dictatorship, which would topple, twelve years later, with another sacrifice of his people.

Clemente Marroquín Rojas and Alfredo Schlesinger provided me with data, documents and photographs that are the graphic history of the red revolution of 1932. With their consent I have used, revised and modified them in order to create the present sketch: "COMMUNIST REVOLUTION," a simple, straightforward exposition of the events, for the purpose of averting the violent clash of classes that is beginning to occur in Guatemala.

This publication is a warning to the peoples and governments of Central America; to the latter so that they gradually improve—without outside intromission—the conditions of the workers in the countryside and in the city, giving them what justly and legitimately corresponds to them so that do not take it by force, and to the former, so that they do not let themselves be dazzled by deceptive offers from politicians interested in taking power, at the cost of much innocent blood, by taking advantage of the ignorance and naiveté of the masses.

Communist agitation in El Salvador began in the capital and in the departmental seats, where the movement's leaders were living. As long as their activities were limited to the cities they were less dangerous, given that the highest aspiration of our artisans is to become independent and set up their own workshops, in order to gradually become small property owners with the product of their labor.

With the dissemination of propaganda among the rural workers, whose misery is greater, their means of subsistence more difficult, the social injustice more striking, their ignorance general and their credulity accentuated, their vehement demands transformed into an armed insurrection, in order to obtain by force the lands and economic independence promised them by the propagandists.

Guatemala, an essentially agrarian country where the majority of the population is landless indigenous people, is even more perilous ground, given that when the rebellion happens, demands of a social and economic order will be aired, unleashing the bloodiest, most implacable of racial hatred.

This will come to pass, as presaged by the events in Patzicia, Villa Canales, Camotán, and San Marcos that were published in the press, if opportune governmental provisions do not arrest the process of social decomposition.

Against slavery, Christianity rose up with the humanitarian philosophy of "love one another," which translates today into the concept of universal fraternity; against feudalism, the medieval wars arose; against the privileges of the nobility, the revolution of 1789; against the tyranny of czarism, the social movement of 1917, and against the age-old oppression of the dispossessed, in El Salvador the red revolution of 1932, and all these broke out because of the lack of comprehension and inhumanity of the political leaders of those times.

It corresponds to the governments of Central America to guide the masses, peaceably and gradually, toward the uplifting of their moral, social and economic conditions, by means of just laws, assistance and social action appropriate to the Indo-Hispanic character, promoting family decency, purity of customs, work, economic, and juridical liberty; without forgetting that the social institutions, the foundation of coexistence—religion, law, family, and property—must also be protected in order to prevent chaos and demoralization, because any violent transition from democracy to a proletarian regime destroys lives, property, and culture.

The mission of the governments consists of harmonizing the relationships between capital and labor and preventing class struggle, the consequence of which shall always be a "tragic toll."

In Guatemala—regrettably—the first acts of anarcho-terrorist violence have broken out. There is still time to prevent the consequences...

The Communist Revolution of El Salvador teaches us just how far an oppressed, hungry people could go, encouraged by promises of immediate social vindication, and history repeats itself.... [End of Introduction]

This ideal geographic location facilitated the close relationships between the propagandists of the red creed and the leaders of the proletariat in the neighboring countries and the intense propaganda in the same country; but these advantages for the propagation of communist doctrine were offset by the love and traditional dedication to work and lack of concern over political and social problems of seventy-five percent of the population. However, those characteristics did not serve to impede the activities of the communist agents for one overwhelming reason: Because the sermon was not aimed as in other countries, at the proletariat in the cities, but instead at the workers in the countryside. The motive behind this tactic is based on the plain and simple fact that the Salvadoran nation is eminently agrarian, and therefore, since the economic problem lies in the land, it was easier to inflame ambitions in those who have the custom of facing, unconcerned, the harsh reality of labor.

Another distinguishing fact that makes the geographic factor stand out in communist propaganda is that this took hold, with greater ease, in the western rather than the eastern regions of the country. The causes lie in the fact that the peasants of the east, descendants of Lencas, are apathetic, of an indolence slightly less than primitive, and that more land is available for crops and the population is less dense.

In contrast, the peasants of the western region (departments of Sonsonate, Ahuachapán, and Santa Ana), descendents of the hardened Pipil, Mam, and Pocomam, communists from atavism and turbulent by nature, sixty-five percent of whom are pure-blooded indigenous, reduced to a small area where the lands are occupied for the most part by the so-called *latifundistas* for growing coffee and sugar cane and for the cattle industry, presented fertile ground for accepting catechization by the revolutionary agents. It should be added to these idiosyncrasies the fact that a good number of the peasants in the country's central and eastern regions are small landowners, while those of the western region of the same category are Indian day workers, and even though some are owners of small plots of land, their restless spirit lends itself to their supporting political exploits.

The meddling of the peasants in politics is more effective in the country's west because they have maintained strong racial unity through the religious confraternities, whose chiefs, within the norms of a concentrated caciquism, have managed to hold onto the power of the old caciques....

Martí, upon his return from Nicaragua, planned the revolt of 1932. He calculated that the people would now heed the call, to make things easier, he thought, and this is what he explained to his friends, that it was expedient to put in the presidency of the Republic a man who, due to his ignorance in the affairs of government, would be an unconscious collaborator of the red cause. Martí was not inclined toward any of the candidates who were on the political stage in 1930; he felt them to be inadequate for the advancement of his cause. And it was in a heated argument among his compañeros when, finally, he pointed to Araujo as the man most useful for enabling the realization of his projects. In his shadow, exploiting his weaknesses and taking advantage of his disorientation, they would be able to go even further than their intentions. Thus it was that communism identified its cause with the aforementioned candidate....

[Juayúa]

It is worthwhile mentioning the communist regime that the triumphant warriors established: The product of the total sacking of the barracks, public granary, and kitchen for its distribution. There they prepared all the food for the red army and on the rustic grinding stones, decent women from the village were forced to grind the corn for the tortillas that would be the food for the heroes.

In the midst of this frenetic spree, a spell of sensuality overcame all the groups of lecherous men, and over the honorable homes, over the prepubescent girls, loomed the terrible weight of a mass rape. At the insistent requests of the men of the red cause, the improvised communist authorities arranged what the popular mind has given to calling *the wedding night*, and this would be the fourth night after their triumph. During this night, all acts of barbarity would be permitted. But the fatal plans of the lascivious soldiers of the Soviet would not come to be; the troops, with their timely arrival, saved the honor of the residents of Juayúa.

DOCUMENT 6-5
"How Is a Dictatorship Born?" editorial from *La Tribuna*, 1952

This editorial appeared in the newspaper La Tribuna *in 1952, to commemorate the twentieth anniversary of the Matanza at a time when the memories of Martínez's downfall and the beginning of 1948 "Revolution" were still fresh. During the period of military reformism it was not unusual for intellectuals to present alternative versions of the events of 1932. This article does not mince words about the horrors of the repression and interprets it as the reason why General Martínez was able to consolidate his hold on power. The editor of the newspaper, Joaquín Castro Canizales, was intimately familiar with the events since he had helped put General Martínez in power.*[21]

Our counterpart "La Prensa Gráfica," in its column "Twenty Years Ago Today," which we cite, has already offered the first news on the tragedy in its two most recent editions, on the 23rd and the 24th.

The one on the 23rd states:

"The General Command of the Army has ordered the Departmental Commanders to discharge ALL THOSE WHO HAVE PRIVATE INTERESTS TO DEFEND (upper case is ours) so that they can defend themselves from the communist attacks on their own."

"The Commission that will organize the Salvadoran capital against communism, in a calm, vigorous and well-guided campaign, was formed with Mssrs. Rodolfo Duke, Angel Guirola, Dr. Francisco A. Lima and Tato Meardi."

The one on the 24th states:

"The Government is putting down the communist movement with an iron hand in Ahuachapán, Sonsonate, Colón, and other places. In all these places, the reds are being swept away by the government forces, which have the situation under control. Last night San Salvador remained in a state of alarm. In view of the situation and with the facilities given by the Government, hundreds of volunteers are reporting to the barracks in this capital and are enlisting in the anticommunist ranks. The red ranks are committing acts of true vandalism, which has the population terrorized. In Colón, Dr. Colocho Bosque, his wife and children, and Mr. Victor Durán were killed by the communists. The capital remains on an emergency footing."

Part of the presidential Manifesto in this time of trial states the following:

"The Salvadoran people may rest assured that the Government is capable of vigorously cutting down any revolutionary outbreak, but it expects for this purpose the unanimous and efficacious cooperation of all the social classes, during such grave and trying times for the future of the fatherland."

The paragraphs transcribed above speak for themselves about the overall drama. The details are even more frightful and it is advisable to draw a veil over them. Those details speak of mass executions, recorded in Izalco, Nahuizalco, Ataco, Apaneca, Soyapango, etc. They point to the body of Ama the Indian, hanging from a ceiba tree in Izalco for three days, as a lesson, just like 120 years ago the head of Aquino the Indian was publicly pilloried in San Vicente, as a lesson to those who at that time rose up for causes more or less identical to these. Because, since time immemorial that is the way our most serious problems have been resolved: cutting the disease out at the root. And the root tends to be, for these blind men who act that way, the branches already laden with poisonous fruit. And they believe that by razing the bad crop, they will have gotten it all. Crass error...!

Between us, the communist outbreak was not the root, rather the flowering of unrest that had been sown much earlier. Just as Aquino the Indian's movement, in the past century, had been nothing other that the angry protest against the unpleasant aftertaste of the Colonial period that still weighed on the Indians, in a nation that was considered to be democratic and republican, and that had expunged from its laws the word SLAVERY.

The orgy of blood in 1932 was cruel, horrifying. The illiterate peasants cut down innocent lives out in the countryside and in the cities they ruled, and the illiterate citizens, organized in a "Civic Guard" corps, also cut down innocent lives in the cities. The first, because they were ignorant, because they were desperate and blinded by hatred; the second because they were educated people, who were defending their interests; because they were learned men who had gone through the University; because they were department-store employees who were defending the interests of their employers.

The Martial Law of January, February, and March of 1932 was applied with excess in the cities. How many old scores were settled on that occasion! Gossip against another person was enough to land him in the Police cells and from those cells to oblivion.

An employee of Mr. Juan Luders, proprietor of "El Fenix," was killed just when he was going out to the sidewalk to bring in a little dog that had gotten out of the house, and two youngsters who at five-thirty in the morning were going to go swimming in El Coro were likewise riddled with bullets by the "Cívicos."

Youngsters practiced their aim on dogs, on vultures and...on the poor folk who did not watch out. How many drunkards, who had been caught out in the streets on a binge, were not cold by dawn, on the sidewalks, pierced by the bullets of the Cívicos...!

The excesses, then, were committed by both sides, with the only difference being that those—the illiterate—acted while seized by hatred and by rage, while these—the literate—acted with serenity. Therefore, later on, when the particulars of the tragedy became known, the country was seized with fright and a sort of "guilt complex" took hold of all those who felt responsible for what had happened and that is how, when it was said that General Martínez was the Provisional President, and not the Constitutional one and that elections had to be called in order to elect a successor, they began feverishly to draw up documents petitioning the Congress to declare him Constitutional President, so that Mr. Araujo's term could end.

The original documents should be in the Congressional archives, with the signatures of thousands of citizens from around the country, who were demanding the Constitutional Presidency for their savior. And due to that collective "Guilt Complex," a dictatorship of 13 years was installed in the country.

This is the way that History is written...!

DOCUMENT 6-6
Enrique Córdova, Memoir, "General Maximiliano Hernández Martínez", ca. 1960s

EXCERPT

The following text is an excerpt from the memoirs by Dr. Enrique Córdova, a prominent lawyer who had been a candidate for the presidency in 1931. This is the main instance in his memoirs where he mentions the insurrection of 1932. He limits his focus to the financial arrangements to pay for the repression rather than offering any extended discussion of the uprising or massacre. In other words, he whitewashes the events, a common occurrence in conservative renditions of the events prior to the consolidation of the hard-line anticommunism in the late 1970s and 1980s. It is also worth noting Córdova's nationalist tone in regard to Martínez's decision to stop payments of the international debt after the uprising in order to pay for the upkeep of public order.[22]

Since his youth, General Maximiliano Hernández Martínez was known as an enthusiast of study and work. Due to these traits, he enjoyed esteem, obtained promotions and became a professor for officers who needed to pass exams in order to rise in the ranks.

One would think that this position as teacher won him friends amongst the officers and led him to aspire to the Presidency of the Republic. To obtain the office, he launched his candidacy toward the end of the presidential term of Dr. Romero Bosque and, upon convincing himself that he did not have a sufficient number of supporters in order to win, he joined with Don Arturo, accepting the candidacy for Vice President, it is said, on the advice of Don Pío.

Don Arturo was victorious and appointed him Minister of War. He was in that position when the putsch of December 2, 1931 overthrew Don Arturo.

Given that Martínez held the Presidency for so long, I shall limit myself to referring to only a few incidents of that interesting era in our national life.

It is a task beyond my powers to refer to and critique all of his administrative acts, in which there was much good and not a little bad. I must make some reference, however, and with the greatest impartiality, since I was neither an opponent nor a supporter of that regime that has so stirred public opinion.

A state of siege is decreed and the debt service is suspended.

During the term of the Military Directory that was constituted upon the fall of Don Arturo, communist uprisings occurred in Sonsonate, Juayúa and other towns.

The communists committed excesses, but defeated by the Government forces, they were swiftly controlled.

Due to these disturbances, the Government decreed a state of siege and the leader Martí and the students Zapata and Luna were arrested, the three being executed shortly thereafter.

In the face of the communist threat, General Martínez invited several capitalists to the Presidential Palace, extending the invitation to General Claramount and to myself, doubtlessly for having been candidates in the past elections. I attended that meeting but not as a capitalist.

Therein, the President expounded on the danger that society was facing with the reds and the little confidence he had that the Army officers could control an insurrection of the troops if they were not equipped with handheld machine guns. He read the documents found in the power of the conspirators and ended his discourse asking for economic aid for the urgent purchase of machine guns.

The price of coffee was quite low and therefore the economic crisis was continuing that had so distressed the Araujo Government and farmers in general. Among those present was Mr. Jaime Hill, a large-scale coffee grower and a man of obvious talent. He asked to speak and made the President see that the economic situation was so depressed that it was not possible to easily gather the sum of money necessary, but that the Government could suspend the service on the foreign borrowing, quite rightly so, given that a primordial duty of the state is to conserve its existence.

"I am a bond holder," said Don Angel Guirola, "but I approve of the suspension of the service on the debt that Mr. Hill has proposed, because it is a patriotic measure."

The others present unanimously supported the idea.

Martínez had to accept it; but he insisted on appointing a Committee that would procure the raising of funds.

Public opinion gave the appointed Committee the nickname "Public Health Committee," because, more than raising funds, it worked on advising on security measures…

All those present, for the most part coffee growers, spoke out in favor of the suspension of the service on the foreign debt and there was no lack of those who called for the death penalty for the communists.

Martínez promised that he would punish them with the full weight of the law, but he insisted that funds be raised for the purchase of machine guns and for this end he created on the 4th of February of 1932 the Council on Law and Order.

At my suggestion, the minutes of the meeting were drawn up, for the purpose of putting on record that the Government had the backing of all those present for the suspension of the debt service.

On the 23rd of January of that same year of 1932 the suspension of payment of the foreign debt was decreed, with Mr. Pedro S. Fonseca, Under Secretary of the Treasury Section, still the Acting Minister. But days later, Dr. Miguel Tomás Molina was appointed Minister, who, as one of his first measures, by Decree dated the 19th of February, published in the Official Gazette on the 20th of said month, set aside "the impounding of funds that had been decreed," that is, the suspension of the foreign debt service.

The desire of the Martínez Government to pay the foreign debt is not surprising. The Government had not been recognized, because at that time there was an international agreement that prevented the recognition of governments arising out of military movements and Martínez had against him that when the coup occurred he was the Minister of War of the overthrown government. Naturally, the desire to improve international relations was added to the patriotic fervor of "maintaining the country's standing."

For my part, I thought that the Moratorium Law was justified, because of the crisis that was burdening the debtors, the same reason for suspending the service on the foreign debt.

DOCUMENT 6-7
"Is Confrontation Inevitable?" editorial by Sidney Mazzini in *Diario de Hoy*, 1977

The columnist Sidney Mazzini, a lawyer from the western region, explains in this op-ed piece the parallels between the conditions in El Salvador in 1977 and the crisis of 1932. By 1977, references to 1932 had become commonplace and, as the columnist makes clear, the memories of the past played a powerful role in defending a strong repressive approach to any perceived threats to the state. The columnist ends his article with an appeal to the army to recover the spirit of 1932 and act accordingly.[23]

The title of this article that we are writing, Is Confrontation Inevitable?, is not meant to frighten or alarm anyone; it is, in the form of a question, something that, God willing, should not happen. But, evidence exists that leads us to think otherwise; not only our own thoughts, but rather those of others principally; that we are heading into an inevitable confrontation of a cunning class struggle, or why not say it, into an internal civil war—without beating around the bush and using euphemisms—of tremendous consequences that are difficult to predict.

The latest events serve to confirm it: the "occupation" of a government ministry that went almost unnoticed (since the splendid, brand-new penal code with its latest reforms was not enforced), the series of murders of renowned, decent men and humble agents of authority, the possible "occupations" of other ministries and other High Powers of State—since things are escalating—until eventually reaching the final escalade, the seizing of central power, the unfurling of the international red flag over the Presidential Palace, as the supreme symbol of authority and command, replacing the glorious blue and white standard, traditional flag of our struggles for independence starting in 1811, with the distant tolling of bells on a 5th of November. We shall fall then under the bloody tyranny of the so-called "dictatorship of the proletariat," just like in Cuba, Viet Nam, Cambodia, etc., with the ensuing endless death, misery, and atrocities.

This issue is important and is not to be looked at askance. At all hours of the day, one hears talk and comments of all kinds, in streets, plazas, and professional cliques, commercial establishments, in the privacy of homes, etc. They say that the situation is going from bad to worse, that there is a dearth of authority and order, that life is becoming unlivable. We are under severe nervous strain, there is anxiety, unease, there is no peace, and, it seems, the promises made have not been kept. Things are not done the same way they used to be, there is no security, the future of El Salvador is uncertain. There is a downward trend in investments, no one is thinking about investing anymore, and if possible, they want to get their money out of the country, sell properties, etc. This is the reality posed as constructive criticism; it is not an exaggeration.

The situation is worse than the one in 1932 because now power is beginning to yield, it is beginning to be "taken"; the correlation of forces is tipping in favor of Marxism, despite the "silent majority." We know that in 1932 a serious confrontation took place, a 100-hour civil war with incalculable casualties. The confrontation that is unfortunately on the horizon will be of greater proportions, corrected and augmented. Things resemble what happened in Chile in Allende's time, or are starting to look like things in Lebanon, which drifted into a bloody civil war, which still continues and never ends. Its army did not do anything to control the looming crisis—under the principle that an ounce of prevention is worth a pound of cure—and now that country, Lebanon, has been invaded by Syria, Israel, or by Arabic League troops. The massacres and destruction have been unimaginable. From the flourishing, progressive foundation that Lebanon had, it has turned into a little less than a human wretch.

In the great outpouring of grief by the thousands of people who accompanied the mortal remains of he who in life was Raúl Molina Cañas, several slogans were chanted and one of them said: "El pueblo quiere paz, gobierno, ¿dónde estás?" [The people want peace, government, where are you?] This is eloquent proof of the mood of the citizenry in general. The truth, and this should be clearly spelled out, is that this does not have to do with defending small-minded class interests of a badly named oligarchy or selfish bourgeoisie, which exist only in the sick minds of those who are suffering from a complex or are social malcontents. No. What is of interest above all other things, is saving the Fatherland, saving El Salvador, from this new tidal wave of evil, from this difficult crossroads the Republic is facing and is crossing. We must put aside or completely ignore famous images or what they will say abroad, or the "advice" given from the outside as part of the famous "human rights packages" that are causing and will cause so much harm to the peoples of Latin America and their economies, all to the benefit of the cause of Soviet imperialism that is only waiting for each Republic in Latin America to fall one by one, in order to turn us into colonies or satellites just like Cuba, Angola, Mozambique, Ethiopia, etc., to mention the most recent.

We hope and we have faith (there is still room) that things will not turn out this way. That we will be saved once more by our beloved *Colocho*—our Savior—and by the Armed Forces and that we will stabilize for another forty years, an era of peace, work, and progress.

We are at a grave juncture, which is at the same time the solution. Either we continue on as we have, going from bad to worse, from jolt to jolt, from crime to crime, coexisting with the "system" that is going to destroy us once and for all, with its arms crossed and without firing a shot, or we use the legal arm that is established and ordered in the Constitution that is in full force and effect. The Article of the Constitution to be applied is 112, which in essence states: "The Armed Forces are established in order to defend the integrity of the territory and the Sovereignty of the Republic, to enforce the law, maintain law and order and guarantee constitutional rights." Among the ultimate—authentically human—rights are those set forth in Art. 163, which states, in capital letters: "ALL THE INHABITANTS OF EL SALVADOR HAVE THE RIGHT TO BE PROTECTED IN THE CONSERVATION AND DEFENSE OF THEIR LIFE, HONOR, LIBERTY, WORK, PROPERTY, AND POSSESSIONS." Nothing more: the Commander General of the Armed Forces has the next word. May God enlighten him, saving our Fatherland and our people from a confrontation between Salvadorans that appears inevitable.

NOTES

Notes to Introduction

1. Dalton, *Miguel Mármol*. The book was published in English translation in 1987: Kathleen Ross and Richard Schaaf, trans., as *Miguel Mármol* (Willimantic, CT: Curbstone Press, 1987). We will treat the Curbstone edition as the "official" English translation of the book, and thus for the purposes of continuity throughout the remainder of this book, all citations to *Miguel Mármol* will refer to the English-language Curbstone edition, unless otherwise stated.
2. *Diario Latino*, January 23, 1932; and *New York Times*, January 24, 1932, p. 1.
3. Fitzpatrick, *History's Memory*.
4. Ibid., p. 7.
5. Sociologist Margaret Sommers has provided well-developed discussions of the meaning of metannarrative in her "What's Political or Cultural About Political Culture and the Public Sphere?" pp. 113–44; and in "Narrating and Naturalizing Civil Society and Citizenship Theory," pp. 229–74.
6. Assmann, *Moses the Egyptian*, p. 12.
7. Many works have influenced our understanding of historical memory and narrative, including Hamilton, *Terrific Majesty*; and J. Smith, "No More Language Games," pp. 1413–40. Additional works are cited in this Introduction, and a more extensive list of works can be found in citations in our Conclusion.
8. Assmann, *Moses the Egyptian*, p. 9.
9. Halbwachs's seminal work appears in Halbwachs, *On Collective Memory*. The first edition of Halbwachs's work was published as *Les Cadres sociaux de la mémoire* in 1925.
10. Ricoeur, *Memory, History, Forgetting*, p. 21.
11. Interview with ARENA deputy, whose identity is being kept anonymous upon request.
12. Binford, *El Mozote Massacre*, p. 105. Example also cited in Wood, *Insurgent Collection Action*, p. 34.

13. "Language is not a fully open system in which people can create any discourse they like, but neither is it a closed system that preempts people's abilities to say what they want to say." Parker, *Idea of the Middle Class*, p. 12.
14. Saussure's main work was published posthumously in 1916 as *Course in General Linguistics*. It was first translated into English in 1959 and published by Oxford's Pergamon Press and New York's McGraw Hill. Bakhtin, *Dialogic Imagination*.
15. Schacter, *Seven Sins of Memory*.
16. Ibid., p. 139.
17. See Bet-El, "Unimagined Communities"; and Jedlicki, "Historical Memory."
18. Bet-El, "Unimagined Communities," p. 206.

Notes to Chapter One

1. T. Smith, "Notes on Population," p. 373; Wallström, *Wayfarer*, pp. 60–61.
2. Tschiffely, *Southern Cross*, p. 304.
3. Beals, *Banana Gold*, p. 87.
4. T. Anderson, *Matanza*, pp. 137–38.
5. MacNaught, "Horrors of Communism."
6. Méndez, *Los sucesos comunistas*, pp. 98–99.
7. M. Figueroa, local commander of Salcoatitán, to Departmental Commander, Sonsonate, March 14, 1932, AGN, MG, SS, Box 4.
8. Méndez, *Los sucesos comunistas*, p. 27.
9. T. Anderson, *Matanza*, pp. 151–52. Méndez, *Los sucesos comunistas*, p. 129.
10. T. Anderson, *Matanza*, pp. 138–42.
11. Méndez, *Los sucesos comunistas*, pp. 33–51; T. Anderson, *Matanza*; Ching, "In Search of the Party," 204–39.
12. Telegram from Francisco Brito, Alcalde of Nahuizalco, to Sonsonate, January 29, 1932, AGN, MG, SS, Box 1.
13. M. Figueroa, local commander of Salcoatitán, to Departmental Commander, Sonsonate, March 14, 1932, AGN, MG, SS, Box 4.
14. Interview with Salvador Pérez, Salcoatitán, July 23, 2000.
15. Circular from the Minister of Health to the Alcaldes of Sonsonate Department, February 9, 1932, AGN, MG, SS, Box 3.
16. MacNaught, "Horrors of Communism."
17. Zamosc, "Landing that Never Was," p. 143.
18. T. Anderson, *Matanza*, pp. 147–51.
19. Juan Rivera, Alcalde accidental (as replacement for Miguel Call) to Departmental Governor of Sonsonate, February 4, 1932, AGN, MG, SS, Box 4.
20. Reported in *Diario del Salvador*, September 13, 1932, contained in the collection of press clippings in AGN, MG, SI, Capitulo 1, Caja 17.
21. From the Community of Indians of Asunción Izalco to General Maximiliano Hernández Martínez, February 26, 1933, AGN, MG, SS, Box 2.

22. Enrique Uribe, Nahuizalco, to Departmental Comandante, Sonsonate, March 4, 1932, AGN, MG, SS Box 3.
23. The SRI was a sort of Communist Red Aid. It provided aid to workers and their families who suffered from what the SRI called "white terror," repression by police, the military, or capitalists who opposed workers' efforts to achieve or more equitable distribution of wealth. Like the Communist Party, the SRI had organizational headquarters in New York and Moscow. It received some nominal financial support for those international sources, but the local chapters in a place like El Salvador depended almost entirely on donations from the sale of local membership cards (*carnets*).
24. M. Figueroa, local commander of Salcoatitán, to Departmental Commander, Sonsonate, March 14, 1932, AGN, MG, SS, Box 4.
25. Alcalde of Armenia to Governor of Sonsonate Department, February 3, 1932, AGN, MG, SS, Box 4. (Note the document is dated January 3, but that was a typographical error made by the typist.)
26. The General Instructions document was first published in Sáenz, *Rompiendo cadenas*. It more famously appeared in Schlesinger, *Revolución comunista*. The documents were also given to U.S. diplomats, and they appeared in USNA, WNRC, G-2 Military Reports, Box 763, folder 3000–3020, Political, "Memorandum: The Story of Communism in El Salvador," written in 1943, p. 13.
27. Sáenz, *Rompiendo cadenas*, p. 231.
28. Secretary of the Central Committee of the PCS to the Caribbean Bureau, October 8, 1931, Russian State Archive of Social and Political History (RGASPI), Moscow, Russia, formerly named the Russian Centre for the Preservation and Study of Documents of Most Recent History (RTsKhIDNI), Fond 495 Opis 119 Inventory (or File) 7, page 15—hereafter abbreviated as 495:119:7, p. 15.
29. Ismael Hernández, secretary general of the SRI, San Salvador, to the Secretariat of the Caribbean SRI, New York, November 29, 1931, RGASPI, 539:3:1060, p. 9.
30. Ibid.
31. Gregorio Ramírez, Santa Ana, April 22, 1931, to Compañero A. Herclet, Paris, France, RGASPI, 534:7:455, p. 18.
32. RGASPI, 495:119: 4, p. 23.
33. On the PCS, see report from Anaya in Guatemala to Caribbean Bureau, April 9, 1931, RGASPI, 500:1:5, pp. 18–21. See also the informe from Luis Guerrero to the subcommittee of the CSLA (Confederación Sindical de Latino América), New York, April 7, 1931, RGASPI, 495:119:11, pp. 14–19. An SRI leader commented in July 1932 on the nadir of membership in SRI chapters in March 1931: Informe de la sección de El Salvador, rendido por el camarada Hernández de la junta del secretariado del caribe del SRI, 12 de julio, 1932; RGASPI, 495:119:12, pp. 25 and 30.

34. RGASPI, 495:119:7, p. 25; also mentioned by Comrade H in RGASPI, 495:119:4, p. 22.
35. RGASPI, 495:119:4, p. 48.
36. RGASPI, 495:119:7, p. 1.
37. RGASPI, 495:119:4, pp. 5 and 55.
38. Informe del VI Congreso, May 1930, RGASPI, 495:119:10, p. 19; see also p. 119.
39. RGASPI, 495:119:10, p. 10.
40. RGASPI, 495:119:4, p. 2.
41. RGASPI, 495:119:4, p. 15.
42. RGASPI, 495:119:4, p. 2.
43. RGASPI, 495:119:1, p. 20.
44. RGASPI, 495:119:1, p. 21
45. RGASPI, 495:119:4, p. 67.
46. Ching, "In Search of the Party," pp. 230–37.
47. Nullification request for January 1932 municipal elections, Nahuizalco, AGN, CN, Box 9.
48. Nullification request for December 1929 municipal elections, Izalco, AGN, CN, Box 7.
49. For examples, see Gould and Lauria, "They Call Us Thieves," pp. 191–237; and Gould, "Revolutionary Nationalism," pp. 138–71. Gould and Lauria are working on a book-length project on this topic.
50. Méndez, *Los sucesos comunistas*; T. Anderson, *Matanza*; M. Figueroa, local commander of Salcoatitán, to Departmental Commander, Sonsonate, March 14, 1932, AGN, MG, SS, Box 4.
51. "La situación actual del Salvador," ca. June 1930, RGASPI, 495:119:11, p. 12. Informe from Anaya, Guatemala, to Caribbean Bureau, October 12, 1930, RGASPI, 495:119:12, p. 13.
52. Lauria, *Agrarian Republic*. Lauria provides a more comprehensive list of rural insurrections in his dissertation, "Agrarian Republic."
53. From the poem "All," Dalton, *Poems*, originally published in *Las historias prohibidas del Pulgarcito*.
54. For a discussion of the various arguments on ethnocide in 1932, see Tilley, *Seeing Indians*.
55. General Maximiliano Hernández Martínez went by his maternal name only, Martínez, which is how most scholarship also refers to him. Throughout this study, we refer to him as Martínez, and only rarely as Hernández Martínez.
56. The British diplomatic correspondence can be found in a variety of reports exchanged between the consul in El Salvador, Rodgers, and the Foreign Office, contained in the Public Record Office, including A379/9/8, A400/9/8, A 500/9/8, A525/9/8, and A537/9/8. The U.S. diplomatic correspondence is contained in USNA, RG 59, Box 5509. The U.S. correspondence also makes copious references to Rodgers's analyses and the corresponding responses of the British government.

57. Zamosc, "Landing that Never Was," p. 138.
58. The most readily available access to the Canadian/British reports is in Zamosc, "Landing that Never Was." The original reports are found in the British Public Record Office in, Hose, Chief of Naval Staff, Ottowa, to Commander in Chief, American and West Indies Station, Bermuda, forwarded to Foreign Office, April 20, 1932, A 4077/9/8, FO 371 15814.
59. From Lammers, Navy Department to Commanding Officers of U.S.S. Philip and Wickes, January 23, 1932, USNA, RG59, 816.00 Revolutions/108.
60. Confidential telegram from Commanding Officer of U.S.S. Wickes, January 25, 1932, USNA, RG59, 816.00 Revolutions/99.
61. From the diary of Henry Stimson, U.S. Sect. of State, January 25, 1932. Yale University Manuscripts Collections. Cited in Astilla, "Martínez Era."

Notes to Chapter Two

1. On the Conquest and colonial-era slavery, see MacLeod, *Spanish Central America*; Sherman, *Forced Native Labor*; Adams, "Conquest Tradition of Meso-America," pp. 114–36; Browning, *El Salvador*; and Ministerio de Educación, *Historia de El Salvador*, vol. 1.
2. On the colonial economy, see Fernández, *Pintando*; Wortman, *Government and Society*; and Martínez-Peñate, *El Salvador*.
3. On the issue of ethnicity and the construction of racialized identities during the colonial era, see Gómez and Herrera, *Mestizaje*.
4. On issues of religion and cofradías during the colonial era, see MacLeod, *Spanish Central America*; Browning, *El Salvador*; and Ministerio de Educación, *Historia de El Salvador*, vol. 1.
5. On land tenure during the colonial era, see MacLeod, *Spanish Central America*; Browning, *El Salvador*; and Ministerio de Educación, *Historia de El Salvador*, vol. 1.
6. On the issue of administration and bureaucratic decentralization during the colonial era, see Wortman, *Government and Society*.
7. For an overview of the Napoleonic era as it relates to Spain and the Spanish Empire, see Lynch, *Revolutions in Spanish America*.
8. On independence in El Salvador and the Federation period, see Lynch, *Revolutions in Spanish America*, pp. 333–40; M. Rodríguez, *Cádiz Experiment*; Turcios, *Los primeros patriotas*; and Ministerio de Educación, *Historia de El Salvador*, vol. 1, ch. 11.
9. On the nineteenth-century economy and land tenure, see Lindo-Fuentes, *Weak Foundations*; Lauria, *Agrarian Republic*; Gudmunson and Lindo-Fuentes, *Central America 1821–1871*; and Ministerio de Educación, *Historia de El Salvador*, vol. II.
10. On the privatization decrees and their impact on land and labor relations throughout western El Salvador, see Lauria, *Agrarian Republic*.
11. On politics in the late nineteenth and early twentieth centuries, see P. Alvarenga, *Cultura y ética*; P. Alvarenga, "Los indígenas," pp. 363–94; Ching,

"From Clientelism to Militarism"; and Holden, *Armies Without Nations*.

12. On the era immediately preceding the 1932 insurrection, see T. Anderson, *Matanza*; and Greib, "U.S. and the Rise of Maximiliano Hernández Martínez," pp. 151–72.

13. For overviews of the military regimes in El Salvador, see Williams and Walter, *Militarization and Demilitarization*; Stanley, *Protection Racket State*; Castro Morán, *Función política del ejército*; and Ministerio de Educación, *Historia de El Salvador*, vol. II.

14. On politics during the Hernández Martínez years, see Luna, "Análisis de una dictadura fascista latinoamericano"; and Castellanos, *El Salvador 1930–1960*; Ching, "Patronage and Politics," pp. 50–70; Ching and Tilley, "Indians, the Military, and the Uprising of 1932 in El Salvador," pp. 121–56; and Elam, "Appeal to Arms"; Astilla, "Martínez Era"; and Williams and Walter, *Militarization and Demilitarization*. On issue of ethnicity during the Martínez era, especially as it relates to birth records, see Tilley, *Seeing Indians*.

15. On economic policies during Hernández Martínez, see Luna, "Analisis de una dictadura;" and Bulmer-Thomas, *Political Economy*.

16. On Hernández Martínez's eccentricities, see the interview with him by U.S. journalist William Krehm in the 1940s, in Krehm, *Democracies and Tyrannies;* and Astilla, "Martínez Era."

17. On the downfall of Martínez, see Parkman, *Nonviolent Insurrection*. On the era of the 1940s in Latin America and the impact of WWII, especially on issues relating to democracy, see Rock, *Latin America in the 1940s*; and Bethell and Roxborough, *Latin America*.

18. For politics during the period 1944–48, see Cárceres, "Discourses of Reformism"; Ministerio de Educación, *Historia de El Salvador*, vol. II.

19. On the 1948 "Revolution" and the 1950 Constitution, see Turcios, *Autoritarismo y modernización*; Cárceres, "Discourses of Reformism"; and Gallardo, *Las constituciones de El Salvador*.

20. On the Osorio and Lemus regimes, see Turcios, *Autoritarismo y modernización*; Cárceres, "Discourses of Reformism"; and Griffith and Gates, "State's Gendered Response to Political Instability," pp. 248–92.

21. On the impact of the Cuban Revolution on diplomacy and politics throughout the Western Hemisphere, see Wright, *Latin America in the Era of the Cuban Revolution*.

22. For an overview of the 1960s, see Valle, *Siembra de vientos*.

23. On the Soccer War, see T. Anderson, *War of the Dispossessed*; Durham, *Scarcity and Survival*; and Jiménez Pérez, *La guerra no fue de fútbol*.

24. On intraleft factionalism in the late 1960s and early 1970s, see Valle, *Siembra de vientos*; Cienfuegos, *Crónica entre los espejos*; and Prisk, *Comandante Speaks*; and Harecker, *con la mirada*.

25. Nairn, "Behind the Death Squads."

26. On ORDEN and some of the early death squads in the 1960s, such as La Mano Blanca (the White Hand), see Valle, *Siembra de vientos*. For other

examinations and descriptions of the death squads, see Armstrong and Shenk, *El Salvador*; Americas Watch Committee, *Analysis of the Department of State*; Amnesty International, *El Salvador: 'Death Squads'*; and Dickey, "Behind the Death Squads."

27. For a good description of the initial stages of grassroots liberation theology and the paramilitary response, see Alas, *Iglesia, tierra y lucha campesina*.
28. On politics in the 1970s, including the two presidential elections in 1972 and 1977, the development of mass mobilization, and the juntas of 1979–81, see Dunkerley, *Long War*; Duarte, *Duarte: My Story*; Webre, *Jose Napoleon Duarte*; and Menjívar, *Tiempos de locura*. On the issue of liberation theology in El Salvador, see Berryman, *Religious Roots of Rebellion*; Whitfield, *Paying the Price*; and Dennis, Golden, and Wright, *Oscar Romero*.
29. On the demise of the Somoza regime and the Sandinista Revolution in Nicaragua, see Kagan, *Twilight Struggle*; and Walker, *Revolution and Counterrevolution*.
30. For studies on the civil war in El Salvador, see Lauria and Binford, *Landscapes of Struggle*, sect. 2; Byrne, *El Salvador's Civil War*; Montgomery, *Revolution in El Salvador*; Wood, *Insurgent Collective*; Dunkerley, *Long War;* Armstrong and Shenk, *El Salvador;* Lungo Uncles and Keene, "El Salvador in the Eighties." On the massacre at El Mozote, see Danner, *Massacre at El Mozote*; and Binford, *El Mozote Massacre*.
31. On U.S. policy toward El Salvador during the war, see Diskin, *Impact of U.S. Policy*; Leonard, *Central America and the United States*; and Bonner, *Weakness and Deceit*. On the specific issue of social movements in the United States against policy in El Salvador, see Gelbspan, *Break-ins*; North American Congress on Latin America, *Central America*.
32. On the signing of the peace accords and the transformation of the military, see Walter, *Las fuerzas*. On the death of the Jesuits, see Whitfield, *Paying the Price*. On the human costs of the war, see United Nations, *From Madness to Hope*; and Americas Watch, *El Salvador's Decade of Terror*. On some of the challenges facing El Salvador in the postwar era, see Popkin, *Peace Without Justice*; Lauria and Binford, *Landscapes of Struggle*; and Tilley, *Seeing Indians*.

Notes to Chapter Three

1. Besides *Miguel Mármol* some of Dalton's poetry has been translated and published in English: Dalton, *Small Hours of the Night*; Dalton, *Clandestine Poems*; Dalton, *Poems*. His translated poetry appears in numerous anthologies. There is a recent biography of Dalton by Luis Alvarenga, *El ciervo perseguido*. Another good source of biographical information on Dalton is Cañas Dinarte, *Diccionario de autoras y autores de El Salvador*. For literary analyses of Dalton, see Lara-Martínez and Seager, *Otros Roques*; see also Lara-Martínez, *La tormenta*.
2. Colindres, *Fundamentos económicos*.

3. Dalton, *Poetry and Militancy*, p. 11. Originally published as "Poesía y militancia en América Latina." Dalton also included a remarkable collection of anecdotes about his experience at the Externado de San José in his autobiographical novel, published posthumously in 1976, *Pobrecito poeta que era yo...*

4. Dalton's fond memories of Father Landarech are expressed in one of his poems: "Acepto que mi poesía no es ya la misma de antes, la que gustaba tanto/al Padre Landarech. El bueno de Tapón, insistía en convencer/a todo el mundo, de que su querida oveja negra era el poeta lírico más importante/de la historia de la literatura nacional [...] recuerdo [...] que le envié por correo el primer poema de amor que hice en Cuba." (I accept that my poetry is not what it was, what Father Landarech liked so much. Good "bottlestopper," he insisted in persuading everyone that his dear black sheep was the most important lyrical poet in national literature [...] I remember [...] mailing him the first love poems that I wrote in Cuba.) *Los Hongos IX* (1966–72). See Lara-Martínez, *En la humedad del secreto*, p. 528. L. Alvarenga, *El ciervo perseguido*, pp. 31–32. Alvarenga notes that Alvaro Menen Desleal claims that Dalton maintained correspondence with Landarech from Cuba.

5. "La vida escogida," in García Verzi, *Recopilación de textos*, p. 38.

6. *Sábados de Diario Latino*, July 28, 1956, p. 3. Dalton erased this poem from the manuscript "Poesía completa I (1961–1965)" and the revised version of *La ventana en el rostro*, probably because of its Nerudian influence.

7. Dalton, *Poetry and Militancy*, p. 15.

8. "Poems in Love to Lisa. II," in Dalton, *La ventana en el rostro*, p. 104.

9. In *Cultura* 89 (January–April 2005): 31.

10. Dalton, *Poetry and Militancy*, p. 19.

11. Ibid., p. 22.

12. "Desde hace algunos años siempre me propuse escribir de prisa, como si supiera que me van a matar al día siguiente... Es terriblemente ridículo ser un escritor salvadoreño, y tal vez lo sea sólo por la haraganería y el egoísmo nacional."*Recopilación de textos sobre Roque Dalton*, p. 47.

13. Dalton, *Miguel Mármol*, p. 34. He compares his encounter with Miguel Mármol to his meeting with Regis Debray a year before when he shed what was "European and soothing" in him. In talking with Mármol, Dalton felt that he was recapturing the "historical, intellectual, sentimental" time and space of his childhood (Dalton, *Miguel Mármol*, p. 34). The meeting with Debray is described in Dalton, "La noche que conocí a Regis," pp. 124–26.

14. Dalton, *Poems*, p. 67. The poem "Crock Logic" originally appeared in *Poemas clandestinos*.

15. Cienfuegos, *Crónica*, pp. 100–120. Another excellent source on Dalton's death is the series of articles published in the electronic weekly *El Faro* (www.elfaro.net) by Miguel Huezo Mixco. There is also an excellent

summary provided in a lengthy email blog by Catrina Monti from El Salvador, http://www.weblog.com.ar/000017.html.
16. One of the names mentioned most often was that of Joaquín Villalobos, who became a legendary commander of the ERP during the civil war of the 1980s. He denies the accusation, pointing out that at the time of Dalton's death the leader of the ERP was Alejandro Rivas Mira. Villalobos, book review, p. 586. Roque Dalton's family has not let Villalobos off the hook, especially Juan José Dalton, who has publicly criticized Villalobos for his lack of forthrightness regarding the assassination. One example of Juan José Dalton's criticism can be found online at: http://encontrarte.aporrea.org/teoria/perfiles/26/
17. For information on members of the Committed Generation, see Hernández Aguirre, "La nueva poesía."
18. Dalton, *Pobrecito poeta que era yo...*, cited in L. Alvarenga, *El ciervo perseguido*, p. 10. "Un país es otro país después que le matan 30 mil hombres en un par de semanas."
19. Hernández Aguirre, "La nueva poesía," p. 79.
20. Salvadoran politics during this period are discussed in Elam, "Appeal to Arms"; and Parkman, *Nonviolent Insurrection*. A Latin American context for the 1940s can be found in Rock, *Latin America in the 1940s*; and Bethell and Roxborough, *Latin America*.
21. Dalton, "Otto René Castillo," p. 9.
22. Canales "La Generación Comprometida," p. 60.
23. Waldo Chávez Velasco, "Discurso del Dr. Waldo Chávez Velasco en su ingreso como Miembro de Número a la Honorable Academia Salvadoreña de la Lengua correspondiente de la Real Academia de la Lengua Española," San Salvador, August 30, 2002.
24. According to Roberto Armijo, the group included himself, Roque Dalton, Otto René Castillo, Manlio Argueta, José Roberto Cea, Alfonso Quijada, José Rodríguez Ruiz, Miguel Angel Parada, Italo López Vallecillos, René Arteaga, Manuel Barba Salinas, Orlando Fresedo, Luis Argel Salinas, Elmer Trujillo, Tirso Canales, Danilo Velado, José Roberto Cea, René Araujo Solís, and Abel Salazar Rodezno. Armijo "Recordando a Juan Felipe Toruño," *Diario CoLatino* III, May 4, 1996, cited by Toruño in "Juan Felipe Toruño."
25. In Hernández Aguirre "La nueva poesía," p. 87.
26. See Handy, *Revolution in the Countryside*; and Cullather, *Secret History*.
27. Canales "La Generación Comprometida," p. 56.
28. Ibid., p. 50.
29. See "Discurso del Dr. Waldo Chávez Velasco."
30. Dalton, "Otto René Castillo," p. 11.
31. The poem was entitled "Messenger pigeons for black man Martí." Cited by Hernández Aguirre p. 82.
32. Dalton et al., *El intelectual y la sociedad*.

33. Ibid., p. 23.
34. Vásquez, *Bibliografía histórica*.
35. Méndez, *Los sucesos comunistas*, pp. 14 and 27.
36. Ibid., p. 47.
37. Ibid., p. 70.
38. Ibid., pp. 39–40.
39. Ibid., p. 61.
40. Buezo, *Sangre de hermanos*, p. 68.
41. Ibid., p. 52.
42. Ibid., p. 40.
43. Ibid.
44. Ibid., p. 43.
45. Ibid., p. 67.
46. Ibid., p. 82.
47. Ibid., p. 83.
48. A biography of the conservative Guatemalan journalist Clemente Marroquín Rojas contains information on the way in which Marroquín Rojas and Alfredo Schlesinger (Jorge's brother) received the papers from General Martínez. See Díaz Lozano, *Aquí viene un hombre*, chs. XIV and XV. We thank Héctor Pérez Brignoli for bringing this source to our attention.
49. Alegría, *Cenizas de Izalco*, published in English as *Ashes of Izalco*; Alemán Bolaños, *El oso ruso*; Machón Vilanova, *Ola roja*.
50. The classic study of this aspect of Latin American literature is D. Sommer, *Foundational Fictions*.
51. As one example of the 1932 uprising portrayed as a government conspiracy, see Cuenca, *El Salvador*, p. 105. "La insurrección, hábilmente provocada por el gobierno, que se negó a reconocer el triunfo de los trabajadores en unas elecciones municipales, estalló en varios departamentos el 22 de enero de 1932." For another example, see P. Alvarenga, *Cultura y ética*.
52. Vázquez Olivera, "'País mío no existes.'" See also Arias's book written shortly before his death in memory of Roque Dalton, *En memoria de Roque Dalton*.
53. Arias, *Farabundo Martí*, chs. 13 and 14. The reference to "spontaneity" is found on p. 132.
54. Luna, "Un heroico y trágico suceso de nuestra historia," p. 64.
55. Luna, "La insurrección de 1932," p. 6.
56. Dalton, *El Salvador*; and Dalton, *El Salvador: Monografía*.
57. The items linked to either the Salvadoran or Cuban Communist Parties included *Documentos Estadísticos del FUAR*, articles from *La Verdad*, the PCS's newspaper, a publication by Jorge Arias Gómez—a communist professor at the UES—and another article from *Prensa Latina*, the official press agency of the Cuban Revolution. The rest of the sources are traditional histories of El Salvador.

58. In Hernández Aguirre "La nueva poesía," p. 87.
59. Dalton, *Monografía*, p. 146.
60. Dalton, *El Salvador*, p. 29.
61. Dalton, *Monografía*, p. 23.
62. Dalton, *El Salvador*, p. 30.
63. Dalton, *Monografía*, pp. 72–73.
64. Ibid., p. 95.
65. Dalton, *El Salvador*, p. 45.
66. Dalton, *Monografía*, p. 112.
67. Dalton, *El Salvador*, p. 46.
68. Dalton, *Monografía*, p. 115.
69. Ibid., p. 117.

Notes to Chapter Four

1. Menchú, *Me llamo Rigoberta Menchú*; Barrios de Chungara and Viezzer, *Let Me Speak!*; Alvarado and Benjamin, *Don't Be Afraid, Gringo*.
2. Tirado, *Celsa's World*, p. 25.
3. Menchú, *Me llamo Rigoberta Menchú*, p. 30.
4. Galeano, *Memoria del fuego*.
5. For a concise summary of the embrace of testimonial literature by academics, see Denegri, "Testimonio and its Discontents," pp. 228–38.
6. Gugleberger, *Real Thing*.
7. Denegri, "Testimonio and its Discontents," p. 231.
8. Arias, *Rigoberta Menchú Controversy*; Stoll, *Rigoberta Menchú*; Canby, "Truth About Rigoberta Menchú." See also the Website dealing with the Stoll/Menchú controversy assembled by Dr. Allan Webb of Western Michigan University: http://www.wmich.edu/teachenglish/subpages/literature/rigobertamenchu.htm.
9. Menchú, *I Rigoberta Menchú*, p. 247.
10. Letter from Miguel Mármol to Roque Dalton, Prague, June 1, 1966, Dalton family archive.
11. Gugleberger, *Real Thing*, p. 81.
12. Dalton, *Miguel Mármol*, p. 39.
13. Lewis, *Children of Sanchez*.
14. From Roque Dalton's notebooks compiled during his interview with Miguel Mármol in Prague, 1966. Hereafter abbreviated, as "Cuaderno," p. xiii.
15. Dalton, *Miguel Mármol*, p. 36.
16. Cuaderno, xiii.
17. Ibid.
18. Ibid.
19. Ibid. These points appear in the finished manuscript in Dalton's introduction written in Havana in 1971; see Dalton, *Miguel Mármol*, p. 39.
20. Jorge Arias Gómez discussed Dalton's expressed discontent with the traditional PCS line during their reunion in Prague in 1966. See Arias Gómez,

En memoria, p. 20.
21. Dalton, *Miguel Mármol*, p. 37. On that same page in the introduction, Dalton claimed that after Prague he and Mármol "fell out of touch with one another," owing to the political situation and the need for party leaders to remain clandestine.
22. More specifically, the two sections being referred to are on pp. 240–50 and 285–320 in Dalton, *Miguel Mármol*.
23. Dalton, *Miguel Mármol*. The two quotes are found on pp. 318 and 312. For similar comments see also pp. 321 and 322.
24. Cuaderno, p. xiii.
25. Dalton, *Miguel Mármol*, p. 196.
26. Ibid., p. 288.
27. Ibid., p. 247.
28. Interview with Giovani Galeas, San Salvador March 14, 2005.
29. I. Rodríguez, "Organizaciones populares," pp. 85–96.
30. Arias Gómez, *En memoria*, p. 29.
31. Cuaderno, pp. 35–36.
32. Cuaderno, pp. 1–4.
33. Dalton, *Miguel Mármol*, pp. 45–73.
34. Dalton, *Miguel Mármol*, pp. 53 and 54.
35. Letter from Miguel Mármol to Roque Dalton, Mexico, June 23, 1966. Dalton family archive.
36. Dalton, *Miguel Mármol*, pp. 321–22.
37. Ibid., pp. 320–22.
38. Italics are in original. Dalton, *Miguel Mármol*, p. 286.
39. Ibid., p. 288.
40. Ibid., p. 293.
41. Ibid., p. 290.
42. These various references are drawn from the Cuaderno, pp. v, 29, 41, and 42.
43. Dalton *Miguel Mármol*, p. 307.
44. Ibid., 302.
45. Cuaderno, p. 43.
46. Gould, *To Die in this Way*.
47. Tilley, *Seeing Indians*.
48. Cuaderno, p. 5.
49. Dalton, *Miguel Mármol*, pp. 80–81.
50. For reasons of space, we did not elaborate on this issue in the last chapter. But in both *El Salvador* and *Monografía*, Dalton exhibited a recurrent anticlericalism and criticized the Catholic Church for being a principal cause of El Salvador's hierarchical and unjust social system. In a passage from *El Salvador*, Dalton claimed, "Roman Catholicism is the main religion in El Salvador. It has been used to keep, mainly the great peasant masses, away from revolutionary ideology and willing to accept the horrible conditions of exploitation to which they are subjected. Nonetheless, in

the last few years the Catholic Church has lost much of its reputation in the eyes of the people, taking off its mask in repeated occasions due to its complicity with the anti-popular actions of North American imperialism and its tyrannical governments" (p. 22).
51. Cuaderno, p. 40.
52. Dalton, *Miguel Mármol*, pp. 337–38.
53. Ibid., p. 275.
54. Ibid., p. 188.
55. Cuaderno, p. 19.
56. Dalton, *Poetry and Militancy*, p. 40, originally published as "Viejuemierda," in Dalton, *Las historias prohibidas del Pulgarcito.*
57. Dalton, *Miguel Mármol*, p. 305.
58. Cuaderno, p. 43.
59. Dalton, *Miguel Mármol*, pp. 266, 306, 308, 309, and 338.
60. Ibid., 297.
61. Ibid. The document is reprinted on pp. 297–300.
62. RGASPI, 495:119:4, 47.

Notes to Chapter Five

1. Cuenca, "La fisura en el FMLN," pp.19–21. *Primera Plana* 1:4.
2. It should be noted that we limit our analysis in the present chapter to those groups that fit under the category of "revolutionary leftist factions," or in other words, those groups who adhered to a Marxist-Leninist notion of historical evolution that obligated them to launch an armed insurrection when the material conditions in their country mandated that they do so. There were other moderate leftist traditions and movements in El Salvador that did not accept the inevitability of armed insurrection or advancing to the stage of communism. Some of them even made significant political gains, such as the Movimiento Nacional Revolucionario (MNR, National Revolutionary Movement), which was founded in 1966 by a group of reform-oriented intellectuals and professionals. Another example could include Fabio Castillo Figueroa, who was a presidential candidate in 1967 and who did not belong to the Communist Party at the time, but who then went on to join the "group" (*el grupo*) that was the progenitor of the ERP, a militant faction that broke away from the PCS in 1972. When the factionalism and fissuring within the left became rampant in the early 1970s, many individuals moved back and forth in their ideological positioning and even organizational affiliation, which complicates attempts at categorizing. But to reiterate, the present chapter focuses on the leftist factions that remained Marxist-Leninist in their orientation, believed that El Salvador, like the rest of the world, would eventually move onto a stage of communism, and that almost inevitably the advance from capitalism to socialism would require armed revolution. It was these various groups, which included the Communist Party and the various factions that broke

away from it in the first half of the 1970s, that tended to invest the greatest amount of energy in analyzing and remembering the insurrection of 1932. They wanted to determine if the uprising of 1932 was a noble failure based on an accurate assessment of the situation or a fundamentally flawed proposition from the beginning. (The authors would like to thank Jaime Barba of the University of El Salvador for his insights on this issue in a letter sent to Erik Ching, dated June 26, 2006.)

3. Dalton and Miranda, "Present Phase," pp. 56, 53, and 57.
4. Sánchez, "Social Developments." "Los cambios sociales y la política del Partido Comunista de El Salvador."
5. See, for example, Comité Central del Partido Comunista de El Salvador, *45 años de sacrificada lucha revolucionaria*, p. 1.
6. Dalton and Miranda, "Present Phase," p. 57.
7. Anaya went by his maternal name. Documents relating to the congress are found in RGASPI, 534:7:455. The congress is also mentioned extensively in the first major document put out by the PCS in May 1930 495:119:10. For the expulsions, see 534:7:455, pp. 8–14. For further elaboration on the expulsions, see Ching, "In Search of the Party," p. 212.
8. RGASPI, 495:119:4, 16.
9. "Informe de la sección de El Salvador, rendido por el camarada Hernández de la junta del secretariado del Caribe del SRI," July 12, 1932, RGASPI, 495:119:12, p. 25.
10. "Informe de la sección de El Salvador." See also RGASPI, 495:119:12, p. 16, for Anaya's earlier report citing the number of SRI locales in 1930.
11. Figueroa Ibarra, "El 'bolchevique mexicano,'" p. 220; see also Anaya's own testimony in Anaya, "La fundación del Partido Comunista," p. 237. Anaya's criticism of Martí is also located in a report from Anaya to Alberto Moreau, Sect. General of the Colonial Department of the Communist Party USA, RGASPI, 495:119:12, p. 8.
12. Gregorio Ramírez, Santa Ana, April 22, 1931, al Compañero A. Herclet, Paris, Francia, RGASPI, 534:7:455, p. 18.
13. RGASPI, 495:119:4, p. 59.
14. See Dalton, *Miguel Mármol*, p. 240; and Cuaderno p. 37.
15. RGASPI, 495:119:1, p. 18.
16. RGASPI, 495:119:1, p. 3.
17. May 16, 1932, letter from Carlos Castillo in RGASPI, 539:3:1060, p. 13.
18. Ching, "Clientelism to Militarism," pp. 380–85.
19. Dalton, *Miguel Mármol*, pp. 372–74.
20. Informe rendido por los camaradas de El Salvador, September 1936, RGASPI, 534:7:455, p. 26.
21. See, for example, the parties' two reports celebrating its thirtieth and forty-fifth anniversaries, Sánchez, "Social Developments"; and Comité Central del Partido Comunista de El Salvador, *45 años de sacrificada lucha revolucionaria*. Another source from the party's thirty-fifth anniversary is a typed

manuscript in Roque Dalton's archive by Alberto Gualán, "Años de lucha heroica: El 35 aniversario del Partido Comunista de El Salvador." In his 1972 history of the Communist Party (see below), also contained in his archive, Dalton claims that Gualán was the "máximo dirigente actual del PCS," and that the article was published in *Revista Internacional* in 1965 (see pp. 254 and 283 of his archive). The Gualán article bears page numbers 173–98 in Dalton's archive. Alberto Gualán is a pseudonym; the original Gualán was a party member in the early 1930s who was killed in the Matanza.

22. Dalton Archive, pp. 265–66. This is contained in Dalton's 1972 history Communist Party of El Salvador (see below).

23. Informe rendido por los camaradas de El Salvador, September 1936, RGASPI, 534:7:455, pp. 23–28.

24. Breves apuntes históricos del movimiento sindical de El Salvador, Library of Congress (LC), Manuscript Collection, Guatemala Documents Collection (GDC), 1944–1954, Reel 8019, Personal Papers of Victor M. Gutiérrez. Mármol's involvement with the CTG is based on another document from the same LC collection dated October 21, 1944 (which is a typographical error and should be 1946), in which Mármol is listed as a delegate from the CTG to a worker's conference in Mexico.

25. Dalton, "Otto Rene Castillo," pp. 11, 18, and 22; and Comité Central del Partido Comunista de El Salvador, *45 años de sacrificada lucha revolucionaria*, pp. 20, 22, and 23.

26. Gualán, "Años de lucha histórica," p. 179. The author also says that between 1960 and 1963 repression by military against mass sectors increased dramatically. On pp. 188–90, he describes the party's growing belief in the existence of a potentially revolutionary situation. See also, Comité Central del Partido Comunista de El Salvador, *45 años de sacrificada lucha revolucionaria*, pp. 14 and 15, for more commentary from a secretary general of the party on the belief that a revolutionary situation was emerging between 1961 and 1963. On the formation of GAR and FUAR, see also Menjívar, *Tiempos de locura*, pp. 27–29.

27. Gualán, "Años de lucha heroica," p. 188.

28. Luna, "Un heroico y trágico suceso de nuestra historia," p. 65.

29. Ibid., quote taken from typed rendition in Dalton archive, p. 172.

30. Luna, "Un heroico y trágico suceso de nuestra historia," quote take from typed rendition in Dalton archive, p. 168.

31. See Harnecker, *Con la mirada en alto*. Also see http://www.ucm.es/info/cecal/encuentr/areas/politica/2p/martin

32. See Menjívar, *Tiempos de locura*, pp. 27–28. Menjívar relies on a 2005 interview with Domingo Santacruz, member of the Political Commission of the Communist Party in the 1960s for his analysis of FUAR, Carpio, and ideological debates within the party at that time.

33. It is worth noting that Rafael Menjívar downplays the seeming paradoxical

shifts of Carpio's approach to armed insurrection in the 1960s by saying that he adhered consistently to the ideology of "guerra popular prolongada" (prolonged popular war), and that his on-again, off-again embrace of armed action remained true to that principle. Menjívar also points out that another armed branch emerged in 1969. See Menjívar, *Tiempos de locura*, p. 28.

34. The proceedings of the party's fifth congress are found in Sánchez, "Los cambios sociales."
35. Sánchez, "Los cambios sociales," p. 18.
36. Roque Dalton identified Gualán in his personal notes as a pseudonym for a party leader, p. 254 of the Dalton archive.
37. Gualán, "Años de lucha heroica," p. 175.
38. Ibid., p. 189.
39. Ibid., p. 189.
40. Ibid., p. 191.
41. Ibid., p. 195.
42. Ibid., pp. 4 and 20.
43. Comité Central del Partido Comunista de El Salvador, *45 Años de sacrificada lucha revolucionaria*, p. 4.
44. Ibid., p. 23.
45. Ibid., p. 15. See also Shafik Handal's article, "Class Struggles in Latin America," p. 56.
46. Dalton Archive, p. 290.
47. Ibid., p. 267.
48. Ibid., p. 269.
49. Ibid., p. 256.
50. Ibid., p. 292.
51. Ibid., p. 258.
52. Ibid., p. 297. The work Dalton referred to is Lissagaray, *History of Paris Commune*, first published in Brussels in 1876.
53. Handal, "Inseverable Interconnection," p. 19. Emphasis in original.
54. From the sixtieth anniversary, p. 31.
55. Handal, "We Have no Alternative to Armed Struggle," p. 14.
56. Handal, "He Died for a Noble Cause," p. 62.
57. Only the ERP did not join the unification at that time.
58. Handal, "We Have no Alternative," p. 13.
59. Zamora, *La izquierda partidaria Salvadoreña*, p. 44.
60. Armstrong and Shenk, *El Salvador*, pp. 135–36, citing *Miami Herald*, January 25, 1980.
61. Handal, "PCS: 60 años," p. 11.
62. Cuaderno, p. 20.

Notes to Chapter Six

1. *La Prensa*, January 13, 1932, p. 1.

2. *La Prensa*, January 29, 1932, p. 1.
3. *El Día*, February 5, 1932, p. 1.
4. "Monseñor Belloso y nuestro palpitante problema social," *El Día*, January 20, 1932, p. 4.
5. Gabino Mata hijo, "Comunismo o no Comunismo," *El Día*, February 4, 1932, p. 4.
6. Aristipo, "Al margen de la situación," *El Día*, February 18, 1932, p. 4.
7. *La Prensa*, January 31, 1932, p. 1.
8. *El Día*, January 27, 1932, p. 4.
9. "Existe un partido comunista?" *El Día*, January 28, 1932. The editorialist overestimated the age of the party; it had been founded in March 1930.
10. G. González y Contreras, "Los orígenes del comunismo salvadoreño," *Diario Latino*, February 2, 1932.
11. "Manifiesto del ejército a la nación," San Salvador, January 27, 1932.
12. "Mensaje del Señor Presidente de la Republica, General Maximiliano Hernández Martínez leído ante la Asamblea Nacional, en el acto de la apertura de su periodo de sesiones ordinarias, el día 4 de febrero de 1932."
13. *La Prensa*, March 29, 1932.
14. Méndez, *Los sucesos comunistas*.
15. Ibid., p. 36.
16. Ibid., p. 199.
17. Ibid., p. 60.
18. Ibid., p. 46.
19. "Cómo Nació la Dictadura," *La Tribuna*, January 25, 1952.
20. Izalco, "La Matanza de 1932 en El Salvador." Juan de Izalco is obviously a pseudonym. The article was written in 1941 and sent to the magazine in 1943.
21. Izalco, "La Matanza de 1932 en El Salvador," p. 86.
22. Schlesinger, *Revolución comunista*.
23. A biography of the conservative Guatemalan journalist Clemente Marroquín Rojas has information on the way in which Marroquín Rojas and Alfredo Schlesinger (Jorge's brother) received the papers from General Martínez. See Díaz Lozano, *Aquí viene un hombre*, chs. XIV and XV.
24. Schlesinger, *Revolución comunista*, p. 20.
25. For accounts of the CIA intervention in Guatemala, see Kinzer and Schlesinger, *Bitter Fruit*; Immerman, *CIA in Guatemala*; and Cullather, *Secret History*.
26. "La Política de la Indiferencia," *Tribuna Libre*, January 24, 1952.
27. "Como Nació la Dictadura," *Tribuna Libre*, January 25, 1952.
28. Bustamante Maceo, *Historia militar*, p. 106.
29. Aguirre Cardona, *La historia constitucional*, p. 143.
30. Alas García, *Historia para el Tercer Curso*.
31. Ibid., p. 201.
32. Lardé y Larín, *El Salvador*, p. 214.
33. Alberto de Mestas, *El Salvador*, p. 494. (His bibliography includes

Schlesinger's *Revolución comunista*.)

34. Another excellent example of a conservative informant ignoring the Matanza is found in the memoirs of Enrique Córdova, a life-long insider from the 1920s until the 1950s. His memoirs make copious references to Martínez and the uprising, but ignore almost completely the Matanza. Córdova, *Miradas retrospectivas*. His memoirs were not published until twenty-seven years after his death in 1966.
35. González Ruiz, *El Salvador de hoy*, p. 11.
36. "La Tragedia Comunista de 1932," *El Diario de Hoy*, January 15 to February 12, 1967.
37. "La Tragedia Comunista de 1932," *El Diario de Hoy*, January 15, 1967.
38. "Quieren otra Cuba en Centroamérica," *El Diario de Hoy*, February 3, 1967. See also February 9, 1967.
39. "Obispo Ratifica su Excomunión al PAR," *El Diario de Hoy*, January 20, 1967.
40. United States of America, Central Intelligence Agency, "The President's Trip to Central America: Security Conditions," Special National Intelligence Estimate (hereafter cited as SNIE), 82/83–68, July 3, 1968, p. 4.
41. *El Diario de Hoy*, January 3, 1972.
42. See López Jiménez. "El espectro de 1932 se alza amenazante. Los ofrecimientos de repartos de tierras," *El Diario de Hoy*, February 7, 1972. Sidney Mazzini V. "La historia, ¿vuelve a repetirse? *El Diario de Hoy*, February 10, 1972. Escobar, "La caída de Don Arturo y la verdad histórica," (three-part article), *El Diario de Hoy*, January 21–24 1972. (A four-part article in *La Prensa Gráfica* devoted to instances of communist influence in El Salvador did not mention the 1932 events at all. See *La Prensa Gráfica*, January 14–18, 1972.)
43. "Forty years ago the communists called to arms and murdered thousands of innocents."*El Diario de Hoy*, February 11, 15, 16, 1972.
44. See "Recordando la huelga" in Castro Ramírez, *Camino de la esperanza*, p. 203.
45. See, for example, Castro Ramírez, *Camino de la esperanza*.
46. See, for example, Baloyra, *El Salvador in Transition*, ch. 2.
47. A clear example of the revolutionary regime's repressive side can be seen in a document produced by the office of the presidency in March 1951 in which it lays out communism as a threat to the state. See Office of the President, *Maquinaciones contra el estado*.
48. ANEP "Planteamiento al Gobierno de la Republica: La Trágica Realidad que vive El Salvador,"*Diario Latino*, November 16, 1977, pp. 16–17.
49. Faro "La Violencia Institucionalizada o el Evangelio Según San Marx," *Diario Latino*, November 22, 1977, p. 21.
50. *Diario Latino*, March 27, 1978, p. 3.
51. *Diario Latino*, March 29, 1978, p. 3.
52. *Diario Latino*, November 24, 1977.
53. *El Diario de Hoy*, Sidney Mazzini, "¿Un enfrentamiento es inevitable?"

November 17, 1977, p. 4.
54. *El Diario de Hoy*, "Satisface a Dr. Mazzini Nombramiento en la OEA," December 2, 1977, p. 17.
55. *El Diario de Hoy*, October 4, 1977, p. 25.
56. http://www.fuerzaarmada.gob.sv/heroes-militares/Heroes%20todos.htm December 2004.
57. "FPL atribuyese muerte de Aguirre y Salinas," *El Diario de Hoy*, July 14, 1977, p. 3.
58. Buckley, *Violent Neighbors*, p. 5.
59. Castro Morán, *Función política del ejército*.
60. Ibid., p. 110.
61. Ibid., p. 149.
62. Ibid., p. 138.
63. Kirkpatrick, "Hobbes Problem," p. 506.
64. This is a reference of the thirteen years of the Martínez dictatorship. General Martínez was toppled by a widespread urban movement in 1944.
65. Galindo Pohl, *Recuerdos de Sonsonate*.
66. Kuny Mena and Cañas Dinarte, *Centuria*, pp. 35–37.
67. http://www.elsalvador.org/home.nsf/culture
68. Panamá Sandoval, *Los guerreros de la libertad*, p. 17.
69. Ibid., p. 17.
70. Del Camino, "Estampas. Pensemos en El Salvador," p. 51. "La leyenda maldita crecerá y para estos pueblos ignorantes habrá siempre la voz que en los instantes graves haga recaer en el comunismo todas las desgracias que los devoran. El suceso ocurrido en El Salvador es digno de la más honda reflexión precisamente porque hace de la palabra comunista un déspota de la superstición humana."

Notes to Conclusion

1. Renan, "What Is a Nation?" pp. 8–22.
2. Ibid., p. 11.
3. Some precedent-setting works for historians on the issues of memory, narration, and tradition include Hobsbawm and Ranger, *Invention of Tradition*; B. Anderson, *Imagined Communities*; and Said, *Orientalism*. Included in the wave of recent of studies in on historical memory is Yuhl, *Golden Haze of Memory*. See especially footnote 35 to Yuhl's introduction for an extensive list of related works in U.S. history. See also Kaiser, *Postmemories of Terror*. See footnote 39 to Kaiser's introduction for another list of relevant works from a different geographical region than that of Yuhl. See also Assmann, *Moses the Egyptian*; Johnson, *Death, Dismemberment, and Memory*; Hodgkin, *Contested Pasts*; Herzog, *Sex After Fascism*; Amadiume and 'Abd Allah Ahmad, *Politics of Memory*; Coombs, *History After Apartheid*; Ashplant, Dawson, and Roper, *Commemorating War*.

4. Kaiser, *Postmemories of Terror*; M. Hirsch, "Projected Memory," p. 8.
5. Passerini, "Introduction," p. 2.
6. Kaiser, *Postmemories of Terror*, p. 22.
7. On general studies of trauma and historical memory, see H. Hirsch, *Genocide and the Politics of Memory*; Bartov, Grossmann, and Nolan, *Crimes of War*; and Edkins, *Trauma and the Memory of Politics*. As a small representation of the vast body of works on the Holocaust and historical memory, see Ely, *Goldhagen Effect*; Hilberg, *Politics of Memory*; Kramer, *Politics of Memory*; and Rosenfeld, *Thinking About the Holocaust*. On the Vietnam War, see Hixson, *Historical Memory and Representations of the Vietnam War*; and Sturken, *Tangled Memories*. On the "Dirty War" in Argentina, see Kaiser, *Postmemories of Terror*. On Stalinist Russia, see K. Smith, *Mythmaking in the New Russia*. On U.S. slavery and its legacy, see Yuhl, *Golden Haze*; Osagie, *Amistad Revolt*; and Fabre and O'Meally, *History and Memory in African American Culture*.
8. Kaiser, *Postmemories of Terror*, p. 198.
9. Schlesinger, *Revolución comunista*; and Luna, "Un heroico y trágico suceso de nuestra historia."
10. The Fundación Ama (FAMA), a recently formed Indigenous organization in Izalco, is especially concerned with historical issues and in particular with telling the story of 1932 from a more ethnic perspective. A clear example of its approach can be seen in Daniel Flores Ascensio's film, *Ama: memoria del tiempo* (Huevos Indios Productions, 2003), which employs oral testimonial to revise the story of the 1932 uprising and massacre in Izalco. Another organization is La Asociación Nahuizalqueña para el Rescate de la Cultura Indígena (ANARSIS, the Nahuizalco Assocation for the Preservation of Indigenous Culture). A long article about ANARSIS and its approach to the memory of 1932 can be found in *Diario CoLatino*, Suplemento Cultural *Tres Mil*, January 29, 2005. An online version can be seen at www.diariolatino.com/tresmil/3000-785.pdf.
11. Jan Assmann attributes his notion of historical memory to Freud. Assmann, *Moses the Egyptian*, p. 152.
12. Email circular from Daniel Flores Asencio on behalf of the AMA Foundation, February 7, 2006, announcing the planned commemoration of 1932 on January 22, 2006, the creation of new Indigenous Rights Organization, the Concilio de Pueblos Indígenas (CPI) de Occidente, and the organization of a International Forum on Genocide (Foro Internacional Sobre el Genocidio El Salvador, 1932), January 19–22, 2007.

Notes to Appendix

1. Excerpt is Dalton, *El intelectual y la sociedad*, p. 23.
2. Excerpt is Dalton, *El Salvador*, p. 45.
3. Excerpt is Dalton, *El Salvador: Monografía*, p. 19.

4. Excerpt is Dalton, *El Salvador: Monografía*, p. 67.
5. Excerpt is Dalton, *Historias prohibidas del Pulgarcito*, p. 112.
6. Excerpt it Dalton, *Miguel Mármol*, pp. 240–47.
7. Cuaderno, pp. 27, 28, and 29.
8. RGASPI 495:119:12, pp. 8–10.
9. The English is taken from an English translation from Russian of this article at http://www.marxists.org/archive/lenin/works/1917/oct/08.htm. However, we have changed a couple of places where Anaya's letter uses "insurrection" and Lenin uses something else, such as "armed uprising."
10. RGASPI, 495:119:4, pp. 11, 12, 13, 27, 55, 56, 60, 61, 62, 63, and 67.
11. RGASPI, 495:119:1, pp. 6, 7, 8, and 22.
12. RGASPI, 495:119:4, pp. 1, 2, and 5.
13. Informe rendido por los camaradas de El Salvador (RGASPI, 534:7:455, pp. 23–26).
14. Miguel Mármol, "Breves apuntes históricos del movimiento sindical de El Salvador," March 30, 1948, Guatemala, from Library of Congress, Manuscript Collection, Guatemala Documents Collection, Reel 8019, Personal Papers of Víctor M. Gutiérrez.
15. Luna, "La insurrección de 1932," an eight-part article published in the newspaper *Tribuna Libre* 1963 over eight days (Part 1: December 12, pp. 6 and 12; Part 2: December 13, pp. 6 and 12; Part 3: December 16, pp. 6 and 7; Part 4: December 17, pp. 6 and 12; Part 5: December 18, pp. 6 and 12; Part 6: December 19, pp. 6 and 14; Part 7: December 20, pp. 6 and 12; and Part 8: December 23, p. 6). The following excerpts are drawn from Parts 2, 3, 4, and 8—December 13, p. 12; December 16, p. 6; December 17, p. 6; and December 23, p. 6.
16. Roque Dalton's roughly one-hundred-page, typed, double-spaced, unpublished manuscript on the history of the Communist Party of El Salvador, Havana, January, 1972, from the personal archive of Roque Dalton provided by the Dalton family. Excerpts taken from pages 267–69, 273, 292, 296, and 297.
17. Méndez. *Los sucesos comunistas.*
18. "Mensaje del Señor Presidente de la República, leido ante la Asamblea Nacional, en el acto de la apertura de su periodo de sesiones ordinarias, el día 4 de febrero de 1932," published as a booklet by the Imprenta Nacional, found in AGN, in a collection of bound and unclassified presidential addresses.
19. Méndez, *Los sucesos comunistas*, pp. 10, 11, 12, 13, 60, 61, 140, and 141.
20. Schlesinger, *¿Revolución comunista*, pp. 3, 10, 11, 40, 193, and 194.
21. "Cómo Nació la Dictadura," *La Tribuna*, January 25, 1952.
22. Córdova, *Miradas retrospectivas*, p. 281.
23. *El Diario de Hoy*, November 17, 1977, p. 4.

WORKS CITED

Books

Aguirre Cardona, Francisco Osmín. *La historia constitucional de El Salvador y el movimiento unionista centro americano.* Talca, Chile: Talleres Gráficos Poblete, 1954.

Alas, Jose Inocencio. *Iglesia, tierra y lucha campesina: Suchitoto, El Salvador, 1968–1977.* El Salvador: Asociación de Frailes Franciscanos, 2003.

Alas García, José. *Historia para el Tercer Curso de Plan Básico.* 4th ed. Santa Ana, El Salvador: Tipografia Comercial, 1960.

Alegría, Claribel. *Cenizas de Izalco.* Barcelona: Seix Barral, 1966. Published in English as *Ashes of Izalco,* Willimantic, CT: Curbstone Press, 1989.

Alemán Bolaños, Gustavo. *El oso ruso: Historia novelada del primer levantamiento comunista en América.* Managua, Nicaragua: Editorial Atlántida, 1944.

Allende, Isabel. *My Invented Country: A Nostalgic Journey Through Chile.* New York: Harper Collins, 2003.

Alvarado, Eliva, and Medea Benjamin. *Don't Be Afraid, Gringo: A Honduran Woman Speaks from the Heart. The Story of Elvia Alvarado.* San Francisco: Institute for Food and Development Policy, 1987.

Alvarenga, Luis. *El ciervo perseguido.* San Salvador, El Salvador: Dirección de Publicaciones e Impresos, 2003.

Alvarenga, Patricia. *Cultura y ética de la violencia. El Salvador 1880–1932.* San Jose, Costa Rica: EDUCA, 1996.

Amadiume, Ifi, and Naim 'Abd Allah Ahmad. *Politics of Memory: Truth, Healing and Social Justice.* London: Zed Books, 2000.

Americas Watch. *El Salvador's Decade of Terror: Human Rights Since the Assassination of Archbishop Romero.* New Haven, CT: Yale University Press, 1991.

Americas Watch Committee. *Analysis of the Department of State Report on the Situation in El Salvador.* New York: Americas Watch Committee, 1983.

Amnesty International. *El Salvador: 'Death Squads'—A Government Strategy.* London: Amnesty International, 1988.

Anderson, Benedict. *Imagined Communities: Reflections on the Origin and Spread of Nationalism.* London: Verso, 1983.
Anderson, Thomas. *La Matanza: El Salvador's Communist Revolt of 1932.* Lincoln: University of Nebraska Press, 1971.
———. *The War of the Dispossessed: Honduras and El Salvador, 1969.* Lincoln: University of Nebraska Press, 1981.
Arias, Arturo. *The Rigoberta Menchú Controversy.* Minneapolis: University of Minnesota Press, 2001.
Arias Gómez, Jorge, et al. *Farabundo Martí.* 1972. 2d ed. San José, Costa Rica: EDUCA, edition, 1996.
———. *En memoria de Roque Dalton.* San Salvador, El Salvador: Editorial Memoria, 1999.
———. *El proceso político Centroamericano.* San Salvador, El Salvador: Editorial Universitaria, 1964. This publication is the proceedings of the Seminario de Historia Contemporánea de Centroamérica held in 1963.
Armstrong, Robert, and Janet Shenk. *El Salvador: The Face of Revolution.* Boston: South End Press, 1982.
Ashplant, T. G., Graham Dawson, and Michael Roper. *Commemorating War: The Politics of Memory.* New Brunswick, NJ: Transaction Publishers, 2004.
Assmann, Jan. *Moses the Egyptian: The Memory of Egypt in Western Monotheism.* Cambridge, MA: Harvard University Press, 1997.
Bakhtin, Mikhail. *The Dialogic Imagination: Four Essays.* Austin: University of Texas Press, 1981.
Baloyra, Enrique. *El Salvador in Transition.* Chapel Hill: University of North Carolina Press, 1982.
Barrios de Chungara, Domitilia, and Moema Viezzer. *Let Me Speak!: Testimony of Domitila, a Woman in the Bolivian Mines.* New York: Monthly Review Press, 1978.
Bartov, Omer, Atina Grossmann, and Mary Nolan. *Crimes of War: Guilt and Denial in the Twentieth Century.* New York: W. W. Norton, 2002.
Beals, Carleton. *Banana Gold.* Philadelphia, PA: J. B. Lippincott Co., 1932.
Berryman, Phillip. *The Religious Roots of Rebellion: Christians in Central American Revolutions.* Maryknoll, NY: Orbis Books, 1984.
Bethell, Leslie, and Ian Roxborough. *Latin America Between the Second World War and the Cold War.* New York: Cambridge University Press, 1992.
Binford, Leigh. *The El Mozote Massacre: Anthropology and Human Rights.* Tucson: University of Arizona Press, 1996.
Bonner, Raymond. *Weakness and Deceit: U.S. Policy and El Salvador.* New York: Times Books, 1984.
Borges, Jorge Luis. "La noche de los dones." In *El libro de arena.* Buenos Aires: Emecé Editores, 1975. Translated into English by Norma Di Giovanni as *The Book of Sand,* New York: E. P. Dutton, 1977.
Browning, David. *El Salvador: Landscape and Society.* Oxford: Clarendon Press, 1971.

Buckley, Tom. *Violent Neighbors*. New York: Crown, 1984.
Buezo, Rodolfo. *Sangre de hermanos*. Havana, Cuba: Editorial Universal, 1944.
Bulmer-Thomas, Victor. *The Political Economy of Central America Since 1920*. Cambridge: Cambridge University Press, 1987.
Bustamante Maceo, Gregorio. *Historia militar de El Salvador*. 1935. 2d ed. San Salvador, El Salvador: Imprenta Nacional, 1951.
Byrne, Hugh. *El Salvador's Civil War: A Study of Revolution*. Boulder, CO: Lynne Rienner, 1996.
Castellanos, Juan Mario. *El Salvador 1930–1960: Antecedentes históricas de la guerra civil*. San Salvador, El Salvador: Dirección de Publicaciones y Impresos, 2001.
Castro Morán, Mariano. *Función política del ejército Salvadoreño en el presente siglo*. San Salvador, El Salvador: UCA Editores, 1984.
Castro Ramírez, Manuel. *Camino de la esperanza*. Artículos, Discursos y Conferencias. San Salvador, El Salvador: Talleres Gráficos Cisneros, 1945.
Cienfuegos, Fermán, pseudonym of Eduardo Sancho. *Crónica entre los espejos*. 2d ed. San Salvador, El Salvador: UFG Editores, 2003.
Colindres, Eduardo. *Fundamentos económicos de la burguesía Salvadoreña*. San Salvador, El Salvador: UCA Editores, 1977.
Coombs, Annie. *History After Apartheid: Visual Culture and Public Memory in a Democratic South Africa*. Durham, NC: Duke University Press, 2003.
Córdova, Enrique. *Miradas retrospectivas*. San Salvador, El Salvador: Imprenta Ricaldone, 1993.
Cuenca, Abel. *El Salvador: Una democracia cafetalera*. Mexico City: Ala Revolucionaria Radical Centro Editorial, 1962.
Cullather, Nick. *Secret History: The CIA's Classified Account of its Operations in Guatemala, 1952–1954*. Stanford, CA: Stanford University Press, 1999.
Dalton, Roque. *Clandestine Poems: Poemas Clandestinos*. Edited by Barbara Paschke. Willimantic, CT: Curbstone Press, 1990.
———. *Las historias prohibidas del Pulgarcito*. Mexico City: Siglo Veintiuno Editores, 1974.
———. *En la humedad del secreto: Antología poética de Roque Dalton*. Edited by Rafael-Lara Martínez. San Salvador, El Salvador: Dirección de Publicaciones e Impresos, 1994.
———. *Miguel Mármol*. Translated by Kathleen Ross and Richard Schaaf. Willimantic, CT: Curbstone Press, 1987.
———. *Miguel Mármol: Los sucesos de 1932 en El Salvador*. San Jose, Costa Rica: EDUCA, 1972.
———. *Pobrecito poeta que era yo....* San Jose, Costa Rica: EDUCA, 1976.
———. *Poemas Clandestinos*. San Jose, Costa Rica: EDUCA, 1976.
———. *Poems*. Translated by Richard Schaaf. Willimantic, CT: Curbstone Press, 1984.
———. *Poetry and Militancy in Latin America*. Translated by Arlene Scully and James Scully. Williamatic, CT: Curbstone Press, 1981.

———. *Recopilación de textos sobre Roque Dalton*. Havana, Cuba: Casa de las Américas, 1986.

———. *El Salvador*. Havana, Cuba: Casa de las Américas, 1963.

———. *El Salvador: Monografía*. Havana, Cuba: Enciclopedia Popular, 1965.

———. *Small Hours of the Night: Selected Poems of Roque Dalton*. Edited by Hardie St. Martin. Willimantic, CT: Curbstone Press, 1996.

———. *La ventana en el rostro*. Mexico City: Ediciones De Andrea, 1961.

Dalton, Roque, René Depestre, Edmundo Desnoes, Roberto Fernández Retamar, Ambrosio Fornet, and Carlos María Gutierrez. *El intelectual y la sociedad*. Mexico City: Siglo XXI Editores, 1969.

Danner, Mark. *The Massacre at El Mozote*. New York: Vintage, 1994.

Dennis, Marie, Renny Golden, and Scott Wright. *Oscar Romero: Reflections on his Life and Writings*. Maryknoll, NY: Orbis, 2001.

Díaz Lozano, Argentina. *Aquí viene un hombre*. 2d ed. Mexico City: B. Costa-Amic, 1968.

Diskin, Martin. *The Impact of U.S. Policy in El Salvador, 1979–1985*. Berkeley: Institute of International Studies, University of California, 1986.

Duarte, José Napoleón. *Duarte: My Story*. New York: G. P. Putnam's Sons, 1986.

Dunkerley, James. *The Long War: Dictatorship and Revolution in El Salvador*. London: Junction Books, 1982.

Durham, William. *Scarcity and Survival: The Ecological Origins of the Soccer War*. Stanford, CA: Stanford University Press, 1979.

Edkins, Jenny. *Trauma and the Memory of Politics*. Cambridge: Cambridge University Press, 2003.

El Salvador, Office of the President. *Maquinaciones contra el estado: Comunismo y reacción pretendieron subvertir el orden en el país*. San Salvador, El Salvador: Imprenta Nacional, 1951.

———. Ministerio de Educación. *Historia de El Salvador*. 2 Vols. San Salvador, El Salvador: Ministerio de Educación, 1994.

Ely, Geoff. *The Goldhagen Effect: History, Memory, Nazism—Facing the German Past*. Ann Arbor: University of Michigan Press, 2000.

Fabre, Geneviève, and Robert G. O'Meally. *History and Memory in African American Culture*. New York: Oxford University Press, 1994.

Faulkner, William. *Requiem for a Nun*. New York: Vintage, 1975.

Fernández, José Antonio. *Pintando el mundo de azul*. San Salvador, El Salvador: Concultura, 2003.

Fitzpatrick, Ellen. *History's Memory: Writing America's Past, 1880–1980*. Cambridge, MA: Harvard University Press, 2002.

Galeano, Eduardo. *Memoria del fuego*. Madrid: Siglo Veintiuno, 1984–86.

Galindo Pohl, Reynaldo. *Recuerdos de Sonsonate: crónica de 1932*. El Salvador: Tecnograff, 2001.

Gallardo, Ricardo. *Las constituciones de El Salvador*. Madrid: Ediciones Cultura Hispanica, 1973.

García Verzi, Horacio, *Recopilación de textos sobre Roque Dalton*. Havana, Cuba:

Casa de las Américas, 1986.
Gelbspan, Ross. *Break-ins, Death Threats, and the FBI: The Covert War Against the Central America Movement.* Boston: Southend Press, 1991.
Geoffroy Rivas, Pedro. *Vida, pasión y muerte del anti-hombre.* San Salvador, El Salvador: Dirección de Publicaciones, 1978.
Gómez, Ana Margarita, and Sajid Alfredo Herrera, eds. *Mestizaje, poder y sociedad: Ensayos de historia colonial de las provinicias de San Salvador y Sonsonate.* San Salvador, El Salvador: FLACSO, 2003.
González Ruiz, Ricardo. *El Salvador de hoy.* San Salvador, El Salvador: Talleres Martínez, 1952.
Gould, Jeff. *To Die in this Way: Nicaraguan Indians and the Myth of Mestizaje, 1880–1965.* Durham, NC: Duke University Press, 1998.
Gudmunson, Lowell, and Héctor Lindo-Fuentes. *Central America 1821–1871: Liberalism Before Liberal Reforms.* Tuscaloosa: University of Alabama Press, 1995.
Gugleberger, Georg, ed. *The Real Thing: Testimonial Discourse and Latin America.* Durham, NC: Duke University Press, 1996.
Halbwachs, Maurice. *On Collective Memory.* Translated by Lewis A. Coser. Chicago: University of Chicago Press, 1992.
Hamilton, Carolyn. *Terrific Majesty: The Powers of Shaka Zulu and the Limits of Historical Invention.* Cambridge, MA: Harvard University Press, 1998.
Handy, Jim. *Revolution in the Countryside: Rural Conflict and Agrarian Reform in Guatemala, 1944–1954.* Chapel Hill: University of North Carolina Press, 1994.
Harnecker, Marta. *Con la mirada en alto: Historia de las Fuerzas Populares de Liberación Farabundo Martí a través de entrevistas con sus dirigentes.* San Salvador, El Salvador: UCA Editores, 1993.
Hart, Stephen, and Richard Young. *Contemporary Latin American Cultural Studies.* London: Arnold, 2003.
Herzog, Dagmar. *Sex After Fascism: Memory and Morality in Twentieth-Century Germany.* Princeton, NJ: Princeton University Press, 2005.
Hilberg, Raul. *The Politics of Memory: The Journey of a Holocaust Historian.* Chicago: Ivan R. Dee, 1996.
Hirsch, Herbert. *Genocide and the Politics of Memory: Studying Death to Preserve Life.* Chapel Hill: University of North Carolina Press, 1995.
Hixson, Walter. *Historical Memory and Representations of the Vietnam War.* New York: Garland, 2000.
Hobsbawm, E. J., and T. O. Ranger. *The Invention of Tradition.* Cambridge: Cambridge University Press, 1983.
Hodgkin, Katharine. *Contested Pasts: The Politics of Memory.* New York: Routledge, 2003.
Holden, Robert. *Armies Without Nations: Public Violence and State Formation in Central America, 1821–1960.* Oxford: Oxford University Press, 2004.
Immerman, Richard H. *The CIA in Guatemala: The Foreign Policy of*

Intervention. Austin: University of Texas Press, 1983.
Jiménez Pérez, Eddy. *La guerra no fue de fútbol.* Havana, Cuba: Casa de las Americas, 1974.
Johnson, Lyman, ed. *Death, Dismemberment, and Memory: Body Politics in Latin America.* Albuquerque: University of New Mexico Press, 2004.
Kagan, Robert. *A Twilight Struggle: American Power and Nicaragua, 1977–1990.* New York: Free Press, 1996.
Kaiser, Susana. *Postmemories of Terror: A New Generation Copes with the Legacy of the "Dirty War."* New York: Palgrave, 2005.
Kinzer, Stephen, and Stephen Schlesinger. *Bitter Fruit.* Garden City, NY: Doubleday, 1982.
Kramer, Jane. *The Politics of Memory: Looking for Germany in the New Germany.* New York: Random House, 1996.
Krehm, William. *Democracies and Tyrannies in the Caribbean.* Westport, CT: Lawrence Hill, 1984.
Kuny Mena, Enrique, and Carlos Cañas Dinarte. *Centuria: Los hechos y personajes del siglo XX en El Salvador.* San Salvador, El Salvador: El Diario de Hoy, 1999.
Lara-Martínez, Rafael, and Dennis Seager, eds. *Otros Roques: Ensayos sobre la poética múltiple de Roque Dalton.* New Orleans, LA: University Press of the South, 1999.
Lardé y Larín, Jorge. *El Salvador. Historia de sus pueblos villas y ciudades.* San Salvador, El Salvador: Departamento Editorial, 1957.
Lauria, Aldo. *An Agrarian Republic: Commercial Agriculture and the Politics of Peasant Communities in El Salvador, 1823–1914.* Pittsburgh, PA: University of Pittsburgh Press, 1999.
Lauria, Aldo, and Leigh Binford, eds. *Landscapes of Struggle: Politics, Society, and Community in El Salvador.* Pittsburgh, PA: University of Pittsburgh Press, 2005.
Leiken, Robert S., and Barry Rubin, eds. *The Central American Crisis Reader.* New York: Summit Books, 1987.
Leonard, Thomas. *Central America and the United States: The Search for Stability.* Athens: University of Georgia Press, 1991.
Lewis, Oscar. *The Children of Sanchez: Autobiography of a Mexican Family.* New York: Random House, 1961.
Lindo-Fuentes, Héctor. *Weak Foundations: The Economy of El Salvador in the Nineteenth Century, 1821–1898.* Berkeley: University of California Press, 1990.
Lissagaray, Prosper-Olivier. *History of the Commune of 1871.* Translated by Eleanor M. Aveling. 1887. Reprint, London: Reeves and Turner, 1986.
Lynch, John. *Revolutions in Spanish America, 1808–1826.* 1973. Reprint, New York: W. W. Norton, 1986.
Machón Vilanova, Francisco. *Ola roja.* Mexico City: self-published, 1948.
MacLeod, Murdo. *Spanish Central America: A Socioeconomic History, 1520–1720.*

Berkeley: University of California Press, 1973.
Magaña, Alvaro, ed. *El Salvador: La República.* 2 vols. San Salvador, El Salvador: Fomento Cultural Banco Agrícola, 2000.
Martínez-Peñate, Oscar. *El Salvador: Historia general.* San Salvador, El Salvador: Editorial Nuevo Enfoque, 2002.
Marx, Karl. *Communist Manifesto.* New York: Bantam Books, 1992.
Menchú, Rigoberta. *Me llamo Rigoberta Menchú y asi me nació la conciencia.* Mexico City: Siglo XXI, 1983. Published in English as *I, Rigoberta Menchu: An Indian Woman in Guatemala.* London: Verso, 1984.
Méndez, Joaquín. *Los sucesos comunistas en El Salvador.* San Salvador, El Salvador: Imprenta Funes y Ungo, 1932.
Menjívar, Rafael. *Tiempos de locura: El Salvador, 1979–1981.* 2d ed. San Salvador, El Salvador: FLACSO, 2006.
Mestas, Alberto de. *El Salvador: País de lagos y volcanes.* Madrid: Ediciones Cultura Hispánica, 1950.
Minc, Rose, ed. *Literature in Transition: The Many Voices of the Caribbean Area.* College Park, MD: Hispamérica & Montclair State College, 1982.
Montgomery, Tommie Sue. *Revolution in El Salvador: From Civil Strife to Civil Peace.* 2d ed. Boulder, CO: Westview, 1995.
Müller, Jan-Werner, ed. *Memory and Power in Post-War Europe: Studies in the Presence of the Past.* Cambridge: Cambridge University Press, 2002.
Nin, Anais. *The Diary of Anais Nin, 1944–47.* New York: Harcourt Brace Jovanovich, 1971.
Osagia, Iyunolu Folayan. *The Amistad Revolt: Memory, Slavery and the Politics of Identity in the United States and Sierra Leone.* Athens: University of Georgia Press, 2000.
Panamá Sandoval, David Ernesto. *Los guerreros de la libertad.* Andover, MA: Versal Books, 2005.
Parker, D. S. *The Idea of the Middle Class: White Collar Workers and Peruvian Society, 1900–1950.* University Park: Penn State University Press, 1998.
Parkman, Patricia. *Nonviolent Insurrection in El Salvador: The Fall of Maximiliano Hernández Martínez.* Tucson: University of Arizona Press, 1988.
Partido Comunista de El Salvador. *45 Años de sacrificada lucha revolucionaria.* March 1975. 2d ed. San Salvador, El Salvador: Publicaciones del Partido Comunista de El Salvador, March 1976.
Popkin, Margaret. *Peace Without Justice: Obstacles to Building the Rule of Law in Salvador.* University Park: Penn State University Press, 2000.
Prisk, Courtney, ed. *The Comandante Speaks: Memoirs of an El Salvadoran Guerrilla Leader.* Boulder, CO: Westview Press, 1991.
Ricoeur, Paul. *Memory, History, Forgetting.* Chicago: University of Chicago Press, 2004.
Rock, David, ed. *Latin America in the 1940s: War and Postwar Transitions.* Berkeley: University of California Press, 1994.

Rodríguez, Mario. *The Cádiz Experiment in Central America, 1808–1826.* Berkeley: University of California Press, 1978.
Rosenfeld, Alvin. *Thinking About the Holocaust After Half a Century.* Bloomington: Indiana University Press, 1997.
Sáenz, Vicente. *Rompiendo cadenas: Las del imperialismo norteamericano en Centro América.* Mexico City: CIADE, 1933.
Said, Edward. *Orientalism.* New York: Pantheon, 1978.
Saussure, Ferdinand de. *Course in General Linguistics.* Edited by Charles Bally and Albert Sechehaye. Translated from the French by Wade Baskin. London: P. Owen, 1959.
Schacter, Daniel. *The Seven Sins of Memory: How the Mind Forgets and Remembers.* New York: Houghton Mifflin, 2001.
Schlesinger, Jorge. *Revolución comunista: ¿Guatemala en peligro?* Guatemala: Unión Tipográfica Castañeda Avila, 1946.
Shanahan, Timothy. *Philosophy 9/11: Thinking About the War on Terror.* Chicago: Open Court, 2005.
Sherman, William L. *Forced Native Labor in Sixteenth-Century Central America.* Lincoln: University of Nebraska Press, 1979.
Smith, Kathleen. *Mythmaking in the New Russia: Politics and Memory in the Yelstin Era.* Ithaca, NY: Cornell University Press, 2002.
Sommer, Doris. *Foundational Fictions: The National Romances of Latin America.* Berkeley: University of California Press, 1991.
Stanley, William. *The Protection Racket State: Elite Politics. Military Extortion and Civil War in El Salvador.* Philadelphia, PA: Temple University Press, 1996.
Sturken, Marita. *Tangled Memories: The Vietnam War, the AIDS Epidemic, and the Politics of Remembering.* Berkeley: University of California Press, 1997.
Stoll, David. *Rigoberta Menchú and the Story of All Poor Guatemalans.* Boulder, CO: Westview Press, 1998.
Tagore, Rabindranath. *My Reminiscences.* New York: Macmillan Company, 1917.
Tilley, Virginia. *Seeing Indians: A Study of Race, Nation, and Power in El Salvador.* Albuquerque: University of New Mexico Press, 2005.
Tirado, Thomas. *Celsa's World: Conversations with a Mexican Peasant Woman.* Tempe: Center for Latin American Studies, Arizona State University, 1991.
Trouillot, Michel-Rolph. *Silencing the Past: Power and the Production of History.* Boston: Beacon Press, 1995.
Tschiffely, A. F. *Southern Cross to Pole Star: Tschiffely's Ride.* 2d ed. London: William Heinemann, 1933.
Turcios, Roberto. *Autoritarismo y modernización: El Salvador, 1950–1960.* 1993. Reprint, San Salvador, El Salvador: Concultura, 2003.
———. *Los primeros patriotas: San Salvador, 1811.* San Salvador, El Salvador: Ediciones Tendencias, 1995.
Tyson, Timothy. *Blood Done Sign My Name.* New York: Three Rivers Press, 2004.
United Nations. *From Madness to Hope: The 12-Year War in El Salvador. Report of the Commission on the Truth for El Salvador.* New York: The United

Nations and El Salvador, 1993.
Valle, Victor. *Siembra de vientos: El Salvador, 1960–69*. San Salvador, El Salvador: CINAS, 1993.
Vásquez, Mario R. *Bibliografía histórica de El Salvador*. San Salvador, El Salvador: Editorial Universitaria, 1995.
Walker, Thomas. *Revolution and Counterrevolution in Nicaragua*. Boulder, CO: Westview Press, 1991.
Wallström, Tord. *A Wayfarer in Central America*. London: Arthur Barker Ltd., 1955.
Walter, Knut. *Las fuerzas armadas y el acuerdo de paz: La transformación necesaria del ejército salvadoreño*. San Salvador, El Salvador: Fundación Friedrich Ebert, 1997.
Webre, Stephan. *Jose Napoleon Duarte and the Christian Democratic Party in Salvadoran Politics, 1960–1972*. Baton Rouge: Louisiana State University Press, 1979.
Whitfield, Theresa. *Paying the Price: Ignacio Ellacuría and the Murdered Jesuits of El Salvador*. Philadelphia, PA: Temple University Press, 1994.
Williams, Philip J., and Knut Walter. *Militarization and Demilitarization in El Salvador's Transition to Democracy*. Pittsburgh, PA: University of Pittsburgh Press, 1997.
Williams, Robert. *States and Social Evolution: Coffee and the Rise of National Governments in Central America*. Chapel Hill: University of North Carolina Press, 1994.
Wood, Elisabeth Jean. *Insurgent Collective Action and Civil War in El Salvador*. Cambridge: Cambridge University Press, 2003.
Wortman, Miles. *Government and Society in Central America, 1680–1840*. New York: Columbia University Press, 1982.
Wright, Tom. *Latin America in the Era of the Cuban Revolution*. Rev. ed. Westport, CT: Praeger, 2001.
Yuhl, Stephanie. *The Golden Haze of Memory: The Making of Historic Charleston*. Chapel Hill: University of North Carolina Press, 2005.
Zamora, Rubén. *La izquierda partidaria Salvadoreña: Entre la identidad y el poder*. San Salvador, El Salvador: FLACSO, 2003.

Scholarly Articles and Chapters

Adams, Richard. "The Conquest Tradition of Meso-America." *The Americas* 46:2 (October 1989).
Alvarenga, Patricia. "Los indígenas y el Estado: alianzas y estrategias políticas en la construcción del poder local en El Salvador, 1920–1944." In Darío Euraque et al., eds., *Memorias del mestizaje: Cultura política en Centroamérica de 1920 al presente*, pp. 363–94. Antigua, Guatemala: CIRMA, 2004.
Armijo, Roberto. "Recordando a Juan Felipe Toruño." *Diario CoLatino III*, May 4, 1996.

Arrieta Gallegos, Valentín, S.J. "Hacia una construcción urgente del orden social en Centroamérica." *Estudios Centro Americanos* I:3 (June 1946).

Barrios, Jaime. "Combat Drive and Political Initiative." *World Marxist Review* 26:3 (March 1983).

Bet-El, Ilana R. "Unimagined Communities: The Power of Memory and the Conflict in the Former Yugoslavia." In Jan-Werner Müller, *Memory and Power in Post-War Europe: Studies in the Presence of the Past.* Cambridge: Cambridge University Press, 2002.

Camino, Juan (Octavio Jiménez Alpízar). "Estampas: Pensamos en El Salvador..." *Repertorio Americano* 24:4 (January 30, 1932): 51–52.

Canales, Tirso "La Generación Comprometida y su tiempo (1956–1996)." *Realidad y Reflexión* 3:8 (Segundo Cuatrimestre 2003).

Cañas Dinarte, Carlos. "Roque Dalton." In *Diccionario de Autoras y Autores de El Salvador.* San Salvador, El Salvador: Dirección de Publicaciones e Impresos, 2003.

Canby, Peter. "The Truth About Rigoberta Menchú." *The New York Review of Books* 46:6 (April 8, 1999).

Chávez Velasco, Waldo. "Discurso del Dr. Waldo Chávez Velasco en su ingreso como Miembro de Número a la Honorable Academia Salvadoreña de la Lengua correspondiente de la Real Academia de la Lengua Española." San Salvador, August 30, 2002.

Ching, Erik. "Patronage and Politics Under General Maximiliano Hernández Martínez, 1931–1939: The Local Roots of Military Authoritarianism in El Salvador." In Aldo Lauria Aldo and Leigh Binford, eds., *Landscapes of Struggle: Politics, Society and Community in El Salvador,* pp. 50–70. Pittsburgh, PA: University of Pittsburgh Press, 2005.

———. "In Search of the Party: The Communist Party, the Comintern and the Peasant Rebellion of 1932 in El Salvador." *The Americas* 55:2 (October 1998).

Ching, Erik, and Virginia Tilley. "Indians, the Military and the Rebllion of 1932 in El Salvador." *Journal of Latin American Studies* 30 (1998): 121–56.

Cuenca, Breny. "La fisura en el FMLN: Diferencias ideológicas o pugna de poder?" *Tendencias* (San Salvador) no. 31 (June 1994).

Dalton, Roque. "La noche que conocí a Regis." *Casa de las Américas* (Havana) no. 40 (July–August 1968).

———. "Otto René Castillo: Su ejemplo y nuestra responsabilidad." In Otto René Castillo, *Informe de una injusticia: Antología poética.* San Jose, Costa Rica: EDUCA, 1975.

———. "Poesía y militancia en América Latina." *Casa de las Americas* (Havana), nos. 20–21 (September–December 1963).

Dalton, Roque, and Victor Miranda. "Present Phase of the Revolutionary Movement in Latin America." *World Marxist Review* 10:5 (May 1967): 48–57.

Denegri, Francesca. "Testimonio and its Discontents." In Stephen Hart and Richard Young, eds., *Contemporary Latin American Cultural Studies.* London: Arnold, 2003.

Dickey, Christopher. "Behind the Death Squads: Who They Are, How They Work, and Why No One Can Stop Them." *New Republic*, December 26, 1983.
Gould, Jeff. "Revolutionary Nationalism and Local Memories in El Salvador." In Gil Joseph, ed., *Reclaiming the Political in Latin American History: The View from the North*. Durham, NC: Duke University Press, 2001.
Gould, Jeff, and Aldo Lauria. "They Call Us Thieves and Steal Our Wage." *Hispanic American Historical Review* 84:2 (May 2004).
Greib, Kenneth. "The U.S. and the Rise of Maximiliano Hernández Martínez." *Journal of Latin American Studies* 3:2 (1970).
Griffith, Kati, and Leslie Gates. "A State's Gendered Response to Political Instability: Gendering Labor Policy in Semiauthoritarian El Salvador, 1944–1972." *Social Politics* (summer 2002).
Handal, Shafik. "He Died for a Noble Cause." *World Marxist Review* 19:6 (June 1976).
———. "Inseverable Interconnection." *World Marxist Review* 21:5 (May 1978).
———. "We Have no Alternative to Armed Struggle." *World Marxist Review* 23:10 (October 1980).
Hernández Aguirre, Mario. "La nueva poesía salvadoreña: 'La Generación Comprometida,'" *Revista Cultura* 20 (April–June 1961).
Hirsch, Marianne. "Projected Memory: Holocaust Photographs in Personal and Public Fantasy." In Mieke Bal et al., eds., *Acts of Memory: Cultural Recall in the Present*. Hanover, NH: University Press of New England, 1999.
Izalco, Juan de. "La Matanza de 1932 en El Salvador." *Repertorio Americano* XLI:4 (March 11, 1944) and XLI:6 (April 29, 1944).
Jedlicki, Jerzy. "Historical Memory as a Source of Conflicts in Eastern Europe." *Communist and Post-Communist Studies* 32:3 (September 1999): 225–33.
Kirkpatrick, Jeane. "The Hobbes Problem." In Robert S. Leiken and Barry Rubin, eds., *The Central American Crisis Reader*. New York: Summit Books, 1987.
Luna, David. "Análisis de una dictadura fascista latinoamericano: Maximiliano Hernández Martínez, 1931–1944." *La Universidad* (San Salvador) 94:5 (1969).
———. "Un heroico y trágico suceso de nuestra historia." In *Seminario Contemporánea de Centro América: El Proceso político Centroamericano*. San Salvador, El Salvador: Editorial Universitaria, 1964.
Lungo Uncles, Mario, and Anna Mary Keene. "El Salvador in the Eighties: Counterinsurgency and Revolution." *Journal of Latin American Studies* 30:2 (1998).
MacNaught, Roy. "The Horrors of Communism in El Salvador." *Central American Bulletin* (Dallas), no. 181 (March 1932).
Montes, Victor. "What Is Happening in El Salvador?" *World Marxist Review* 20:12 (December 1977).
Nairn, Allan. "Behind the Death Squads." *The Progressive* (May 1984).
North American Congress on Latin America. *Central America: North American Congress on Latin America (NACLA) Archive of Latin America*. 16 microfilm reels. New York: Scholarly Resources, 1997.

Passerini, Luisa. "Introduction." In Luisa Passerini, ed., *Memory and Totalitarianism*. New York: Oxford University Press, 1992.
Renan, Ernest. "What Is a Nation?" In Homi Bhabha, ed., *Nation and Narration*. 1990. Reprint, London: Routledge, 1994.
Rodríguez, Ileana. "Organizaciones populares y literatura testimonial: los años treinta en Nicaragua y El Salvador." In Rose Minc, ed., *Literature in Transition: The Many Voices of the Caribbean Area*. College Park: MD: Hispamérica & Montclair State College, 1982.
Sánchez, José. "Los cambios sociales y la política del Partido Comunista de El Salvador (Social developments in El Salvador and the policy of the Communist Party)." *Revista Internacional* 8:8 (1965).
Sánchez, Rubén, and Orlando Millas. "Revolutions Are Never the Same." *World Marxist Review* 25:4 (April 1982).
Smith, Jay M. "No More Language Games: Words, Beliefs and the Political Culture of Early Modern France." *American Historical Review* 102:5 (December 1997).
Smith, T. Lynn. "Notes on Population and Rural Social Organization in El Salvador." *Rural Sociology* 10:4 (December 1945).
Sommers, Margaret. "Narrating and Naturalizing Civil Society and Citizenship Theory: The Place of Political Culture and the Public Sphere." *Sociological Theory* 13:3 (November 1995).
———. "What's Political or Cultural about Political Culture and the Public Sphere? Toward a Historical Sociology of Concept Formation." *Sociological Theory* 13:2 (July 1995).
Toruño, Rhina. "Juan Felipe Toruño como figura histórica en el desarrollo de la literatura salvadoreña." Paper presented at the V Congreso Centroamericano de Historia, San Salvador, July 2000.
Villalobos, Joaquín. Book review of *Revolutionary Movements in Latin America: El Salvador's FMLN and Peru's Shining Path*. *Journal of Latin American Studies* 32:2 (May 2000).
Zamosc, Leon. "The Landing that Never Was: Canadian Marines and the Salvadoran Insurrection of 1932." *Canadian Journal of Latin American and Caribbean Studies* 21 (1986).

Archives

The Dalton Family Archive of Roque Dalton.
The documents of the archive facilitated by the Dalton family fall into four categories:
(1) An almost final typewritten version of *Miguel Mármol* labeled "Miguel Mármol. Testimonio bibliográfico-político. (Redacción final, introducción, notas, selección de documentos y apéndices de R. D.) Praha 1966-La Habana 1971."
(2) A series of typewritten documents related to the events of 1932, most of which were used for the production of the testimonial:

Glosario de salvadoreñismos.
El espíritu de los trabajadores!!!
Circular firmada por Miguel Mármol. Circular No. 2 Segunda Epoca
Prosa dedicada a una joven maestra directora de la escuela de Santa Elena,
    Departamento de Usulután. 1932
Poema de la clandestinidad. Usulután, junio de 1933
Pensamiento dirigido a un militante de la organización revolucionaria cubana
    "Joven Cuba" retenido en El Salvador en 1935, para rehacerle el ánimo que
    se le miraba abatido, En las celdas de la Policía Nacional. 1935
Poema a la madre desde la prisión. 1935, en la Policía Nacional
Carta declaratoria de huelga de hambre dirigida al Director General de la
    Policía Nacional, Coronel Francisco Merino Rosales. 12 de Noviembre
    de 1935
Carta de despedida de Miguel Mármol al autor después de finalizada la serie
    de entrevistas y sesiones de trabajo que sirvieron de base al relato
    autobiográfico. Praga, 10 de Junio de 1966
Carta de Miguel Mármol al autor desde México. México, D.F., 20 de julio de 1966
Sobre la estrategia huelguista. San Salvador, 13 de enero. 1930
Plan de trabajo modelo para los sindicalistas de la FRT de El Salvador (Dic. 1930)

Documents relating to the activities of Red Relief International (Socorro Rojo
    Internacional) in El Salvador

Estatutos del Socorro Rojo Internacional
Secretario General de la Sección Salvadoreña del Socorro Rojo Internacional.
    Secretario General de la Sección Guatemalteca del mismo. San Salvador,
    22 de septiembre de 1930
Socorro Rojo Internacional. New York, 14 de octubre de 1930
Socorro Rojo Internacional. New York, 14 de octubre de 1930
New York, 5 de noviembre de 1930
The 21 November 1930
Partido Comunista de El Salvador. Sección de la Internacional Comunista, El
    Salvador, C. A. 15 de diciembre de 1930
"Fines del Socorro Rojo Internacional" Propaganda leaflet from 1931
Comunicación de una militante para el Socorro Rojo Internacional—Sonsonate.
    Enero 14 de 1931. Julia Mojica
Circular del SRI desde Nueva York. New York City, 28 de enero de 1931
El problema de las finanzas del SRI. 8 de febrero de 1931
Al Comité Ejecutivo. New York, 26 de febrero de 1931
Mensaje del Secretariado del Caribe del SRI a la Sección Salvadoreña. New York,
    26 de febrero de 1931
Socorro Rojo Internacional. Secretariado del Caribe. New York, 13 de marzo
    de 1931
Socorro Rojo Internacional. Secretariado del Caribe. New York, 13 de marzo de

1931. Circular no. 68

Datos de un carnet de miembro del Socorro Rojo Internacional, Sección de El Salvador

Socorro Rojo Internacional. Secretariado del Caribe. "Los crímenes de la reacción salvadoreña"

Socorro Rojo Internacional. Sección de El Salvador. Comité Ejecutivo Nacional. (Confidencial y urgente)

La propaganda audiovisual de los comunistas salvadoreños de los años 30: esquemas de divulgación y propaganda marxista-leninista.

Salvadoran Communist Party documents:

Manifiesto del PCS con motivo de la masacre de mayo en Sonsonate y la detención de Farabundo Martí

Carta al Comité Pro—Candidatura Comunista en las elecciones municipales de Santa Tecla. Nueva San Salvador, 31 de diciembre de 1931

Nota de la Comisión Nacional de política electoral del PCS. San Salvador, 2 de enero de 1932

Partido Comunista de El Salvador, Sección de la Internacional Comunista. Comité Central. San Salvador, 5 de enero de 1932

Manifiesto comunista para los soldados de Ahuachapán. Ahuachapán, 7 de enero de 1932

Candidatos a diputados por el Partido Comunista en las elecciones de enero de 1932

Instrucciones electorales del PC en enero de 1932

De Comité Central al Comité departamental de Santa Ana sobre las elecciones. 8 de enero de 1932

Plan que desarrollará el Comité Militar Revolucionario el día... del actual (enero) en la lucha por la toma del poder por los obreros, campesinos y soldados, por resolución del Comité Central del Partido Comunista de El Salvador

14 de enero de 1932. Por qué el soldado debe tomar parte en la revolución proletaria.

Dos comunicaciones de militantes dirigidas al Comité Central del Partido en los días anteriores a la insurrección y una información dirigida al Comité Militar Revolucionario de San Salvador.

San Salvador, 15 de enero de 1932. Al Comité Militar Revolucionario.

Credencial de Comandante Rojo

Instrucciones del 16 y 19 de enero de 1932

Manifiesto del Partido Comunista de El Salvador a los soldados del ejército. San Salvador, enero 20 de 1932

Manifiesto del Comité Central del Partido Comunista a las clases trabajadoras de la República: obreros, campesinos y soldados (Interview published in *La Verdad*, publication of the PCS, January–February 1963).

Transcript of the discussions at the Seminario de Historia Contemporánea de Centroamérica, held at the University of El Salvador in 1963

Excerpts of "Años de lucha heróica (El 35 aniversario del Partido Comunista Salvadoreño)," by Alberto Gualán

"Los partidos políticos." Editorial of "La Estrella Roja," órgano del Grupo Marxista de la Universidad de El Salvador y del Grupo de Revolución Universitaria, 19 de diciembre de 1931

(3) The "Cuaderno" (notebook) of interview notes labeled "'Miguel Mármol.' Manuscrito. 37 páginas."

A total of sixty-one pages with the notes taken by Dalton during the interview with Miguel Mármol. These notes constituted the main "raw material," for the testimonial.

(4) A ninety-eight-page typewritten history of the Communist Party, dated in Havana January 1972.

Archivo General de la Nación, San Salvador, El Salvador

Ministerio de Gobernación, Sección Sonsonate, Boxes 1, 2, 3, and 4
Ministerio de Gobernación, Colección de Nulos, Boxes 7 and 9
Sección Indiferente, Capitulo 1, Caja 17

Library of Congress
Manuscript Collection, Guatemala Documents Collection (GDC), 1944–1954, Reel 8019, Personal Papers of Victor M. Gutíerrez

National Archives, Washington, DC, United States

USNA, RG 59, Box 5509
USNA, RG 59, 816.00 Revolutions/99
USNA, RG 59, 816.00 Revolutions/108</list>

Washington National Records Center, Maryland, G-2 Military Reports, Box 763, folder 3000–3020, Political. "Memorandum: The Story of Communism in El Salvador," written in 1943

Public Records Office, Kew Gardens
A 4077/9/8
A379/9/8, A400/9/8, A 500/9/8, A525/9/8 and A537/9/8. A379/9/8, A400/9/8, A 500/9/8, A525/9/8, and A537/9/8
A 4077/9/8
FO 371 15814

Russian State Archive of Social and Political History (RGASPI), Moscow, Russia, formerly named the Russian Centre for the Preservation and Study of Documents of Most Recent History (RTsKhIDNI):
Fond 495 Opis 119 Inventory (or File) 1, hereafter abbreviated as 495:119:1
495:119:4
495:119:7
495:119:10
495:119:11
495:119:12
500:1:5
534:7:455
539:3:1060

Yale University Manuscripts Collections

Diary of Henry Stimson, U.S. Sect. of State, January 25, 1932

Dissertations

Astilla, Carmelo. "The Martínez Era: Salvadoran-American Relations, 1931–1944." PhD diss., Louisiana State University, 1976.

Cárceres, Jorge. "Discourses of Reformism: El Salvador 1944–1960." PhD diss., University of Texas, Austin, 1996.

Ching, Erik. "From Clientelism to Militarism: The State, Politics and Authoritarianism in El Salvador 1840–1940." PhD diss., University of California, Santa Barbara, 1997.

Elam, Robert V. "Appeal to Arms: The Army and Politics in El Salvador, 1931–1964." PhD diss., University of New Mexico, 1968.

Lauria, Aldo. "An Agrarian Republic: Production and the Peasantry in El Salvador, 1740–1920." PhD diss., University of Chicago, 1990.</bibtxt>

Interviews

Salvador Pérez (born in 1914), Salcoatitán, July 23, 2000.
Giovani Galeas, San Salvador, March 14, 2005.
Anonymous ARENA deputy, National Assembly Building, San Salvador, El Salvador, May 9, 2004.

Newspapers

El Día
El Diario de Hoy
Diario Latino
Diario del Salvador
La Prensa
Primera Plana
La Tribuna

Pamphlets and Ephemera

"Mensaje del Señor Presidente de la Republica, General Maximiliano Hernández Martínez leído ante la Asamblea Nacional, en el acto de la apertura de su periodo de sesiones ordinarias, el día 4 de febrero de 1932."

"Manifiesto del ejército a la nación." San Salvador, January 27, 1932.

Websites

http://encontrarte.aporrea.org/teoria/perfiles/26/
http://www.elsalvador.org/home.nsf/culture
http://www.fuerzaarmada.gob.sv/heroes-militares/Heroes%20todos.htm
http://www.marxists.org/archive/lenin/works/index.htm
http://www.ucm.es/info/cecal/encuentr/areas/politica/2p/martin
http://www.weblog.com.ar/000017.html.
http://www.wmich.edu/teachenglish/subpages/literature/rigobertamenchu.htm
Primera Plana. 1: 4. San Salvador: 7/13 Octubre 1994. http://lanic.utexas.edu/project/lasa95/arreaza1_fn.html#fn20
Vázquez Olivera, Mario. "'País mío no existes.' Apuntes sobre Roque Dalton y la historiografía contemporánea de El Salvador." In the electronic journal *Istmo* <http://www.denison.edu/collaborations/istmo/articulos/pais.html>.
www.elfaro.net

Films

Consalvi, Carlos Henríquez, and Jeff Gould. *1932: Cicatriz de la memoria*. Museo de la Palabra y la Imagen, 2003.

Flores Ascensio, Daniel. "*Ama: Memoria del tiempo.*" Huevos Indios Productions, 2003.

INDEX

Abyssinia, 324
Acajutla, 40, 64, 276–77
Acelhuate River, 245, 276
Adams, Richard, 130
Africans, 19, 73, 141, 169–70, 252
Aguiñada Carranza, Rafael, 212
Aguirre Cardona, Osmín, 232
Aguirre y Salinas, Osmín, 85, 109, 230, 232, 241
Ahuachapán: Comrade M's report from, 305–7; counterattack in, 36, 350; PCS in, 49, 57, 189, 286, 293, 305; peasants in, 348; rebel attack to, 1, 28–29, 33, 41, 339; union organizing in, 321
Air Force garrison, 286, 288, 293
Alegría, Claribel, 124–25
Alemán Bolaños, Gustavo, 124–25
Allende, Salvador, 236, 240, 357
Alliance for Progress, 87–88, 113, 235
Alvarado, Pedro de, 71
Ama, Feliciano: alliances of, 58, 59; in Dalton's notebook, 167–68, 295; execution of, 244, 261, 351; and interethnic conflict, 60; local leadership of, 30, 36; as revolutionary, 326
Ama Foundation (Fundación Ama, FAMA), 378

American Enterprise Institute, 243
American exceptionalism, 10
American Revolution, 19
anarcho-syndicalism, 167, 326
Angola, 240, 358
anticommunism: 1932 narrative and, 4, 12, 21, 123–25, 175, 226–27, 233–34, 254–55, 351; ARENA Party and, 17, 246; and Cold War, 197; military regimes and, 86–88, 96, 112, 217; as motive for Matanza, 63; and Reagan administration, 92; and Red Scare, 6–8; and U.S. policy makers, 94, 231
April and May Revolutionary Party, 268
Aquino, Anastasio: in Dalton's work, 101, 132, 270–72; and interpretations of 1932 events, 231, 351
Araujo, Arturo: and 1931 elections, 59, 80, 303, 315; and 1932 events, 230–31, 245, 294, 303, 309, 349; in Dalton's work, 256; fall from power, 81, 352
Arbenz, Jacobo, 109, 112, 201, 231
ARENA party: and legacy of 1932 events, 95, 242; and memory of 1932 events, 14–15, 17, 245,

261; and neoliberalism, 246, 248
Arévalo, Juan José, 109, 201, 228
Argentina, 252, 258, 305
Arias Gómez, Jorge, 127, 149, 155, 166, 204, 273, 325, 368n57, 369n20
Armenia, 44, 59, 279
army: anticommunism of, 86; role in Arturo Araujo's fall, 80–81; and beginnings of military regime, 82, 85, 110; and civil war, 16, 91–96, 242; communist infiltration in, 285–86, 292–93, 310, 330; and consolidation of the state, 77, 269; in Dalton's historical interpretation, 103, 133, 153, 178; and historical memory, 116, 118–19, 125, 198, 202, 227, 241, 243; and Matanza, 194–95, 278–80; and modernization of the regime, 110; and murder of Jesuit martyrs, 257; narrative of 1932 events, 223, 241; repressive tactics of, 84, 93, 208, 213–14, 242; role in 1932 events, 1, 5, 7, 14–15, 17, 23, 36–37, 40, 43, 56, 62, 127, 194–95, 223, 225, 230, 289, 291, 357
Asia, 203, 228
Asociación de Beneficiadores de Café (Association of Coffee Processors, ABECAFE), 240
Asociación Nacional de la Empresa Privada (National Association of Private Enterprise, ANEP), 239
Assmann, Jan, 1, 12–13, 23, 260, 378n11
Asunción Izalco, 31–32, 36
Ataco, 351
Atiquizaya, 315
Atlacatl battalion, 16

Aztecs, 71, 326
Azuehillo, 321

Bakhtin, Mikhail, 16–17
balsam, 72, 233
Banco Agrícola Comercial, 299
Bará, Ernesto, 32, 341
Bay of Pigs invasion, 87, 112
Bet-Al, Ilana R., 19
Binford, Leigh, 16,
Bolivia, 9, 106–7, 139, 186
Bolsheviks, 6, 43, 171, 191, 301
Bonaparte, Joseph, 75
Bonaparte, Napoleon, 75
Brito family, 35, 60
Buezo, Rodolfo, 121–25, 152, 198, 200–201
Burgos-Debray, Elizabeth, 142–43
Bush, George H. W., 94
Bustamante Maceo, Gregorio, 133, 179, 231, 277

Caffrey, Jefferson, 64
Calderón, José Tomás, 37, 275, 277, 291
Call, Miguel, 29, 32
Calvo, Tito, 36–37
campesino. See peasant
Campos, Domingo, 34
Canadian navy, 40, 64–66
Canales, Moisés, 31
Canales, Tirso, 110, 113, 367n24
Cañas, José Enrique, 288, 294
Carías Andino, Tiburcio, 345
Caribbean Bureau: inquiry, 53, 57–58, 190, 192–94, 196; records, 44, 48, 199; reports to, 49, 224, 296, 302–14
Carpio, Salvador Cayetano, 205–7, 373n32, 374n34
Carter, Jimmy, 92, 240
Casa de las Américas, 104, 106
Castaneda Castro, Salvador, 85, 109, 244

Castillo, Carlos, 194
Castillo, Fabio, 116, 126, 371n2
Castillo, Otto René, 101, 109–10, 202, 367n24
Castillo, Pedro Pablo, 131
Castro, Fidel. *See* Cuban Revolution
Castro Canizales, Joaquín, 350
Castro Cárcamo, Rafael, 32
Castro Morán, Mariano, 242–43
Catholic Church, 73, 91, 172, 370n50
Cenáculo de Iniciación Literaria (Literary Initiation Group), 111
Cenizas de Izalco (Ashes of Izalco), 124
Central American Common Market, 86, 88–89
Central American Federation, 76
Central Bank, 83
Central Committee of the Communist Party: criticism of, 199; decisions prior to uprising, 34, 55–56, 152, 163, 191, 193, 285–95, 305; and Farabundo Martí, 57; leadership of uprising, 311; party history by, 203, 210, 302
Central Intelligence Agency (CIA), 107, 112, 203, 236
Centuria, 245
César Vallejo, 104
Chalchuapa, 32
Chávez, Eusebio, 30
Chávez Velasco, Waldo, 110, 113
Chicas, Eugenio, 161–62
Chicas, Francisco, 161–62
Chile, 100–101, 111, 236, 240, 357
China, 203, 324
Christian Base Communities, 91
Christian Democratic Party, 90–91
Cienguegos, Fermán (Eduardo Sancho), 107–8
Cihuanaba, 162, 171–74
Círculo Literario Universitario (University Literary Circle), 101, 111
Civic Guard, 40–42, 277–79, 318, 351
Civil Rights movement, 10, 19
civil war: 1932 narrative and, 2, 4, 7, 184, 242, 247, 253; account of, 93–94; and communist party strategy, 186, 187; and ethnic issues, 11
Claramount, Antonio, 354
coffee: cultivation, 25, 27–28, 77–80; during great depression, 52, 63; and economic conditions, 86–87, 112; ethnic conflict and, 60; Hernández Martínez policies, 83; and neoliberalism, 247–48; in western region, 32, 50; workers, 45, 49, 53, 314, 321, 323
cofradías, 26–27, 73–74
Cojutepeque, 105
cold war: after Cuban Revolution, 87, 112; and civil war, 93; and communist causality argument, 9–11, 260; end of, 5; onset of, 7
Colocho Bosque, Jacinto, 351
Colón, 28–29, 33–34, 276, 339, 350–51
Colonial Department, Communist Party U.S.A., 296
colonos, 50–51
Comintern, 6, 47–48, 51–52, 188–89
Comintern Archive, 5, 44, 47, 61, 178
Committed Generation, 108–14, 263
communal lands, 27, 50, 69, 74, 76, 78, 168
Communist Party (Salvadoran): and 1931 elections, 81; and civil war, 212–13; Dalton and, 102–3, 106–7, 210–11; Dalton's history of, 328–33; factionalism in, 51–52, 89, 183–87; Fifth Congress, 188, 205–8; foundation, 189, 267; Jorge Arias

Gómez and, 128–29
Compañía Salvadoreña de Café, 83
Comrade H, 52–53, 57–58, 192–93, 199, 215, 302, 308, 311
Comrade R, 54–55, 193–94, 308, 312, 314
Confederation of Workers of El Salvador, 267–68
Congress of Workers and Peasants, 188
Consejo de Gobierno Revolucionario, 86
consensus history, 10–11, 14
Constituent Assembly, 110
Constitution, 84–86, 110, 268, 358
Coordinadora Revolucionaria de Masas (Revolutionary Coordinating Committee of the Masses, CRM), 213
Córdova, Enrique, 303, 353, 376n34
Coro, El, 352
Cortés, Hernán, 71
countermemory, 12
counternarrative, 12, 119–20, 123–25, 219, 226, 246
coup d'etat: of 1931, 63, 81; of 1944, 230; of 1948, 85, 109; of 1960, 87, 103; of 1979, 92
creole, 75
cuaderno. *See* notebook
Cuba, 103, 104, 129
Cuban Revolution: and anticommunism, 7, 86; and cold war, 87; and committed generation, 203; and communist causality, 11, 219, 255; and communist factionalism, 89, 204; and popular movement in El Salvador, 112, 202–3, 268
Cuenca family, 57
Cuenca, Max, 284, 288–89, 292, 294
Cultura, 116

D'Aubuisson, Roberto, 246

Dalton, Roque: and 1932 as watershed, 133, 198; adding/subtracting narrative elements, 158–77; on Aquino rebellion of 1833, 132, 271–73; archive 13, 138, 147; and changes to Mármol testimonial between 1966 and 1971, 137–81; changing views on insurrection, 21, 106–7, 123, 126, 128, 135, 149, 187, 202–4, 208–12, 260; and hidden quotations, 177–79; as historian, 114–17, 129–34, 179, 267–71; interview with Miguel Mármol, 2–3, 105–6, 134, 137–81, 291–95; life history, 97–109, 258; and linear chronology, 156–58; member of Generación Compometida, 108–14, 263–65; and *Miguel Mármol* excerpt, 284–91; and narrative reconfiguration, 153–56; as novelist and literary figure, 62, 94, 101, 176, 273–83; relations with Jorge Arias Gómez, 127, 133, 149; and testimonial literature, 4, 144–47; and unpublished history of Communist Party in 1972, 210–12, 214
Dalton, Roque, works. *See names of individual books*
Dalton, Winnal, 84, 98–99
De Mestas, Alberto, 233
death squads, 5, 8, 90–92, 126, 242–44
delayed insurrection strategy: 1932 debate on, 190, 325; Dalton and, 135, 149–50, 187, 329; *Miguel Mármol* narrative and, 163, 166; Miguel Mármol support of, 201; PCS debates on, 202–8. *See also* factionalism
Delgado, José Matías, 115, 131

Día, El, 220, 222
Diario de Santa Ana, 333
Diario Latino, 111, 223
Díaz, Luis, 52
Dirección de Publicaciones, 115–16
Directorio Cívico Militar, 103
Dirty War, 252, 258
Dolores Izalco, 31–32, 36
Don't Be Afraid, Gringo, 139
Duarte, José Napoleón, 91, 208, 237
Dueñas family, 53
Duke family, 53
Duke, Rodolfo, 350
Durán, Víctor, 351

Ecuador, 72
Ejército Revolucionario del Pueblo (People's Revolutionary Army, ERP), 106–8, 126, 208, 367n16
ejido, 106, 208
El Salvador: Dalton's view of ethnicity in, 169; Dalton's view of history in, 149; historical interpretation in, 129–35, 166; and *Miguel Mármol*, 138, 172, 177, 179
El Salvador: Monografía: Dalton's view of ethnicity in, 169; Dalton's view of history in, 149; excerpts of, 269, 271; historical interpretation in, 129–35, 166; and *Miguel Mármol*, 138, 172, 177, 179
elections: municipal of, 1932, 59, 81; presidential of 1931, 58, 80, 303–4; presidential of 1944, 84; presidential of 1950, 86; presidential of 1962, 87; presidential of 1967, 218; presidential of 1972, 90, 208, 212, 236, 237; presidential of 1977, 92; presidential of 2004, 184, 245
England, 50, 80, 267

Escuela Normal España, 111
Estrada Cabrera, Manuel, 295
Estrella Roja, 121
ethnic conflict, 9–12, 76. *See also* Indians: conflicts with Ladinos
ethnicity, 26, 49–50, 72–73, 134; as counternarrative, 6, 8–10, 11–13, 21, 60, 119, 123–24, 219, 246, 259, 325; exclusion of, 54, 123, 128, 131, 170, 223–24, 239, 243, 256, 260, 271; and historical memory, 15, 20; and *Matanza*, 66, 119–20, 246; in Roque Dalton, 124, 130–31, 166–69
ethnocide, 62–63, 246, 260
ethnography, 142–43
Externado de San José, 99–100, 232, 257, 384n3

factionalism, 51, 184–88, 195, 206, 314. *See also* delayed insurrection strategy
Farabundo Martí Liberation Front (FMLN), 93–95, 184, 213–15, 245–46
fascism, 7, 82, 224, 297–300
Federación Regional de Trabajadores Salvadoreños (Regional Federation of Salvadoran Workers, FRTS), 43
Ferdinand VII, 75
Fernández Anaya, Jorge, 188, 199, 205, 295, 315, 317–18, 325–26
Fifth Congress of the PCS, 205–6
Final Offensive, 93, 184
Fitzpatrick, Ellen, 11
Fonseca, Pedro S., 355
fourteen families, 53, 98
France, 139, 142, 185
Franco, Francisco, 233, 281
Frente Agrario de la Región

Oriental (Agrarian Front of the Eastern Region, FARO), 239
Frente Farabundo Martí para Liberación Nacional (Farabundo Martí National Liberation Front, FMLN), 93
Frente Nacional de Orientación Cívica (National Front for Civic Organization, FNOC), 203
Frente Unido de Acción Revolucionaria (United Revolutionary Action Front, FUAR), 134, 204
Fuentes, Carlos, 141
Fuerzas Armadas de Liberación (Armed Forces of Liberation, FAL), 213
Fuerzas Populares de Liberación Farabundo Martí (Farabundo Martí Popular Liberation Forces, FPL), 207

Galdámez, Marcelino, 36
Galeano, Eduardo, 140
Galindo Pohl, Reynaldo, 244
García Márquez, Gabriel, 141
García Medrano, María, 99
Geoffroy Rivas, Pedro, 114
Germán, Juan, 41
Germany, 83, 282, 324
globalization, 72, 95
Gómez Zárate, Alberto, 58–59, 303
Gorki, Maxim, 264
Gould, Jeffrey, 61, 170
Great Britain, 5, 40, 64–66, 135, 267
Great Depression, 8, 52, 79–83, 133, 227
Grupos de Acción Revolucionaria (Revolutionary Action Groups, GAR), 204
Gualán, Alberto, 206, 373n21
Guardia Cívica. See Civic Guard

Guatemala: colonial period in, 71, 76; democratic period in, 109–10; CIA sponsored coup in, 112; and Schlesinger's narrative of 1932 events, 123, 228, 229, 344–49; Mármol in, 200–201
Guatemalan Workers' Confederation, 201
Guevara, Ernesto (Che), 106–7, 109, 186, 253, 266, 294
Guillén, Nicolás, 103
Guirola, Angel, 350, 354
Gulag, 19

hacienda, 73
Halbwachs, Maurice, 14, 17
Handal, Shafik, 95, 184, 205–6, 212–14
Havana, 106, 114, 265–66
Hernández, Ismael, 188
Hernández, Miguel, 113
Hernández Martínez, Maximiliano: policies, 81–84, 195; Dalton's view of, 132; and Indian population, 62; in narratives of 1932 events, 228–29, 232–33; rationale for Matanza, 63–66, 81; as right-wing icon, 218, 222, 240, 244, version of 1932 events, 223–25
Hijos de Sánchez, Los, 144
Hikmet, Nazim, 113
Historia militar de El Salvador, 133, 179, 231, 277
Historias prohibidas del Pulgarcito, 106, 273
historical memory, 12–20, 97, 246, 251–52
Hitler, Adolf, 7, 83, 282
Hoja, 111
Holocaust, 19, 252
Honduras, 88–89, 173, 194, 307

I Rigoberta Menchú, 4, 139, 142–43, 180
Ilopango, 156, 159–61, 286, 288, 290, 299
imperialism, 132–33, 266–69
Independence movement, 75–76, 115–16, 131
Independiente, El, 101
Indian(s): communities, 26–27; leaders, 30; targets of Matanza, 40–43; PCS views of, 49–50, 52, 54; and ethnocide argument, 62; under Spanish rule, 71–74; after independence, 76–79; in Aquino rebellion, 101, 271–73; in narratives of 1932, 119–20, 123–25, 221–22, 224–32, 243–47, 259–60, 334, 336–37, 340, 342–44, 351; in Dalton's work, 130, 132, 162–68, 279–80; Guatemalan, 139–40; and mestizaje, 169–70; conflicts with ladinos, 9, 35, 59–60, 81; role in events of 1932, 23, 28, 58
indigo, 27, 72, 75, 77, 247, 272
insurrectionary strategy. *See* delayed insurrection strategy; factionalism
Intelectual y la sociedad, El, 114, 265
International Red Aid, 43, 361n33; and 1932 uprising, 45–49, 53, 58–61; in Anaya's report, 297–98; in cuaderno, 292; definition of, 189–90, 361n23; factional disputes with PCS, 190–94; narratives after 1932, 194–95, 199–200; in *Revolución comunista*, 123, 345; in *Sangre de hermanos*, 121, 200
Italy, 83, 224, 282
Izalco: Indians in, 27; rebel activity in, 28–32, 34, 36, 339–41; Matanza in, 41, 276, 279; ethnic conflict in, 58, 60; commemoration of Matanza in, 245–46, 261

Jiquilisco, 276
Jodarria, La, 101
John of the Cross, Saint, 103
Juárez, Carlos, 34
Juayúa, 169, 276–77, 339, 354; as home of Emilio Redaelli, 242; in "A Landowner's Account," 333–37; in *Revolución comunista*, 344, 349; in *Los sucescos comunistas*, 342
Juventud Comunista de El Salvador (Communist Youth, J.C.), 297–98, 303

Kaiser, Susana, 258, 377n3
Kennedy, John F., 87, 235
Kirkpatrick, Jeane, 243–44
Kosovo, battle of, 19

La Libertad department, 34
La Libertad port, 275, 306
Labor Party: British, 80; Salvadoran, 134
Ladinos, 9, 76, 78, 91, 224, 343; and 1932 uprising, 23, 30; in cuaderno, 167–68; as elites, 28, 35, 41–43, 79, 119–20, 333–37; in elite narratives, 221, 256; and gender, 226, 237; in Izalco, 31; as mestizaje, 26, 62; in Nahuizalco, 59–61; and PCS membership, 50–52, 58; as peasants, 26, 28, 63
land privatization, 78
land reform, 91, 92, 239
land tenure, 73–74, 256, 363n5, 363n9; and Indian communities, 76; in Western

countryside, 50
Landarech, Alfonso María, S.J., 100, 366n4
Landowners, 50–51, 71–71, 348; and coffee 27; as elites, 78–79, 81–83, 85, 88, 91–92, 221, 225–27, 238–39, 261, 281; and the Great Depression, 63; as postwar narrative, 247–48
Lanzas, Irma, 111, 113
Lardé y Larín, Jorge, 116, 233
Las Moras, 34
Latin American Congress of Culture, 100
Lauria, Aldo, 61
Lebanon, 240, 357
Lemus, José María, 87, 103–4, 197, 203
Lencas, 71, 348
Lenin, 185–87, 191–92, 210, 212, 214, 255, 285, 292, 300–301, 329
Leninism, 12, 47, 169, 203, 207, 241
Let Me Speak!, 139
Lewis, Oscar, 144–45
Liberation Theology, 91, 122, 239, 365n27–28
Lima, Francisco, 350
Lissagaray, Prosper-Olivier, 212
López, Luis, 294
López Vallecillos, Italo, 111
Luders, Juan, 352
Lue, Timoteo, 120
Luna, Alfonso, 122, 276, 288–89, 294, 354
Luna, David, 127–29, 133, 163–64, 204–5, 215, 259–61; 325–28; and Roque Dalton, 164–66

Maceo, Antonio, 133
Machón Vilanova, Francisco, 124–25
Magical Realism, 141
Mam, 348
Mao, Zedong, 186
Mármol, Miguel, 137–81, 188, 196, 245, 278–82; and 1948 document from Guatemala, 21, 200–201, 215, 320–25, 373n24; as communist, 147–48, 169, 180; and interview with Roque Dalton, 3, 13, 20, 98, 106, 108, 124, 134, 179, 192, 205, 209, 258, 266n13, 270n21; and storytelling, 156–58; and religious upbringing, 171; surviving firing squad, 2, 151; views on *Miguel Mármol*, 154–56
Marroquín, Dagoberto, 116
Marroquín Rojas, Clemente, 346, 368n48
Martí, Farabundo, 61, 199, 247, 276, 284, 354; arrest, 55, 57, 152, 274; conflicts with Anaya, 191–94, 295–302; in cuaderno, 291–95; execution, 5; as inspiration to authors, 114; as leader of SRI, 189, 190, 322; in *Miguel Mármol*, 284–91; as namesake to FMLN, 93, 184, 213, 242; as namesake to FPL, 207; in report from Santa Ana comrades, 214–320; in report by Comrade H, 302–7; in *Revolución comunista*, 349; role in 1932, 56, 58; in *Sangre de hermanos*, 121–23, 200–201; as subject of Arias Gómez biography, 127
Martial Law, 157, 306, 352
Marx, Karl, 185–86, 191–92, 210, 214, 218, 255, 264, 300–301; modernist concept of time, 158; theory of revolution, 6, 8, 9; theory of history, 185
Marxism 6, 12, 129, 185, 203, 215, 239, 241, 256, 330, 357; and Communist Party of El Salvador (PCS), 49, 61; in Dalton's writings, 266–68,

332; as Eurocentric, 185; and Farabundo Martí, 199, 317; and intraleft debates over revolution, 187, 189, 192, 197; and Miguel Mármol, 147, 169, 214, 324; relationship to rebels in 1932, 43, 47, 246; and Roque Dalton, 100–103, 115, 158, 169, 170, 172; and U.S. foreign policy, 88
Masferrer, Alberto, 134, 176, 268
master narrative, 4, 138
Mata, Gabino, 120
Matanza 2, 5, 37–43, 61–66, 69, 125, 206, 242, 256–57, 314–15, 324, 333, 350; and Ama's lynching, 58; as army conspiracy, 127; in Dalton's writings, 271, 281; ethnic dimensions of, 119, 236, 260–61; interpretations by leftists, 133–35, 228; interpretations by rightists, 224, 227, 233, 237, 244–45; and Mármol's execution, 173–74; narratives of, 14–15, 17, 185, 231, 233, 236, 253–54; number of killed, 14; in Revolución comunista, 123; shame associated with, 226, 233–34; silence surrounding, 4, 218; as watershed in El Salvador's history, 71, 108–9, 249
Maximiliano Hernández Martínez Brigade, 5, 242
Mazzini, Sidney, 240, 356
McNaught, Roy, 30–31, 40, 63
Meardi, Tato, 350
Medrano, José Alberto, 89, 90
Mejoramiento Social, 63, 101, 224, 232
Meléndez-Quiñonez dynasty, 79
membership, 48, 49; *Miguel Mármol* and 138, 147–49, 152–53, 163–66, 284; and narrative of 1932 events, 12, 43, 45, 194, 197–98, 214; records, 5, 23, 44; Rodolfo Buezo and, 121; role in uprising, 4, 47–48, 54–61, 123, 133, 295–328; Seventh Congress, 213; University of El Salvador, 126–27
Memoria del fuego, 140
memory, 4, 5, 11, 21, 97, 137, 217, 252; and 1932, 89, 117, 198, 200, 254–55, 260–62; collective, 137, 253–355, 258; and Dalton's notebooks, 145, 329; historical 12–20, 181, 251, 258; historiographies of, 359n7, 377n3; leftist debates over, 183–215; rightist debates over, 217–49; and trauma, 252
memory communities, 17, 257
memory groups, 18, 138, 181, 215, 218, 257–59
Menchú, Rigoberta, 4, 139–43; and Stoll controversy, 180
Méndez, Joaquín, 30–32, 45, 118–25, 225–27, 230, 244, 340–44
Merlos, Salvador, 286, 293
mestizaje, 131, 169, 170
mestizo, 9, 92, 130; in cofradías, 73; and ladinos 26; and mestizaje, 169–70
metanarrative, 11–12, 24, 117, 122, 125, 218, 259, 340
Mexican Regional Labor Confederation, 321
Mexican Revolution, 9, 238, 327
Mexico 9, 71, 75–76, 124, 168, 321, 327, 373n24; and Che Guevara, 109; and Dalton's exile, 103–4; and Oscar Lewis's *Children of Sanchez*, 144; and the Peace Accords of 1992, 95
Michaux, Henri, 103
Miguel Mármol, 3, 13, 97, 115, 118,

124, 129, 137–38, 183, 195, 242, 284–91; and communist causality, 153; and cuaderno 13, 137–81, 291–95; and Dalton's evolving politics, 114, 128, 149, 152, 209, 273–74, 328–33; and Dalton's literary style, 132; and ethnicity, 166–69; and intra-left debates, 185; and narrative reconfiguration, 153–56, 180; as polarizing text, 5; as testimonial literature, 138–46, 179, 181; in translation, 94
Military Fraternity of El Salvador, 241
Milosevic, Slobodan, 19
missile crisis, 87, 203
Molina Cañas, Raúl, 357
Molina, Arturo Armando, 88, 91–92
Molina, Mariano, 32, 341
Molina, Miguel Tomás, 355
Montevideo, 321
Morán, Tiburcio, 31
Moratorium Law, 355
Morazán department, 16
Moreau, Alberto, 296
Moscow: relations with leftists in El Salvador, 48, 52, 188–89, 196, 199; role in 1932 uprising, 65, 225; as site of Comintern archive, 5, 23, 44, 257, 361n28; as site of Third Communist International/Comintern, 6, 44, 189–90, 361n23
Mozote, El, 16, 93
Mussolini, Benito, 7, 224, 282
Myth of Mestizaje, The, 170

Nahuizalco, 41, 278n10; ethnic demographics of, 26–27; ethnic politics in, 59–61, 81; and Matanza, 39, 42–43, 229, 276, 351; as target of 1932 rebels,

28–9, 33, 35–37, 118, 334–36, 339, 343
Napoleonic wars, 75
narrative reconfiguration, 138, 153, 162, 177, 180, 291
National Assembly, 14, 84, 212, 223, 227, 337
National City Bank, 299
National Guard, 46, 89–90, 213, 226, 277–80, 307, 339
National Opposition Union (UNO), 208, 212
National Republican Alliance Party. *See* ARENA party
National Unemployment Council, 304
nationalism, 75, 89, 170, 225, 227, 246, 301
neoliberalism, 246
Nerio, Rosalío (Felipe), 30, 35
Neruda, Pablo, 100, 113–14
new historicism, 10–11
new nationalism, 141
New York City, 44, 47, 52, 190–91, 194, 196, 199, 200, 296, 302, 361n23
New York Times, 7
Nicaragua, 77, 124, 190, 254, 275, 349; mestizaje in, 170; Revolution of 1979, 92, 213, 241; and U.S. occupation in 1930s, 65
Nicaraguan Revolution. *See* Sandinista Revolution
Nonualcos, 272–73
Nora, Eugenio de, 263
notebook (Dalton's), 20, 137–81, 209, 291

Obando Sánchez, Antonio, 316
Ola roja, 124
Opinión Estudiantil, 101
Orantes, Benjamín Inocente, 31
ORDEN. *See* Organización Democrática Nacionalista

Organización Democrática
    Nacionalista (ORDEN),
    89–90
Organization of American
    States, 240
Ortíz, Juan, 279, 321
Oso ruso, El, 124
Osorio, Oscar, 86–87, 112, 157, 234,
    238, 268

Panama Canal, 64, 324
Panamá Sandoval, David Ernesto,
    246, 248
Partido Pro Patria, 82
Partido Revolucionario de
    Trabajadores
    Centroamericanos
    (Revolutionary Party of
    Central American Workers,
    PRTC), 209
patronage, 9, 58, 79
patrullas cantonales, 90
Patzicia, 347
PCS. *See* Communist Party of
    El Salvador
Peace Accords, 86, 95, 184
peasant leagues, 48, 193, 309
peasants, 24–28, 47–48, 55, 58, 62,
    78–79, 89, 91–92, 101, 188, 203,
    208, 212, 214, 223, 238, 284–93;
    in Christian-based unions,
    239; as paramilitaries, 90; as
    rebels before 1932, 132, 273; as
    rebels in 1932, 1, 23, 66, 81,
    119–23, 153, 192–93, 231–33,
    237, 245, 248, 275, 308–10,
    321–22; as targets during civil
    war, 16; as targets of Matanza,
    37–38, 41–43, 61, 194, 267–70,
    279–80; in testimonial litera-
    ture, 139
Pérez, Salvador, 38
Pérez Alvarado, Francisco, 31
Pérez Brignoli, Héctor, 368n48

petty bourgeoisie, 51, 286, 293, 311
Pineda, Gustavo, 234–35
Pipiles, 71, 272
Platero, Francisco, 36
Pobrecito poeta que era yo..., 105–6,
    108, 366n3
Pocomam, 348
Popular University, 324
Prado, Mariano, 272
Prague, 2–3, 13, 97–98, 105–8, 129,
    134, 138, 143, 149, 178–81,
    205, 209
Prensa, La, 35, 220, 222, 263, 350
Prensa Latina, 132

Ramírez, Gregorio, 191
Ramírez, Gumercindo, 172
Ramos, Juan, 41
Raza cósmica, La, 170
Reagan, Ronald, 92–93, 242–43
Real Thing, The, 140
Recinos, Luis Felipe, 189, 199,
    200, 318
*Recuerdos de Sonsonate: crónica de
    1932*, 244
Red Commanders, 54–56, 118, 285
Red Scare, 6–7, 46
Redaelli, Emilio, 29–31, 242, 245,
    336, 337
Redaelli, Mario, 242
Regalado family, 53
Renan, Ernest, 13, 17, 251–52, 261
Repertorio Americano, 120, 228, 229
Resistencia Nacional (National
    Resistance, RN), 108, 208
Revista Internacional, 105, 187, 205–6
*Revista Salvadoreña de Ciencias
    Sociales*, 117
Revolution of 1948, 85, 109–10, 112,
    203, 230, 232, 238, 244, 350
Ricoeur, Paul, 14, 17
Ríos, Lorenzo, 31
Rivas Mira, Alejandro, 108, 367n16
Rivas, Félix, 34

Rivas, Rafael, 29
Rivera, Diego, 100
Rivera, Julio, 87–88
Rodríguez, Ileana, 155
Rodríguez, Rosenda, 31
Romero Bosque, Pío, 79, 81–82, 195, 230, 296, 300, 353
Romero, Arturo, 85, 230, 241
Romero, Carlos Humberto, 213, 240
Romero, Monsignor Oscar Arnulfo, 92, 213, 242
Roosevelt, Franklin Delano, 83
Ruiz, Narciso, 284, 292
Russia, 6, 9, 12, 19, 43, 51, 124–25, 252; and Revolution of 1917, 8–10, 47, 85; as site Comintern and Comintern Archive, 5, 23, 44, 178, 188, 361n28
Russian Revolution, 6, 8–10, 47

Saint-John Perse, 103
Salaverría family, 31
Salcoatitán: as a center of 1932 uprising, 28–38, 44
San Marcos, 347
San Martín, Joaquín, 272
San Salvador, 33, 40, 90, 92, 105, 131, 188, 213–14, 221, 239, 245, 276; as the capital city, 26, 60, 64, 76; as home of Miguel Mármol, 2, 148, 171; population of in 1932, 29; as the stronghold of the PCS and SRI in 1932, 48–54, 57, 61, 81, 123, 151, 163, 189, 191, 195, 200, 290–91, 303–7
San Vicente: department, 213; city, 272–273, 351
Sánchez, Chico, 30, 167–68, 226, 279
Sánchez Hernández, Fidel, 88
Sandinista Revolution, 92, 213, 241, 365n29
Sandino, Augusto César, 65, 190, 253, 275, 324

Sangre de hermanos, 121–22, 152, 198, 200
Santa Ana, 227, 276–77, 288, 294, 303, 333, 348; in 1932, 29, 306; document from the comrades in 1936, 196–200, 215, 314–20; as focal point for PCS organizing, 49, 189, 305, 321
Santa Cruz Michapa, 286, 293
Santa Tecla, 33–36, 156, 276, 286, 293–94, 339; as focal point for PCS organizing, 49, 189, 305–6, 321
Santayana, George, 261
Santiago Nonualco, 272
Santo Domingo, 213
Saussure, Ferdinand de, 16–17
Schacter, Daniel, 17–18
Schlesinger, Alfredo, 346, 369n48, 375n23
Schlesinger, Jorge, 12, 39, 45–46, 59, 123–25, 178–79, 229–30, 235, 244–45, 260
Seminario de Historia Contemporánea de Centroamérica, 116
sharecroppers. *See* colonos
smallholders, 50–52
Society of Commercial Employees, 267
Socorro Rojo Internacional. *See* International Red Aid
Sol family, 53
Sonsonate, 32, 35–37, 40, 60, 65, 168, 220, 244, 339; in 1932, 1, 28–29, 33, 48, 291–93, 311, 340, 349, 354; as focal point of PCS organizing, 49, 57, 189, 284, 286, 292, 305–6, 321
Sonzacate, 28–29, 32–33, 36–37, 167, 339
Soviet Union, 6–7, 102, 167, 184, 186, 198, 203, 205, 246
Spain, 72, 74–76, 111, 124, 139, 157,

233, 324
Stalin, Josef, 9, 184
state of siege, 86, 222, 289, 294, 338, 354
Stoll, David, 142
Straits of Magellan, 77
strikes, 53, 80–81, 88, 315, 317
Sucesos comunistas en El Salvador, Los, 118–19, 225, 229, 340
Sumpul River massacre, 93

Taberna y otros lugares, 106
Tacuba: in 1932, 28–30, 33–34, 37, 220, 307, 339; as focal point for PCS organizing, 57, 133
Taracena, Arturo, 142
Tegucigalpa, 320
Tepetitán, 272
Testimonial literature, 3–4, 106, 138–44, 155, 179, 181
Testimonios, Los, 104
Third Communist International, 6, 186
tierras realengas, 74
Tilley, Virginia, 170
Tirado, Thomas, 139
Tribuna Libre, 128, 325
Tribuna, 231, 350
Turno del ofendido, El, 103
Typographical Alliance, 267

U.S. State Department, 83, 240
Ubico, Jorge, 109, 228, 345
Un libro levemente odioso, 106
Union Confederation of Latin America, 321
United States 7, 19, 25, 77, 79, 92, 323; and anticommunism during cold war, 86–88, 91, 93; consensus historiography, 10–11, 14; as imperialist power in El Salvador, 131–32, 267, 282; relations with El Salvador during civil war, 94, 184, 240–44; relations with Martínez in 1932, 64, 66, 81–82, 225, 229, 281, 345; as a superpower, 10; as trading partner with El Salvador, 83, 246, 248
Universidad Centroamericana José Simeón Cañas (UCA), 239, 257
Universidad, La, 117
University of El Salvador, 101, 103, 110–11, 113, 116–17, 121, 126, 149, 197, 204, 231, 283, 325
Urgent General Instructions, 45, 56, 177–79, 237
Uribe, Enrique, 42
USSR. *See* Soviet Union
Usulután, 167, 173–74, 286, 293

Vallejo, César, 114
Vasconcelos, José, 170
Ventana en el rostro, La, 103
Verdad, La, 131
Vietnam, 203
Vietnam War, 10, 252
Villa Canales, 347

Washington Treaties of 1923, 64, 82
World War I, 79
World War II, 83, 267

Young Communist League, 287, 297, 303, 309–10
Yugoslavia, 19

Zacatecoluca, 174, 272
Zapata, Mario, 122, 276, 288–89, 294, 354
Zapote, El, 286, 293
Zaragoza, 315, 321